NORTH CAROLINA STATE FLAG.

May 20, 1775. Mecklenburg Declaration of Independence. April 12, 1776. Delegates to the Philadelphia Convention selected at Halifax, N. C., and instructed to vote for American Independence.

History of Mecklenburg County
—NORTH CAROLINA—
and
The City of Charlotte
from 1740 to 1903

by

D. A. Tompkins

Author of *Cotton and Cotton Oil; Cotton Mill, Commercial Features; Cotton Values in Textile Fabrics; Cotton Mill, Processes and Calculations;* **and** *American Commerce, Its Expansion.*

This Edition Contains Two Volumes in One
Volume One: Narrative; Volume Two: Appendix

HERITAGE BOOKS
2008

HERITAGE BOOKS
AN IMPRINT OF HERITAGE BOOKS, INC.

Books, CDs, and more—Worldwide

For our listing of thousands of titles see our website
at
www.HeritageBooks.com

A Facsimile Reprint
Published 2008 by
HERITAGE BOOKS, INC.
Publishing Division
100 Railroad Ave. #104
Westminster, Maryland 21157

Copyright © 1903, 1904 D. A. Tompkins

— Publisher's Notice —
In reprints such as this, it is often not possible to remove blemishes from the original. We feel the contents of this book warrant its reissue despite these blemishes and hope you will agree and read it with pleasure.

International Standard Book Numbers
Paperbound: 978-0-7884-1345-2
Clothbound: 978-0-7884-7527-6

"All hail to thee, thou good old State,
    the noblest of the band!
Who raised the flag of Liberty, in
    this our native land!
All hail to thee, thy worthy sons were
    first to spurn the yoke,
The tyrant's fetters from their hands,
    at Mecklenburg they broke."

EXPLANATION.

This history is published in two volumes. The first volume contains the simple narrative, and the second is in the nature of an appendix, containing ample discussions of important events, a collection of biographies and many official documents justifying and verifying the statements in this volume. At the end of each chapter is given the sources of the information therein contained, and at the end of each volume is an index.

INTRODUCTION.

History of a county is closely associated with history of the State, as the health of an arm is with the condition of the whole physical structure. An account of the life of a prominent man in a community is a history of that community in the same way that the history of a representative county is a history of the commonwealth. This book is written primarily to preserve Mecklenburg history for the inspiration of present and future generations of Mecklenburg people, but the aim extends further than this on the presumption that this is a typical southern county and hence, by deductive reasoning, its growth portrays the effects subsequent to certain industrial activities throughout the South.

Prominent among the author's incentives was the desire to investigate, from an industrial standpoint, regarding the lack of industries until within the last half century and the causes of business revival since. He had no personal opinions to illustrate, but investigated and brought forth this accumulation of facts so that he and others might be enabled to form opinions based on truth. The history preaches no doctrine and leans to no side. It is the result of five years of almost continuous work, of painstaking and laborious investigations, of considerable financial expenditure, and of a guiding desire to learn and to record the historical events of the county.

The author is not a native of Mecklenburg. He was raised on a farm in South Carolina, and was educated at the South Carolina College and at Rensselaer Polytechnic Institute in Troy, New York, and though active participation in Charlotte life in recent years has made him a thorough citizen, he feels that he can view in an impartial manner the events herein discussed. The *data* was gathered from a library of North Carolina history and literature, unpublished State and county records and manuscripts, the Colonial and State Records, private correspondence and diaries and business records, testimony of aged and reliable citizens, and files of Charlotte newspapers from 1824 to 1903.

D. A. TOMPKINS.

October 1, 1903.

CONTENTS.

                                                                                       Page.

CHAPTER I............................... 1

        THE COLONISTS.

An Account of the Settlement of the Original Colonies and of the Causes Which Prompted Emigration to North Carolina and to the Piedmont Section.

CHAPTER II.............................. 7

      INDIANS OF THIS SECTION. (1753 to 1763.)

Troubles Between White People and Indians—Full Report of a Peace Conference—Wars Among Different Indian Tribes—The Cherokees and the Catawbas.

CHAPTER III............................. 15

        EARLY SETTLERS. (1740 to 1762.)

Original Homes of the Immigrants—Their Nationalities—Traits of Character—Religious Persecutions in the Old Country, and Subsequent Removal to America and Mecklenburg County.

CHAPTER IV............................. 22

      INDUSTRIES AND CUSTOMS. (1745 to 1762.)

How the Settlers Built Their Homes—Their First Mills and Occupations—Trading—Social Life and Diversions.

CHAPTER V.............................. 28

        FORMATION OF THE COUNTY. (1762.)

Creation of Mecklenburg from Anson—Origin of the Names of the County and the City of Charlotte—Physical Description of the Country at that Time.

CHAPTER VI............................. 31

        BEGINNING OF CHARLOTTE. (1762 to 1772.)

Influences Which Tended to the Necessity for a Town—Difficulty in Obtaining a Charter—The First Court House—Laws of the New Town.

x   HISTORY OF MECKLENBURG COUNTY.

CHAPTER VII ....*Page* 35

EARLY TROUBLES AND REGULATORS. (1762 to 1772.)

Annoyances on Account of a Disputed Boundary Line—The McCulloh Land Riots—Surveying the Cherokee Boundary—Oppressive Taxes and Unjust Officers, and the Battle of Alamance.

CHAPTER VIII.............................. 41

THE APPROACHING STORM. (1772 to 1775.)

England's Position With Regard to America—Affairs in the Colonies. —Governor Martin's Dissensions With the Assembly—Rifle Factory in Charlotte—Polk Calls the Convention.

CHAPTER IX................................ 46

DECLARATION OF INDEPENDENCE; MAY 20, 1775.

Manner of Election and Assembling of the Delegates—Excitement. —The Addresses and the Committee on Resolutions—News of the Battle of Lexington—Declaration Unanimously Adopted—Temporary Form of Government Provided.

CHAPTER X................................. 52

GOVERNMENT BY THE COMMITTEE. (1775 to 1776.)

Adjourned Meeting Held May 31—Adopts Rules of Government Until "Laws are Provided by Congress"—Proceedings Supplementary to Previous Convention—The Two Official Declarations Compared.

CHAPTER XI................................ 56

THE REVOLUTION. (1776 to 1780.)

Organization of the State Military Forces—Prominent Parts Taken by Mecklenburg Men—Scovilite and Tory Campaigns—The Continental Troops—Governor Caswell in Charlotte.

CHAPTER XII............................... 60

THE HORNETS' NEST. (1780 to 1782.)

Surrender of Charleston—Battle of Ramsour's Mill—Davidson and Davie Harass the British—Reception of Cornwallis in Charlotte. —Surprise at McIntyre's, Battle of King's Mountain and Departure of the British—General Davidson Killed at Cowan's Ford.

CONTENTS. xi

CHAPTER XIII ....*Page* 65
CLOSE OF THE EIGHTEENTH CENTURY. (1776 to 1800.)
War Times and County Affairs—Lawyers and Legislative Proceedings—Monetary System—Public Buildings and Industries—Andrew Jackson and James Knox Polk Born in Mecklenburg. —George Washington in Charlotte.

CHAPTER XIV............................. 70
EDUCATION BEFORE 1800.
First Teachers and Schools in Mecklenburg—Qualifications of Teachers and Nature of Instruction—Grammar and Classical Schools. —Queen's College, Queen's Museum and Liberty Hall.

CHAPTER XV.............................. 75
RELIGION AND CHURCHES FROM 1748 TO 1800.
Presbyterians Most Numerous in the Early Times—Rev. Hugh McAden, Rev. John Thompson and Rev. Alexander Craighead the First Preachers—Seven Noted Churches and Some of Their Customs.

CHAPTER XVI............................. 80
DOCTORS AND MEDICINES BEFORE 1800.
First Physicians in the County and the Leading Ones of the Period. —Methods of Practice and the Medicines Used—Prevalence of Witchcraft and Its Treatment.

CHAPTER XVII............................ 84
SLAVERY BEFORE 1800.
Introduction of the System Was Slow—Conditions of Labor—No One Owned More Than a Dozen Slaves—Prices, Habits and Ability of the Negroes—Only a Few Were Skilled Laborers.

CHAPTER XVIII........................... 89
FIRST YEARS OF THE NINETEENTH CENTURY. (1800 to 1825.)
Statistics of Wealth and Population of the County and City—Improvements in Public Buildings—Proceedings and Methods of the Courts—Richest Man in the County Worth $10,700.

CHAPTER XIX ....*Page* 94

INTRODUCTION OF THE COTTON INDUSTRY. (1790 to 1825.)

First Planting in the Colonies Was Experimental—Little Progress Made Previous to the Invention of the Cotton Gin—Two Thousand Saws in Use in Mecklenburg in 1803—Rapid Development Thereafter.

CHAPTER XX................................. 97

EFFECT OF SLAVERY ON INDUSTRIES.

Occupations of First Settlers and the Causes—They Made All They Used—Slavery Induced Them to Turn Their Entire Attention to Agriculture—Comfortable and Peaceable Conditions Prevailed.

CHAPTER XXI............................. 101

LIFE IN THE OLD SOUTH.

A Study of the Negro—Dispositions of Planters and Systems of Agriculture—Description of the Plantations, the "Big House" and the Cabins—Treatment of the Slaves—Social Diversions.

CHAPTER XXII............................. 107

CHURCHES BEFORE THE CIVIL WAR.

Growth of the Congregations in the County and the Building of the First Churches in Charlotte—Something of the Most Noted Ministers and Their Great Influence—Revivals and Various Religious Incidents.

CHAPTER XXIII............................. 111

EDUCATION BEFORE 1860.

First Chartered Schools—County Academies—Ministers Conducted Excellent Schools—Beginning of the Public System—Military Institute—Male and Female Institutes—Davidson College.

CHAPTER XXIV............................. 117

GROWTH AND DEVELOPMENT FROM 1825 TO 1860.

Population, Wealth and Taxes—Trades and Improvements—Laws and Courts—Newspapers—Mecklenburg's Part in the Mexican War—Smallpox—Fairs and Public Exhibitions—The Census of 1840.

CONTENTS.   xiii

CHAPTER XXV ....*Page* 124
    RAILROADS AND INDUSTRIES FROM 1830 TO 1860.
    Realization of Necessity for Better Means of Travel and Commerce.
    —Work on the Catawba River—Railroad Agitation in 1833—The
    Old Stage Coach—First Passenger Train in 1852—County Road
    Commissioners—Varied Industries.

CHAPTER XXVI............................ 129
    MINING AND THE MINT BEFORE 1860.
    Discovery of Gold in 1790—First Attempt at Mining in 1825—Foreign
    Investors Take Active Interest—Most Noted Mines and Their
    Productions—Mint Established in Charlotte in 1837, and Its
    Record Since.

CHAPTER XXVII............................ 133
    SLAVERY, POLITICS AND SECESSION. (1825 to 1861.)
    Dividing Issues Discussed—Customs Regarding Slaves—Political
    Animosity—Mecklenburg Strongly Southern in Feeling—County
    Declares for Secession Twenty Days Before South Carolina.
    —North Carolina Secedes.

CHAPTER XXVIII........................... 138
    CIVIL WAR. (1861 to 1865.)
    Mecklenburg Soldiers Among the First to Volunteer—Were Promi-
    nent in the Formation of the First or "Bethel" Regiment—Dis-
    tinguished Officers From Mecklenburg—Conditions in the County
    During the War—Last Meeting of Confederate Cabinet Held in
    Charlotte.

CHAPTER XXIX............................ 143
    RECONSTRUCTION. (1865 to 1875.)
    Mecklenburg Escaped the Worst Evils of Those Days—Federal
    Officers and Troops in Charlotte—Editor Waring Indicted for
    Espousing the Southern Cause—Conduct of the Negroes Com-
    paratively Peaceable—Elections in the County.

CHAPTER XXX............................. 149
    FIRST DECADE WITHOUT SLAVERY. (1865 to 1875.)
    County Affairs in War Times—Emancipation Forced White Men to
    Work—Attention Diverted to New Things—This Section an In-
    viting Field for Investors—Reasons for the Progress Made.
    Death of a Woman Who Remembered May 20, 1775.

HISTORY OF MECKLENBURG COUNTY.

CHAPTER XXXI ....*Page* 154
INDEPENDENCE CENTENNIAL CELEBRATION. (May 20, 1875.)
Preparations and Committees for the Event—Great Men Present. —Marshals Were Confederate Generals—Immense Crowd in Charlotte—The Proceedings and Interesting Incidents.

CHAPTER XXXII............................ 158
LAST QUARTER OF THE CENTURY. (1875 to 1900.)
Public Improvements—Public Buildings—Medical Society—Law Association—Newspapers—Farms.

CHAPTER XXXIII........................... 162
THE CHURCHES FROM 1860 TO 1903.
Short Sketches of the Growth of the Principal Congregations of the Leading Denominations in the City and County, and of the Other Religious Organizations.

CHAPTER XXXIV............................ 166
EDUCATION FROM 1860 TO 1903.
Development of County Public School System—Charlotte Graded Schools First in the State—Presbyterian, Elizabeth, Davidson and Medical Colleges—Charlotte Military Institute—Biddle University and St. Michael's Training and Industrial School.

CHAPTER XXXV............................. 173
MINING, BANKING AND THE ASSAY OFFICE. (1860 to 1903.)
Use of Improved Mining Machinery After the War—The Miners and the Products—Minerals Found in the County—Receipts of Gold and Silver at the Assay Office—History of the Office. —Charlotte's Leading Banking Institutions.

CHAPTER XXXVI 176
ROAD BUILDING FROM 1880 TO 1903.
Influences Which Made Better Roads Necessary—Original Methods and Subsequent Progress—Cost of Roads—Convict Labor Satisfactory—Lessons Taught by Experience.

CHAPTER XXXVII.......................... 180
DEVELOPMENT OF MANUFACTURES. (1865 to 1900.)
Iron Substituted for Wood in Machinery as a Result of the Abolition of Cheap Labor—Necessity Forces Improvements—First Cotton Mill Built in 1881 and First Cotton Oil Mill in 1882—Cotton Compresses—Industrial Progress Attendant Upon Manufacturing—Situation in 1900.

CONTENTS. xv

CHAPTER XXXVIII.......................*Page* 185

MECKLENBURG AND CHARLOTTE IN 1903.

Population, Taxable Real Estate, Personal Property, Railroads and Banks—Expenses and Receipts of County and City—Social and Business Organizations—Incorporated Towns—Farm Products. —New Buildings.

CHAPTER XXXIX............................ 187

MECKLENBURG'S GREAT CITIZENS.

Sketches of the Lives of President Andrew Jackson, President James Knox Polk and Senator Zebulon Baird Vance.

CHAPTER XL............................... 193

SUMMARY.

Explanation of the Growth and Development of Mecklenburg and Charlotte Under Diverse Conditions in Different Periods, in Comparison With the United States and North Carolina.

INDEX TO ILLUSTRATIONS.

North Carolina State Flag..................*Frontispiece*
Map of Mecklenburg Outlines.................... 1
Queen Charlotte 29
First Court House............................... 31
News of the Battle of Lexington................ 47
Sketch of Catawba River........................ 57
Receipt for Tuition in Queen's Museum.......... 71
Bill for Teaching, 1771......................... 73
Receipt Dated in 1810........................... 89
Cotton Plant in September....................... 91
Cotton Plant in November........................ 91
Whitney's Original Model 95
Holmes' Saw Gin................................ 97
Cotton "Square" and Bloom...................... 99
Matured Boll and Opening Boll.................. 99
Open Boll and Empty Boll....................... 99
The "Big House"................................ 101
Spinning Wheel 103
Spinning Wheel and Yarn Reel................... 103
Ante-Bellum Bed Room........................... 105
Slaves and Their Cabin, 1850................... 105
Subscriptions to Charlotte Academy, 1823....... 111
Davidson College, Main Building, 1857.......... 115
Gin House and Screw............................ 119
Modern Steam Cotton Ginnery.................... 119
Bill of Sale 123
Notice of Sale 123
County Court House, 1888....................... 159
County Court House, 1898....................... 159
City Hall, 1888................................ 159
City Hall, 1898................................ 159

Railroad Station, 1888......................*Page* 159
Railroad Station, 1898......................... 159
Average Road, 1888............................ 159
Average Road, 1898............................ 159
First Presbyterian Church..................... 163
Tryon Street Baptist Church................... 163
Tryon Street M. E. Church, South.............. 165
Catholic Church 165
Davidson College Campus....................... 167
Presbyterian College 169
Elizabeth College 171
Road Machinery 179
Cotton Mill and Cotton........................ 181
Cotton Mill Operatives 183
Wheat 185
Corn 185
Grapes 187
Cattle 187
Andrew Jackson 189
Jackson's Birthplace 189
James Knox Polk 191
Polk's Birthplace 191
Zebulon Baird Vance 191
Diagram 193

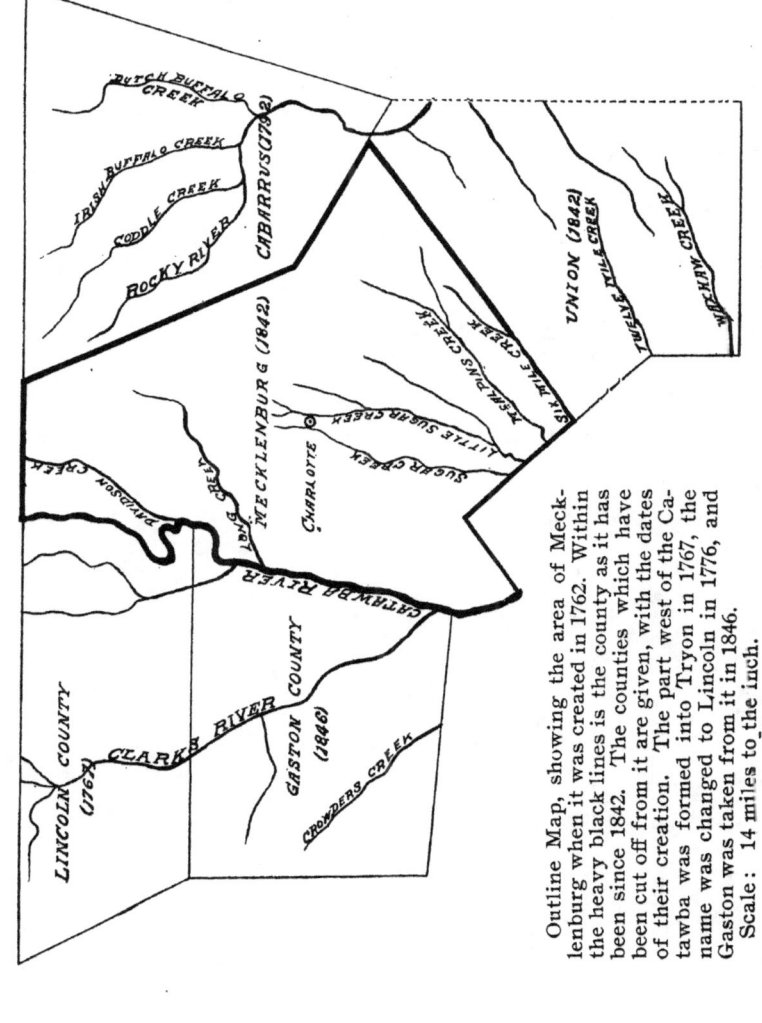

Outline Map, showing the area of Mecklenburg when it was created in 1762. Within the heavy black lines is the county as it has been since 1842. The counties which have been cut off from it are given, with the dates of their creation. The part west of the Catawba was formed into Tryon in 1767, the name was changed to Lincoln in 1776, and Gaston was taken from it in 1846.
  Scale: 14 miles to the inch.

CHAPTER I.

THE COLONISTS.

An Account of the Settlement of the Original Colonies and of the Causes Which Prompted Emigration to North Carolina and to the Piedmont Section.

October 12, 1492, Christopher Columbus landed on one of the Bahama Islands named by him San Salvador. He never touched the main land of North America, though on his third voyage he visited the coast of South America. In 1499, Americus Vespucius, a bold and intelligent navigator, published a map of the coast of North America, and wrote vivid descriptions of the lands he visited, so that his contemporaries named the continent America, in his honor. In 1497, an Englishman, John Cabot, discovered the continent of North America, and hence England assumed the right of exclusive possession on account of prior discovery. In 1498, John Cabot and his son, Sebastian, explored the whole coast line from Labrador to the mouth of Chesapeake Bay.

The Spaniards were the first settlers of the new land—along the coast of the Gulf of Mexico, in what is now Mexico. In 1535, Jacques Cartier, a Frenchman, sailed up the St. Lawrence as far as Montreal, and planted a fort on the heights of Quebec in 1541. In 1562, and the years following, the French Huguenots made a settlement in Florida, but were destroyed by the Spaniards, who had established St. Augustine in 1565, from which the French were unable to drive them. The French planted more settlements in what is now Nova Scotia—then called Acadia, and all the way up the St. Lawrence, at the beginning of the Seventeenth century. From the year 1600, France and England were the only real rivals for the colonization of North America. The resistance of the Dutch in the Netherlands and the destruction of the Spanish Armada broke the power of Spain.

In 1578, the English fitted out an expedition to settle Labrador. But the hundred settlers were afraid to be left alone on that bleak coast, and the colony returned without accomplishing anything. In 1583, Sir Humphrey Gilbert and Sir Walter Raleigh, as representatives of England, went through the form of claiming New Foundland, whose valuable fisheries were already supplying Europe with fish, a hundred and fifty vessels from France and forty from England being engaged in that trade. In 1584, Raleigh sent out two ships to take a more southerly course from England, and they came to Roanoke Island, North Carolina. The whole country then between the parallels of 33 degrees and 45 degrees north latitude was named by Raleigh, Virginia, in honor of England's virgin queen, Elizabeth. The first colony on Roanoke Island was of men only, and it failed. The idea was exploration rather than colonization. The second colony, on the same island, contained women and men, and here, April 18, 1687, the first white child born in America, Virginia Dare, first saw the light. The colony was left in good condition with promises of succor from England. But when the ships came, the colonists had all disappeared. The Indians of Roanoke Island had been described by one of these colonists to be "most gentle, loving and faithful, and such as live after the manner of the golden age." The disappearance of the colony has remained a mystery, though it is claimed that the whites intermarried with the Indians, and that the Croatan Indians of Robeson county are the descendants of the mixed race. This is the only answer that has ever been given to the question, "What became of the lost colony?"

In April, 1607, the first permanent English settlement in what is now the United States, was made at Jamestown, in Virginia. The Spaniards had been upon the very spot eighty years before, but they had given up, and the English remained permanently. After Jamestown came Henrico, Hampton, New Bermuda, and other settlements in Virginia. In 1619, a Virginia Assembly met. In that year also a

Dutch vessel brought the first negro slaves, twenty of them, to America. The Puritans landed on Plymouth Rock the next year, in 1620, making a permanent colony there. Between them and the Virginia Colony the Dutch had established themselves in the New Netherlands. As early as 1610, they built a fort on the Hudson at Albany, and had put up a few log huts on Manhattan Island, which they called New Amsterdam. Captain Argall was sent from Virginia to subdue New Amsterdam and did so, but so soon as he went back the Dutch threw off the English yoke. In 1651 they conquered a Swedish colony and became the rivals of the Puritans in trade with the Indians. The Dutch extended their settlements from Connecticut to the Delaware. In 1664, they gave up their town, New Amsterdam, to Colonel Nicholas, acting for the Duke of York, and both New Netherlands and New Amsterdam changed their names to New York.

In 1633, the Colony of Maryland, with its liberal charter, was founded by Lord Baltimore, and it was settled from Virginia, from the New Netherlands and by the Catholic immigrants from England. Delaware had been first settled by the Swedes, who had acknowledged the authority of the Dutch. The Swedes had also been the first settlers of Pennsylvania. In 1681, Charles the Second granted a charter for the whole country to William Penn, the Quaker, and named it Pennsylvania. The same year a party from Germany settled in what is now known as Germantown. The Quakers, who were persecuted in England, came over in great numbers. Other Germans followed and colonized Western Pennsylvania. From about this time began the immigration of the Scotch-Irish, from Ulster county, Ireland, in scattering bands, into New England, in larger numbers into New York and New Jersey, and by the thousand into Pennsylvania, settling Philadelphia and then going beyond the German settlements still farther west.

In 1670, a few emigrants from England settled at Port

Royal, South Carolina, moving the next year to the western bank of the Ashley river and again to Oyster Point, at the junction of the Ashley and Cooper rivers where, in 1680, the foundations of Charleston were laid. They were reinforced in 1673 by an immigration of Dutch from New York, seeking new homes after the English conquest of the New Netherlands. In 1686 there was a large immigration of the Huguenots who fled from religious persecution in France. After long controversies between the English and these Dutch and French dissenters, the latter were admitted to all the rights and privileges of the former. The South Carolina Colony was constantly threatened by the Spaniards to the south of them. Later in history, Georgetown became an important point. The Scotch-Irish also made Charleston a port of entry. A large Swiss settlement was made near the coast, but was so much reduced by the too great change in climate from their native mountains that the survivors moved westward toward the up country.

"The Carolinas" is the name given by the French who explored them in 1563, in honor of Charles the Ninth. The first permanent settlements in North Carolina were made from Virginia and by English immigrants, along the Chowan river, adjacent to Virginia. Some of these lands, although lying in North Carolina, were deeded by Governor Berkeley, of Virginia, as the boundary line of 36 degrees and 30 minutes was not determined until 1728. The first settlements of importance were made in 1653. All along the border of eastern and middle North Carolina, the Virginia settlers poured over the line. The land grants in this colony were more desirable and the taxes and levies less than in Virginia. But for sixty years the population was mostly confined to the territory north of Albemarle Sound, which gave its name to Albemarle county, one of the two divisions of the colony. A colony from the Barbadoes settled at the mouth of the Cape Fear in 1665, but in 1690 the last of these settlers left and moved south to Charleston. This colony was called the county of Clarendon. In 1663 the counties of Clarendon and Albemarle were united under the government of Lords Proprietors. There was an open revolt in Albemarle until the people were persuaded that their liberties would be preserved. This was in 1669, when there met an Assembly composed of the Governor and his Council and twelve delegates elected by the people. In 1709 and 1710, several thousand Swiss and German immigrants from the Palatinate settled at New Bern, which was named for the Swiss city. Baron De Graffenreid was their leader. There was a dreadful massacre by the Indians in 1712, in which many of these and other settlers lost their lives. So the progress of the colony was slow. In 1717, the taxable inhabitants numbered only 2,000, and in 1729 the number had grown to 13,000. Then the tide of immigration began to pour in all at once, and on account of late settlement, the foreign population was greater in North Carolina, and the immigration from the other colonies as compared with English immigration was also larger. The population of 20,000, including the negro slaves, in 1730, had grown to 393,000 by 1790. This growth was largely by immigration from the other colonies.

The first known land grant was made in 1633 to a Quaker named Durant, at the mouth of the Little and Perquimans rivers, which became the nucleus for a large Quaker settlement—a refuge for those who were persecuted in both Virginia and New England. Other dissenters, from Nansemond county, Virginia, one colony being composed of sixty-seven persons, settled in the territory just over the line.

After Bacon's Rebellion, especially, "fugitives from arbitrary tribunals, non-conformists, and friends of popular liberty, fled to Carolina as their common subterfuge and lurking place." In 1672, there was organized resistance against England for the oppressive laws, taxing tobacco a penny a pound and requiring its shipment to England for taxation before it could be sent elsewhere. The people arrested the Deputy Governor and Council and elected a Governor of their own, an Englishman named Culpepper. Says Bancroft of this incident: "Are there any who doubt man's capacity for self-government—let them study the history of North Carolina. Its inhabitants were restless and turbulent in their imperfect submission to a government imposed on them from abroad; the administration of the colony was firm, humane and tranquil when they were left to take care of themselves. The uneducated population of that day formed conclusions as just as those which a century later pervaded the country."

The main settlers in Eastern Carolina were English from Virginia, and as the country was settled along the coast they gradually moved westward. Henry McCulloh settled a colony of Scotch-Irish direct from Ireland in Duplin county in 1736. From the year 1740 a stream of Scotch-Irish and German immigrants from Pennsylvania and the Valley of Virginia poured southward along the whole of the Piedmont section. In 1746 occurred in Scotland the Battle of Culloden, in which the Scotch Highlanders, who were still loyal to the House of Stuart, were defeated. In the following year and for years afterward colonies of these Highlanders came to Wilmington and then up the Cape Fear, settling what are now Bladen, Sampson, Cumberland, Harnett, Moore, Robeson, Richmond and Scotland counties. In 1750, the Moravians purchased 100,000 acres of land from Lord Granville, in Surry County. In the meantime there began an immigration over the southern line of the colony from Charleston and Georgetown as ports of entry, and from the several nationalities that had already settled South Carolina. This northward movement from South Carolina and the migration westward from the settled portions of the eastern counties, and the movement southward from Pennsylvania and Virigina, met and mingled in the southern Piedmont region now occupied by Mecklenburg and adjacent counties.

CHAPTER II.

INDIANS OF THIS SECTION. (1753 to 1763.)

Troubles Between White People and Indians—Full Report of a Peace Conference—Wars Among Different Indian Tribes—The Cherokees and the Catawbas.

American Indians were much the same everywhere. In the days when the white people began to settle this section, they found the American Indian in possession of the land. It is not necessary to discuss Indian characteristics or to lament the exit of the Red Man from the field of action, or to accuse our ancestors of barbarity in their treatment of this race of people. The Indian was not capable of civilization, and he, for that reason more than all others, is not with us today. But the Indian character in its general features was the same everywhere, and needs no special discussion for the reason that the Indians originally living in this section displayed no marked differences from those found all over the country when the English began to found their colonies.

Originally, the Catawba Indian nation inhabited the valleys of the Catawba river and its tributaries, and claimed all the country adjacent thereto as far west as the Blue Ridge mountains. West of the Blue Ridge the Cherokees held sway. The Catawbas, like other Indians, delighted in pomp and show, painted their faces and wore feathers and showy trinkets. Their religion consisted largely in warding off evil spirits by charms, totems and incantations. They burned off their hair with live coals, wore furs, used the bow and arrow and the stone axe. The conjurer and the medicine man were little less than gods among these people. The dance and the masquerade were similar to those held everywhere by Indians. Their feasts and their methods of warfare were the same as among other tribes. Hence, it seems that these Catawbas were no better Indians than were to be found elsewhere on the American continent. If they were sometimes well disposed towards the whites, it was for reasons other than those springing from innate goodness, as their history will show.

In order to get an idea of the Indian and his doings in this section, it will be necessary to note the Indian troubles which took place here from 1750 and up to and after the organization of this county. The first thing to be noted is that foreign Indians were always passing back and forth through this section, committing all kinds of lawlessness upon the English settlers at the instigation of the French. Generally, these roving bands were small in numbers. As early as June, 1753, three "French Indians" and five northern Indians met thirteen Catawbas about two miles from Salisbury and fought a small battle. The Catawbas killed five of their enemies, suffering no loss themselves. The white people who lived along the routes taken by these roving bands always suffered either personal violence or loss of property.

June 16, 1754, Colonel John Clark, of the Anson Militia Regiment, reported that the Indians had recently killed sixteen white persons on Broad river. This proceeding was the work of the Catawbas or the Cherokees, and was thought to be the beginning of an attempt to cut off the frontiers from the more thickly settled portions of the province. This event, as well as the threatening attitude of all the Indians in this section, led the whites to cultivate closer friendship with the Catawbas than ever before. The Governor of the province, at the solicitation of the whites of this section, appointed James Carter and Alexander Osborne, of Rowan, to treat with the Catawbas and settle the troubles then existing between the two races. Accordingly, on the 29th day of August, 1754, the commissioners met "King Hagler and sundry of his head men and warriors" at Matthew Toole's house, and proceeded to discuss affairs relating to the whites and the Catawbas, Toole acting as interpreter. At this meeting the whites presented their grievances against the

Indians and the Indians explained the cause of their own offenses, and in turn presented their grievances against the whites. The Indians were accused of going to the mill of one William Morrison and attempting to throw a pail of water in the meal trough, and, when Morrison tried to prevent them, of attempting to strike the miller over the head with their guns. The Indians replied to this charge, that they only intended to put a few handfuls of meal in the pail to make a drink, according to their custom.

The whites then brought up the murder of a little girl below the Waxhaw settlement by Indians. Hagler said that his warriors had killed the drunken Indian who had committed this crime, forcing the Indian's own cousin to kill the murderer in the presence of an assembled band of warriors and whites, thus demonstrating to the white people that the Indians were willing to punish such an offender. Other charges were then preferred by various persons, accusing the Indians of taking bread, meat, clothes, of trying to carry away a child, and of attempting to stab men and women who opposed them in the commission of such petty lawlessness. In reply to these latter charges, Hagler said that the Indians were often at war with their enemies, and that it was not always possible for them to hunt and to get bread for themselves; that under such circumstances they had gone to the houses of white people and had asked for something to eat, but that the whites would hide everything from them and say there was nothing for them. Hagler, continuing, said the Indians under such circumstances had often searched the houses of the whites for food and found it. He averred that one of his wild young men merely pretended he was going to carry away the child mentioned by the whites in order to surprise the child's parents and have a joke at their expense.

The whites then accused Hagler's warriors of other acts of theft, and Hagler replied that he had some warriors who had stolen knives, clothes, and the like, although cautioned not to do so. Hagler told the whites that they themselves were responsible for many of the crimes they charged against the Indians, as they rotted grain in tubs and made strong drink of it and sold and gave it to the Indians, causing them to get very drunk and to commit all manner of excesses. Hagler recommended that the whites take some steps to prevent the selling of liquor to the Indians.

The commissioners then presented the charge of horse stealing against the Indians, a crime which they said was punishable by death among the whites. Hagler replied by saying that the Indians had also had many of their own horses stolen by white people; that they had lately caught one white man with some of their horses and carried him before a South Carolina justice of the peace, but the man was not punished.

The Indians made many speeches during this meeting, all professing friendship for the whites. In one of his talks Hagler said that the Great Man Above made us all, as well as this island; that he fixed the Indian's forefathers here; that in the early days the Indians had no instruments to make a living, only bows and arrows of stone; that they had no knives, and cut their hair by burning it off their heads and bodies with live coals of fire; that they had only stone axes; that they bled themselves with fish teeth, and wore clothes of skin and furs. But now Hagler said that his brethren enjoyed the clothes which they got from the whites, as well as many other conveniences, and that the Indians wished to live in peace with their white neighbors. Hagler was very urgent in calling the attention of the commissioners to the selling and giving away of whiskey to the Indians, and asked that such practices be stopped. The chief said that many of his warriors had lately died from the effects of whiskey, and that many of the crimes committed by his people were directly traceable to the use of liquor. The conference broke up and a better understanding between the Catawbas and whites seems to have resulted.

During the year 1755, Governor Dobbs visited this section and selected a site for a fort on Fourth creek, in the territory between Salisbury and the present town of Statesville. This fort, named in honor of the Governor, was erected and a company of soldiers under Hugh Waddell sent to occupy it and to guard the frontiers. It was built of oak logs, fifty-three by forty feet, twenty-four and a half feet high, with three floors in it, and room for the discharge of one hundred muskets at one time. It is said that a garrison of forty-eight men remained there during the year 1756.

During 1756, a fort was begun at the Catawba nation. Governor Dobbs visited the Catawbas in 1755, and no doubt selected the site for this fort, as well as the one in Rowan. The government of the province procured a tract of six hundred and forty acres, on which to erect the fort, at a cost of £60, but it appears that the work was never completed, as the Catawbas did not like the idea of its erection so near them, thinking, no doubt, the whites would use it to oppress them. When the Indians became restless on account of its erection, they were, by the Governor's order, given presents amounting to £42 12s. 9d. The work done at the fort was finally abandoned after something like £1,000 had been expended.

While the white people were busy trying to erect the fort at the Catawba nation, the settlers on Broad river sent another complaint to the Legislature, reciting the perpetration of several robberies by strolling bands of Indians, presumably Cherokees, headed by some French and Northern Indians, who hoped thereby to provoke the settlers to some violence that they might have a pretext to murder or to bring on a general Indian war. These acts of villainy continued all through the summer of 1756, and until late in the fall. The people on the frontiers said that the garrison at Fort Dobbs and the militia aiding that garrison could do little in case of a general Indian uprising, and hence the back settlers were being forced to retire from their lands and take up their residence in the inner settlements. Many of the settlers, forced from their homes, took refuge, in the fall of 1756, with the Moravians at Bethabara, which town was enclosed with palisades.

Notwithstanding the Catawbas had been well treated by the whites and had been given guns, clothing and presents of various kinds, and even a fort had been begun in their border as a protection both to themselves and to the whites, and had been abandoned at their behest, these Indians became restless and cruel in the year 1757, and began to insult the whites and do many acts of petty violence. They went so far in their violence as to go to Salisbury while the District Court was in session and insult the Chief Justice.

In May, 1758, the Rowan people informed the Assembly that the frequency of Indian outrages on the head waters of the Dan river had caused the settlers on the forks of the Yadkin to leave their homes and retire "farther inland." Outrages on the Dan continued, as well as murders and robberies all along the western frontiers, during the year 1758 and in the spring of 1759, so much so that Governor Dobbs laid the condition of the frontier settlers before the Assembly and Colonel Hugh Waddell was given two companies of provincial troops and power to order out the militia of Anson, Rowan and Orange counties to punish the Cherokees.

In the fall of 1759, Governor Lyttleton, of South Carolina, appealed to Georgia, North Carolina and Virginia to aid him in an expedition against the Cherokees. Colonel Waddell was requested by Governor Dobbs to order out the militia of Orange, Rowan and Anson counties and join the militia with his regular troops and march to the aid of the South Carolina Governor. But the great body of the militia refused to leave the borders of the province, only eighty out of five hundred militiamen remaining with Colonel Waddell; the others either deserted or went home without leave, an action on their part which Governor Dobbs attributed to lack of education and schools and a pious clergy. Waddell's remaining force was, however, met and turned back, as Governor Lyttleton had made peace with the Indians and no fighting became necessary, the treaty being signed October 26, 1759. The Indians soon broke this peace, the garrison at Prince George Fort, where the Cherokee chiefs were imprisoned as hostages, being enticed away and murdered. This was the signal for a general Cherokee uprising, and massacre and assassination began. The Creeks were drawn into the war. Fort Loudon fell and the frontiers of this province were again at the mercy of the Cherokees.

In 1760 the Cherokee depredations forced the Moravians to guard their town day and night. Refugee settlers in large numbers crowded into Bethabara, which forced the building of Bethany, three miles from Bethabara, for the accommodation of these refugees and the protection of the Moravians themselves. Only extreme vigilance and the constant ringing of the church bells prevented an Indian attack. But the Cherokees were not content to rob and murder the frontier people and to threaten the Moravians and their refugees; they openly attacked Fort Dobbs February 27, 1769, and were repulsed by Waddell and his garrison. Ten or twelve Indians were killed or wounded, one white boy was killed and two white men were wounded, one of whom was scalped.

These events determined the whites to put an end to Indian outrages. Troops from Virginia and both Carolinas were assembled, the North Carolina troops under Waddell. The Virginians and North Carolinians entered the upper Cherokee country, while Colonel Grant, with the South Carolinians, entered the lower country of the Cherokees. Grant's forces met the Indians near the present town of Franklin and defeated them. During the next month the whites destroyed the Indian towns and corn fields and inflicted such a heavy blow upon the Cherokee nation that it was forced to sue for peace. This Indian campaign of 1761 broke forever the power of the Cherokees and reduced their strength so much that they, like the Catawbas, became friends of the whites, as they knew it was now to their advantage.

These Indian troubles had continued for seven years. Many of the settlers were driven away, some were killed, others were scalped. Farming and home-building were much retarded, and new settlers who would have moved in from Pennsylvania and other colonies were frightened away. It was not until the beginning of 1763 that the frontier people began to take up life again where it had been interrupted, and the militia of Mecklenburg and adjoining counties could be said to be able once more to feel that Indian troubles had ended.

CHAPTER III.

EARLY SETTLERS. (1740 to 1762.)

Original Homes of the Immigrants—Their Nationalities—Traits of Character—Religious Persecutions in the Old Country, and Subsequent Removal to America and Mecklenburg County.

Immigrants to Mecklenburg county came from three directions. One wave rolled southward from Western Pennsylvania and Virginia—the Scotch-Irish, who had had large experience in the selection of good lands. These were followed closely by the Germans from the same region, who settled mainly the territory now occupied by Cabarrus, Lincoln and Gaston counties, but who also peopled Mecklenburg proper and passed over into South Carolina with the Scotch-Irish, settling the northwestern portion. This wave of immigrants was met by another wave a little later from the south, coming by way of Charleston and Georgetown—a mixed multitude of English, Scotch, Germans, Huguenots and Swiss, who found in the low country by the sea too great a contrast to their own mountain homes. While these two waves were mingling, the third wave rolled in from the east, mainly English, and finding the best lands taken, settled the next best or passed through into the lands to the west and south. The sections which were settled by these different peoples retain the traces of nationality in their names and in the churches; the Scotch-Irish and Huguenots with the English dissenters uniting to build Presbyterian churches, while the Lutheran and German Reform churches mark the German settlements. By the beginning of the Revolutionary War the representatives of these different nationalities were fast intermingling by marriage.

A petition to the Council concerning the lands which were at first considered in Mecklenburg and then were put in

South Carolina show 140 names of English origin, 47 Scotch, 7 German and 6 French.

In 1755, Governor Dobbs visited the present county of Cabarrus, where he owned large tracts of land, and he found seventy-five families already settled on his lands. He reported that these families contained eight or ten children each, and that some "Irish Protestants" had settled together in order to have a preacher and a school teacher of their own. There were also twenty-two German and Swiss families on his lands. The actual settling of Mecklenburg county by permanent home-seekers began about 1748. From that time on a stream of settlers poured in from the north. In 1754, they had settled on Broad river and were asking for protection from the Indians. In 1757 the Selwyn tracts of land, one of which is now partly occupied by the city of Charlotte, contained something less than 400 souls.

In 1755, Rev. Hugh McAden made a missionary visit through Mecklenburg. He found the Scotch-Irish settled at Rocky River, Sugar Creek, in the Waxhaws, and on what is now Broad river, in South Carolina. The earliest land grants are dated 1749, but between 1750 and 1758 many hundreds of such grants were issued. There was probably only a short time generally between the issuing of the grant and the settlement of the land. Rocky river and its tributaries were the first water courses occupied by the settlers, and by 1762 all the streams mentioned in the first chapter are recorded in land grants, patents and deeds.

To understand and appreciate the history of the people of Mecklenburg, we must know something of the origin and history of these early settlers. John Knox, the great Scottish reformer, was not only the apostle of religion, but of liberty as well, to his people. When he said, "If princes exceed their bounds they may be resisted by force," he set the rights of the people over against the right claimed for the king and sometimes called the "Divine right of kings." Mr. Froude calls this saying "the creed of republics in its first hard form." Knox was also the apostle of popular education. Carlyle says of him: "He sent the schoolmaster into all corners, saying, 'let the people be taught.'" Scotland was a different land after the life and labors of John Knox.

In the reign of James the First, of England and Scotland, two Irish nobles rebelled against him, and the king took possession of their lands in the north of Ireland. He wished to settle this region, about half a million acres of land, with Protestants, to balance the Catholic power which held the rest of Ireland, and so he offered inducements to the Scotch to emigrate to North Ireland. This country was called Ulster. Rev. Andrew Stewart, one of their ministers, wrote: "The king had a natural love to have Ireland planted with Scots, as being of a middle temper, between the English tender and the Irish rude breeding, and a great deal more likely to adventure to plant Ireland."

The Scotch emigrated to Ireland in great numbers. In the first fifty years of their settling they numbered 200,000. By the beginning of the Eighteenth century they numbered a million, and they carried with them to Ireland their fondness for education and their love of liberty. They were thrifty and industrious and they prospered. Their prosperity excited the jealousy of their English rivals in manufactures, and the British Parliament began to pass laws restricting their woolen trade, so the Scotch-Irish, as they were afterwards called, began to leave Ireland. In 1698, 20,000 of them left Ulster for America. Not content with oppressive taxation, the Parliament began to interfere with the religion of the Ulsterites. They were forbidden to have school teachers of their own and forbidden to hold any office higher than that of petty constable. Their ministers were forbidden to perform the marriage ceremony, and when they did, the marriage was declared to be illegal. So the Scotch left their Irish home in an exodus that has been compared to the exodus of the Israelites from Egypt.

In 1727 six emigrant ships full of Scotch-Irish arrived at Philadelphia in one week, and all through the first half of the Eighteenth century it was not uncommon for two or three emigrant ships a day to reach America from Ireland. Then just a little after Mecklenburg county was organized, the rents of the tenants who were left in Ireland were raised and thousands of them driven from their farms by force. Two years after this, 30,000 Scotch-Irish came to America in one year.

Some of them went to New England and settled there. There was one Scotch-Irish church which had 750 members. They settled a good part of New York. They peopled New Jersey. They took possession of the Quaker City, Philadelphia, and filled up Western Pennsylvania, with Pittsburg as the centre of their colony. Then as the Pennsylvania lands were taken, they moved southward and westward. They were among the pioneer settlers of Kentucky and Tennessee. They occupied the fertile Valley of Virginia and peopled the western counties so that they soon outvoted their cavalier brethren in the eastern counties. Thomas Jefferson said of Patrick Henry, whom he styled "Our leader in the measures of the Revolution in Virginia," that "his influence was most extensive with the members from the upper counties."

As these upper counties of Virginia were filled and the best lands taken, the Scotch-Irish moved southward, as we have seen, into North Carolina, through Guilford, Orange, Alamance, Rowan, Iredell, Cabarrus and Mecklenburg counties. Mecklenburg was the centre of this emigration southward from Virginia and Pennsylvania. Everywhere these Scotch-Irish people were advocates of education and of liberty. When we come to Revolutionary times, we learn that the great majority of the patriots in New York were Scotch-Irish; that the Scotch-Irish, numbering in Pennsylvania a third of the whole population, stood as a unit for independence and contributed a majority of the troops of the Keystone State. General Washington said that if he had been

EARLY SETTLERS. 19

defeated at Yorktown, he would have fallen back upon the Scotch-Irish of the Valley of Virginia. We shall see that the Scotch-Irish of Mecklenburg were of the same spirit, and simply gave earlier expression to it than their brethren elsewhere.

The first Germans known to have reached this section were three young farmers. They were all probably Redemptioners. This term was used in connection with white apprentices, and afterwards applied to poor emigrants who were not able to pay their passage to America and were willing to enter into contracts in order to pay back the funds advanced for their passage across the ocean. The names of these three Germans were Barringer, Smith and Dry. When they had worked out their term of service they started on their perilous march from Pennsylvania to the South, passing by a savage Indian camp and the French frontiersmen, following the old buffalo trail, known as the Indian trading path, until they reached the Yadkin at the trading fort; but when they crossed the Yadkin they were surprised to find that the Scotch-Irish were just ahead of them, having taken up the choicest spots up and down the Catawba; so these Germans turned to the left, following the right bank of the Yadkin, and finally located on the high ground between the present Cold Water and Buffalo creeks. This was then Bladen county.

About the year 1745 the news of the good land of freedom went back to Pennsylvania and then reached the millions of the Fatherland. They came from all directions, chiefly from Pennsylvania, but often from Charleston and Wilmington, settling the northeastern borders of Mecklenburg as well as Rowan and Stanly. These Germans came from the upper regions of Germany, Wurtenburg, Baden, and especially from the Palatinate, which had been so mercilessly ravaged by Louis the Sixteenth. They were intelligent, labor loving, industrious Protestants, who fled from persecution. They built their houses here on high ground, often on the tops of the hills, after the fashion of the ancient German castles. They were hardy, self-reliant, frugal and courageous. They clung to Luther's translation of the Bible. They tolerated no idlers among them. The children were trained and skilled in all hard labor and handicraft, and they defended their homes heroically when they were summoned to vindicate the rights which they had secured. They took part in almost every expedition against the Indians, and a very active part in General Rutherford's march against the Cherokees in 1776, a young German called Matthias Barringer being one of the very few killed. The Germans traded with Salisbury on the north and with Cross Creek, now Fayetteville, on the east, rather than Charleston. They did not figure as prominently in the affairs in which Charlotte was concerned on account of the rivalry which grew up between the Charlotte and Cabarrus sections.

These German Protestants respected just authority, were God-fearing, peaceful and law-abiding. They had their sports and their amusements, their Easter holiday and their Chris Cringle frolics. They were guiltless of dissipation and debauchery, and even their amusements partook rather of skill and labor than of useless sport. Their quiltings, corn shuckings, log rollings, house raisings, all tended to develop manliness and womanliness as well as to cultivate the social virtues. Their family government was excellent, combining for them the State, the Church and the School, and their thrift and economy laid the foundations for comfort and wealth.

The French settlers were mostly Huguenots who were also the victims of religious persecution in the Old World and sought freedom of conscience in the New. The Swiss were from the Palatinate and near akin to their German neighbors in religious belief. A large colony of Swiss in South Carolina was almost destroyed by the fever of the lowlands near the coast, where they first settled, and the mention of the Swiss families by Governor Dobbs is probably the explanation of what became of the survivors. They would naturally tend toward the hill country, as more nearly like their own home.

Authority:—General Rufus Barringer's Address and Wheeler's Sketches and Old Records.

CHAPTER IV.

INDUSTRIES AND CUSTOMS. (1745 to 1762.)

How the Settlers Built Their Homes—Their First Mills and Occupations—Trading—Social Life and Diversions.

The early settlers of Mecklenburg were not idlers and many of them were skilled in various industrial arts. They had everything to do for themselves in the wilderness in which they made their home. When they came, there were no cleared fields, no roads, no schools or churches, no mills to grind their corn and wheat, no shops to make their hoes and plows and axes, and not even houses to shelter them. There were no saw mills and no brickyards. But the settlers had something that was even better than the possession of all these things. They had the knowledge and the skill to make the wilderness blossom as the rose. They knew how to make things and they made them.

As early as 1750, some of them were doing business with Charleston. In order to buy what they could not make, they must have something to sell. They sent to Charleston over an Indian trail, which passed near Charlotte and which is now the route of the Charlotte & Columbia Railroad, the products which their cattle yielded—tallow, cheese, butter and hides. Then as they began to raise grain and fruits, they manufactured whiskey and brandy. With these they bought in Charleston salt, iron, and household goods, with now and then a slave to help in the work on the plantation. As the farmers could not afford to go to Charleston often, there began to be built country stores in the different neighborhoods—in Paw Creek, Hopewell, Steele Creek, Providence, Sugar Creek, Rocky River.

The people made their own hats and shoes, and wove their own cloth. They were hatters and shoemakers and weavers and tailors. They raised indigo for dyeing. They raised flax and made it into linen. They raised tobacco and it became quite a profitable crop, as the world was then learning how to smoke. But at first it was easier to raise cattle than anything else, and the settlers not only sent them to Charleston, but drove them to Philadelphia. Later Virginia bought all the cattle sent northward.

These pioneer settlers slept in their wagons until they built a house to shelter them, cutting down the trees of the forest and hewing the logs into shape. They daubed the spaces between the logs with clay and covered the roof with boards riven out of the logs. These houses had one room and one door and one window. Sometimes the people could afford a glass window. Generally they let in the air with the light and shut out both with a wooden shutter. When they did not have planks for a floor, they used the floor they found there—the ground. Inside the house were probably two beds, a trunk, some pewter dippers and plates, a dozen spoons, some wooden trenchers and piggins, and a few stools or chairs. The farmer would have a few plow irons, a hoe or two, a mattock, some harrow teeth, an axe, a broad-axe, an iron wedge, two or three mauls, a chisel, and an auger. These were all he needed at first, and he brought them with him from North or South. He would have fifty head of cattle, three or four horses, twenty hogs, and a few sheep and geese. The sheep gave their wool and the geese their feathers to make the folk comfortable by day and night. When the family began to buy cups and saucers, and glass and china ware from Charleston, they were considered wealthy.

The things they brought with them began to wear out and so the blacksmiths built their shops, and the weavers set up their looms and the tailor brought out his goose. And the hides were not all carried to Charleston to trade for leather, but tanneries were built to make leather at home. Then rude mills were set up on the water courses to grind the wheat and corn, and the carpenters and blasksmiths together built saw mills to turn the logs into boards. One of the first saw mills and flour mills was built on Rocky river and owned by

Moses Alexander. Richard Barry had a tanyard in operation in Hopewell. Thomas Polk had a saw mill and grist mill near Charlotte before 1767. The mills did a good business and leather and flour began to be sold in Charleston instead of hides and wheat. The settlers were learning the great law of prosperity—that they could keep their money at home by manufacturing things for themselves and that the manufactured products brought more money in the markets than the raw products.

In January, 1767, John McKnitt Alexander made "a great coat" for Andrew Bowman, which had nine large and three small buttons, the seam sewed and the button holes worked with mohair thread. Three yards and three inches of broadcloth were used, costing two pounds and fifteen shillings; the buttons and thread cost two shillings. The charge for making the coat was seven shillings, and Mr. Bowman was no doubt sumptuously arrayed when he donned this raiment. The women made all their own dresses and the material for them. They spun the wool and cotton and wove it into linsey and checks and colored it according to their own fancy. When Jeremiah McCafferty set up his store in Charlotte, in 1770, he sold persian, camblett, mits, forrest cloth, oznaburgs, and calico. But with calico at eight shillings a yard, these were materials that only the wealthy could afford. Buttons, thread and pins were very costly, and the housewives had to be very economical with salt and sugar, as they were high priced and difficult to get.

Early title-deeds show the occupations of the people who bought and sold the lands in Mecklenburg, and it is recorded that these hardy pioneers were weavers, joiners, coopers, wheelwrights, wagon makers, tailors, teachers, blacksmiths, hatters, merchants, laborers, wine makers, miners, rope makers, surveyors, fullers and "gentlemen." "Gentlemen" denoted then a certain rank rather than the possession of certain qualities. The first Mecklenburgers were producers. They believed that any work, so it were faithfully and honestly done, was worth doing, and that manhood was more than wealth. Mecklenburg could have existed comfortably cut off from the rest of the world. That makes a people feel independent. And when a man has built his home in the woods with his own hands, and furnished it, and cleared his own little plot of ground, and is beginning to be comfortable, he does not feel much like paying taxes out of his small earnings to a King or a Parliament over the seas, without any representation in the matter for himself and his rights.

Nearly every farm had a distillery for turning grain and fruit into whiskey and brandy. These liquors were used freely by all, but it would be a mistake to suppose that the people were intemperate. Spirits were deemed a necessity on the plantations. It was cheaper to distill than to buy. Moreover, the distance from the markets, Charleston being the nearest, was so great that it was easier to carry the products of the granaries and orchards in liquid form than in bulk. Every teacher's account with the farmers contains a credit of whiskey, and the preachers were also temperate drinkers. Among the effects of Rev. Alexander Craighead, sold at his sale, were a punch bowl and glasses. One custom that seems singular to us was the use of liquor at funerals. The people came a long distance and refreshments were served at the graveyards and churches. Whiskey played a leading part in these refreshments, though wine, which was more expensive, was also used. In 1767, seven gallons of whiskey were consumed at one funeral, costing five shillings to the gallon, the same being charged to the estate. Another occasion on which whiskey was used was at the "vendue" or sale of an estate. The amount of whiskey charged to the estate varied with the size of the sale and the number in attendance. It seems to have been taken for granted that a liberal use of the beverage would be repaid in the higher price the buyers would bid under the mellowing effect of the liquor.

One of the famous institutions of these early days was the old time tavern. The taverns sprung up along all the public roads. There were several in Charlotte. There was a good deal of travel through this section, between the North and the South, from early times. The tavern was not only a lodging place where meals were served, but a public house as well, where all kinds of liquors were served and where the punch bowl was an indispensable piece of furniture. From the variety of the liquors one is reminded of Dickens' tales of merry England in the stage coach days. The host of these early days was a genial and popular fellow, and the tavern became a meeting place for the men of the community, where they exchanged their ideas or confirmed their prejudices as the case might be, getting now and then from the travelers passing through, the news of the outside world.

Horse racing, the game of "long bullets," shooting matches and other outdoor sports of like nature were the diversions for the early settlers. "Long bullets" was a famous game, played with a large iron ball, the effort of one side being to keep the ball from passing their goal and at the same time to force it beyond the goal of the adversary. One of the first ordinances passed by the town of Charlotte forbade this game being played in the streets. Betting at horse races was common, there remaining to this day evidences of money borrowed on occasions of this kind in order to indulge the gambling propensity at Thom's or Campbell's Race Tracks. But while gambling was permitted, profanity was sternly forbidden, and was frequently punished by the county courts. After 1774, there are numerous instances of people being fined for profane swearing, the amount of the fine depending upon the number of oaths of which the culprit was convicted.

At the four county courts each year people came together from all parts of the county, and the court meetings were great occasions for trading wares and exchanging views. Then there was an annual election of the members of the Provincial Assembly, which was the signal for a gathering of all the leading men. The most prosperous of the people frequently visited Charleston and even Philadelphia, and they brought back with them newspapers and publications of the day. But one of the greatest institutions for bringing the people together was the muster. While this was at first nominally a military assembly, it soon became a social and political occasion. The military companies were kept in efficient condition for muster day, and it grew to be the chief opportunity for the public discussion of political issues. Such questions as the McCulloh land disturbances, the boundary dispute, the vestry and marriage acts, the Regulation troubles, and all the questions relating to the issues between the colonies and the mother country were discussed at the muster meetings. So the people were by no means ill-informed as to what was going on in the world. The children generally received six months of "schooling" for two or three years, and at the outbreak of the Revolution there was a fair number of college-bred men in the community, perhaps more in proportion to the population than at present.

The first settlers of the county from Virginia and Pennsylvania doubtless brought the currency of those colonies with them, and this was probably the first paper money put in circulation in this section. The "hard money" of that day consisted of English, Spanish and German coins, with now and then one of French mintage. From the account of a loan to Jean Cathey by George Cathey, we learn that "ten silver dollars" were valued at four pounds English money, while "one dubloone in gold" was worth six pounds. After Charleston became the principal market for Mecklenburg, South Carolina currency became common, but there was never a sufficient volume of currency for the needs of the population. Chief Justice Hasell, who held Salisbury Court in 1776, says that there was scarcely any specie circulating among the people, not enough to pay the stamp tax.

Authority:—County and Private Records.

CHAPTER V.

FORMATION OF THE COUNTY. (1762.)

Creation of Mecklenburg from Anson—Origin of the Names of the County and the City of Charlotte—Physical Description of the Country at that Time.

In North Germany are two little duchies that go by the name of Mecklenburg, Mecklenburg-Schwerin and Mecklenburg-Strelitz. From Mecklenburg-Strelitz, in the year 1761, went a young princess to be the wife of George the Third and Queen of England, and her name was Charlotte. The marriage was a popular one, and there was great rejoicing in England, and after a while the news of it reached the Piedmont section of North Carolina, where the people were just about to make two counties out of one. The name of the old county was Anson, named for the Admiral Anson whose good ship carried the young princess, Charlotte, to England. The new county was named Mecklenburg in honor of the queen who had come from old Mecklenburg, in Germany, and to do her still more honor, they called their town Charlotte. It must have been very pleasant to the king to think how loyal to the mother country and the royal family were the people of Mecklenburg and its "Queen City" of Charlotte, in St. George's Parish, in the Colony of North Carolina. It was his own fault if he afterwards had cause to change his mind about them.

The year 1761 was memorable in the history of the world. England and France had been fighting on land and on sea, and some of the land fighting had been done in America. During the war the Americans learned that they could fight as well as or better than the English soldiers could in this wild forest-land. In the year 1762, the war was finished and the Treaty of Paris was signed. By that treaty the French practically gave up North America to the British, and Spain

CHARLOTTE
PRINCESS OF MECKLENBURG.
Later Queen of England by marriage to George III.
Hence Charlotte, Queen City, Mecklenburg County,
NORTH CAROLINA.

Copyright 1901 by D. A. Tompkins

gave England part of Florida in return for Havana, in Cuba. The colonists observed another thing in the war, and that was that they were not so dependent as before upon the protection of the mother country, now that the French armies did not threaten them. They began to talk more independently. In England, there was at that time, and is now, an "Established Church" supported by taxes levied on the people. This was the Church of England, or what is now known in America as the Protestant Episcopal Church. At home, its bishops and other clergy had the right to levy church taxes or tithes, and this system was put into operation in the American colonies. The next year after the passage of the act creating Mecklenburg county, a young lawyer stood up before the judges, in Hanover county, Virginia, to defend the rights of the people against the oppressive taxation by the clergy. His name was Patrick Henry, and the jury that heard his eloquent defence gave the parsons "penny damages," and the brave words of the young lawyer rang throughout the colonies.

Arthur Dobbs was Governor of the colony, James Hasell was President of the Council and John Ashe was Speaker of the Assembly, when the act was passed creating the county of Mecklenburg, December 11, 1762. The bill had been introduced by Anthony Hutchins into the Assembly, accompanied by a petition "of several of the inhabitants of Anson county;" and Nathaniel Alexander, afterwards Governor of North Carolina, who represented the Rocky river section, used his influence in having the wishes of his constituents carried out as to the new county. December 31, of the same year, at the meeting of the Governor's Council, Alexander Lewis, Nathaniel Alexander, John Thomas, Robert McClenahan, Paul Barringer, Henry Foster, Robert Miller, Robert Harris, Richard Barry, Martin Phifer, Robert Ramsey, James Robinson, Matthew Floyd, Abraham Alexander, Thomas Polk and James Patton, were appointed His Majesty's Justices of the Peace for the new county, and they represented the Rocky River, Clear Creek, Sugar Creek, Waxhaw, Hopewell and Broad River settlements. And when, on the 26th of February, 1763, Moses Alexander, as High Sheriff, and Robert Harris, as Clerk of the Court and Register of Deeds, took charge of their respective offices, the history of the county may be said to have begun.

This Piedmont country was being rapidly settled, and the people did not want to travel so far to the county seat to have their legal business transacted. So, just as Anson was formed out of Bladen, then the most westerly county, and just as Rowan and Mecklenburg grew out of Anson, so in November, 1768, a bill, introduced by Martin Phifer, was passed dividing the original Mecklenburg county into two, one called Mecklenburg county and St. Martin's Parish, and the other Tryon county and St. Thomas' Parish. Later still, in 1792, Cabarrus county was cut off from Mecklenburg, and again in 1842, Union county was made out of Mecklenburg territory. But as Mecklenburg included both Cabarrus and Union during the whole Revolutionary period, the history of one is the history of all three.

It was a wild and strange country which the early settlers found. There was probably little cleared land, though some accounts speak of the country between Sugar creek and Rocky river as a fertile plain, covered with pea vines and grass. But the hills and probably most of the valleys were covered with primeval forests. The old title-deeds mention as marks on the dividing lines, an ash, an oak, post-oak, white oak, black oak, red oak or water oak, a maple, a poplar, a beech, or a hickory. Through these forests roamed deer and buffalo, and in the dense undergrowth, panthers, wild-cats, black bears, and wolves made their lairs. There were squirrels and turkeys and pheasants in abundance. There were beaver dams on Paw creek and Steele creek. The only road was one Indian trail through Mecklenburg, from the Yadkin river to the Catawba nation, with here and there the beaten path of the buffalo herds.

Authority:—State and County Records.

FIRST COURT HOUSE.

CHAPTER VI.

BEGINNING OF CHARLOTTE. (1762 to 1772.)

Influences Which Tended to the Necessity for a Town—Difficulty in Obtaining a Charter—The First Court House—Laws of the New Town.

Mecklenburg county, as at first constituted, contained all of the present county, Cabarrus, Gaston, Lincoln and a part of Union. The total area was four or five times as great as it is today. In 1766, the population of Mecklenburg was about five thousand, and this grew to six thousand within the next two years. Increase in population and development of the natural resources were rapid and continuous after government was firmly established.

In the latter part of 1765, Henry Eustace McCulloh donated a tract of three hundred and sixty acres of land to John Frohock, Abraham Alexander and Thomas Polk, as commissioners, to hold in trust for the county of Mecklenburg, on which to erect a court house, prison and stocks. McCulloh was the agent of Augustus Selwyn, who owned several immense tracts of land on a grant from the king, making it obligatory upon him to settle them with an average of one person to every two hundred acres. He foresaw that the interests of his employer would be advanced by the location of the county seat on his land. The courts before this time had been held at Spratts, just outside the present city limits, and as the proposed town was near the centre of the county, circumstances were apparently favorable to his plans, but objection was made by the people in the Rocky river section, who desired the court house to be located nearer to them.

The first representatives of Mecklenburg in the General Assembly were Martin Phifer, from Rocky river; and Thomas Polk, who favored the new town. In 1766, Mr.

Phifer introduced a bill to enable the commissioners of Charlotte to lay off the town in squares and streets and lots, and to erect a court house, prison and stocks. Nothing was said about the county seat or where courts should be held, and on this account, the bill was defeated by the friends of Charlotte led by Polk.

In this year, there was a large increase of population west of the Catawba river, and a new county was proposed. It was evident that if this plan succeeded, Charlotte would not then be in the centre of Mecklenburg, but her partisans, with a wise foresight, took advantage of the opportunity and erected a court house at their own expense. The building was erected at the intersection of Trade and Tryon streets, which were named about that time, and was in the centre of the square. It was a long structure, supported by pillars ten feet high, and a stairway was on the outside; the upper room was for court and public meetings, while the space below was used for a market. Martin Phifer, however, succeeded in having passed his bill creating Tryon county, but Thomas Polk had attached to it an amendment providing that the courts of Mecklenburg should for a period of seven years be held in the Charlotte court house. It is very probable that the county seat would have been located elsewhere had there not been a court house already built in Charlotte.

Previous to the passage of this bill, all efforts to have Charlotte incorporated had failed, but the objections were now withdrawn and the bill making Charlotte a town legally was enacted and became a law in November, 1768. This act added Richard Barry and George Allen to the old commissioners, and these five men were instructed to lay off one hundred acres of the town in half-acre lots and to carry out the requirements of the charter, but no provision was made for ordinances of the town government. Thomas Polk was required to give a bond as treasurer.

The law stipulated that for every town lot taken, an annual rent of one shilling should be paid to the town treasurer, and a dwelling should be erected on the lot within three years on penalty of forfeiture. Eighty lots had already been taken, and on some of them dwelling houses had been built. The ordinary house was made of sawed or hewn logs, and the cracks were filled with mud and straw or sticks. There was one large room twenty feet square, with high roof, and sometimes the bedrooms were partitioned off from this room with curtains or planks. Light was admitted through one window, which was generally closed with a wooden shutter, but sometimes with glass panes. The common chimney was made of stones, the better one of brick, and the poorer one of logs covered on the inside with mud. The roof was made of clap-boards fastened with home-made iron spikes or nails.

Those early issues of our history occasioned much partisan strife and considerable bitterness. In 1769, Martin Phifer was succeeded in the Assembly by Abraham Alexander, who, with Thomas Polk, continued to represent the county until 1773, when they were succeeded by Martin Phifer and John Davidson. Mr. Davidson introduced a bill to erect a permanent court house at Charlotte, and it passed both houses of the Assembly, but was vetoed by Governor Martin. The next year, Phifer was succeeded by Thomas Polk, and the agitation in favor of Charlotte continued. The temporary arrangement of seven years was about to end and some action was necessary. In December, 1773, Polk introduced a bill making Charlotte the permanent county seat and providing a regular town government, but the bill was not acted upon because of the dismissal of the Assembly by Governor Martin.

Polk re-introduced the bill at the next session, and it became a law in March, 1774. Its passage settled the question for all time, and allayed much of the bitter feeling that had been engendered. This act repealed the law of 1768 requiring the erection of a building on every town lot, unless the lot was located on Tryon or Trade street. Jeremiah McCafferty, William Patterson and Isaac Alexander were added to the commissioners in place of some who were dead or removed from the province. The commissioners were given power to require every taxable person in the town to work on the streets six days each year; any one failing to so work was to be fined five shillings for each day of such failure.

Before this time there had been considerable agitation regarding road-building, and efforts had been made to have roads laid off and worked from Charlotte to Charleston and from Charlotte to Fayetteville. Commissioners were appointed for the latter work in 1771, and others were put in their places two years later.

In 1774, Charlotte covered less than one hundred acres of land, but the population increased steadily, and in 1778, the law was revised to permit the laying off of eighty more lots, as all the original ones had been taken and most of them well improved with good buildings. The reasons assigned for the growth were that Charlotte was well situated for the inland trade and that Liberty Hall drew in many people to educate their children.

August 2, 1766, Governor Tryon wrote that this province was being settled rapidly and that more than a thousand emigrant wagons from the North had passed through Salisbury within a few months. These settlers were reported to be strong, healthy and industrious, and capable of various occupations.

The government of Mecklenburg was vested in a Sheriff, Clerk of the Court and sixteen Justices of the Peace. Charlotte was governed by the Board of Town Commissioners, but it seems that there were but few law-breakers, for the courts were occupied almost entirely with collecting quit-rents and settling disputes regarding conflicting claims to land.

Authority:—Colonial and County Records, old Deeds and Official Papers, and Hunter's Sketches.

CHAPTER VII.

EARLY TROUBLES AND REGULATORS. (1762 to 1772.)

Annoyances on Account of a Disputed Boundary Line—The McCulloh Land Riots—Surveying the Cherokee Boundary—Oppressive Taxes and Unjust Officers, and the Battle of Alamance.

When Mecklenburg county was created, the boundary lines were not definitely determined. The line between North Carolina and South Carolina had been surveyed toward the west only so far as the Salisbury and Charleston road, near Waxhaw creek. This left in dispute practically all the southern boundary of Mecklenburg, and troubles of various kinds naturally resulted.

For several years, the sheriff of Anson had been openly defied. On one occasion he raised a posse to assist him, and a riot resulted that continued several days, during which time the sheriff was captured and imprisoned. The people causing this disturbance were a lawless element who had been driven out of South Carolina and other provinces, and had drifted to this region because of the protection afforded them by the disputed boundary. When North Carolina sheriffs called on them, they plead loyalty to South Carolina, and when officers from that section called, they claimed to be citizens of North Carolina. A militia company was organized on authority of a commission from the Governor of South Carolina. There were in the unsettled region many honest men who refused to pay their taxes until it was legally determined to which province they owed allegiance, fearing that if they paid to one, they would be later forced to duplicate the fees to the other.

In June, 1764, Henry Eustace McCulloh came to Mecklenburg to survey the Selwyn tracts of land, to grant titles to those deserving them and to eject those who refused to comply with the requirements. When he arrived, he was given to understand that many of the settlers "would hold to the South" and oppose the running of any lines, and was threatened with personal violence if he attempted to carry out his plans. McCulloh suggested that the "South Men" hold a meeting and select a committee to confer with himself regarding a peaceable adjustment of the differences. This was accordingly done, and the committee, composed of James Norris, Thomas Polk, James Flennegin and George Allen, met the agent, and, after a long conference, reported to the people they represented that the terms proposed by Selwyn's agent were just and reasonable, and should be accepted.

McCulloh thought the troubles were now settled, and left the county, intending to return soon and complete his work, but when he came back in the following February, he discovered more opposition than at the previous time. Large bodies of armed men, sometimes numbering two hundred, and usually led by Thomas Polk, interfered with the surveying parties, broke the chains and continued to make threats. One party of good men who were surveying on one of the Selywn tracts, was set upon and beaten severely. McCulloh was brave and persevering, and the opposition to his work began to weaken. Thomas Polk was the only really able man associated with the "South Men," and he appears to have done so in order to force the attention of the proper authorities to the necessity of surveying the boundary line. In 1765, he became friendly with McCulloh and was appointed one of Selwyn's surveyors for this county.

Open war with the Cherokee Indians ended in 1761, but for several years thereafter great annoyance was caused by the lack of a definite dividing line between Mecklenburg and the Cherokee country. In May, 1767, Governor Tryon yielded to the persistent entreaties and marched with one hundred men to perform the work. The troops in this expedition were commanded by General Hugh Waddell; and Colonel John Frohock, of Rowan, and Colonel Moses Alexander, of Mecklenburg, were among the subordinate officers. While this survey could have been made by half a dozen men, yet. Governor Tryon's military display had a salutary effect on the Indians, who cheerfully accepted the line as run and gave no further trouble until the white people began once more to encroach upon their territory. The Governor was, nevertheless, subjected to criticism because of the expense of the expedition, which some attributed solely to his well-known love for military glory.

William Tryon, in his first public utterance as Governor of North Carolina, said he was here to serve the people, but his actions soon gave ample proof that he was here to serve the Lords Proprietors and to execute their wishes. That he did his duty to his employers to the best of his ability, no one can deny. Just as he was ingratiating himself in the good graces of the people, he was called upon to enforce the provisions of the Stamp Act. The good people of Eastern North Carolina attended to this matter so that it never much concerned the people of Mecklenburg, but it had two results of far-reaching consequence to all the province. First, Governor Tryon harshly resolved to regain the lost dignity of his administration in whatever way he could; second, the people thereafter looked with suspicion upon anything originating with the Governor.

The trouble which culminated in the battle of Alamance began in 1761. The central counties complained of cruel and unjust officers, Tryon's extravagance in building his palace, extortion, corrupt courts, and of being compelled to pay taxes in money of which there was not a sufficient quantity in circulation. These charges were justified in some counties, but Mecklenburg was happily free from nearly all of it. This county had not been established long enough for the Governor to fill the offices with his favorites, so the sheriff and clerk and justices were among the most honored and trusted men.

Resistance to the officers in Orange, Anson, Rowan and other counties grew until it assumed a serious aspect. Men who were unable to defend themselves alone, banded together for self-protection and to work together for the regulation of the injustices. In this way they came to be known as Regulators. From this state of affairs, Herman Husbands, a Quaker preacher, organized the discontented men into a systematic association. Meetings were held and petitions presented to the Governor, but they were refused or ignored.

It was inevitable that unlawful acts should result from the bitterness between the opposing parties. One day, in the summer of 1768, a horse was taken from a Regulator who had ridden into Hillsboro on business. That night the friends of the offended man regained the horse by force, and the same night some one fired into Edmund Fanning's house. Soon thereafter Husbands and several other Regulators were arrested and their trial set for the September court. Fanning was to be tried at the same time for collecting illegal fees, and both sides to the controversy expected trouble.

In August, Governor Tryon came to Mecklenburg to review the militia, which numbered nine hundred. During his stay in the county he was entertained by the Alexanders and Polks and other good families. He reviewed the troops and secured three hundred volunteers to go to Hillsboro to maintain order during the sessions of court. These men began the march September 12, and returned in October, the expected trouble having been averted. Husbands was acquitted of the charge against him and Fanning was found guilty, but was let off with a nominal fine. Before the Mecklenburg troops disbanded, they were complimented by the Governor for their splendid behavior.

The situation developed steadily, and in the Spring of 1771, each side prepared for a final test of strength. Husbands, having failed to get satisfaction by law and petitions, determined to make a show of force. Governor Tryon sent General Hugh Waddell through Rowan and Mecklenburg to raise troops for his cause, but General Waddell obtained only one hundred in this county. These, with nearly two hundred Rowan volunteers, were intercepted at the Yadkin river and turned back by a superior force of Regulators, so they did not join the Governor until after the battle.

Meanwhile, Governor Tryon was marching westward with his army ten or twelve hundred strong. On the 17th of May, he was met near Alamance creek by a large body of the Regulators led by Husbands, who presented the cause of his followers. Tryon obstinately refused to make any promises or concessions, and seemed resolved to fight, even though he had no better reason than to send back to England the news of a "glorious victory."

The Regulators outnumbered Tryon's soldiers, but the latter had the advantage of military training and were well armed. Some of the followers of Husbands were not prepared for battle, and none of them had more than a dozen rounds of ammunition, but they fought like men until all hope was gone. After the battle ended, Governor Tryon ordered the immediate execution of a half-witted ignorant boy named James Few, and six of the prisoners taken were afterwards hung for treason. A number of Mecklenburg men were in the ranks of the Regulators, but as they had no organization among themselves, it is not possible to estimate their number.

Mecklenburg people recognized the justice of the cause for which the Regulators shed their blood, but they did not deem it prudent to make open resistance to authority at that time. The Phifers, Alexanders, Polks and other prominent citizens were not the kind of men who strike without carefully considering the consequences, but from May 17, 1771, independence of thought steadily developed into independence of action.

The young men were not so conservative as their fathers, and they did not hesitate to express sympathy for the men who were struggling against oppression. Col. Moses Alexander was commissary for General Waddell, and while his wagons, laden with powder, were passing through the county, they were captured and the powder was destroyed by nine boys who have since been known as "The Black Boys of

Mecklenburg." They blacked their faces and disguised themselves as Indians before attacking the wagons, and from this they gained their name. These boys were afterwards noble soldiers in the Revolution.

Authority:—Colonial Records, Original Official Documents, Court and County Records, Caruther's Old North State, Waddell's Address on the Regulation, and Jones' Defense of North Carolina.

CHAPTER VIII.

THE APPROACHING STORM. (1772 to 1775.)

England's Position With Regard to America—Affairs in the Colonies.
—Governor Martin's Dissensions With the Assembly—Rifle Factory in Charlotte—Polk Calls the Convention.

When England was confronted by the American disturbances, it was not the first time she faced the problem of conciliating a discontented dependency. Three precedents by which she might have been guided were the reclamation of Ireland, Wales and Chester. The four were analogous cases, each being governed by force without mercy until it became apparent that such government was hopeless; then the three were won by concessions and the fourth was lost by obstinacy.

Throughout the colonies, the five years preceding actual hostilities was a time of emotion and intense suspense. The feelings of the people were aroused in apprehension of the final struggle for their abstract rights. England's import taxes imposed upon the colonies had been practically suspended, but the Americans were plainly told that it was for expediency and not because of principle, and it was the principle for which the patriots contended. British troops were quartered on American soil at the beginning of 1775, and early in that year military strength superseded civil authority in Massachusetts.

When Josiah Martin became Governor of North Carolina, in 1771, he immediately began dissensions with the Assembly. The State's finances were in good condition and some of the taxes, being plainly unnecessary, were repealed by the Assembly. Though the bill was passed unanimously, it was promptly vetoed by the Governor, and from that time forth he waged continual war with the representatives of the people.

The Assembly of December, 1773, was dismissed by Governor Martin after having been in session only a few days. Before adjournment, however, a committee of nine good citizens was appointed to carry on correspondence with similar committees in the other provinces. Martin Phifer and John Davidson, representatives of Mecklenburg, were both present at this session. At this time, Thomas Polk was engaged in the work of surveying the boundary line between North Carolina and South Carolina.

Governor Martin having determined that no more Assemblies should convene until the people came to his way of thinking, John Harvey was authorized to call a congress of the people when he deemed it prudent. Accordingly, the call was issued for an election of representatives to a Provincial Congress to meet in New Bern in August of 1774. Governor Martin was astounded at this bold stroke, but his threats were unavailing and the Congress met at the appointed time. Mecklenburg county was represented by Benjamin Patton. Richard Caswell, William Hooper and Joseph Hewes were elected delegates to the Continental Congress, which met in Philadelphia, but at the same time a resolution was adopted declaring loyalty to the king.

The Governor was now in an embarassing situation as he felt the reins of government slipping through his fingers, and, yielding to his Council, he called the Assembly to meet in New Bern in April, 1775. John Harvey called the second Provincial Congress to meet at the same time and place. With but few exceptions, the members of the two bodies were the same, and Harvey was Speaker of the Assembly and Moderator of the Congress. Nothing was accomplished at this session except the return of the same delegation to the Philadelphia Congress and the agreement of the members to not trade with British ports. Mecklenburg was not represented.

Mecklenburg people had distinguished themselves for conservatism, and it was quite evident that they favored no offensive action before affairs assumed a more definite shape.

County government had been established little more than a decade, the homes were hewn from primitive forests, industries were developing, and just as the people were prepared to enjoy the blessings of liberty and abundance, they were loath to accept the rumors of war.

They were, however, thinking of the issues of the day and were preparing to meet them. Edmund Burke, in his speech on "Conciliation," delivered in Parliament March 22, 1775, ascribed the independence of Americans politically in a considerable degree to their independence in religion. If it be true that independence was more rife among dissenters than others, this partially explains the action of Mecklenburg in that year, for it is probable that no where in the colonies did the Church of England have fewer followers. Both Governor Martin and Governor Tryon wrote of the discouragements to the Church in this section.

One phase of industry which had much influence on the trend of events, was the development of the rifle. The people of this region needed a serviceable weapon for aggressive use, and from the old New England blunderbuss they developed a long, well-made rifle that was inferior to none in the world. At the outbreak of the war, there were only three rifle factories in the colonies, and one of them was in Charlotte. The iron was obtained near High Shoals, and was blasted there. Then the barrel was shaped, bored carefully and rifled. The wooden stock extended clear to the end of the barrel, which was four feet in length. General Washington was presented with one of these Charlotte rifles in 1787, and he praised it very highly. The excellence of the weapon and the ability with which it was used played an important part in the war of the Revolution.

It had now become apparent to all observing people that a rupture of the ties binding the colonies to England was imminent. Preparations for war were being made and the Congresses of the people were the real governing bodies. Troops were being massed by America and England, but the Continental Congress yet asserted loyalty to the crown, and Thomas Jefferson and his followers were endeavoring to effect a compromise with the mother country.

That North Carolina was among the foremost advocates of liberty is evidenced by a letter written to James Iredell by William Hooper, who was one of our delegates to the Continental Congress. He wrote, April 26, 1774: "With you I anticipate the important share the colonies must soon have in regulating the political balance. They are striding fast to independence, and ere long will build an empire upon the ruins of Great Britain; will adopt its Constitution purged of its impurities, and from an experience of its defects will guard against the evils which have wasted its vigor and brought it to an untimely end."

Governor Martin had lost all control of the government of the province and was preparing to go on board a British man-of-war. Rumors were rife of legislation by Parliament that would subdue the colonies. The best statesmen of England ralized and admitted the injustice of the taxation of people by a governing body in which the people themselves had no representative. Yet it was apparent to all that the participation in Parliament of far distant America was a practical impossibility. The only logical alternatives were self-government with a mild form of protection or absolute independence. England declined to concede the first; America fought for the second.

During these troublous times, the Charlotte court house was the regular meeting place for the men of this section, and they often assembled to discuss news of interest. Royal government in North Carolina ended in June, 1775, and there was no semblance of royal authority in Mecklenburg for some time prior to that date. Several meetings were held among the leading citizens to decide what should be done. It was necessary to take some definite action, and to provide a system of government.

Thomas Polk was military commander of the county and was a leader among the people. He was authorized to call a meeting of delegates from each militia district whenever, in his opinion, the proper time had come to act. The first of May, 1775, Thomas Polk, in accordance with these instructions, issued notice for each district to elect two delegates to an Assembly to be held in the court house in Charlotte on the nineteenth day of May.

Authority:—Colonial Records, Burke's Speech on Conciliation, County Records, Moore's History, Johnson's Reminiscences and Hunter's Sketches. The item about the Rifle Factory in Charlotte was obtained from an article by W. H. Robarts in the Washington *Post,* June 16, 1901.

CHAPTER IX.

DECLARATION OF INDEPENDENCE; MAY 20, 1775.

Manner of Election and Assembling of the Delegates—Excitement.
—The Addresses and the Committee on Resolutions—News of the Battle of Lexington—Declaration Unanimously Adopted—Temporary Form of Government Provided.

Colonel Polk, by authority of the power previously vested in him, issued the notice for the election of two delegates by each of the nine militia districts in the county. There should, therefore, have been eighteen delegates to the convention. When it assembled on the 19th of May, however, so many prominent men were present that a dispute arose as to who should be termed delegates, and a compromise list containing the names of twenty-seven of the best citizens was finally accepted. Rev. Humphrey Hunter, in his memoirs, says he was present, being twenty years of age, and that half of the men in Mecklenburg county were in Charlotte that day.

Delegates and some other leading citizens obtained seats in the court house, while those who could not get in gathered in groups and discussed the issues among themselves. Organization was perfected by the election of a chairman in the person of Abraham Alexander, who had been a magistrate and chairman of the Inferior Court and a representative of Mecklenburg in the General Assembly. John McKnitt Alexander, who was also an honored magistrate, was made secretary.

Excitement was intense, as it became apparent that the proclamations of the King and the Governor made necessary some decisive action on the part of the people. Every one realized the importance of deliberate consideration before making a declaration that could never be recalled. Rumors

NEWS OF THE BATTLE OF LEXINGTON.

were plentiful of offensive legislation by Parliament and of other efforts to subdue the colonists and to quench the spirit of freedom so rife among them. The colonies were preparing for war, and the time had come for all men to choose between England and America. Mecklenburg promptly decided between the two, and then she went further in the belief that if war must come, it should be fought for a purpose rather than for a grievance. A revolution was more to be desired than was an insurrection.

The addresses made to the convention demonstrated that all the delegates were searching for truth and eagerly desiring to know what was proper to be done. Among the leading speakers and advisers were Colonel William Kennon, a distinguished lawyer of Salisbury; Rev. Hezekiah J. Balch, an honored Presbyterian minister, and Dr. Ephraim Brevard. The chief topics considered were the alarming condition of the province which was being threatened yet was not arming, the restraint of provincial and export trade, unjust taxation and the necessity for a form of government.

While the convention was thus occupied and the spectators were intent upon the proceedings, a horseman galloped into town, shouting as he came, the news of the battle of Lexington. When he reached the court house, the people surrounded him and listened with amazement to the news in detail. Just one month before, the British troops had fired upon a crowd of Americans and more than a score of them were killed. Then the minute men responded and the British troops were forced to beat a precipitate retreat.

This news had a double effect on the delegates: the sacrifice of the patriots incited their sympathy, and the rout of the British encouraged them in making a bold stroke for liberty. Men who had cautioned against aggressive action now shouted for a positive declaration of independence. The last doubt was conquered and opposition was useless. A committee composed of Dr. Brevard, Colonel Kennon and

Rev. Hezekiah Balch, was appointed to draw up resolutions for the consideration of the convention.

During the absence of the committee, a new phase of the situation developed. This was occasioned by an inquiry as to how the delegates were to avoid the obligation of the oath of loyalty imposed upon them after the defeat of the Regulators. Some replied that the question did not deserve consideration, but others discussed it seriously. The consensus of opinion was that the king absolved the obligation of loyalty on the part of the Americans by declaring them in a state of insurrection and out of his protection.

The various suggestions and resolutions were carefully considered by the committee, and as a result, their report was not submitted until after midnight. It was read by the secretary and apparently gave entire satisfaction to the delegates, as they at once began clamoring for its immediate adoption. At 2 o'clock in the morning of May 20, the chairman put the question to a vote and the delegates and spectators shouted: "Aye, Aye." The twenty-seven delegates then went forward and signed the document as representatives of all the people. It was agreed that the Declaration should be proclaimed from the court house steps at noon, and at that time it was read by Colonel Polk in the presence of several thousand persons, who cheered the resolutions with great enthusiasm.

Captain James Jack was deputized to go to Philadelphia, where the Continental Congress was sitting, and give copies of the Declaration to the President of Congress and to each of North Carolina's representatives. When he arrived in Salisbury, he was induced by Colonel Kennon to tarry there in order to allow the Declaration to be read in court, which was in session. All who heard the reading expressed approval except two lawyers, Dunn and Booth, who called it treason and endeavored to prevent Captain Jack's intended trip to Philadelphia. They were foiled in the attempt and were afterwards brought to Charlotte and punished for "unfaithfulness to the common cause." George Graham and Colonel J. Carruth were among the dozen men who went to Salisbury and arrested the lawyers.

Meanwhile, Captain Jack arrived in Philadelphia June 23, the day that General Washington left to take command of the Continental army. He was met that day by William Alexander, of Mecklenburg, who was there on business, and who in his old age often told that he met Captain Jack at that time and the Captain said he was there with copies of the Mecklenburg Declaration of Independence adopted May 20. Congress was then preparing the address to the king, which was agreed to July 8, and which declared loyalty to the king and repudiated the charge of a desire for independence. Hence it was not deemed prudent to publicly consider the Mecklenburg Declaration of Independence, and Captain Jack so reported the views of the President and our representatives.

June 30, Governor Martin inclosed in a letter to the Earl of Dartmouth a copy of the Cape Fear *Mercury* containing the Mecklenburg Resolves of May 31. The Governor wrote that the proceedings of that convention "surpasses all the horrid and treasonable publications that the inflammatory spirits of this continent have yet produced, and your Lordship may depend its authors and abettors will not escape my due notice, whenever my hands are sufficiently strengthened to attempt the recovery of the lost authority of government. A copy of these resolves, I am informed, were sent off by express to the Congress at Philadelphia as soon as they were passed in the committee." August 8, he issued a proclamation denouncing the action of the Mecklenburg people as "most infamous" and "treasonable."

The Declaration, as signed, was as follows:

"1st. *Resolved,* That whosoever directly or indirectly abets or in any way, form or manner, countenances the invasion of our rights as attempted by the Parliament of Great Britain, is an enemy to his country, to America, and the rights of man.

"2d. *Resolved,* That we, the citizens of Mecklenburg county, do hereby dissolve the political bands which have connected us with the mother country; and absolve ourselves from the allegiance to the British Crown, abjuring all political connection with a nation that has wantonly trampled on our rights and liberties, and inhumanly shed the innocent blood of Americans at Lexington.

"3d. *Resolved,* That we do hereby declare ourselves a free and independent people, that we are and of right ought to be a sovereign and self-governing people under the power of God and the general Congress; to the maintenance of which independence we solemnly pledge to each other our mutual co-operation, our lives, our fortunes and our most sacred honor.

"4th. *Resolved,* That we do hereby ordain and adopt as rules of conduct, all and each of our former laws, and the crown of Great Britain cannot be considered hereafter as holding any rights, privileges, or immunities amongst us.

"5th. *Resolved,* That all officers, both civil and military, in this county, be entitled to exercise the same powers and authorities as heretofore; that every member of this delegation shall henceforth be a civil officer, and exercise the powers of a justice of the peace, issue process, hear and determine controversies according to law, preserve peace, union and harmony in the county, and use every exertion to spread the love of liberty and of country, until a more general and better organized system of government be established.

"6th. *Resolved,* That a copy of these resolutions be transmitted by express to the President of the Continental Congress assembled in Philadelphia, to be laid before that body.

EPHRAIM BREVARD.	CHARLES ALEXANDER,
HEZEKIAH J. BALCH,	ZACCHEUS WILSON,
JOHN PHIFER,	WAIGHTSTILL AVERY,
JAMES HARRIS,	BENJAMIN PATTON,
WILLIAM KENNON,	MATTHEW MCCLURE,
JOHN FORD,	NEIL MORRISON,
RICHARD BARRY,	ROBERT IRWIN,
HENRY DOWNS,	JOHN FLENNEGIN,
EZRA ALEXANDER,	DAVID REESE,
WILLIAM GRAHAM,	JOHN DAVIDSON,
JOHN QUEARY,	RICHARD HARRIS,
HEZEKIAH ALEXANDER,	THOMAS POLK,
ADAM ALEXANDER,	ABRAHAM ALEXANDER,

JOHN MCKNITT ALEXANDER."

Authority:—Same as Previous Chapter, Jones' Defense, Wheeler's History, Wheeler's Reminiscences, and Special Investigations in the Libraries of Charleston, S. C., and London, England.

CHAPTER X.

GOVERNMENT BY THE COMMITTEE. (1775 to 1776.)

Adjourned Meeting Held May 31—Adopts Rules of Government Until "Laws are Provided by Congress"—Proceedings Supplementary to Previous Convention—The Two Official Declarations Compared.

It will be observed that the Declaration did not make adequate provisions for the government of the county. In the convention of May 20, the all-absorbing topic of interest was the dissolution from Great Britain, and it remained for the next meeting to complete the arrangements for laws and officers. The adjourned meeting was held May 31, and twenty resolutions were then adopted. These resolutions are generally known as the "Resolves," while those of May 20 are termed the "Declaration."

The Declaration was divided into five different parts or resolutions. The first asserted that the cause of the Declaration of Independence was "the unchartered and dangerous invasion of our rights, as claimed by Great Britain." The second dissolved the political bands connecting us with the mother country, while the third declared our independence. The fourth revoked all British authority and laws, but adopted the latter "as a rule of life," and the fifth ordained that each delegate present should thereafter be a "Justice of the Peace in the character of a committeeman."

This document and the minutes of the various meetings were in possession of John McKnitt Alexander, and were lost in the fire that destroyed his house in 1800. Several copies of the Declaration had been previously made: one which was sent to Dr. Hugh Williamson, the historian, was lost, but another sent to Judge Martin, which is known to have been in his possession in 1793, was preserved. Soon after the fire, John McKnitt Alexander re-wrote the Declaration from memory, and this production is almost word for word like the Martin copy, thus showing Mr. Alexander's familiarity with the famous document. The proceedings of the convention of May 31 were printed in the *Cape Fear Mercury* in June, 1775, but the only known copy of the paper was borrowed from the British Colonial Office by Hon. Andrew Stevenson, the United States Minister to Great Britain, in the year 1837, and was not returned.

The Resolves were also published in June in the *South Carolina Gazette and Country Journal,* and copies of this paper are now preserved in Charleston and in London. These Resolves extend the actions of the convention of May 20, accepting as settled the new order of affairs following the separation from England. The Resolves were drawn up by Dr. Brevard, and signed by him as clerk by authority of the committee, and they superseded the fourth and fifth resolutions of May 20 and supplemented the Declaration of Independence by definitely defining the authority under which the county should be governed.

Independence having been declared eleven days previously, the Resolves begin with the reasons for the establishment of the forms of government therein contained. The first paragraph recites that all previous laws and commissions were established by the authority and consent of the king, and that they were suspended when the king declared the colonies out of his protection, and therefore could not be in effect unless re-established. Recognizing the legitimate authority of the Continental and Provincial Congresses, the laws and regulations following were enacted "for the internal government of this county, until laws shall be provided for us by the Congress."

It was then stipulated that each militia company should assemble at some convenient point and choose from their own number two men to serve as "Selectmen." A Selectman had jurisdiction over all matters of a civil nature wherein not more than twenty shillings was concerned, and two Selectmen sitting together could try cases involving as much as forty shillings. One constable was provided for each of these officers, and authority was given them also to commit to confinement any person accused of petit larceny.

The eighteen Selectmen in the county were to meet four times a year to try all cases not in the jurisdiction of any of them separately, and to hear appeals. All money for rents and public and county taxes was to be paid into the hands of the chairman of the committee and "disbursed as required by public exigencies." The militia was advised to equip themselves with arms and accoutrements, and hold themselves in readiness to execute the commands of the general Congress or of the committee, and Thomas Polk and Dr. Joseph Kennedy were directed to purchase three hundred pounds of powder, six hundred pounds of lead and one thousand flints.

Thus it will be noted that the Convention of May 20 reinstated the old laws and officers with a few changes, and the Resolves allowed these officers to be elected by the people. The officers and laws, however, remained practically as before the Declaration, though it was expressly stated that the officers should "exercise their powers independent of the Crown of Great Britain."

Ample provision was made for the collection of debts. Persons owing so much as forty shillings could be prevented from leaving the county, and property could be levied on for the amount. Any Selectman could issue the warrant upon oath of the creditor. The government was strong and efficient, and there was but little opposition to it. When a person desired to leave the county, a certificate was given him stating that he was a friend to the "common cause."

The third Provincial Congress met in Hillsboro August 20, 1775, and Mecklenburg was represented by Thomas Polk, John Phifer, John McKnitt Alexander, Samuel Martin, Waightstill Avery and James Houston, the four first named having signed the Mecklenburg Declaration of Independence. At this session, a provisional government was instituted for the State, with Cornelius Harnett at the head, and the State was divided into six general militia districts. The Battle of Moore's Creek Bridge was fought February

27 following, at which time the Patriots won a decisive victory over the Tories.

John Phifer, Robert Irwin and John McKnitt Alexander represented the county in the Congress that convened April 12, 1776, and they were instructed by the county committee to declare for independence. The Congress took this action, and was the first of the thirteen to so instruct her representatives in Philadelphia. The Constitution of North Carolina was adopted December 18, 1776, and this provided for committees of safety to govern each county. While the government of Mecklenburg was not modified, yet this action superseded the authority of the conventions held in May, 1775, and the laws then adopted "until laws shall be provided for us by the Congress."

Authority:—Same as Previous Chapter, and an Original Copy of the *South Carolina Gazette and Country Journal* of June 13, 1775.

CHAPTER XI.

THE REVOLUTION. (1776 to 1780.)

Organization of the State Military Forces—Prominent Parts Taken by Mecklenburg Men—Scovilite and Tory Campaigns—The Continental Troops—Governor Caswell in Charlotte.

The Provincial Congress of August, 1775, arranged for three classes of military troops in the State. First were two continental regiments under Colonels Moore and Howe, and in the first of which George Davidson and George Graham, of Mecklenburg, were officers. Six battalions of minute men were provided for, each battalion to consist of two companies of fifty men each, and Mecklenburg's levy was one hundred men. Of the county militia, the officers were Colonel Thomas Polk, Lieutenant-Colonel Adam Alexander, Major John Phifer and Second Major John Davidson. April, 1776, four additional continental regiments were organized, and Colonel Polk became commander of the Fourth regiment. At the same time the militia was reorganized on account of resignations and because some of the first officers were disloyal. The Mecklenburg officers were promoted after Colonel Polk left the militia, and George A. Alexander became Second Major. In November of 1775, a bill was passed authorizing a company of volunteer rangers in the county, and the officers were Captain Ezekiel Polk and Lieutenants Samuel Watson and William Polk.

Thomas Polk was one of the most active men in the State, and he and William Kennon were on the committee to prepare a temporary plan of government. Waightstill Avery was a member of the Provincial Council of thirteen, of which Cornelius Harnett was chairman. There were six district committees of safety, and Mecklenburg was represented in the Salisbury district committee by Hezekiah Alexander and Bejamin Patton. Then there were thirty-six county

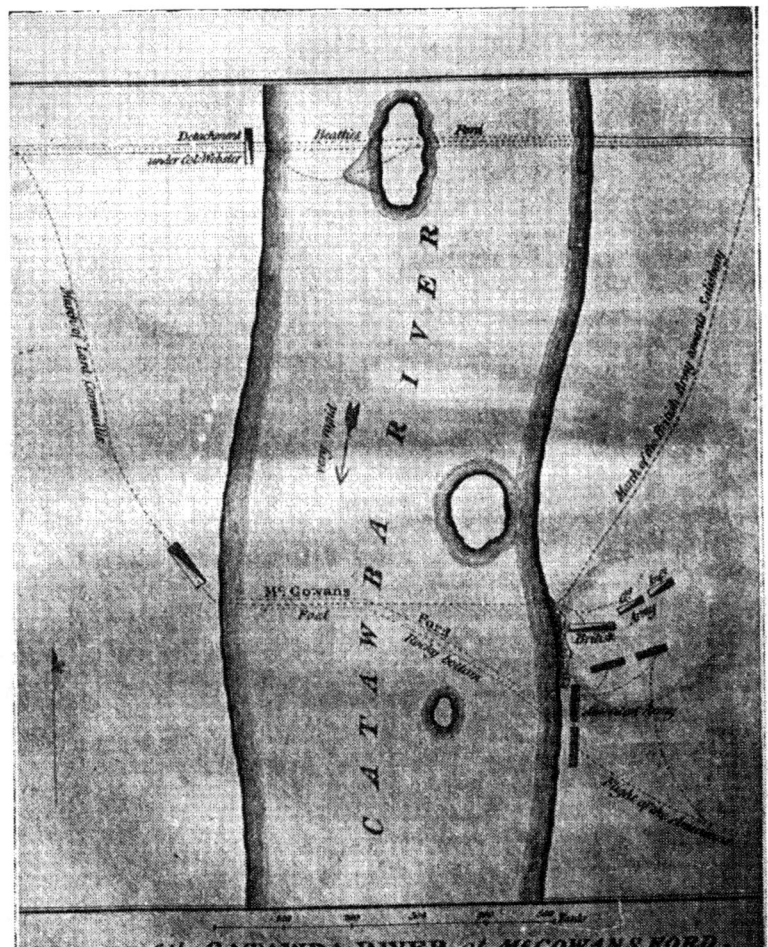

committees of 21 members each, which met four times a year to take action against Tories, and to attend to questions of confiscation and other military affairs. Two companies of "light horse" were raised in the Salisbury district, and Martin Phifer was captain of the Second. May 11, 1776, the Provincial Council was superseded by the State Council of Safety, of which Hezekiah Alexander was a member.

In December, 1775, Colonels Rutherford, Graham, Caswell, Martin and Polk, with six hundred men, went to South Carolina and assisted General Richardson in his campaign against the Scovilites, a lawless band of men who defied all authority. This was called the Snow Camp Campaign on account of the snow falling so heavily during the march. A notable declaration made at this time was by the young ladies of Mecklenburg, who resolved to have nothing to do with any boys who had not volunteered for the march against the Scovilites.

In the summer of 1776, General Rutherford was engaged in a campaign against the Cherokee Indians. Several skirmishes were fought in the neighborhood of the present town of Franklin, and the Indians were reduced to quietude and signed a treaty of peace in the following May. On this expedition, Captain Charles Polk commanded a company of Mecklenburg militia which was accompanied by Dr. Ephraim Brevard. Colonel Adam Alexander, Lieutenant-Colonel John Phifer, Major John Davidson and Jesse A. Alexander also participated in the expedition. Waightstill Avery was active in the work of preparing a constitution and the laws for State government, and became Attorney General immediately after the constitution was adopted, December 18, 1776.

The North Carolina brigade of 9,400 men, was formed at Wilmington in July, 1776. William Davidson was at this time Lieutenant-Colonel of the Third regiment, William Polk was Major in the Ninth, and Charles Alexander was a Lieutenant in the Fourth regiment, of which Thomas Polk was Colonel. The brigade remained in North Carolina and

South Carolina until March, 1777, when it was ordered north and arrived in Philadelphia the first of July. The Mecklenburg troops were in the battles of Brandywine and Germantown, and in the latter, Major William Polk was slightly wounded. They spent the winter with General Washington at Valley Forge, and in May, 1778, they were consolidated into four regiments, numbering in all only 1,157 officers and men. Three thousand North Carolina militiamen were drafted in the continental service for nine months, and, with Washington's army, took part in the campaign in the winter of 1778-1779.

When the continental regiments were consolidated, Colonel Polk resigned his commission and returned to his home. He did not hold a position of prominence again until September 15, 1780, when he was appointed Commissary-General by General Green, who succeeded General Gates, in Charlotte, December 3, 1780, but in the meantime he was active in county affairs and in the defense of the home people. The notable services of Polk and of his sons are worthy of all honor. Captain Thomas Polk, Jr., was killed at Eutaw Springs while fighting bravely September 8, 1781. William Polk was wounded in the Scovilite campaign and also at Germantown, and Captain Charles Polk was active throughout the war. During Colonel Polk's service as commissary for General Greene's army, money was scarce and Colonel Polk expended all his private funds in the public cause, part of it, however, being afterwards returned to him.

In February, 1779, a Tory insurrection gained considerable strength in Tryon county, and troops were collected to suppress it. David Wilson commanded a company of Mecklenburg "light horse" in this campaign, which was in every way successful. May 1, a levy for clothing for the continental troops was made, and this county was called upon to supply 72 hats, 144 pairs of shoes and stockings, 304 yards of linen and 144 yards of woolen or double-woven cloth.

The term of service of nearly all the North Carolina troops expired in April, 1779, and the soldiers returned to

THE REVOLUTION.

their homes. The General Assembly directed the Governor to draft 2,000 of the militia, most of whom were to be sent to the defense of Charleston. Governor Caswell and the State Council came to Charlotte April 10, and here reviewed the soldiers who were to go to Charleston, and the next day, General Butler, with 700 troops, began the march. While here the Governor commissioned William R. Davie a lieutenant in the light horse company, of which William Barnett was captain.

During these trying times, the men of Mecklenburg were nobly doing the duty of true patriots. This county sent soldiers to fight under Washington, to help South Carolina and Georgia, to drive back the Indians and to suppress insurrections; and when the task of defending their homes devolved upon them, they put up a fight that is one of the noblest in history. While the men were doing these things, the women were no less zealous in their patriotism. They made clothes for the soldiers, nursed the sick and wounded and encouraged the feeble-minded by their sacrifices and their courage.

Authority:—Colonial Records, Personal Correspondence, Eggleston's History of the United States, and Johnson's Reminiscences of the Revolution.

CHAPTER XII.

THE HORNETS' NEST. (1780 to 1782.)

Surrender of Charleston—Battle of Ramsour's Mill—Davidson and Davie Harass the British—Reception of Cornwallis in Charlotte.—Surprise at McIntyre's, Battle of King's Mountain and Departure of the British—General Davidson Killed at Cowan's Ford.

Charleston surrendered to the British forces May 12, 1780. At this time General William Caswell and Colonel Buford were at Lanier's Ferry, on the Santee river, with 400 men each. The British marched from Charleston to Camden, and Caswell fell back to Cross Creek, N. C., where he was June 2. Buford, with his small force, retreated towards Charlotte, but was intercepted at Waxhaw by Lieutenant-Colonel Tarleton with a superior force, and his detachment was cut to pieces on the 29th day of May. Shortly after this engagement, Mrs. Jackson, the mother of Andrew Jackson, moved with her children from Waxhaw and lived for some time with a widow at Sugar creek, and Andrew was often in Charlotte.

The patriots in the vicinity of Charlotte, as well as all in North Carolina, were much discouraged. Nearly the entire military strength of the State had been surrendered at Charleston, leaving the country practically without any means of defense against the approaching invaders. General Rutherford, with a small body of troops, was watching General Rawdon at Hanging Rock when he received intelligence of a Tory uprising in the neighborhood of Ramsour's Mill. Being unwilling to leave Charlotte unprotected, he ordered Colonel Francis Locke to raise troops to quell the Tories, he himself intending to join Locke before the attack. Colonel Locke, with several capable assistants, collected about 400 men, and without waiting for reinforcements, fell upon the 1,100 Tories June 20, and inflicted upon them a crushing defeat. General Rutherford appeared on the scene before the battle had ended, and his cavalry assisted in the pursuit of the vanquished Tories. William and Ezra Alexander were captains in General Davidson's battalion at this event.

Rutherford's command now joined General Gates, and participated in the battle of Camden August 16, which resulted in the disastrous defeat of the Americans, General Rutherford being taken prisoner. The command of Rutherford's brigade thereupon devolved upon General Davidson, who camped eight miles below Charlotte to recuperate his troops. Caswell and Sumner formed a camp of militia in Charlotte, but retreated toward the north when Cornwallis left Camden September 8. Davidson and Davie, with their inferior forces, were all that opposed the entry of Lord Cornwallis into the State, but they prepared to defend their homes to the bitter end.

These intrepid soldiers did all in their power to harrass the British, and succeeded in impeding their progress considerably. They captured sentries and spies, and so alarmed Cornwallis by capturing small foraging parties that he would not send out less than a regiment for that purpose. Every step of the British march was greeted with a rifle shot from the woods and the determined persistent opposition did much to dishearten the conquering army.

Major Davie surprised the British at Captain Wahab's, near the South Carolina line, September 21, and inflicted damage upon them, the killed and wounded numbering about 60. At various other times he attacked and routed small bodies of foragers and guards, and he was continually near the British army. September 10, he, with General Davidson, annihilated a body of Tories two miles from the British camp, which was then at Waxhaw. General Davidson then located at McAlpin's creek, eight miles south of Charlotte, with 400 men. At midnight of September 25, Davie, with one hundred and fifty cavalry, entered Charlotte, where he was joined by Major Joseph Graham, the young hero who had done much fighting with a small band of volunteers. Cornwallis left Waxhaw September 24, and about 11 o'clock September 26, his advance guard entered Charlotte, approaching from the south by Trade street.

Davie and Graham had made ample provision for a strong resistance, and it is superfluous to mention the bravery of these patriots who resisted so gloriously a victorious army outnumbering them 15 to 1. Major Graham was in command of a company that advanced along East Trade street, protected by the houses and fences and trees on each side. Another company was dismounted and placed behind the stone wall surrounding the space underneath the court house, while the others were held in reserve. Tarleton's cavalry, under the immediate command of Major Hanger, formed in line within three hundred yards of the court house, and were supported by solid ranks of infantry. The order to charge was given and obeyed, and then the Americans, who had kept quiet, calmly delivered a galling fire which threw the attacking party into such confusion that they turned and galloped back in disorder. Two other charges were similarly repulsed, but meanwhile the British infantry had steadily advanced, and it became apparent that the work of the day was about completed, and the retreat was begun. The noble defenders were vigorously pursued, but under cover of nightfall, succeeded in avoiding capture. Lieutenant George Locke and four privates were killed, and Major Joseph Graham and five privates were wounded, and the enemy lost 45 in killed and wounded.

Cornwallis remained in Charlotte sixteen days, during which time his position fully justified him in naming the town "The Hornets' Nest." As an illustration of the respect he had for his enemies, he sent Major Doyle with 450 cavalry and forty wagons on a foraging expedition, October 3. The country people saw them passing gaily along the road, and Captain James Thompson and Captain George Graham, with about a dozen armed men, followed them to McIntyre's farm. Here the foragers began loading the wagons with the fat of the land; the dogs were set to chasing chickens, a bee hive was turned over and the bees chased the soldiers, and altogether it made a merry scene. A red faced captain was standing on the doorsteps laughing boisterously, when one of the men in ambush said to his companions, "I can't wait any longer; let every one pick his man; the captain is mine." At the fusillade that followed, the British were confused and ran madly about the yard looking for a place of refuge from what appeared to be a complete ambuscade. Major Doyle hurried up and the troops at once set out toward Charlotte; patriots all along the road took up the fight, and the flight was precipitate and disorderly until Charlotte was reached.

October 5, 1780, General Sumner retreated across the Yadkin, leaving the enemy in force in this county. Two days later, the Board of War wrote to Governor Nash that Josiah Martin, who called himself Governor of North Carolina, was in Charlotte signing official papers and offering inducements to Tories. The battle of King's Mountain was fought October 7. Colonel Patrick Ferguson, an able and a favorite officer of Lord Cornwallis, had been sent out some time before to head off the Whigs, who were retreating toward the mountains, and his command, which originally consisted of 110 regulars and about the same number of Tories, included a full thousand men at the time of the battle. Colonels Campbell, Shelby, Hambright, Sevier, Winston, McDowell, Cleveland and Williams combined and raised a force to "catch Ferguson," who was openly boasting of things he was going to do. These officers, with an army nearly as large as Ferguson's, pursued him and came upon him on King's Mountain. The fighting began about 3 o'clock in the afternoon, and in little more than an hour, Ferguson was killed and all his men killed, wounded or captured.

These events so affected Lord Cornwallis that he resolved to leave this section, and on the twelfth day of October, he departed from Charlotte, leaving behind much plunder that he was unable or unwilling to carry with him. Though he had been very unwelcome, he was not even allowed to depart in peace, for General Davidson, who had been at Camp McKnitt Alexander, in the northern part of the county, began to impede his progress, and he was ably assisted by Davie, Graham and others.

General Rutherford was released from prison about this time, and he at once raised three companies of dragoons and two hundred cavalry. Assisted by Colonel Robert Irwin and Major Joseph Graham, he marched toward Wilmington, defeated the Tories at Raft swamp and another body near Wilmington, and Colonel Gagney near Lake Waccamaw. In December, Major Joseph Graham enlisted fifty riflemen, captured the British guard at Hart's Mill, was with Lee at Pyle's hacking match and Clapp's mine, and with Colonel Washington at Whitsell's mill. February 1, 1781, the Grahams and the Polks were with General Davidson when he, with three hundred men, intercepted Cornwallis at Cowan's Ford, where the Americans were defeated and General Davidson was killed. Richard Barry, David Wilson and other soldiers took the body of the dead general to the home of Samuel Wilson, Sr., where it was prepared for burial and interred by torchlight in the Hopewell cemetery.

Authority:—Same as Previous Chapter, Wheeler's History and Hunter's Sketches.

CHAPTER XIII.

CLOSE OF THE EIGHTEENTH CENTURY. (1776 to 1800.)

War Times and County Affairs—Lawyers and Legislative Proceedings—Monetary System—Public Buildings and Industries—Andrew Jackson and James Knox Polk Born in Mecklenburg.—George Washington in Charlotte.

The transition of the power of government from the king to the people occasioned no marked change except in the authority. There was no revolution in laws and officers in Mecklenburg, but affairs remained much as they were before the Declaration of Independence. People in this county were fortunate from the first in having officers of their own choosing, it being customary for several good men to be suggested to the Royal Governor for his selection for each office.

During the war, confiscation commissioners were appointed at different points in the county, their duty being to seize any property of Royalists and to watch suspected parties. The old county court, composed of the justices of the county, met four times each year to try appeals and cases out of the jurisdiction of themselves separately. It was their duty also to elect the sheriff and register and clerk of the court. Another department of the government was the commissioners for the poor. They employed a man as superintendent to look after the destitute, and in 1872, he reported his expenses for the year at $80.

Counties were then divided into sections called militia districts. There was a captain of the militia, a tax lister and two magistrates in each one; taxes were listed during the last six "working days" of July. In 1775, there were only nine of these districts, but the number was increased to seventeen in 1777, and to nineteen in 1784, at which number it remained to the close of the century.

Mecklenburg did not lack for lawyers in the early days. In 1774, when Charlotte contained less than 200 inhabitants, there were five local lawyers, and at every court several from other counties were present. Waightstill Avery came about 1767, and he was the leading lawyer during the Revolution and for some time afterwards. At the court held in October, 1778, Spruce McKay presented a license to practice law, signed by Judges Samuel Spencer and Samuel Ashe. Wm. R. Davie was the attorney for the State at the October term, 1779, and in 1783, Adlai Osborne was county attorney, and his pay was £10 for every court attended. Within the last quarter of the century, about thirty lawyers were licensed to practice in the Mecklenburg court, but not more than ten or twelve lived in the county at any one time.

Fees to lawyers were not different from what they now are. In 1764, Richard Henderson was paid £34 for prosecuting Berry for the murder of Hugh Irwin. November 12, 1773, Wm. Smith received £7 for services as administrator of an estate. In 1794, Daniel Brown was paid two guineas for prosecuting two suits for John Bigham in the Lancaster, S. C., court, and in 1796, Wm. J. Alexander received £4 from Allen Reed for fees in a suit in chancery.

Legislatures were much occupied during this period with local laws. In 1779, the Rocky river fish law was enacted, prohibiting obstructions in the river which had been built to catch the fish, and in 1786, several other rivers were included in the provisions of the act. In 1779, the county was divided into two military divisions on account "of Charlotte being in an uncentral position and the necessity for all men to attend court-martials and other military duties." When water overflowed as a result of a mill dam, and damaged land, the law provided that the land owner should give ten days' notice and make application to the county court to order the sheriff to make an investigation and assess the amount of damages to be paid by the mill owner.

Until the United States monetary system was organized, there was great inconvenience caused by the money in circulation. Paper money was subjected to all manner of fluctuations during the war times, and was not worth its face value in "solid money" at any time. Gold and currency were used here with the stamp of North Carolina, South Carolina, Continental, Spanish and English, and exchange was consequently very annoying. The amount in circulation was also insufficient, and before and after the war, efforts were made to have certain commodities made legal tender for debts and taxes, but the plan did not meet with general approval.

The permanent location of the capital of the county in Charlotte, in 1774, was the first impetus to progress that the town received. The second incentive was the incorporation of Liberty Hall Academy in 1777. These events contributed much to the growth of Charlotte, causing people to purchase lots and move to the village for purposes of trade and to enjoy the educational advantages not to be obtained in the country.

Public buildings in the town in 1775 consisted of a jail, court house and stocks. In the county charges of 1774, fifty pounds was taxed for a jail, and in the next year an equal amount was again expended on the buildings. The court house, which was built in 1767, was repaired in 1773 and again in 1774. In July, 1778, the county court ordered Sheriff Thomas Harris to employ workmen to make such "alterations and repairs within the court house as he may think proper in order to render the same more convenient for lawyers and other officers of court to execute their respective duties without interruption or confusion."

In October, 1779, Thomas Polk and Duncan Ochiltree were appointed commissioners to "impale or otherwise inclose the under part of the court house" in order to make it agreeable as an exchange, and a stone wall was accordingly built around it. The court house was so damaged at the time of the British invasion and occupation of 1780 and 1781, that court was held in Joseph Nicholson's house until April of 1782.

In September, 1786, the total population of Charlotte was 276. Of these 123, or nearly one-half, were negroes; of the remaining 153 white people, 69 were females and 84 were males. The population of the entire county at this time was about 9,000, which increased to 19,439 by the close of the century. The value of town property in 1796 was returned as $4,264. In 1795, the number of acres of land listed for taxation was 211,533, and in 1797, it was 273,284. The variance in the figures is accounted for by the failure of some to list their property.

There was no United States postoffice in Charlotte before 1792, in which year the local officers for the first time took the oath of allegiance to the Federal government. Edward Waine and Ephraim B. Davidson held the position as postmaster before 1800.

The only industries in Charlotte at the close of this period were a flour mill, saw mill and a blacksmith shop. Besides these, however, might be mentioned a number of taverns, a maker of rifles, and the merchants, tailors, weavers and hatters. Jeremiah McCafferty opened a store in Charlotte as early as 1771, and three others were doing business prior to the Revolution. The firm of Ochiltree, Martin & Co. were merchandising as late as 1780, and in 1783, the same firm was doing business under the name of Ochiltree & Polk, and there were many other traders in the town and county.

Andrew Jackson, seventh President of the United States, was born in the southeastern part of Mecklenburg, six miles from the present town of Waxhaw, in what is now Union county, March 15, 1767, and soon after his birth, his widowed mother moved with her children into South Carolina. In the records of the October term of the county court in 1787, is this entry:

"W. Copples, Andrew Jackson and Alexander McGinty, Esquires, come into Court and produce License from the Honorable, the Judges of the Superior Court of Law and Equity, authorizing them to practice as Attorneys in the several County Courts within this State, and having taken the oath of office, ordered that they be admitted accordingly."

November 2, 1795, James Knox Polk, eleventh President of the United States, was born between Hopewell and Huntersville, at the home of his mother's parents, Mr. and Mrs. James Knox. His father, Samuel Polk, was a son of Ezekiel Polk, and in 1806, when James Knox Polk was eleven years of age, moved with his family to Tennessee.

George Washington was in Charlotte May 25, 1791, being on a tour through the South. He dined with Gen. Polk with a party of the most prominent citizens of the county, who had been invited to meet the distinguished guest.

Authority:—Colonial and County Records. The birthplace of Jackson was decided definitely by Parton's Biography. Appleton's Encyclopedia, the Land Records and Col. S. H. Walkup's Publication.

CHAPTER XIV.

EDUCATION BEFORE 1800.

First Teachers and Schools in Mecklenburg—Qualifications of Teachers and Nature of Instruction—Grammar and Classical Schools.—Queen's College, Queen's Museum and Liberty Hall.

The first school teachers in Mecklenburg of whom there are any records, were at their work in 1762, about the time the county was established. So that, properly, the history of education in Mecklenburg begins with the history of Mecklenburg itself. February 9, 1762, Charles Moore, who lived in the lower part of the county, which is now in South Carolina, gave to Andrew Armon a receipt for four pounds and fifteen shillings in full payment of a note from his father for "schooling." As this teacher was practicing his vocation in a part of the county then most thinly settled, it is within the bounds of proper inference to say there must have been teachers before that time in the neighborhoods of Rocky river, Sugar creek, Steele creek, and Providence. Moses Ferguson taught near where the Barringers lived, and later at Steele creek before 1762, and he was one of the teachers mentioned by Governor Dobbs in 1755 as being employed by a number of Irish Protestant families who had banded together in order to have their children educated.

There were but few school houses in the county before the Revolution, it being the custom for the teachers to work at their homes or at the homes of the patrons. By 1775, however, there were school buildings in Charlotte and at Rocky river, Clear creek, Sugar and Steele creeks, Providence, Hopewell, Beatty's ford and one between Providence and the present town of Monroe. The Sugar creek grammar school was one of the most noted in this section. Some teachers would teach in one community a few months, and then move to another, and in this way were engaged in their

Received from Mr. James Alexander this 17th of July the sum of Sixteen Pounds So. Currency, at the rate of forty eight Shillings for a ten Pounds Bill being in part payment for a Years Tuition of his Brother Joseph Alexander in Queens Museum, Charlotte. I say rec'd

pr. Jos. Alexander

RECEIPT FOR TUITION IN QUEEN'S MUSEUM.

work during the whole year. They did not depend for their living entirely upon tuition, as records are plentiful of teachers "crying sales" and "trading horses."

Writing, reading, spelling and arithmetic were the subjects taught in these first schools. The Bible was often used as the text book for reading, but considerable difficulty was encountered in securing a sufficient number of arithmetics. The teacher, of course, possessed one, and he or the pupils would copy portions of it for the use of the school. Some books were kept for sale by the merchants in Mecklenburg, but these were of a religious character, and the text books were usually purchased in Charleston and brought back by the traders.

People of those days had practical ideas about everything. It was deemed important that children be taught the rudiments of education, and some were sent north to college, but the things most highly considered were religious and industrial training. Parents believed it essential that their children be given instruction in the Bible, Catechism and religious doctrines, and that each one be trained in some trade. Provisions were made by wills and otherwise for a child to be given a certain amount of "schooling" and to be bound to some man who would agree to instruct him in "the art and mystery of weaving," "tailoring" or any of the similar industries. It was customary for all orphans to be bound in this way until they became twenty-one years of age, and thus each one was fitted to earn an independent living.

There are many records of bills, charges against estates and receipts for "schooling" prior to the Revolutionary war. In September, 1775, John Patterson, schoolmaster, circulated articles of agreement to teach a school in the northern part of the county. The contract stipulated that the master should "well and truly teach, according to custom, spelling, reading, writing and arithmetic," and that the patrons should "cut and lay convenient to the school house a sufficiency of firewood for the year." The school opened October 5, 1775, and continued six months, the teacher's remuneration being "equivalent to six months' wages with board and lodging." Teachers were paid the same wages as common hired men.

After the Revolution there were several popular schools in the county. Dr. McCorkle taught at Thyatira, Dr. Robinson at Poplar Tent, Dr. Wilson at Rocky river, Caldwell at Sugar creek and James Walters at Providence. Besides these men, who were located permanently in their respective neighborhoods, there were many traveling teachers. In 1773, Kerns Henderson taught the two children of Joseph Sample at a "musick school." Elizabeth Cummins, who taught a four months' school in the county in 1774, was Mecklenburg's first lady teacher. Clio's Nursery and Science Hall were taught by Rev. James Hall, the pastor of Fourth creek, Concord and Bethany.

Elijah Alexander taught a school at his home in 1791, and boarded a number of "scholars." In some of the best schools by this date, geography and Latin were added to the usual course of instruction. As early as 1787, John McKemey Wilson was at school away from home, and in 1790, Thomas Polk spoke of James Polk as "soon to leave for Williamsburg for school." Boarding schools in the county were rare, but it was not uncommon by the close of the century for boys to be away from home attending school.

December 5, 1770, Governor Tryon suggested to the Assembly the wisdom of establishing in the back country a school for "higher learning," and the idea met with the prompt approval of the representatives. A committee was appointed to consider the matter, and the chairman, Edmund Fanning, soon presented a bill establishing and endowing Queen's College, in Charlotte, and it was enacted and approved by the Governor January 15, 1771. The board of trustees included the most distinguished men in the county, and they met March 1, 1771, and elected Edmund Fanning president, and three tutors, of whom Rev. Joseph Alexander was one; and Thomas Polk was elected treasurer. This institution began with favorable indications of success, but it

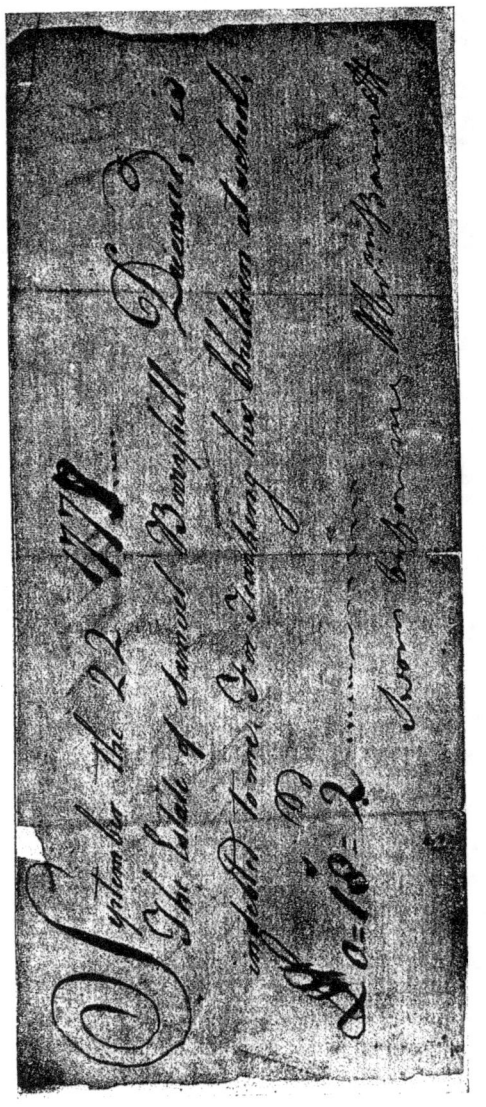

BILL FOR TEACHING, 1771.

was hampered by the dissensions in the county, caused by the court house controversy, land troubles and Regulators. In June, 1773, Governor Martin issued a proclamation giving notice that the king had disallowed the charter. The only apparent reason was that the college, being in a Presbyterian stronghold, would tend to encourage dissenters from the established Church of England. The school continued for some time without a charter, though the patronage was not encouraging.

In 1773, Martin Phifer endeavored to get a new charter for the Charlotte school under the title of Queen's Museum. Though his effort was unsuccessful, the people of the town in the next year began a school under that name as successor to Queen's College, which had been abandoned. Thomas Polk, Abraham Alexander and others, persevered in the face of repeated disaster in their desire to have a high grade school in Charlotte. John McEwen was given a diploma by Queen's Museum in 1776, but about that time the name was again changed, this time to Liberty Hall Academy.

Liberty Hall Academy was incorporated in 1777, and Robert Brownfield, of Mecklenburg, was president for the first year. He was succeeded by Dr. McWhorter, of New Jersey, who held the office until the institution was closed in 1780 on account of Cornwallis' invasion. It enjoyed great prosperity during the first years of its existence, but the war impeded its progress until finally it was forced to suspend.

In 1760, Crowfield Academy was established about two and a half miles northeast of the present site of Davidson College. It continued in great usefulness until the British invasion in 1780, during which time instruction was given to many men who afterwards became prominent.

These first schools of "higher learning" included Latin, Greek, Hebrew, Philosophy and Theology in their course of instruction, in addition to that of the common schools. They were supported by tuition, donations, a tax on liquor, and occasionally lotteries were allowed to assist them. Girls did not attend them, as the necessity for their education equal with boys was not then manifest. and all the instruction they received was merely enough to equip them to study the Bible and Catechism.

The more prominent citizens of these times possessed considerable libraries, but among the poorer classes books were scarce. At the close of the eighteenth century, a few books of a substantial character were owned by almost every family. The Bible was the most popular, and the others generally used were the Westminster Confession among the Presbyterians, Luther's Bible and Catechism among the Germans, and the Book of Common Prayer among the few adherents of the Established Church. The Almanac was about the only current literature obtainable, except in rare instances, when the leading men would go to Charleston to trade and would bring back some newspapers.

Authority:—County Records, Bills, Receipts, Personal Accounts, Raper's Church and Private School History, and Charles Lee Smith's History of Education in North Carolina issued by the Federal Government in 1888.

CHAPTER XV.

RELIGION AND CHURCHES FROM 1748 TO 1800.

Presbyterians Most Numerous in the Early Times—Rev. Hugh McAden, Rev. John Thompson and Rev. Alexander Craighead the First Preachers—Seven Noted Churches and Some of Their Customs.

It has been already stated that the two principal classes of the people who settled Mecklenburg were the Germans and the Scotch-Irish. The Germans were Lutherans and German Reform in their religious beliefs, while the Scotch-Irish, who were their superiors in numbers, were Presbyterians. In 1755, when Governor Dobbs made his visit to this section of the province, he reported that these Scotch-Irish had joined in bands of twenty or more families in order to have teachers and preachers of their own choosing.

A deed recorded in 1765 mentions the "old meeting house" on Rocky river, which was probably built in 1758, as Dobbs would no doubt have recorded the fact had there been a church in the county at the time of his visit. In 1755, however, the congregations of Rocky river and Sugar creek petitioned the New York Synod for a preacher, but none was sent at that time. Rev. John Thompson was preaching in the county in 1752.

In October and November of 1755, Rev. Hugh McAden made a missionary journey through the county, and reported that he preached to "some pretty serious and judicious people," and that "all had great desire for the Gospel and took much interest in spiritual things." He preached at the homes of Moses Alexander, Major Harris, David Caldwell, James Alexander, and in the Waxhaw settlements. November 23, he was at the church "five miles from Henry White's," and this was the first church ever used in the county.

Rev. Alexander Craighead, of Augusta county, Va., accepted the call to the Rocky river and Sugar creek congregations in 1759, and at this time both the congregations had churches. When McAden visited the county he found the Presbyterians divided into two parties, one of which was called the "New Side" and favored the revivalist practices of Whitfield, while the "Old Side" was opposed to them. Craighead was a revivalist and a follower of Whitfield, and a majority were in his favor, but after his death, in 1766, the "New Side" lost prestige and never regained it except for a brief while in 1800, when the great revival swept over this part of the State.

The career of this first minister is full of interest. That he was independent and fearless in thought and action is evidenced by his withdrawal from the Philadelphia Synod in 1741, at which time he was accused of "irregularities" in his teachings, and he in turn accused his accusers of coldness, formality and Pharisaism. He was courageous and felt strongly, but he controlled his feelings within the bounds of reason and order. The Scotch-Irish were loyal to the government, but demanded the right to choose their own religious instructors, believing the prevention of it meant destruction of religious liberty.

The years intervening between 1755 and 1770 may be termed the formative period of the county, in religious affairs as in all others. The unsettled conditions, the boundary dispute, the hostility of the Indians and the fierce struggle for existence in a country with no roads, markets far away and little or no currency, makes it wonderful that even a little was accomplished in the higher walks of life. The settlers of Sugar creek selected a site for a common burial place in 1763, and the oldest marked grave in that hallowed spot bears the date of that year.

Before 1770, there were Presbyterians, Lutherans, German Calvinists, a few Baptists, and some extreme followers of Whitfield known as "New Lights," in Mecklenburg county. Presbyterians and Germans alone had established churches by that time. The churches at Steele creek, Hopewell, Center, Sugar creek, Rocky river, Poplar Tent, New

Providence, Coldwater, the German churches west of the Catawba and the Clear creek church had all assumed a permanent place in our local history and had begun the important part they afterwards accomplished in the development of the county.

With the more perfect organization of the Presbyterian churches and the settlement here of several preachers of that faith who claimed equal authority with ministers of the Established church, the question of removing the restrictions which prevented Presbyterian ministers from performing the marriage ceremony, began to be agitated. A justice of the peace was permitted to perform the ceremony provided a license had been obtained from the clerk of the court, for which a fee of twenty shillings was charged. In January, 1771, the Assembly enacted a law, introduced by Edmund Fanning at the instigation of Thomas Polk, which allowed Presbyterian ministers to solemnize the rites of marriage by publication in their assemblies or by license.

After the coming of Rev. Joseph Alexander to Sugar creek, in 1767, the churches in this county made great progress for several years. This was due to the more frequent preaching, the cessation of Indian outrages, and the end of the old religious controversy. The churches did not enjoy peace even after this, for a new dissension arose over the discussions as to whether or not it was right to sing anything but the Psalms in the churches. Craighead had used no other hymns, and Rev. Joseph Alexander followed in his footsteps, and Rev. H. J. Balch did not raise the question in his day. The question was opened by the advent of Revs. James McRee, Thomas H. McCaule and Robert Archibald, who desired to use Watt's hymns. The agitators finally won, but a new church was formed by some whose consciences would not allow them to sing anything except "inspired psalmody."

During the year 1770, those members of Providence church who lived near Clear creek established a church more convenient to their neighborhood, and united with Providence in securing the services of a pastor. Revs. Reese,

McRee, Archibald and Barr ministered to them until 1792, when Rev. James Wallis became their pastor and served the churches until his death in 1819. Sardis church was formed about 1794 by some members of Providence and Clear creek who were dissatisfied with the introduction of Watt's hymns by Rev. Wallis. Lower Steele creek church was organized in 1794 by Rev. William Blacksocks, of the faith of Associate Reformed Presbyterians.

During the war, especially in 1780 and 1781, the churches were greatly disturbed. After peace was declared, the doctrines of the French skeptics began to be discussed. A society composed of prominent church members was formed for the purpose of considering the new theories, and some men openly avowed disbelief in all things. For ten years the power of the society grew, and the dissensions attracted much attention, but the whole movement was combatted from the very first by all the ministers. Efforts to check the growth of the skepticism were unavailing, and the churches suffered much until the great revival at Providence in 1802, when many of the infidels were converted.

Growth of the churches was attended with many other difficulties, as the worldly-minded were as plentiful then as at any time. Dancing, horse racing, gambling, card playing, drunkenness and neglect of public worship were the sins that enticed the church members. Then there were always some differences of belief. Rev. Robert Archibald was suspended from the ministry in 1794 because he preached the doctrine of universal salvation. In 1779, Little Steele creek church was formed by members who left Lower Steele creek church because of a dispute as to whether it was necessary to fast the day before the administration of the Lord's Supper. Regeneration, baptism, total depravity, original sin, and free moral agency were also discussed. Considering all these difficulties, it is wonderful that the churches made any progress. Their final victory can only be accounted for by the fact that they stood as the representatives of that higher spiritual life without which society can not long exist.

One method used to raise money for church purposes was

RELIGION AND CHURCHES FROM 1748 TO 1800.

the renting of pews. A member was usually appointed every quarter to collect these rents. Thirty-two shillings a year was charged for one seat or pew, but free seats of some kind were provided for those who could not afford to pay. Before 1800, the Presbyterian church had more strength than all other churches in the county combined. The Methodists built their first "meeting house" just before the close of the century, and it is yet Harrison M. E. church, near where the Charlotte and Lancaster, S. C., road crosses the State line. James Jonathan and Daniel Mills were the founders of this organization.

Authority:—Personal Accounts, County Records, Pamphlets and Church Records.

CHAPTER XVI.

DOCTORS AND MEDICINES BEFORE 1800.

First Physicians in the County and the Leading Ones of the Period.
—Methods of Practice and the Medicines Used—Prevalence of
Witchcraft and Its Treatment.

When Mecklenburg county was formed, it is doubtful whether there was a resident doctor in the county, except such as modern science would regard as nurses. The first regular physician of whom there is any record of his practicing in Mecklenburg was Dr. John Newman Oglethorpe, of Rowan, in 1764. In 1766, the administrator of Valentine Dellinger reported that he had paid a "Doctor Cantzon" twelve shillings. Dellinger lived in what is now Lincoln county.

The first resident physician and the first man of medical education who practiced his profession in the present county of Mecklenburg was Dr. Joseph Kennedy. A record of this physician's labors bears the date of 1766, but it is likely that he practiced a few years earlier than that date. Dr. Kennedy died in 1778. The next resident physician was Dr. Ephraim Brevard, who certainly began the practice of his profession as early as 1772, when he began to have accounts against several estates for "medicine and visits."

In 1773 and 1774, "Dr. Newman" practiced in the Hopewell section of the county. He probably lived in Rowan. In 1777, Dr. Felix Pitt was a resident physician. In his account with William Barnett, in 1778, such items as a "visit" at eight shillings, a "large blister Plaister" at fifteen shillings, "seven Aperient powders" at seventeen and one-half shillings, and "a Pectoral Mixture" at one pound two and one-half shillings, were charged.

In 1780, Dr. Thomas Henderson, who was a Mecklenburg school teacher in 1774, appeared in the records as a physician. For nearly thirty-six years afterwards he seems to have been the leading physician in this county, his practice extending to every part of it. About the same time Dr. Henderson began to practice in Charlotte, Dr. James R. Alexander began to practice at Hopewell. When Isaac Alexander's services as teacher in Queen's Museum terminated in the Fall of 1776, he began the study of medicine, but it was not until 1782 that he began active practice. When Dr. Ephraim Brevard's property was sold at public sale in 1782, Dr. Isaac Alexander, Dr. Thomas Henderson, Dr. James R. Alexander and a Dr. Dysart are noted as purchasers of "physic." It is more than likely that they were the only resident physicians in this county at that time.

In 1780, when the smallpox was epidemic in the county, having been brought here by the British and the American armies, Dr. James Alexander vaccinated many of the people of his section. In one family he vaccinated ten persons, charging one pound currency for each "innoculation"—probably depreciated continental currency. While this epidemic was prevailing, Catherine Blackwelder, of Cabarrus, acted as a nurse and no doubt saved many lives by her care and self-sacrifice. Some of those who were the recipients of her attentions paid her, but the money was the almost worthless continental currency of the time, so that she never received any adequate compensation for her heroic efforts to save the lives of her friends and neighbors. Henry Probst, of Cabarrus, in 1789, rendered an account against one of his neighbors for "four fisicks and rideing." He was not a physician, but no doubt had some knowledge of medicine.

It is a fact not now generally known that some of the early settlers in this section regarded many diseases as directly due to the power and influence of witches. These ideas especially prevailed among the ignorant of all nationalities. However, there is no record in this county from which it could be inferred that anyone was ever punished for witchcraft, witches generally being regarded here as spirits of evil influence who made their journeys at night and brought their baneful influence to bear on horses, cattle, and human beings. There were those in every neighborhood who professed to be able to drive away witches or relieve those who had been put under their influence. The methods of these so-called "witch doctors" were often ludicrous. For instance, children who were said to be "bewitched" were subjected to a treatment which consisted in placing a ladder on end against a building and passing the bodies of the children up through the successive rungs of the ladder after the fashion of weaving, then repeating the process from top to bottom.

There are traditional instances which relate how the "witch doctors" tried to cure cases of serious sickness by means of methods which border on those now practiced by the faith healers. In the particular cases referred to, the "witch doctors" began their treatment by reconciling any family differences with neighbors, even to the extent of returning all borrowed property, after which the treatment consisted of "words" or "prayers," sometimes accompanied with anointing the parts of the body which seemed to be the seat of the "witches" with concoctions, the making and compounding of which was a secret to all except those initiated. Even after 1800, they who professed to cure the evils brought on human beings by witches were found in many parts of the original territory of Mecklenburg.

Investigation discloses the fact that women in rare instances were regarded as possessing the power of witches. In such cases they were shunned by the superstitious. Men could teach women how to cure certain diseases attributed to the power of the witches, but men could not initiate men into the mysteries of such an art, that being only possible to a woman. It is not known how the first man acquired the power which enabled him to drive away witches or to relieve the sufferings supposed to be due to their influence.

By the year 1790, three other physicians had begun to practice in this county. They were William Strain, who lived in what is now Cabarrus, and Alexander Cummins, who resided somewhere in the northern part of the county, and Thomas Donnell. A year or two later, Dr. Charles Harris began the practice of his profession. He lived in what is now Cabarrus. Dr. Harris was an educated man, and with Dr. Henderson and Dr. Alexander, seems to have enjoyed a large practice.

Between 1790 and 1800, the other Mecklenburg physicians were Frederick Croner, William Morrison, Joseph McKnitt Alexander, and Cyrus Alexander. Dr. Joseph Ramsey and Dr. John Sibley, both of Rowan, practiced in parts of the county during this period, as well as Dr. Samuel C. Dunlap, of Lancaster county, South Carolina, and Dr. William Kerr, of York county, in the same State.

Of all these men, Dr. Croner, who lived in Charlotte, seems to have taken most pains to display his knowledge of Latin. His accounts were full of such phrases as *per noctem* and *eodem die,* among other peculiarities. All these doctors put great confidence in a drug known as "cooling powders," as well as "blisters," "sulphur," "magnesia," "bark," "unction" and "cream tartar."

During this period there were many women in various parts of the county who had some skill in the treatment of diseases, especially of a disease which the people called "white swelling." Several bills and receipts remain, all signed by women, for services in treating this affection.

Authority:—County Records, Official Papers, Personal Correspondence, Family Traditions and Business Accounts.

CHAPTER XVII.

SLAVERY BEFORE 1800.

Introduction of the System Was Slow—Conditions of Labor—No One Owned More Than a Dozen Slaves—Prices, Habits and Ability of the Negroes—Only a Few Were Skilled Laborers.

The first immigrants to Mecklenburg brought with them but few slaves. Those settlers who came from Pennsylvania and Maryland were searching for a new and freer land wherein to dwell, and in the uncertainty of their ultimate location, it is improbable that they were encumbered with slaves, who would then and for some time afterwards have been more trouble than their services would justify. Those who came from Virginia brought a few slaves; they knew where they were going, were acquainted with the nature of the country and did not have to move so far as those from the North.

Another reason why the introduction of slavery into the county was so slow, was that most of the settlers were poor people and could not afford servants. They were searching for a region where they could live by their own industry without fear of tyrannical and arbitrary interference. The work of pioneers was not suited to the slaves, and the unsettled condition of the country offered too many inducements to them to run away. After government was firmly established and these first settlers had achieved some success in worldly riches, the growth of slavery was steady.

It was so easy in those days to live independently that hired labor of every kind was scarce. Each man built his little cabin and began work for himself. Game was plentiful, and not much industry was necessary for obtaining necessities of life. Hence it was very difficult to hire anyone, and each farmer had to do his own work until he could by diligence and economy save enough to buy a slave. Governor Dobbs said that from 1750 to 1764, "the number of laborers and artificers in comparison with the number of planters was small." Laborers were paid from three to six shillings a day for work which was much less than a day's work in England, so the price of labor in Mecklenburg was higher than in the mother country.

When a farmer accumulated enough money to buy a slave, he would go to Charleston and buy what the first sale lists called a "negro wench" or a negro man; paying for a female an amount about equal to four hundred dollars, and for an able-bodied man perhaps as much as one hundred dollars more. When the county was formed in 1762, there were only a few slave owners in this section. The first recorded sale of a negro at auction in Mecklenburg was at Hugh Irwin's sale in 1764, when a "negro" was sold for seventy-five pounds. Previous to 1774, not more than two slaves were disposed of at any public sale of an estate, though it is certain that some persons owned more than that number before that date. At Moses Alexander's sale in 1774, "a negro wench and child and fellow" were sold for one hundred and seventy-five pounds, "a negro wench and child" for one hundred and thirty pounds, one "negro man" for sixty-nine pounds and another for one hundred and twenty-three pounds, a "negro wench" for eighty-eight pounds and a "negro child" for thirty-six pounds. This was the largest slave sale held in the county before the Revolution, Moses Alexander being the largest slave owner of his day.

By this time, slaves had learned how to run away from their masters. In 1769, George Cathey charged Archibald Cathey three pounds and four shillings for going to Newbern "after runaway negroes." The sparsely settled country then afforded many avenues of escape to the runaways, and their capture was attended with difficulties. There were in the county a few white "indentured servants" who had been sent over from England because of debt or crime, but this class entirely disappeared with the Revolution. One of these, Johnston Clark, was sold at Archibald Cathey's sale in 1777, and was purchased by Josiah Cathey for twenty-one pounds. Hezekiah Alexander freed an "indented slave" in 1772.

Even before the Revolution, there was opposition to slavery because of economic reasons. The Rowan county committee of safety, August 8, 1774, adopted resolutions which fairly expressed the views of a majority of the people of this whole section, declaring: "That the African trade is injurious to this colony, obstructs the population of it by freemen, prevents manufacturers and other useful emigrants from Europe from settling among us, and occasions an annual balance of trade against the colonies." During the Revolutionary war, the progress of slave trade was very slow, and not until after the United States government was fully established did it take on new life.

The British invasion in 1780 and the events of the war during the next year caused slave owners much annoyance in the control of their slaves. The British promised freedom to all slaves who would join their forces, but only a few accepted the invitation and nearly all these were finally regained by their owners. A great number, however, took advantage of the exciting times and endeavored to escape. John Sample owned one who ran away seven times in 1781 and 1782, but was caught every time.

In the year 1791, the county court empowered the sheriff to seize and sell at auction all horses found in the possession of slaves who were off the plantations of their masters. The reason given for this action was that "danger to life and injuries of various kinds would likely result from the possession of horses by negro slaves." Two years later, the court ordered the officers to arrest and confine in the county jail all negroes "ranging at large during public meetings in the town of Charlotte except such as carried passes from their masters," and that "in case of an arrest of this kind, the owner of the slave shall pay all costs of the action." The reason assigned for this proceeding was that "sundry injuries have arisen to the owners of slaves by the promiscuous mingling of the negro population with the whites on public occasions."

In 1791, a negro man named Ben was tried by the court and sentenced to death for burglary, and in 1793 a slave named Simon was similarly sentenced for a like offense. One Sunday in the Spring of 1793, Ben, Joe and Sam, slaves living near Providence, came to Charlotte and stole a ten gallon keg of whiskey from a spring house. After getting drunk, they stole a horse from a pasture and rode off, but were soon apprehended, tried and sentenced to receive fifty lashes on the bare back. Their owners were taxed with all costs, and in this trial slaves served as witnesses, but were not sworn.

During the last decade before 1800, the largest slave owners in the county were T. Hood, John Ford and James Walkup, who owned eight, nine and twelve slaves respectively. The names of slaves are interesting in view of the fact that they often suggested the character and education of the owners. Hood's were named Jacob, Charlotte, Weyer, Dinah, Hannah, Josiah and Prudence; Ford's were Phebe, Dinah, Sylvia, Charlotte, Jack, Dice, Will and Julius. Walkup's slaves were sold in 1798 for prices ranging from twenty-five to four hundred and twenty-five dollars each, and among them were Titus, Farrabo and Prince. Rev. Samuel Kennedy called his: Romulus, Juno, Daphne, Alpheus, Joseph and Terah.

By the will of John Wilson, who died in 1795, it was provided that one of his slaves, a negro man named Plumb, should be given his freedom. The county court in the next year recommended Plumb to the General Assembly as worthy of emancipation and his freedom was secured. This proceeding was not uncommon in Mecklenburg in the latter part of the century.

Before 1800, it was rare that a slave owner taught his slaves to do anything but farm work. In 1785, David Allison charged James Cannon, of the Hopewell section, twelve pounds for one month's work of two negro tailors, and some negroes were employed in wagon shops and other places of the kind, but there was a widespread prejudice against the use of slave labor in occupations of skill on account of its competition with free white labor. With the invention of the cotton gin and the resultant increase in cotton production, slave labor increased to such an extent that it was utilized in nearly all occupations. This left the poor whites no alternative but to work in competition with the slaves trained by the whites in more fortunate circumstances, who had, as a consequence, ceased to work.

Authority:—County and Private Records, Printed Notices, Receipts and Bills.

To Joseph Gales **Dr.**

Printer, Bookseller, Stationer and Proprietor of the Raleigh Register.

To the RALEIGH REGISTER, and North-Carolina Gazette, from

Received Payment,

RECEIPT DATED IN 1810.

CHAPTER XVIII.

FIRST YEARS OF THE NINETEENTH CENTURY. (1800 to 1825.)

Statistics of Wealth and Population of the County and City—Improvements in Public Buildings—Proceedings and Methods of the Courts—Richest Man in the County Worth $10,700.

Statistics recorded in the early years of our history are very conflicting and unsatisfactory, the cause being that the monetary system was unstable and oscillating so that money values were not always the same; a great portion of property was not returned for taxation, people paid taxes where they lived on property wherever it might be, and the difficulty attending travel made the duties of the officers hard to fulfill. Some people would list their taxes one year and omit the duty the next. People living in Charlotte would list all their slaves in the county as though they lived here, thus causing it to appear that the blacks greatly outnumbered the whites in the town.

Tax returns in 1800 for Mecklenburg county included 293,145 acres of land, and town property in Charlotte valued at 2,835 pounds. The county tax was 4 pence on 100 acres of land and 1 shilling on each poll and each 100 pounds valuation of town property. All white men between the ages of twenty-one and fifty were subject to poll tax, and they numbered 1,247; all negroes between the ages of twelve and fifty were subject to the tax, and they numbered 854. James Neel was sheriff of the county in 1800, and continued in that capacity until 1802, when he was succeeded by Robert Barry, who, the next year, was succeeded by William Beatty, who lived but a few months, his unexpired term being filled by John Cook. In those years, the law allowed the county jailor 2s. 6d. a day for each prisoner, and the rations for the prison inmates consisted daily of "one pound of wholesome bread, one pound of good roasted or boiled meat and all the water needed."

At the July term of court, 1802, Thomas Alexander was deputized to erect a whipping post and stocks near the jail, and Edwin Jay Osborne was admitted to the practice of law. James Potts had been licensed the preceding year. The State tax in that year amounted to 627 pounds in Mecklenburg, and of this amount 253 pounds was paid on cotton machinery and three pounds on town property. The tax levied by the State then was 8d. on 100 acres of land, 2s. on 100 pounds valuation of town property, 2s. on each poll, an annual tax of ten pounds on peddlers and a tax on the amount of goods sold by stores. Mecklenburg's State tax in 1803 amounted to 546 pounds, 654 in 1804 and 632 in 1805. In the latter year, 212 pounds tax was paid on cotton gins, Mecklenburg leading all the other counties in the number of gins.

In 1803, David Cowan was appointed standard keeper of weights and measures, and $58 was allowed him with which to purchase the necessary outfit. Samuel Lowrie was appointed State's Attorney at the July court, and Dr. Nathan Alexander, David Cowan and John Sharpe were appointed a committee to investigate and report upon the advisability of building a new jail. They reported in favor of the new building. Cowan resigned as standard keeper in the following year and William Davidson was appointed to the vacancy at the October court. The same court licensed John Beatty to keep a tavern in Charlotte, and sentenced Henry Price to confinement for one-half an hour in the stocks for quarreling, and fined Henry Emberson five dollars for a similar offense.

At the April term of court, in the following year, Gen. George Graham, Capt. William Davidson and Isaac Alexander were appointed commissioners to investigate the condition of the public buildings and the finances of the county. Though they and the sheriff recommended that a new jail should be built, all that was done was to appropriate ten pounds for repairs. John Black was appointed county surveyor. At this time the system of patrolling was in full

COTTON PLANT IN SEPTEMBER.

COTTON PLANT IN NOVEMBER.

force, and six patrols were appointed for the Charlotte militia district, and these patrols were of much service in preventing troubles among slaves and in apprehending the runaways. In 1805, Nathaniel Alexander, of Mecklenburg, was elected Governor of North Carolina, and he occupied the office for one term.

Charlotte's charter was amended by the General Assembly in 1807, and the commissioners appointed were William Davidson, Archibald Trice, Joseph Faires, William Allison and William Carson. They were empowered to make all necessary rules and regulations for the government of the town and to enforce them. The body was also made self-perpetuating; they elected their own successors.

The General Assembly, in 1806, provided for Superior courts, and divided the State into six judicial districts, Mecklenburg being in the sixth. The first Superior court was accordingly held by Judge Francis Locke in this county in the following January. David Cowan was the first Superior court clerk, and Winfield Mason was appointed master in equity. Elections in those times were held at the residences of John Ray, Robert Hood and Margaret Davidson, to provide for all sections of the county, though any resident could vote at the court house if he preferred. The election was held on the Tuesday preceding the second Thursday in August, and began at noon and ended at sunset, when the ballot boxes were sealed and carried immediately to the court house in Charlotte.

Adlai L. Osborne was admitted to the practice of law in 1808, and at the same court several other matters of interest transpired. An additional ten pounds was appropriated for repairs on the jail. Two slaves, Ephraim and Moses, were acquitted of the charge of killing Jack, a negro belonging to Joseph Spratt, and Charles Richmond and James Summers were fined five dollars each for an affray in the presence of the court. The next year, William Carson was appointed standard keeper, George Hampton sheriff, Thomas Alexander treasurer, and John McKnitt Alexander county trustee. Archibald Henderson, an attorney, presented to the court the naturalization papers of John Patterson, this being the first instance of the kind on record. Authority was given to sell the old jail, as provision for a new one had been made. That year is notable for the fact that the United States currency law went into effect, and thereafter transactions were made in dollars and cents. In 1810, at the July court, James Lewis Crawford transferred to William Allison the Mecklenburg rights of Freeman's patent washing machine for a term of fourteen years, and the contract was registered. In this year also, a new court house was erected.

The war with England in 1812-14, did not directly concern the people of Mecklenburg, and the issues were of no material consequence to them. However, this did not prevent the people from assisting to expel the foreign forces, and five companies of Mecklenburg troops served throughout the war and did noble service for their country. There were nearly five hundred men in the five companies. After the defeat of the British at New Orleans, Colonel Joseph Graham was sent with his regiment against the Creek Indians in Alabama, but Gen. Andrew Jackson had completely defeated them when he arrived.

In 1814, there were in Charlotte 237 town lots, valued at $36,000; five stores, seventy-eight white polls and 228 blacks. It is to be borne in mind that most of these negroes were living on farms outside of Charlotte. In 1818, there were seventy families in the town district. In the next year the town lots were valued at $41,400, there were 118 tax payers in Charlotte and there were thirty stores in the county. In 1830, the town property was valued at $46,300, and there were eleven stores in the town.

The court held in July, 1823, ordered that the notices should be published in the *Western Carolinian*. In that year also, the General Assembly incorporated the New Providence Library Association, which was organized for the purposes of general reading and literary culture. The Centre Library Society was incorporated in 1817. In 1825, there were 258 town lots returned for taxation; William Smith was postmaster in Charlotte, and there were ten other post-offices in the county. At that time the population of Charlotte was about seven hundred. The public buildings consisted of the court house, jail and postoffice; there were fourteen stores, several taverns and a number of persons engaged in the industries of tailoring, weaving, wagon making and other employments requiring skill. Mills and shops of various kinds were in operation in the county. There were perhaps ten lawyers in the county and as many physicians. Drs. McKenzie and Caldwell were the leading practitioners. In 1819, William Davidson was the richest man in the county; he owned twenty-three slaves, 1,835 acres of land, and his total assessed property amounted to $10,700. Thomas G. Polk's property was valued at $10,611, and eight others in the county were worth more than five thousand dollars each.

Authority:—County Records and Personal Accounts.

CHAPTER XIX.

INTRODUCTION OF THE COTTON INDUSTRY. (1790 to 1825.)

First Planting in the Colonies Was Experimental—Little Progress Made Previous to the Invention of the Cotton Gin—Two Thousand Saws in Use in Mecklenburg in 1803—Rapid Development Thereafter.

The history of the cultivation of cotton goes back to a thousand years before the Christian era. Details of the first planting, and even the introduction of it into the United States, do not immediately concern us except to demonstrate the wonderful evolution from its cultivation for mere household use to the leading industrial feature of the South. In the course of this phenomenal growth and expansion, there are some points of peculiar interest.

It is well known that the first colonists who came over from England were experimenters and adventurers. They came for the novelty of new experiences, and consequently accomplished but little. When it was realized that the New World needed men who were willing to endure hardships and toil for poor remuneration, the settlers were not so eager to come, but those who did venture to undertake the task of building a new country were of a practical kind. However, they continued to experiment, always hoping to find an easier way to live.

Cotton planting was begun by the first permanent settlers in Virginia in the early part of the seventeenth century. They hoped that something good would come of it, but they were hoping without reason, for cotton was not then a practical industry. The first exportation of cotton, consisting of eight bags weighing 1,200 pounds, was made from Virginia in 1784. When Mecklenburg was settled, between 1740 and 1760, the pioneers were slow to undertake the planting of cotton. They were busy with the building of their homes,

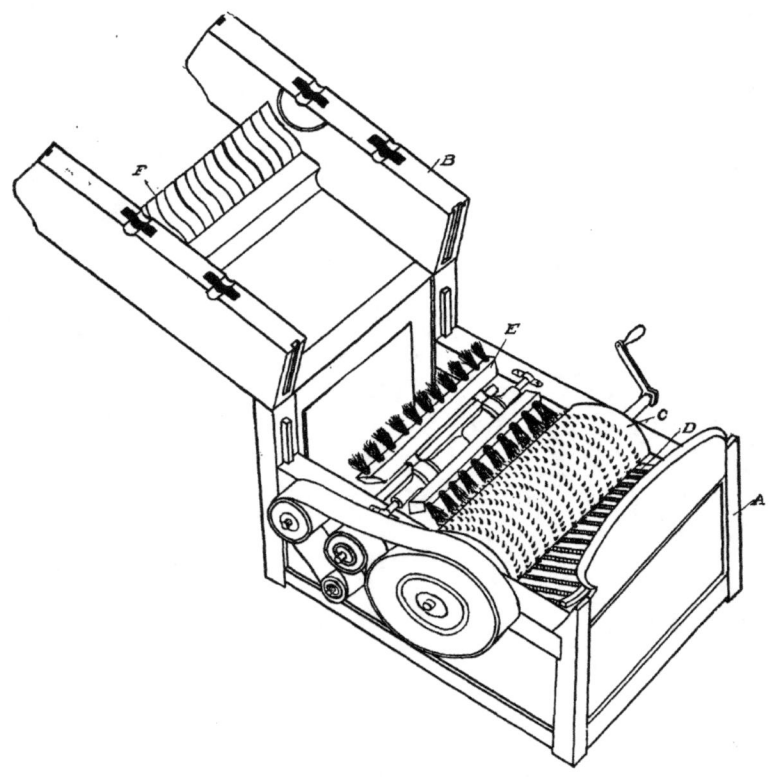

WHITNEY'S ORIGINAL MODEL.

INTRODUCTION OF THE COTTON INDUSTRY.

with their defense and with the sustenance of life. The small amount of ground which was tilled was for the necessities of life, and cotton was not one of them. Nearly everything used by them was produced by the users, and, therefore, there was no use for cotton except in the home. Then the difficulty and tediousness of separating the seed and the lint served to retard the growth of the industry.

Ten years after the county was organized with an established government, the Revolutionary troubles began. During the war, all occupations were more or less paralyzed, and it was certainly no fit time for introducing a new one. After the war, from 1782 to 1795, considerable cotton was planted in the county, though all of it was for use in the family. The lint was laboriously picked from the seed by hand, and was then put into practical form by means of the spinning wheel or spinning jenny and the loom. A demand for cotton goods sprang up and people began to plant it for purposes of sale. The great and constant annoyance was the necessity for picking the cotton by hand; and the importance of a machine to replace this tedious process was plain.

Eli Whitney, a young New Englander, had gone to Georgia to teach school, and was living at the residence of the widow of Gen. Greene, near Savannah. There he heard so much talk of the necessity for the invention that he gave his attention to the matter. In 1793, he made the model of his "gin," and a patent was obtained in the following year. In 1796, Hodgen Holmes, of Augusta, Ga., made a very important improvement by substituting the saw for the wire-spiked roller, and he obtained a patent on his "gin." As a result of these two patents, there was much litigation and ill-feeling, and it was said that Whitney was not treated fairly in the South, though the three States of North Carolina, South Carolina and Tennessee gave him a total of $90,000 for his patent, part of which he utilized in an attempt to form a monopoly west of the Savannah river, and the balance he used as a basis to begin the manufacture of firearms in New Haven. This invention was the first great incentive to the cotton industry, and its growth from that time was rapid and steady. The expansion of cotton planting naturally increased the demand for slave labor, and the increase of slave labor increased cotton planting, so these two forces in southern life were linked together and were, in a sense, dependent upon each other.

In 1802, the Legislature of North Carolina bought the patent right for this State, agreeing to pay Whitney for it by a special tax of two shillings and six pence on each saw used in a gin within the State for a period of five years. The tax was collected and paid to the inventor. It amounted to about thirty thousand dollars. This tax, which amounted to an average of $7,500 a year, indicates that there were about thirty thousand saws in use at that time.

In the settlement of the taxes for Mecklenburg, made November 30, 1802, the amount of cotton gin tax was 253 pounds and 16 shillings, which shows that there were about two thousand saws in use in this county. Mecklenburg led all the other counties in the amount of this tax. In 1803, the tax amounted to only 182 pounds. In 1804, Mecklenburg paid 212 pounds, and Lincoln county was second in the State with 56 pounds. In 1805, the tax amounted to 213 pounds, and Mecklenburg continued at the head of the list of cotton producing counties. This first cotton gin was a primitive affair, being nothing more extensive than a box about three feet long, two feet high, and two feet wide. Inside the box was the simple machinery that separated the seed from the lint about five times as fast as it could be done by hand. The principal feature of Whitney's original model was a wooden cylinder carrying annular rows of wire spikes, which was subsequently superseded by Holmes' improvement, which consisted of shaft carrying collars separating circular saws, which passed through narrow spaces between ribs, through which the seed could not pass.

Authority:—State and County Records, and Photographs and *fac similes* of Original Patents.

HOLMES' SAW GIN.

CHAPTER XX.

EFFECT OF SLAVERY ON INDUSTRIES.

Occupations of First Settlers and the Causes—They Made All They Used—Slavery Induced Them to Turn Their Entire Attention to Agriculture—Comfortable and Peaceable Conditions Prevailed.

It is a well established fact that contentment is not conducive to progress. People who are satisfied with their condition in life have no desire to go forward, or to explore new and untried fields of endeavor. The settlers of this county came here because of dissatisfaction with conditions existing where they had been living, and they were, therefore, willing to risk what little they possessed for a chance of winning more. They built their rude homes in the forest, and were eager to accept any device or any phase of industry that would tend to economize labor or to simplify the difficulties of their existence.

These first citizens became mechanics, carpenters and traders. They built shops and made wagons. They tried to produce everything needed for themselves and something else that might be sold for gain. If they were favored with abundant crops, the surplus was sold in Charleston and the money laid by or invested in property or comforts of life. The crops, however, did not afford sufficient means for trade and industrial expansion, and their attention was turned toward occupations requiring skill or special care. Cattle raising became important, and was developed to large proportions, the cattle being sold in Charleston or in Virginia, and sometimes even in Philadelphia. Weavers, millers and tailors manufactured goods for sale, as did wagon makers, basket makers and coopers. The liquor traffic began quite naturally; poor farmers would raise a few bushels of corn and distill it into liquor, which was easier to carry to market and easier to sell, and commanded a better price than the original product. Inventions and improvements were being made, and the people were progressing into wider channels of commercial intercourse.

"Necessity is the mother of invention," and invention is the avenue to progress. Hence, among the first settlers the scarcity of labor and the distance from market made invention necessary, and thus made advancement and expansion natural and continuous. When there was the work of three men for one man to do, the one man turned his thoughts to other and better modes of doing the work, but when there were three men to do the work of one man, there was but little necessity for thought of any kind. People never focus their mental powers except for cause, and without concentrated mental application, nothing can be created; and we would continue forever in the same old rut if we did not create a new and better one.

Whitney's and Holmes' inventions in connection with the cotton gin had more lasting effect upon the life of our people than any other invention ever made. There was a double necessity for the invention; it greatly reduced the amount of labor required, and did the work better than it could be done by hand. To say that it increased cotton production would but poorly express the truth, because, for all purposes of commerce, the invention of the cotton gin began the cotton industry. The gin reduced the amount of labor needed for the separation of the cotton from the seed, but in the enormous increase of cotton planting, it created a larger demand than ever for slave labor. The farmers realized to what use the slaves could be put, and the slave traffic assumed large proportions. It was evident that there would be a steady market for cotton, and as slaves could do the farm work better than any other kind of work, cotton gradually superseded all other industries until it was not only the leading one, but the only one of any consequence. The shops which had been productive of trading were closed to the public, and were utilized only for what was needed on the plantation. The plantations generally produced a little of everything, but

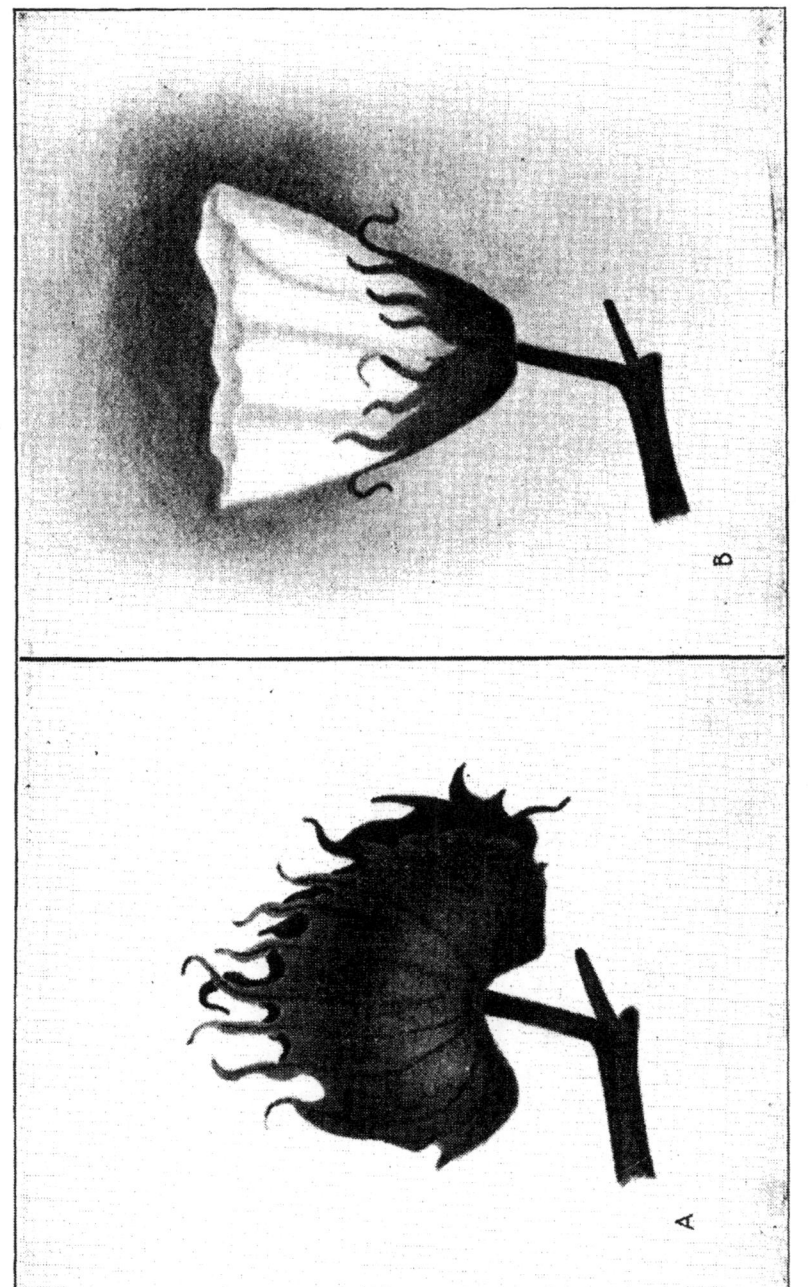

COTTON "SQUARE" AND BLOOM.

MATURED BOLL AND OPENING BOLL.

OPEN BOLL AND EMPTY BOLL.

cotton was the only product for trade and gain. Labor was cheap and plentiful under the domination of slavery, and the controlling element of white people ceased to work for themselves. The result was that there were no industries requiring skill or thought, and there was no necessity for scientific farming or anything else scientific. Nothing was more natural than that the white population should be content with the situation. Slavery not only demonstrated that people will not think unless it is necessary, but also that they will not work unless it is necessary. The planters, of course, were busy and had responsibilities, but riding around and giving orders does not tend to intellectual growth in the direction of material progress.

Within three decades after the invention of the cotton gin, slavery had accomplished its revolution. The people whose minds had been occupied with diversified industries and industrial expansion were narrowed down to the development and growth of cotton. There is no denying the fact that in this period the southern white people were happy and prosperous and contented, but it was discernible that at some time the cotton production would reach its limit, the demand would be supplied, the price would decrease and the backward and retrogressive movement would begin. The mills and shops lay idle, the abundant natural resources were ignored, and everything staked upon one occupation, because it could be carried on by slave labor and the families of the planters could have all they needed without thinking of other means of obtaining wealth. There was simply no need for anything else right then.

The production of cotton with slave labor was an industry requiring much land per capita. It appears that the limit of population under this system was reached about 1830. The system of agriculture also rapidly exhausted the fertility of the soil. These two conditions conduced to a constant emigration to the northwest and southwest. Part of this emigration was of people who wanted to escape the system altogether, and the other part was of people who went where more and better land was to be found, which was necessary to take care of the increasing population in connection with what was practically a single industry—the production of cotton.

The attention of men of education and great mental force was given to the professions, and the South furnished the statesmen for the nation, while the North got rich by the manufacture of the raw product taken from the South. The soil, the climate and the cheap labor were all favorable to agriculture, and particularly to cotton planting, and as the people could easily and comfortably live by this occupation alone, they did not care to engage in manufacturing or anything similar. All the work was done by slaves, and agriculture was the only work for which they were fitted. The capital of the people consisted of slaves, and that was a form of capital that could not be invested except in one department of labor. One of the chief reasons for the peaceable prosperity of the South was the freedom from agitators and struggles between labor and capital, caused by conditions wherein labor and capital were one and the same.

Summarizing, we find that the result of the introduction and growth of the system of slavery was revolutionary; it turned the energies of the people almost wholly to the cultivation of cotton; it practically destroyed all other industries; it developed a landed aristocracy; it gave ample leisure time to the white men for the study of professions; it unfitted the white men for manual labor, and it ultimately resulted in the hazardous risk of making the entire material wealth of a people dependent upon a single issue.

Authority:—County Records and Personal Records and Business Accounts; Newspapers and Statistics of Population and Wealth.

THE "BIG HOUSE."

CHAPTER XXI.

LIFE IN THE OLD SOUTH.

A Study of the Negro—Dispositions of Planters and Systems of Agriculture—Description of the Plantations, the "Big House" and the Cabins—Treatment of the Slaves—Social Diversions.

Discussion of southern plantation conditions before the Civil War must necessarily include the study of the institution of slavery, because the life itself was dependent upon the work of the slaves. Had it not been for the system of slave labor, the noted southern aristocracy would have been impossible.

Measured by Anglo-Saxon standards, a low type of uneducated negro was one bundle of contradictions. He could sleep more and exist with less sleep, eat more and exist with less food, than could ordinary humanity. In honesty and dishonesty, in strong affections and violent passions, in unparalleled loyalty and savage disloyalty—his mood often moving with rapidity from one extreme to another—he was governed by his immediate surroundings and influences.

It is totally at variance with Anglo-Saxon character to live in absolute subjection and yet love the master. On the other hand, the negro was readily submissive and admired and loved his owner. The life on the plantation was one of absolute mastery on one side, and of absolute subjection on the other, with amicable personal relations between the two and affection on each side.

There were as many different types of negroes as there are of whites. Some of the slaves brought to America were totally savage, while others enjoyed a considerable degree of civilization. The highest type included those from the interior of Africa, who had developed a partial civilization and were seldom enslaved; the lowest type was undoubtedly the West Coast Guinea negro, who was entirely savage, and the worst kind of cannibal. These latter in America were called "blue gum niggers," and the other negroes believed that the bite of a "blue gum" was deadly poisonous. The higher class came to be known as the "Dinka" negroes, but much the larger portion caught and brought to this country were naturally of the inferior types.

The slaves, when first brought across the ocean, were filled with terror at the new conditions. They could not understand the strange language and the many wonderful things about them, and expected some such fate as usually befell their tribesmen in Africa when overtaken by misfortune. The planter, living on his plantation, was always at hand to quell disturbances. The influence of his family was of manifest importance in keeping the better nature of the negroes to the fore. The negroes looked upon the whites with awe, and imitation of the ways of the whites was natural. It is easy to comprehend the great power the whites had over the characters of the blacks. A very generous and friendly kindness has an immense and far-reaching influence; that the kindness was real and that it bore fruit is amply proven by the world-astounding loyalty of the slaves to their masters during the Civil War.

Many people who were opposed to slavery have persistently represented the planter as a furious fighter or "fire-eater." Frequent duelling seemed to confirm this belief. As a matter of fact, the average planter, while amply courageous, was the most amiable, friendly, hospitable and unaggressive of men. He was slow to take or to give offence, and never carried a pistol or otherwise went prepared for a fight. When he felt himself offended by an inferior, he afflicted an ordinary chastisement; when his veracity or courage was questioned by an equal, there was a well formulated "Code Duello" printed in book form, in accordance with all the regulations of which he must, as a gentleman, proceed. The idea that the planter was indolent, an indifferent business man, and always a spendthrift, is totally in error. He was ever on the alert, was judicial minded, ener-

SPINNING WHEEL.

 SPINNING WHEEL.

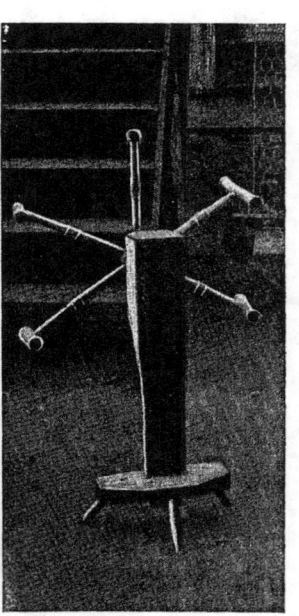 YARN REEL.

getic, usually well educated and always well trained in everything pertaining to the management of a plantation.

The system of agriculture operated by the planter was remarkably successful. Besides developing the production of cotton so as to give the world a better and cheaper supply than ever before, he at the same time produced more grain per capita, more meat per capita and more home supplies than the people of any other part of the United States. The methods of the organizations and of training the organizations were unsurpassed. The farmer before the war raised all the supplies needed at home, and sold his cotton or tobacco for clear gain. The fact that the support of all the humanity was produced on the plantation made profit certain, and even with cotton at 4 cents a pound, the planter would clear from 8 to 10 per cent. on his investment. The crop was generally laid out on the basis of twenty-five acres to one man and one mule. Of this land, ten acres would be put in cotton and the remainder in wheat, corn and oats. About one-half of the labor, including the strongest men, were selected for plow hands, and the older men, the strongest women and the youths did the hoeing, handling of the grain, picking the cotton and all miscellaneous work. The work of the able-bodied men was, of course, not confined to plowing; in season they did the blacksmithing, cleared land, made and repaired farm tools and ginned the cotton and hauled it to market.

The average southern plantation contained about three thousand acres and one hundred slaves, and such a one would be equipped with something like twenty-five plow hands, twenty-five miscellaneous hands, fifty women and children, twenty-five mules, four horses for family use, six hundred hogs, twenty-five head of cattle, one hundred sheep, ten goats and fifteen dogs, and chickens, guineas, peacocks, turkeys, geese and ducks. Then there were the blacksmith shop, wheelwright and other woodworking shops, twenty-five negro houses, a grist and flour mill, and a store. Such a plantation was worth $100,000, would produce about 100 bales of cotton and would make a clear profit of from $10,000 to $20,000 a year, according to the way it was managed. Some planters were thrifty and economical, and accumulated wealth continuously; others employed overseers to look after the estate, and spent the profits in travel or in local extravagance.

It was customary for the planter and his family to live on the plantation, because the maintenance of the organization made their presence necessary. This afforded abundant leisure time to each member of the family, and the plantation home was always a hospitable place. The host and his family had ample service, horses, vehicles, plenty of home-raised food, excellent cooks and various amusements, such as hunting and fishing, with which to entertain their guests. Negroes were fond of music and supplied it whenever called upon, though no compulsion was employed in such cases—none was necessary. A slight suggestion by a young lady from the "big house" would bring forth a tender of services from everyone on the plantation who could play the fiddle or any other instrument. Besides being fond of music, the negroes enjoyed nothing more than the gayety and finery of dances; on such occasions they would stand in crowds on the outside of the open windows and enjoy the scene thoroughly. The publicity of all plantation life was good training for the young men, and accustomed them to appearing in public and contributed to make them public speakers and statesmen.

Previous to about 1845, most of the negro houses were built of logs, and the houses of many planters were similarly constructed. After 1845, most of the houses for planters and for slaves were frame buildings, those for the planter being usually large and pretentious, while those for the slaves were the ordinary little houses with two or three rooms. The log house was covered with boards six inches wide and from two to four feet long, which were riven or split from logs. Frame houses were covered with shingles. All these cabins were periodically whitewashed, and were

ANTE-BELLUM BEDROOM.

SLAVES AND THEIR CABIN, 1850.

generally kept fairly clean. All the slaves had to work when they were able to do so, but at no other time, and they all knew they would be cared for in old age and in sickness. The old negroes were much respected, and each one would have his little cabin, and perhaps a garden, and there, with his family about him, would pass his last days in peace. Some of the negroes would spend their evenings and holidays in hunting; others would work a little plot of garden and produce something and thus earn a little extra money, which would be expended in any way they desired.

Well regulated plantations were generally in the immediate control of the owner, but if he chanced to be a professional man, fond of travel or otherwise engaged away from home, he employed an overseer. There was a wagon shop on nearly every plantation. Wagons had wooden axles and were lubricated with pine tar made in a "tar kiln." In the smithshop they used charcoal made in a "coal kiln." Collars for mules were made at home of corn shucks or poplar bark. Much cotton and wool was spun at home, a small quantity woven, and wool was frequently exchanged at a factory for cloth. The planter's wife overlooked the weaving and making of the clothes, though the work was done by the negroes. The ladies in the family provided the very best attention for the slaves when sick, and guarded carefully against any unavoidable suffering. Nearly all ladies were good horseback riders, and could handle horses not only easily, but so well as to make it a real pleasure. Churches were liberally provided, and master and slave attended services regularly, a gallery being arranged in all churches for the negroes. In the summer, when the crops were "laid by," there would be protracted and camp meetings, which would draw the people from far and near.

Plantation amusements were various and numerous. In all of them the negroes took interest, and in some participated. Fox hunting was very popular. Some few planters kept as many as twenty-five or thirty fox hounds. It was not uncommon for ladies to take part in the chase. Almost every planter kept a few pointer or setter dogs, and hunted partridges. Besides these dogs kept by the planter himself, his sons and the negroes had a miscellaneous collection of rabbit dogs, coon dogs and "possum" dogs. Fishing was common and popular. Horse racing, chicken fighting, wrestling and boxing were all popular and were conducted with decorum. Betting was not common, but sometimes it would be carried to the extreme by some event of unusual interest. House parties, dances and picnics were frequent among the young white people, while the older ones indulged in barbecues with political speaking or impromptu speeches of any kind. The white boys and the negroes hunted rabbits in day time and coons and opossums at night.

Much of the work was turned into frolics. Negroes from different plantations would be gathered together at "corn shuckings," where they would be divided into two parties, each with a huge pile of corn, and with singing and laughter would have an exciting contest. Plenty to drink and eat was supplied, and the white people would stand around and witness the fun. Similar combinations were effected for clearing land, house raisings and log rollings, while the ladies had their quilting parties and other pleasant gatherings.

Authority:—"The Old Plantation," by James Gordon Avirett; Newspapers, and the Recollections and Personal Investigations of the Author.

CHAPTER XXII.

CHURCHES BEFORE THE CIVIL WAR.

Growth of the Congregations in the County and the Building of the First Churches in Charlotte—Something of the Most Noted Ministers and Their Great Influence—Revivals and Various Religious Incidents.

Charlotte, in 1815, set apart a lot on Trade and Church streets to be used for religious purposes and for a cemetery. The people of the town combined and erected a comfortable building, which was for many years used by preachers of all denominations. There had been considerable bitter feeling in the county between the members of the various religious organizations, and this union house of worship in Charlotte began a charitable friendliness among the local churches which has never ceased.

In 1821, the Charlotte members of the Sugar Creek Presbyterian church petitioned to be formed into a separate congregation. Rev. S. C. Caldwell, the pastor at Sugar creek, had been preaching in Charlotte once a month since 1805, and continued to do so until his death in the Fall of 1826. June 8, 1827, Rev. R. H. Morrison was installed as pastor of the congregations of Charlotte and Sugar creek, and he served these churches until April 3, 1833, when his pastoral relation with "the church of Charlotte" was dissolved.

The Presbyterians secured control of the town church in 1832, and in the following year, erected a better building. On the fourth Sunday in August, 1833, the new church was occupied and "David Parks and Nathan B. Carroll were appointed elders." Soon after this, a revival was conducted by Revs. Morrison and Leavenworth, assisted by Revs. Furman and Barnes, of the Baptists. As a result of the meetings, thirty-six new members were received into the church. Rev. A. J. Leavenworth was pastor from 1834 until March

12, 1839. Revs. Thomas Owen, John M. M. Culpepper and Harper Caldwell served from 1839 to 1842; Rev. J. F. W. Freeman from 1842 to 1846; Rev. Cyrus Johnston from 1846 to 1855; Rev. A. W. Miller from 1855 to 1857; Rev. Alexander Sinclair from 1857 to 1865. William Carson, who died November 22, 1846, bequeathed $1,000 to the Presbyterian church and $5,000 and his library to Davidson College.

January 7, 1833, an auxiliary of the American Tract Society was formed in Charlotte. Isaac Alexander was chairman, Rev. A. J. Leavenworth secretary, and David Parks treasurer. The purpose of the society was to circulate tracts and other printed matter for the stimulation of religious interest. January 7, 1834, a Sunday School Union was formed in the town, and $100 raised to promote the work.

Rev. David J. Allen, a Methodist, was stationed in Charlotte in February, 1834, succeeding Rev. J. J. Allison. The Methodist congregation had been organized since 1815, and the town church, which has since become Tryon Street Methodist Episcopal church, grew from the original congregation at Buck's Hill, seven miles northwest of Charlotte, on the Beatty's Ford road. Their first church was erected on Seventh street in 1834, and it served until the present site was occupied in 1859. D. R. Dunlap and Brawley Oates were the leaders in the organization of the congregation in 1815. This church was one of a circuit until 1833, when it was made a station. The Harrison Methodist church, in the southern part of the county, was established in 1785. Another, of which Andrew Moore was founder, was built at "Bethesda," in the western part of the county, about 1810. In June, 1853, there was a Methodist revival and quarterly conference in Charlotte, which was attended by Presiding Elder Durant, Evangelist Baker, of Texas, and Rev. Mr. Jenkins, who had been a missionary in China. The missionary had with him a Chinaman and some Chinese images which excited much comment. Great interest was manifested in the meeting, a large amount was raised for foreign missions, and fifty persons were converted. In April, 1858, another revival, lasting three weeks, added forty-five members.

Rev. Mr. Barnes, of the Baptist denomination, was preaching in Charlotte in 1833. During that year and the next, he and Revs. John Culpepper and Wait preached occasionally in the county court house. In 1839, the church was erected on Fourth street, but it was sold a few years later and a better one was built at the corner of Seventh and Brevard streets.

Rev. G. D. Berkheim was in Charlotte in the early part of 1859, to organize a Lutheran church. The building was erected in March, and Revs. Bittle and Berkheim were the preachers for the congregation. The Episcopal church was organized in 1845, and a new church occupied June 22, 1858. Rev. Mr. Parker, of Salisbury, served the church until a regular pastor was secured.

Rev. Joseph Stokes, in 1824, was the first Catholic priest to visit this section. Rev. John Maginnis succeeded him in Charlotte in 1827. He taught school at his house and preached, and gradually drew around him a Catholic congregation. Rev. J. J. O'Connell was appointed to the mission in 1851, and in the same year built the first Catholic church in Charlotte.

The Associate Reformed Presbyterians did not have a church in Charlotte before 1860, though several of that belief resided in town. In the county, however, they were second only to the Presbyterians in getting started. Gilead church was formed in 1788, and Little Steele creek in 1795, and there were also Associate Reformed Presbyterian churches at Coddle creek, Prosperity, Hopewell and Sardis. Among the able men who served these churches were Revs. James McKnight, John Boyce, Alexander Ranson and John Hunter.

From 1800 to 1860, the noted seven Presbyterian churches of Mecklenburg were all prospering, and new ones were being formed in the county, principally by members of these old churches. Pleasant Hill church was formed by members of Steele creek in 1836, and began with forty-two members. In the latter part of May, 1858, there was a revival at Hopewell, conducted by Rev. S. C. Pharr, the pastor, who was assisted by Rev. R. H. Morrison. As a result of the meeting, fifty members were taken into the fold. In 1831, Sharon church was formed by the members of Providence who lived north of McAlpin's creek.

Camp meetings and revivals were annual events of importance. There was in every section a camp meeting ground with a large arbor for preaching, and little cabins for the accommodation of the people. Many of the people would carry tents with them, and they would remain for weeks at a time. The best preachers were obtained for such occasions, and sometimes the excitement was intense and large numbers were converted.

The ministers were generally well equipped with this world's goods. In 1819, Rev. John Williamson owned 504 acres of land, and his property was valued at $2,312. Rev. S. C. Caldwell owned property amounting to $2,702; Rev. Humphrey Hunter was worth $1,500; Rev. James Wallis $3,526, and Rev. Isaac Grier $1,200. They each owned several slaves and large tracts of land. Rev. S. C. Caldwell had 904 acres of land and eight slaves.

Authority:—Newspapers and Church Records and Sketches.

Charlotte Male and Female Academy.

We the subscribers promise to pay the sums severally annexed to our names, for the purpose of erecting a Male and Female Academy in the Town of Charlotte, Mecklenburg county, which sums we promise to pay to the Trustees, in the following instalments, viz: One-fourth on the 1st of December next, and the balance in two annual payments, that is to say, one-half in December, 1824, the other half in December, 1825. Witness our hands, this 28th day of February, 1823.

N. B. It is agreed by the Trustees, that those who pay their subscriptions in advance, shall have a discount of 10 per cent.

SUBSCRIPTIONS TO CHARLOTTE ACADEMY, 1823.

CHAPTER XXIII.

EDUCATION BEFORE 1860.

First Chartered Schools—County Academies—Ministers Conducted Excellent Schools—Beginning of the Public System—Military Institute—Male and Female Institutes—Davidson College.

There was little difference in the general aspect of Mecklenburg county schools before 1800 and between that time and 1860. At the principal churches in the county, excellent schools were maintained by the ministers, nearly all of whom were accomplished scholars. A number of these schools were chartered and had a regular course of instruction. Previous to the beginning of the public school system, about 1840, there were numerous teachers other than the ministers, who were regularly engaged in school work, and from 1840 the ministers were gradually supplanted in the work by men who could give their entire time to it.

Rocky River Academy was incorporated in 1812, and New Providence Academy was chartered in 1811, at which time James Wallis was principal. A high grade school was maintained there for many years. In 1852, there were two schools in the neighborhood. Miss H. G. Graham was conducting Providence Whitehall Academy, and Miss Sarah J. Parks was principal of Providence Female Academy. In 1853, W. B. Pressly taught at Sugar creek, and two years later the school was under the direction of John B. Parkey. T. M. Kirkpatrick, who had taught at Davidson, began Sharon Female Academy, seven miles from Charlotte, in February, 1849. He continued in charge of it until his death in 1855, being succeeded by Miss Eliza Parker. In 1854, Rev. R. F. Taylor began a classical school at Rock creek, and in 1855, Miss Susan Rudisill was teaching a school for girls at the residence of Mrs. Margaret Grier, in the Paw creek section.

S. W. Irwin was at the head of a classical school at Mallard creek church in 1834, and in the same year, Rev. John Maginnis was teaching a preparatory school on Tryon street, in Charlotte. J. C. Denny, who had taught two sessions in Charlotte, was at Steele creek in 1853. Robert G. Allison began the third session of the Charlotte English and Classical School in October, 1855. Rev. J. M. Caldwell and his wife taught at Sugar creek for several years before 1845. Then Misses Gould and Chamberlain conducted Claremont Academy, near the Sugar creek church, for several sessions, and in 1852, Miss Mary Ann Frew was teaching there. About that time, a daughter of J. R. Alexander was teaching a girls' school at her father's residence, half way between Charlotte and Davidson College. S. D. Wharton, of Alexandriana, was teaching at Hopewell in July, 1850, and in 1853 Mt. Carmel Academy was taught by Miss Brandon. Good schools were also conducted at Harrisburg and Cedar Grove.

Some of the teachers and many of the ministers, about the middle of the century, were highly educated. In June, 1847, Prof. Pliny Miles lectured in the Female Academy on the art of improving the memory. November 16, 1848, Rev. J. W. F. Freeman delivered an astronomical lecture in the Presbyterian church "preparatory to forming a night class for the study of astronomy by aid of Mathison's splendid diagrams." In 1853, Prof. R. H. A. Koch was teaching music in Charlotte, and in the following year Adolphus Evvette, a Frenchman, was giving special instruction to ladies in the "new system of drawing." There was usually a dancing school, and sometimes as many as three or four. September 17, 1839, Mr. A. G. Powers was teaching writing and shorthand in the town.

In 1837, North Carolina received $1,500,000 from the United States as her share of the funds which had accumulated from the sale of public lands. This amount, with some other then on hand, was used as a public school fund, and a literary board was organized consisting of the Governor and three others by him appointed. In 1839, the counties were divided into school districts, six miles square, and each county voted whether or not to have public schools, all but one voting in favor of it. Mecklenburg's vote was 950 for and 578 against, and in Charlotte it was 314 to 51. The county school tax assessed was six cents on the poll and three cents on the $100 valuation of property. The county schools were under the control of a board of seven superintendents, and each school had three committeemen. The income from the State fund was supplemented by a tax levied by the county courts, and the court was authorized to levy, on any district having as many as fifty school children, a tax sufficient to build a school house.

Rather than pay the tax, the people preferred to build the houses, so rough log buildings were erected, though there were a few neat frame structures in the county. Where there had not previously been a school, new teachers were employed, and as they could only be employed for a part of each year at a meagre salary, they were not of the highest order. In other places, however, the public schools were combined with the old schools. In 1849, the public money in district No. 50 was paid to Alexandriana Academy and used wholly for the poor people. Mrs. E. Wilson, the teacher, kept account of the number of days attended by children whose parents were unable to pay tuition, and this was charged to the public fund. Mecklenburg's portion of the public money, together with the county tax, amounted to $2,149 in 1849, and to $3,449 in 1850, in which year it was the second largest county fund in the State. In 1841, there were seventy-seven school districts in Mecklenburg. The salaries of teachers ranged from fifteen dollars to thirty dollars a month, and the books used included Webster's speller, North Carolina reader, Davie's arithmetic and Smith's grammar.

January 8, 1838, the Charlotte Male Academy opened, in charge of Rev. A. J. Leavenworth, and about forty students were enrolled. Mr. Leavenworth was followed by

Thomas A. Avery, and he by Robert G. Allison. Mr. T. C. Pomeroy, of New York, was the next principal.

October 9, 1848, Rev. J. W. F. Freeman was in charge of the Academy. He was followed the next year by Prof. J. W. Harrington, a graduate of Columbia College, of New York, who held the position until 1851. During that time the trustees of the institution were D. R. Dunlap, Leroy Springs and J. D. Boyd. Prof. W. D. Johnston conducted the school from 1854 to 1858.

July 26, 1858, the corner stone of the Charlotte Military Academy was laid with impressive ceremonies, participated in by the Masonic fraternity in a body. V. C. Barringer and Ex-Governor Graham were the orators, and a large crowd was present. The building was erected in the southern part of the city, and is now used by the graded school. It was completed in 1859, and in the fall of that year the school was opened by Gen. D. H. Hill, Gen. Jas. H. Lane and Col. C. C. Lee. R. M. McKinney, C. P. Estill, Marshall and Bynum were also teachers before the war.

An advertisement of the Charlotte Female Academy, in 1832, stated that the course of instruction included the common and higher studies, drawing, painting, music, Latin, Greek, French and Italian. Mrs. S. D. Nye Hutchison was in charge of the school from 1836 to 1839, and Miss Sarah Davidson was music teacher. Rev. A. J. Leavenworth was principal in 1840, and Rev. Cyrus Johnston from 1846 to 1853. August 15, 1849, the school opened with Rev. Johnston, Miss Mary Dayton and Miss Josephine C. Kerr as teachers. The building was burned March 26, 1851, and no effort was made to rebuild until two years later. Then bids were received for erecting a brick building three stories high and 92 by 53 feet in size. The work was completed in 1859.

The Charlotte Female Institute was organized and opened during the fall of 1857, with Rev. Robert Burwell and his wife, who had been conducting a school in Hillsboro, in charge. A good building was provided by the people of

DAVIDSON COLLEGE, MAIN BUILDING, 1857.

Charlotte, and the institution was successful. In 1859, the building was enlarged and completed, and the faculty increased by bringing in J. B. Burwell, a son of the principal, graduate of Hampden-Sidney College, and a teacher of experience. Mrs. J. A. Crittenden was teaching a school for girls in Charlotte in 1838 and 1839. There had been for a long time a school in Charlotte at intervals, known as the Female Institute. In 1838, it was being conducted by Mr. and Mrs. Gustavus Spencer, who were considered excellent teachers.

After the close of Liberty Hall, the people of Mecklenburg did not give up their hope of having an institution of higher learning in the county. The subject was much talked about, and at a convention held at Lincolnton in September, 1820, and attended by North Carolina and South Carolina Presbyterians, the first definite move was made. A board of trustees was selected, and later in the year a charter was obtained for Western College. The reason for the proposed school was "that the more western counties in the State are distant from Chapel Hill, which renders it inconvenient for their youth to prosecute their education there." Friends of the University opposed the new school, and the trustees being unable to agree as to the location, and not having much encouragement, abandoned the project in 1824.

Resolutions tending to the establishment of a Presbyterian college were adopted by the Concord Presbytery, at Prospect church, in the Spring of 1835. The object of the movement was for the promotion of liberal learning "preparatory to the Gospel ministry." The committee appointed to carry out the plans included Revs. R. H. Morrison, John Robinson, Stephen Frontis, Samuel Williamson, and Robert Burton, William Lee Davidson, John Phifer and Joseph Young. In the summer of 1836, William Lee Davidson donated a large tract of land for the building site, and preparations were made to begin the work. Subscriptions to the amount of $30,000 had been secured by Revs. Morrison and P. J. Sparrow. The institution was named Davidson College, in honor of General William Davidson, who was killed at Cowan's Ford, about seven miles from the present site, February 1, 1781. The college was opened in March, 1837, with 66 students and the following faculty: Rev. R. H. Morrison, president, Rev. P. J. Sparrow and M. D. Johnston. The Legislature granted the charter December 28, 1838. The manual labor feature was introduced, but proved unsuccessful and was dispensed with after four years' trial. In 1855, Davidson College was placed on a strong financial basis by the bequest of Maxwell Chambers, of Salisbury, which amounted to $258,000. The institution was prosperous until the beginning of the Civil War. In 1840, Dr. Morrison was succeeded as president by Rev. Samuel Williamson, who served in that capacity until 1854, and was succeeded by Dr. Drury Lane, who continued in office until 1860. It was for a long time customary for the college to hold public examinations semi-annually, at which the exercises consisted of "speaking, both selected and original composition and a debate."

Authority:—Records of the Schools, Official Information and Newspapers.

CHAPTER XXIV.

GROWTH AND DEVELOPMENT FROM 1825 TO 1860.

Population, Wealth and Taxes—Trades and Improvements—Laws and Courts—Newspapers—Mecklenburg's Part in the Mexican War—Smallpox—Fairs and Public Exhibitions—The Census of 1840.

In the first part of the nineteenth century, the country was scantily settled, roads were bad, modes of travel were tedious, and consequently the census taking could not be thorough. Emigration movements often assumed vast proportions and the variability of the slave population would sometimes make the total number of inhabitants at one census much smaller than at a preceding one. Some years nearly all the property was listed and at others only a portion of it. In 1842, Union county was made from portions of Mecklenburg and Anson.

In 1820, the population of Mecklenburg was 16,895; in 1830, it was 20,073; in 1840, 18,273; 1850, 13,814, and in 1860, 17,374. The population in 1825 was about the same as it was in 1860. From 1835 until 1850 there was a great emigration to the West. In 1825, the population of Charlotte was 700, and in 1860, it was 1,336. The census of 1830 disclosed the facts that there were in the county sixty-one unnaturalized foreigners, one white man 105 years old, one white woman 101 years old, and three negroes 100 years old.

Charlotte did a considerable merchandise business during this period. In 1832, the merchants' tax amounted to $220 and the peddlers' tax to $250. The tax on each peddler was $10.00, so there must have been twenty-five men regularly engaged in that work. They traveled into all portions of the country, and did a good business with the people who lived a long distance from town. Stores were in all parts of the county, but they were supplied only with the necessities of life; for anything else it was necessary to come to Charlotte. There were a number of grist and flour mills in the county, and a few saw mills which did work for the public. The merchants knew how to advertise, and stores as early as 1840 were selling their "entire stock of goods below cost." There were usually two or three milliners in the town, and they advertised the latest fashions and best work. The newspapers in 1833 announced that "the balloon sleeves are going out of fashion," and a hope was expressed that the same fate would befall the "ladies' big hats, some of which are two or three feet broad."

The Mansion House was the chief hostelry in town in 1840, and it and the Charlotte Hotel were popular in 1860. Taverns and saloons were noted places for men to assemble for public discussions of all kinds. Licenses were granted to whiskey dealers, and the traffic became so common that in 1833, an organization of the "Sons of Temperance" was effected. The campaign occasioned some excitement and served to retard the growth of the liquor business, but had little other effect. A saloon keeper advertised that he had just received a fine consignment of liquors and one "special preparation for the members of a certain society in this town," and the liquor men said that the doctors were pushing the temperance movement so they could get to sell all the liquor. In 1842, the Washington Temperance Society of Mecklenburg County was organized with 145 members. In 1853, Burton Craige was elected to Congress over James W. Osborne, and the charge was made during the campaign that Osborne was a "Son of Temperance," but it was not proved. The local election in the same year was also fought on the liquor question, and the "dry" candidate was overwhelmingly defeated.

The county tax in 1826, was thirty cents on the poll and ten cents on each $100 worth of property, but in 1836, it was reduced to twenty-five cents and eight cents respectively. In addition, there was a "poor" tax ranging from fifteen to

GIN HOUSE AND SCREW.

MODERN STEAM COTTON GINNERY.

twenty-five cents on the poll, and from five to ten cents on each $100 valuation. In May, 1828, commissioners were appointed to build a poor house, and the work was completed in January, 1833, and a man and his wife employed to take charge of it. In 1829, the old court house, which was erected in 1810, was thoroughly overhauled and repaired, and in 1845, a new building was erected on West Trade street. June 1, 1849, J. B. Kerr, the town treasurer, advertised for sealed bids for repairing the "horse racks and the streets in Charlotte." The first fire engine was purchased in 1830, $100 being paid for it. A regular fire company was kept up, but was very ineffective. In 1858, gas lamps were purchased for the streets and public buildings, at a cost of $1,015.40. In 1803, William Davidson and William Allison had charge of the Charlotte division of the Mutual Fire Insurance Company. In 1855, the Charlotte Mutual Fire Insurance Company was organized with R. C. Cowan president, John Irwin vice president, J. F. Irwin secretary and treasurer, William Johnston attorney, and W. L. Winston agent.

Whipping posts and stocks remained in use until after the war. The laws were rigidly enforced, and whipping and branding were the usual modes of punishment for minor offenses. Courts were always kept busy while in session, and a number of lawyers lived in the county. Among them were J. C. Spears, F. L. Smith, James H. Wilson, S. J. Lowrie, James W. Osborne, V. C. Barringer, A. F. Brevard, F. H. McDowell, W. J. Keahey and William Johnston. In 1835, Rev. Isaac Grier was elected delegate from Mecklenburg to the constitutional convention over William Lee Davidson, the issue being Davidson's announced intention to propose an amendment allowing Catholics to hold office. In 1834, a town ordinance was in effect making it a misdemeanor, punishable by a $5.00 fine, to leave wood boxes on the street, to dig sand or dirt from the street or to keep more than one dog. The first election of town officers by the people was held January 17, 1852, when A. Graham was elected intendant, and six prominent citizens were elected councilmen. Previous to this time, the mayor had been elected by the aldermen.

The dispensation of justice was vested in the county magistrates; a county court presided over by three magistrates, and which met quarterly; and a Superior Court of law and equity, which met twice a year.

In the year 1858, there was snow on the 26th day of April. Snow fell in Atlanta thirteen days before, and on the 15th there was a frost in Mecklenburg. The weather was extremely cold for some time, fires being necessary for comfort until the end of May. April 15, 1849, there had been a similar snow and cold spell, the snow being several inches deep and all the fruit being killed, and in the Spring of 1840, all the fruit was killed by a cold spell. In the Fall of 1858, three comets were reported as being visible, and were objects of much interest to Charlotte people.

Mecklenburg's first newspaper was Holton's *North Carolina Whig,* which was established in 1824. The name was changed to the *Journal* in March, 1832, and back to *Whig* January 26, 1852. Holton remained in charge of it, and from 1852 until 1855, A. C. Williamson was connected with it. June 28, 1834, it appeared in mourning with black ruled columns on account of the death of Lafayette. D. Asbury was one of the editors in 1841.

January 13, 1848, James Fulton succeeded J. W. Hampton as editor of the *Jeffersonian,* and in the next year left to take charge of the Wilmington *Journal.* Samuel C. Crawford edited the *Jeffersonian* in 1844. In 1848, J. L. Badger was connected with the *Journal,* and a year later was publishing the *Hornets' Nest.* The *Hornets' Nest* and the *Journal* were the only papers published in Charlotte in 1850. July 10, 1852, the *Western Democrat* appeared, edited by R. P. Waring, and in 1855, Dr. H. M. Pritchard was editor. In 1854, the *Whig, Democrat* and Wilmington *Journal* engaged in a discussion relative to the Independence Monument Association, which was organized in Charlotte several years previous, and the Charlotte papers said it had been abandoned because some people persisted that the name of a certain Tory should be put on it. May 17, 1859, the *Daily Bulletin* began publication under the management of E. H. Britton & Co.

May 17, 1848, Raymond & Waring's great zoological exhibition appeared in Charlotte, with lions and tigers and a brass band. About the same time, Dr. Shannon advertised that he was in Charlotte for a short time to practice and teach "pathetism," and that the fee for a full course was $10.00. He announced that he would cure headache, toothache and slight cases of rheumatism free; for curing any chronic disease he was to be paid one year after the cure was effected. In 1847, W. Barth passed through the county practicing "animal magnetism." In March, 1833, "Mr. Prosser, the American Fire King," appeared at the Masonic Hall and exhibited "his power of withstanding high degrees of heat, eating melted lead, blazing sealing wax and live coals." April 28, 1852, Mr. John Vane was in the county teaching people how to dectect counterfeit money. Daguerreotype artists often spent several weeks in town and were widely patronized.

Lectures, circuses, shows and exhibitions of all kinds were numerous. The Odd Fellows and Masons generally celebrated on May 20th or July 4th, and the young people held festivities on May day. The Charlotte Jockey Club was the source of much entertainment, and their races, May 1, 1838, were attended by large crowds. At a 4th of July celebration at Providence in that year, a cannon exploded, killing William L. Patton and wounding Jonah Boyes and Hugh Peoples. In October, 1855, the Mecklenburg County Agricultural Society held a fair in Charlotte, and the society was reorganized, and fairs were thereafter held every year until the beginning of the war. May 20, 1848, was the occasion of a large celebration with processions; speeches by Rev. Cyrus Johnston, William S. Harris, of Cabarrus, and Hon. J. W. Ellis; music by the Providence band, and a big dinner.

July 4, 1847, there was a celebration and free barbecue in town. Rev. H. B. Cunningham opened the exercises with prayer, the Declaration of Independence was read by S. Nye Hutchison, James A. Fox delivered the oration, and railroad speeches were made by J. W. Osborne and J. H. Wilson.

North Carolina furnished one regiment of infantry for the Mexican war in 1846, but Mecklenburg had no part in the formation of the regiment. Some of the enterprising patriots volunteered and obtained permission to raise a company of "light horse dragoons." G. W. Caldwell was captain, and E. C. Davidson, J. K. Harrison and A. A. Norman were lieutenants, and D. C. Robinson was a sergeant. They left Charlotte in April, 1847, went to Charleston, and from there to Vera Cruz, where they joined the American forces and engaged in several battles. The Governor of the State at that time was William A. Graham, of Orange county, a son of Gen. Joseph Graham, and it is also worthy of notice that a native of the county, James Knox Polk, was President of the United States.

In November, 1848, a medical society was organized in Charlotte for the purpose of uplifting the profession. In 1850, the smallpox spread throughout the county. In November of that year the doctors published a signed statement declaring that the disease was not smallpox, but in December, Dr. McIlwaine declared that it was smallpox, and demanded that precautions be taken against it. January 3, 1851, a board of health was formed by the authorities and a report was submitted showing that at that time there were 109 cases of the disease in Charlotte, 16 others in the county and that 9 negroes and one white man had died with it. The epidemic continued through 1851, and increased rapidly until the warm weather began. Among the physicians in Charlotte and Mecklenburg from 1830 to 1860, were D. F. Caldwell, C. J. Fox, Pritchard, Taylor, Hutchison, Robert Gibbon, D. R. Williamson, William Parham, J. C. Rudisill, M. O'Reilly, P. C. Caldwell, McIlwaine, J. M. David-

Sept- 16. 1854,

I have today sold to Mr R. M.
Miller the following negroes
One likely mulatto woman
named Julia   £ 925⁰⁰
Her daughter Jane   650⁰⁰
Her son Colston   460⁰⁰
                          ―――――――
       Total   £ 2035⁰⁰

Payable 1/4 cash, 1/4 in
6 mo. 1/4 in 1 year,
deferred payments at
6% interest.
                James Hargrove [LS]
Witness

BILL OF SALE.

Notice!
Negroes for Sale.

On the 18th day of December next, at the Plantation of the late *Obedience Dinkins*, dec'd. I will offer for sale

12 likely NEGROES,

viz: 5 *Men*, 3 *Women*, 2 *Boys*, and 2 *Girls*, a quantity of

Cotton, Corn and Fodder,
1 Horse, 2 Cows and calves,
1 Cotton Gin & Gearing,
Farming Tools,
Household & Kitchen Furniture,

with other articles not mentioned. The sale will continue from day to day, until all are sold. A credit of twelve months will be given. Bond and approved security required.

Sam'l. Cox, *Executor*.

White Hall, N. C., Nov. 19, 1838.

N. B. All persons having claims against the late *Obedience Dinkins*, dec'd., will present them properly attested within the time the law directs, or this notice will be plead in *bar* of their recovery.

SAM'L. COX, *Executor*.

NOTICE OF SALE.

son, E. H. Andrews, a dentist, and J. M. Happoldt, an eye specialist and surgeon, at Providence.

The census of 1840 gives full particulars of Charlotte and Mecklenburg at that time. There were in Charlotte 849 persons, of whom 548 were white and 301 were negroes. Among the other things enumerated are twelve stores, one bank agent, three taverns, one tannery, one printing office, one weekly paper, two academies, one common school, two ministers, six lawyers, six doctors, four miners and fifty mechanics. The population in 1830 was 717, and in 1851 it was 1,186. At this latter date the town property was valued at $122,740, and in addition, the 41,976 acres of land in the militia district was valued at $162,540. The tax lists also included gold and silver plate worth $350, thirteen pleasure carriages, eighty-three gold watches, thirty-eight silver watches and twenty-four pianos.

In the whole county were 11,909 white people and 6,841 negroes; 1,692 persons engaged in agriculture, 234 in manufacturing and trades, 49 in commerce, 94 in mining and 58 in learned professions. One hundred and eighty-seven white persons more than twenty years of age could not read or write. One college had 81 students, 5 academies had 185 and 25 common schools had 475. Only twenty-four pensioners lived in the county. There were 9 tanneries, 15 distilleries, 15 gold mines, 1 carriage factory, 11 flour mills, 23 grist mills, 32 saw mills and 32 stores. In 1850, the county contained 712 town lots, valued at $124,345, and 289,522 acres of land valued at $1,059,968. The total tax was 70 cents on the poll and 30 cents on each $100 valuation of property.

Authority:—Newspapers, County Records, and Census Reports.

CHAPTER XXV.

RAILROADS AND INDUSTRIES FROM 1830 TO 1860.

Realization of Necessity for Better Means of Travel and Commerce.
—Work on the Catawba River—Railroad Agitation in 1833—The Old Stage Coach—First Passenger Train in 1852—County Road Commissioners—Varied Industries.

Many years before the war, the people of Mecklenburg were beginning to realize the importance of diversified industries. The agitation for the proposed railroads and the excitement attendant upon the construction of them, acted as awakening influences. Discovery of gold was an important factor, and much interest was manifested in the establishment of the mint. The great improvement of cotton mill machinery also had its influence. The primary reason, and perhaps the most important one, was that the country was divided into a comparatively small number of landed estates; there were no farms for sale, and hence the new population was forced to give attention to something besides agriculture. An industrial crisis was imminent, and the problem would have solved itself by natural agencies within a few more years, had not sectional differences brought on the war.

As early as 1797, there was legislation for the purpose of rendering the Catawba river navigable. In 1801, a stock company, at the head of which was Waightstill Avery, was formed under the provisions of this law. The capital stock of the company was $15,000, and the income was to be derived from tolls on the river trade. In 1809, the Legislature passed an act allowing a lottery to raise five thousand dollars to aid in the enterprise. In 1817, a resolution was passed relative to a proposed canal to connect Rocky river and the Catawba. The Catawba Navigation Company, in 1829, was given five more years in which to complete the work. As population increased and the necessity for a better mode of transportation became apparent, the Mecklenburg people gave more thought than ever to the river navigation, but about then the railroad talk began, and that at once commanded the attention.

October 7, 1833, a public meeting for the discussion of internal improvements was held in the court house and delegates were appointed to a railroad meeting in Salisbury. At a convention held in Salisbury, October 10, 1836, Mecklenburg and eighteen other counties were represented by a total number of 131 delegates. Resolutions were adopted asking the Legislature to aid in the building of railroads, which was of so great importance to the western counties. About the same time, Mecklenburg sent three representatives to the Knoxville railroad convention, which met to consider the advantages to be secured by building the Charleston and Cincinnati railroad. It was agreed that "It will form a bond of union among the States which will give safety to our property and security to our institutions." Similar conventions were held at short intervals in Charlotte, Salisbury, Knoxville and other interested cities for a number of years.

A regular organization for the promotion of improvements was kept up in Charlotte after 1845, and the committee of correspondence included the best men of the county. April 27, 1847, a railroad meeting was held to take definite action regarding the railroad to Columbia. It was stated that the road would not be built to Charlotte unless a sufficient amount of stock was subscribed by Charlotte people. The work of securing subscriptions was begun at once, and in May, 1849, the contract was made for the grading of the road, which was to be completed by January 1, 1851.

Previous to the advent of the railroad, the public means of travel was the stage coach. There was usually only one trip made each way every week, but on some of the more popular routes, two trips were made. The arrival and departure of the stages were, ordinarily, the chief events of interest. People living on the line from Fayetteville through

Charlotte to Lincolnton, received mail twice a week, it being carried in four-horse coaches. There were other routes from Wilkesboro to Charlotte, Greensboro through Salisbury to Charlotte and on to Yorkville, S. C., and from Charlotte to Camden and Columbia. Mail was not of much importance, as people rarely expected to receive any. In 1831, the Charlotte postmaster advertised eighty letters that had not been called for, some of them addressed to people living in the town. The high rate of postage, and the fact that it had to be paid by the ones who received the mail, probably had something to do with the condition.

The first goods by freight over the road to Charlotte was received by a merchant October 6, 1852, though the track had not then been completed into town. October 21, 1852, the arrival of the first passenger train was greeted with a tremendous celebration. Crowds came from Columbia, Chester, Winnsboro, and the surrounding country, and the newspapers stated that twenty thousand people were present. The Columbia band furnished the music, and John A. Young was chief marshal. Gen. Young made the address of welcome in behalf of Charlotte, and James W. Osborne for North Carolina, and President Palmer, of the railroad, responded to the addresses, and he was followed by Ex-President Goldsden and John W. Ellis. The barbecue was given on the grounds of the Female Academy, and at night there was a dance and a display of fireworks. C. Banknight was the first railroad agent in this city, and, November 3, 1852, he advertised daily passenger trains between Columbia and Charlotte.

In 1856, the road from Goldsboro to Charlotte was completed. Until that time, the Democratic party had opposed State aid to internal improvements, and many persons openly proclaimed that the whole movement was impractical and would eventually fail. Gradually everyone was brought to realize the importance of the innovation, and then there was no further objection to State aid, and the system was extended rapidly. A large number of roads were chartered between 1840 and 1860, but many of them were never carried any further. The two roads put Charlotte into connection with the North and South, and drew the attention of the county to inter-state commerce. It was quite evident that the cultivation of agricultural products was not sufficient for the maintenance of an increasing population, and there was much said and written about the value of manufacturing cotton and wool.

Daniel Alexander announced, July 16, 1833, that he had removed his wool carding machine to his lower mill, on Mallard creek, where he would card wool for six and one-quarter cents a pound. Three years previously, Z. H. Bissell was engaged in rope making at the St. Catherine mine. In 1839, W. H. Neel was conducting the Sugar creek mills, five miles southwest of Charlotte, and was also carding wool. Wilson Parks was running a wool carding machine on McAlpin's creek, eight miles below Charlotte, in 1842. The Rock Island Factory began operations in February, 1849, and in April, 1852, was working two sets of cards, 480 spindles and thirty looms. At this factory, black and gray cassimeres were made, some of which were being sold in Wilmington, in February, 1851, for $87\frac{1}{2}$ cents a yard. Tweeds, jeans and kerseys were also made, and wool was bought at 25 cents a pound. November 14, 1854, steam power was used for the first time in Leroy Springs' mill, which had a capacity of two hundred bushels of flour a day. This was the first steam engine used in Charlotte. Feathers were generally used for beds and pillows, and in 1838, a patent feather renovator was in operation in Charlotte. The Charlotte Gas Light Company was chartered and began supplying gas for lighting purposes in 1858. At that time, W. D. Pinckney & Co. were manufacturing hydraulic presses and other machinery; P. Savers was a local architect and civil engineer; J. D. Palmer was manufacturing candy, and Alexander & McDougal were operating the Charlotte machine shops.

In 1778, there was a regularly organized board of road

commissioners in Mecklenburg. The county was divided into thirty-eight sections, over each of which was a superintendent. Before 1810, the commissioners, at their meeting, had many petitions for roads and bridges to consider. The Salisbury and Camden road was the first one in the county, but even before the Revolution, efforts had been made to have others surveyed. The Legislature, in 1817, provided for a road to be surveyed and opened from Fayetteville, through Mecklenburg to Morganton. In the next year, Thomas G. Polk and others were authorized to lay off and open a road from Milton, in Caswell county, to Salisbury, Charlotte and the South Carolina line. In 1825, all white men between the ages of 18 and 45, and all negroes between the ages of 16 and 50, were required to work the public roads. The county court, in May, 1827, appropriated two hundred dollars for a complete survey of the county roads, bridges, water courses, hills, towns, villages, factories and other details. This work was done by Joab Alexander, Thomas G. Polk and William Lee Davidson. In 1830, there were twenty-five public roads in the county, and when the railroad agitation began, there was much talk of plank roads to connect the railroad stations with the country. In 1849, a plank road from Charlotte to Lincolnton was proposed. In 1851, the road to Taylorsville was begun, and several others were planned and some of them were built.

Authority:—State and County Records and Newspapers.

CHAPTER XXVI.

MINING AND THE MINT BEFORE 1860.

Discovery of Gold in 1790—First Attempt at Mining in 1825—Foreign Investors Take Active Interest—Most Noted Mines and Their Productions—Mint Established in Charlotte in 1837, and Its Record Since.

In 1790, a little son of Conrad Reed, who lived in what is now Cabarrus county, found a large nugget of gold at a place afterwards known as Reed's mine. Soon thereafter, some nuggets were found near Rozzel's Ferry, in Mecklenburg. For twenty years after the discovery of gold, the people did not know of its true value. It was used chiefly for lining the powder holes in rifles, as it would not rust, and though a considerable quantity was found, it was not put to any more practical use. All of it was known as "branch gold," being picked up, for the most part, in creeks.

The first attempt to follow a gold vein was made by Samuel McComb, on his land near Charlotte, in 1825. He operated the mine for several years, and then disposed of it to a mining company. Gold mining machinery was scarce and ineffective, and as a consequence, the development of the industry was slow. The McComb mine was later known as the old Charlotte mine, and still later as the St. Catherine mine, and is located one mile west of the city. It was well equipped for that period, and was considered prosperous for a number of years. Capp's mine was being worked in 1826, and is located five and one-half miles from Charlotte.

In 1830, Chevalier Rivafanoli, an Italian and an agent for a London mining company, arrived in Charlotte to engage in mining. He brought with him several foreigners, who were experienced miners, and he leased the property owned by Bissell & Baker. He possessed considerable capital, and his ventures met with success. About the same time, some northerners came to this section and also took an interest in the search for gold. Immigrants to Mecklenburg were numerous for several years, until the discovery of gold in California in 1847, when the tide of immigration turned the other way.

Some of the newspapers expressed a fear that the mining would have an injurious effect upon agriculture, and would encourage idleness as the natural result of easily secured wealth. On the contrary, it was a stimulus and encouragement to all industrial pursuits. There was an increase of trade and of employment for mechanics, new buildings were erected and all the vacant ones were filled, and as a consequence of the new inhabitants and the temporary speculations, the circulation of money was more general. Value of property increased all over the county, and those who did not wish to sell their lands and buildings, could easily rent or lease them on good terms.

Capp's mine, in 1830, represented an investment of $20,000. The weekly product of gold averaged eight hundred pennyweight, and the weekly expenses amounted to $125. Thirty-eight negroes were employed to do the hardest work. A fourteen horse-power steam engine was used to pump the water from a ninety foot shaft, and it also furnished power for two mills for grinding ore. On Mallard creek, six miles from the mine, were four grinding mills and eighteen pounders, all operated by water power.

The Dunn mine and Rudisill's mine were worked from an early period, and a large number were opened in various parts of the county, most of them being abandoned after a few years. Dunn's mine was first worked by Dr. Samuel Henderson, who was called "the gold pioneer." In 1831, the property was transferred to Fanoli. The cradle and sluice were the only means of recovering gold for many years. Crushing machinery was in use in 1830, and the first stamp in the county was put up at St. Catherine's mine in 1840. This was the work of J. Humphrey Bissell, whose services to the county and to the science of mining were valuable. Among the others who helped to build up the industry were Thomas Penman, Dr. Daniel Asbury, Commodore Stockton and Admiral Wilkes. In 1843, J. Gibson took out a patent for a location on Catawba river, remarking that he cared nothing for the water, but was after the gold in the sand at the bottom. The sand was scooped up with long-handled shovels by men on a float.

March 28, 1834, John Harrison gave to J. B. S. Harris a receipt for $188.12 "for the building of a gold machine." In 1833 and 1834, the Legislature incorporated the Washington, Franklin, Mt. Island, Mecklenburg, North Carolina, Hope, Campbell's Creek, American, and Claremont gold mining companies in Mecklenburg county. The list of incorporators includes nearly all of the leading citizens of the county at that time. There were ten mines in operation in the county in 1850.

W. Morrison was local agent for the Bank of Newbern in 1830, and in January, 1832, a meeting was held in Charlotte to discuss plans for securing a branch of the United States Bank, but the effort was unsuccessful. In 1834, a branch of the North Carolina Bank was secured. Previously there had been so little money in circulation that there was no need for a bank. The gold mining ventures caused an increase in the circulation, and the new citizens agitated the matter until the agency of the State Bank was established. Thomas J. Hogg, of Raleigh, was agent for the bank in 1855, J. J. Blackwood in 1842, W. A. Lucas in 1852, and Thomas W. Dewey in 1853. In 1852, H. B. Williams was local agent for the Bank of Camden. April 19, 1853, the Bank of Charlotte was organized, with an authorized capital of $300,000, divided into shares of $50 each. H. B. Williams was president, W. A. Lucas cashier, and the board of directors consisted of T. H. Brem, J. H. Wilson, D. Parks, S. P. Alexander, A. C. Steele, W. R. Myers, and H. B. Williams. Most of the money used was State bills, and they were generally discounted.

From the time gold was first mined in the county, there

was a demand for a branch of the United States mint in Charlotte, by counties in this section both in North and South Carolina. In 1830, the North Carolina General Assembly appointed a special committee, under the chairmanship of Gideon Glenn, to investigate the subject. Their report stated that the annual production of gold in the State amounted to $500,000, at a cost of $150,000, and recommended the establishment of a mint. Acting upon this recommendation, the United States Congress appropriated $50,000 for the purpose, March 3, 1835. The corner stone was laid with impressive ceremonies January 8, 1836, and the mint was opened December 4, 1837, and did a large amount of business from the start.

Col. John H. Wheeler was the first superintendent, and he was succeeded in 1841 by B. S. Gaither. Green W. Caldwell was appointed to the position in 1844, and resigned two years later to volunteer for the Mexican war. He was succeeded by J. W. Alexander, who served until 1849. James W. Osborne was appointed in 1849, and held the position until G. W. Caldwell was reappointed in 1853. Dr. John H. Gibbon was assayer during the whole period preceding the war. The mint was burned in July, 1844, and most of the machinery was thereby ruined. D. M. Barringer, representative in Congress, secured the passage of a bill appropriating $25,000 for rebuilding, in February, 1845. Superintendent Caldwell received instructions regarding the proposed work on the 18th of April, and within three days had contracted with H. C. Owen to do the work for $20,000, thus saving $5,000 for the government. The mint, during the first year of its existence, coined gold to the amount of $84,165, the expenses being $17,466, and bullion being received to the amount of $131,698. This gradually increased until 1849, when the bullion value was $390,731, and the coinage was $361,229.

Authority:—Records on File in the United States Mint, Newspapers and County Records.

CHAPTER XXVII.

SLAVERY, POLITICS AND SECESSION. (1825 to 1861.)

Dividing Issues Discussed—Customs Regarding Slaves—Political Animosity—Mecklenburg Strongly Southern in Feeling—County Declares for Secession Twenty Days Before South Carolina.—North Carolina Secedes.

The Missouri compromise, which divided the nation into a slavery and a non-slavery section, was effected in 1820. The administration of James Madison, from 1817 to 1825, has gone into history as the era of good feeling, but it was only a calm before the storm. By the time it ended, the term "abolitionist" was being applied to certain inhabitants of "free" States, who were clamoring for the suppression of the slavery system. The North was not directly concerned in the industry which was the chief source of wealth to the South, and to the continuance of which the negro was considered essential. Hence, it was quite natural that the two sections should have different opinions on the subject.

According to the laws of 1826, the time for selling and hiring slaves was the first day of the Superior Court, which met twice a year. The Legislature of the same year made it illegal for free negroes to come into the State. At that time, there were 1,500 negroes in the county, not counting the few free ones. Several persons owned as many as twenty-five salves, and 80 persons owned more than six each. The highest price received for one at sale in that year was $568, and the value ranged from that down to $100 for a small boy. In 1850, there were 678 slave owners in the county, and they owned 2,713 slaves, and 155 men owned as many as six each.

Hiring slaves and the custom of employing overseers gave rise to much trouble. Few overseers were employed in this county, but the practice of hiring out the negroes was common. Such a contract usually stipulated that the lessee should "control the negroes as if owner" for one year, and that he should provide them with articles of clothing, which were mentioned. He was also required to protect their health and strength, and to otherwise care for them.

August 8, 1859, three negroes who belonged to J. H. and W. E. White, discovered that the railroad bridge across the Catawba had been damaged by a storm, and succeeded in stopping the train and thereby saving many lives. They were liberally rewarded by the passengers for this act.

A special tax of 25 cents was levied on each negro to pay the expenses of the patrollers. The value of slaves increased rapidly, and in 1841, Leroy Springs sold a negro shoemaker to Samuel A. Harris for $1,500. By that time, the free negroes were causing trouble by inciting the slaves to run away. September 20, 1852, a public meeting in Charlotte was largely attended to determine what steps should be taken in regard to these matters.

October 25, 1830, an editorial in the Charlotte *Journal* called attention to the state of affairs wherein talk about dissolution of the Union had become so common as not to excite horror, as it once did. The readers were counseled that such things should not be. May 8, 1832, another editorial mentioned the evil effect of "treating" at elections, and said it should be prohibited. Until the secession talk began, the Whigs and Democrats were about evenly matched, but after that, the Democrats led easily, because all Whig secessionists voted with them. The presidential campaign of 1848 was fought on the slavery issue, with particular reference to its exclusion from Texas, and Zachary Taylor, the Whig candidate, was elected, and received a majority in Mecklenburg county, but the county was otherwise Democratic. In the next year, G. W. Caldwell was elected to Congress as an Independent candidate. In 1852, Franklin Pierce, Democrat, was elected President, and Reid, for Governor, received in the county 1,421 votes, to his opponents's 731. Pierce was succeeded by Buchanan, also a Democrat. August 5,

1855, a public meeting was held in Charlotte to discuss the issues of the day, and the idea of secession was popular, though some questioned its expediency and advised against talking of it. There were 1,280 voters in Mecklenburg in 1856, the creation of Union county having reduced the number from more than two thousand.

In 1835, the State Legislature passed resolutions, in view of the proceedings of abolitionists in the Eastern and Middle States, defining the position of North Carolina on the negro question. It was claimed that the States had the sole right to regulate slavery, and that the constitution delegated no such authority to the Federal government. Congress was petitioned to restrict the circulation of incendiary abolitionist literature in the South, and to prevent the abolitionists from stirring up strife.

Gradually the sectional slavery issue became a political issue, and this made the feeling more bitter and more open. The State Democratic convention in 1858 convened in Charlotte, and 477 delegates were present, representing 77 counties. Hon. J. W. Ellis, of Rowan, was nominated for Governor, and was elected in August by 12,000 majority, receiving 553 majority in Mecklenburg. At the same time, W. F. Davidson was elected to the State Senate, and Dr. H. M. Pritchard and M. W. Wallace to the House of Representatives. William J. Yates was appointed a member of the Governor's Council. Governor Ellis was re-elected in 1860; John Walker was elected Senator, and S. W. Davis and J. W. Potts Representatives.

In the presidential campaign of 1860, there were four candidates—Breckinridge, Bell, Lincoln and Douglass. The vote in Mecklenburg was: Breckinridge, 1,101; Bell, 826; and Douglass, 135. The Charlotte *Whig* said that the "Union" party in this section had "gone up higher than a kite." The feeling was strong, as it was generally believed that Lincoln's platform and speeches made it clear that the rights of the South would be ignored. J. E. Herrick, a northerner, was in Charlotte in November, 1860, and it being reported that he had "a touch of abolitionism," he was politely advised to depart from the county.

December 1, 1860, there was held in the court house a public meeting which has but one equal in the history of the county—May 20, 1775. A tremendous crowd was in attendance, the best men coming from every section. James B. Robinson, of Providence, was chairman, and John E. Brown and M. L. Wallace were secretaries. Speeches were made by A. C. Williamson, S. J. Lowrie, W. Kerr, Gen. Young, J. H. Wilson and others. Major Hill and Lieutenant Lee were called upon for speeches and declined, saying they were ready to act, but not to talk. A committee of eleven reported resolutions declaring that the election of Lincoln predicated the subversion of the constitution, and that there should be a State convention to consider what action was necessary. S. W. Davis presented the petition to the General Assembly December 5th. South Carolina seceded December 20th.

January 30, 1861, the Legislature ordered an election to be held February 28th to elect delegates to the convention, and at the same time to determine whether or not there should be a convention. A public meeting, February 9th, nominated James W. Osborne and William Johnson as delegates. The election in the State went against the proposed convention by a small majority, but Mecklenburg's position was clearly presented by the vote, which showed only seven votes in Charlotte and 252 in the whole county against the convention.

Public meetings were frequent, and a State mass meeting in Goldsboro, February 22d and 23d, was largely attended by Mecklenburg people. The assembly adjourned to meet in Charlotte May 20th, and elaborate preparations were made for the event, but it was forestalled by Lincoln's requisition on Gov. Ellis for troops. The Governor at once called the Legislature in special session, and it ordered a convention to convene May 20th. Osborne and Johnson represented Mecklenburg, and on the first day of the proceedings, the ordinance of secession was passed by a unanimous vote.

Authority:—State and County Records and Newspapers.

CHAPTER XXVIII.

CIVIL WAR. (1861 to 1865.)

Mecklenburg Soldiers Among the First to Volunteer—Were Prominent in the Formation of the First or "Bethel" Regiment—Distinguished Officers From Mecklenburg—Conditions in the County During the War—Last Meeting of Confederate Cabinet Held in Charlotte.

Early in 1861, the drilling of soldiers began in Mecklenburg county. There were frequent musters and parades and exhibitions by the military companies. Fort Sumter, in South Carolina, was surrendered by the Federal forces to the State April 12th, and at that time seven States had seceded. Eight days later, the United States mint in Charlotte was seized and occupied by the local militia, under the command of Col. J. Y. Bryce. Just one month later, on the eighty-sixth anniversary of the Mecklenburg Declaration of Independence, the State of North Carolina dissolved the bonds which bound her to the Federal Union.

Mecklenburg county was ready for the crisis, and took a remarkably prominent stand at the very first of the trouble. The Legislature, which met in Raleigh May 1st, provided for the Governor to raise ten regiments of troops for the State. At that time, North Carolina had not decided what stand to take, but as the states north and south of her had seceded, she realized the necessity of being prepared for any emergency, and when President Lincoln's requisition for troops came, the State was ready to cast her lot with the sister commonwealths in the common cause. William Johnson, of Mecklenburg, was appointed commissary-general for the State, and though he held the position but a short time, he did valuable service by his prompt and energetic work.

The entire history of the Civil War does not include a

nobler example of valor and patriotism and efficiency than the First North Carolina Volunteers, commonly known as the "Bethel Regiment," and Mecklenburg county has just cause to feel proud of its remarkable record. The Charlotte Grays (Company C), and the Hornets' Nest Rifles (Company B), were among the first to be mustered into the service of the State. The two companies left Charlotte April 16th, and the occasion of their departure was made memorable by a hearty celebration, and flags were presented to the young captains, E. A. Pass and L. S. Williams, by the young ladies of the county. The faculty and cadets of the Charlotte Military School were all taken to Raleigh to drill the troops, and the regiment was organized in Raleigh by successive orders dating from April 19th to May 16th. D. H. Hill was colonel, Charles C. Lee lieutenant-colonel, James H. Lane major, Rev. E. A. Yates chaplain, all these men going from Charlotte. Three of the companies were in Richmond May 18th, and the other seven arrived three days later, and within the succeeding twenty days they fought and won a battle, and a member of the Edgecombe company shed the first blood for the Confederacy.

The personnel and equipment and general efficiency of the regiment occasioned the highest praise, and the Virginia papers united in the opinion that it was the equal, if not the superior, of any in the nation. It included the best military ability of the State, and its accoutrements were all that any body of troops could desire. The battle of Bethel was fought June 6th. The total number of Confederate troops engaged was 1,408, and 800 of them were members of the First North Carolina Regiment, the others being Virginians. A victory was won over the 4,400 Federal troops, and in the fighting, the two Charlotte companies bore conspicuous parts and were complimented for bravery and discipline. September 3d, Col. Hill was made a brigadier-general, and Lieutenant-Colonel Lee was elected colonel. September 21, Lieutenant-Colonel Lane became colonel of the Twenty-eighth regiment, then being organized at High Point.

October 12th, the "Bethel" regiment was mustered out of service, and reorganized later at High Point as the Eleventh regiment, in which the Mecklenburg men were honored by promotion.

Mecklenburg county furnished one company for the first regiment of artillery, and one for the first regiment of cavalry, known respectively as the Ninth and Tenth North Carolina regiments. Both companies were organized in May, the first by Captain Thomas H. Brem, and the other by Captain J. M. Miller. The Ninth regiment was engaged in one hundred and fifty battles during the war, and the Tenth also took an active part. In these first days of the war, the ladies of the county did their duty as nobly as did the men, and they took as much interest in the conflict. They made clothes and sent provisions of all kinds for the soldiers. During the month of June, the "Jewess ladies" of the town raised $150 to assist the volunteers, and every one did all that could be done.

In the election of 1860, 2,062 votes were cast in Mecklenburg; and between 1860 and 1865, the county furnished for the Confederacy twenty-one companies, which, with recruits, included 2,713 soldiers. Besides these, there were many who joined other commands as privates or officers. The students of the Military Academy were made drill masters, and nearly all of them became officers. Col. Hill was a lieutenant-general at the close of the war, and J. H. Lane was a brigadier-general. Col. C. C. Lee, of the Thirty-seventh North Carolina regiment, was killed at Frazier's Farm, in Virginia, June 30, 1862.

Col. R. M. McKinney, of the Fifteenth, was killed near Yorktown, April 16, 1862. Major E. A. Ross was killed at Gettysburg, July 1, 1863. Hamilton C. Jones was lieutenant colonel of the 57th, which was organized at Salisbury July 6. 1862, and he became colonel of the regiment in 1865; was at the battle of Gettysburg and other important engagements, and served throughout the war. Colonel William A. Owens, who left Charlotte as lieutenant of the Hornets' Nest Rifles, was killed at Snicker's Ford, Va., in August, 1865. Lieut. Gen. Leonidas Polk was a grandson of Thomas Polk of revolutionary fame.

At a public mass meeting held in the Mecklenburg court house, August 29, 1863, the administrations of Governor Vance and President Davis were endorsed by a unanimous vote. The public spirit was active, and when Gen. John H. Morgan passed through the city, December 24, 1863, the citizens of Charlotte raised $4,000 to aid him in equipping a new cavalry force. January 13, 1864, Captain Raphael Semmes delivered an address in the court house, and was enthusiastically received.

Gen. Lee surrendered at Appomattox Court House, Va., April 9, 1865. Johnston surrendered to Sherman near Durham, April 26. Sherman had occupied Raleigh April 13, and Fort Fisher surrendered April 15. President Davis and the Confederate cabinet, accompanied by a thousand cavalry, arrived in Charlotte late in the evening of April 15. Mr. Davis proceeded to the home of Mr. Bates, at the corner of Fourth and Tryon streets, and there made a short talk to the crowd which had assembled. Before entering the house, a telegram was handed to him, and as he read it, he exclaimed, "Can this be true? This is dreadful. It is horrible. Can it really be true?" He then handed the message to Col. Wm. Johnston, who read it and announced to the crowd the first news which had been received in Charlotte of the assassination of President Lincoln.

The Confederate officials were hospitably entertained during their stay in the city. The official headquarters were in the building now occupied by the Charlotte *Observer,* and President Davis' private room is now the office of the chief editor. The last meeting of the cabinet was held at the residence of Mr. William Phifer, on the morning of April 20, and immediately thereafter the cabinet and the cavalry departed from Charlotte. Gov. Vance held a consultation with the President in Charlotte, April 16, but nothing of importance was accomplished. A cast-iron slab marks the spot where the President was standing when the news of Lincoln's assassination reached him. At the close of the war, the Charlotte hospital, under the direction of Dr. Ashby and Rev. F. M. Kennedy, contained twelve hundred sick and wounded soldiers.

July 7, 1863, the General Assembly provided for mobilizing a "Guard for Home Defense," which came to be known as the Home Guard. All able-bodied men between the ages of 18 and 50, who were exempt from Confederate service, were enrolled, except a few stated exceptions. The whole number in North Carolina was 12,500, and each county was commanded by a major if it contained less than five companies, and by a lieutenant-colonel if it contained more than that number. Lieutenant-Colonel T. H. Brem commanded the Guard in Mecklenburg, and did much good in protecting the country from marauders, in enforcing the conscript law and in capturing deserters.

Authority:—Clark's Regimental Histories, County Records and Newspapers.

CHAPTER XXIX.

RECONSTRUCTION. (1865 to 1875.)

Mecklenburg Escaped the Worst Evils of Those Days—Federal Officers and Troops in Charlotte—Editor Waring Indicted for Espousing the Southern Cause—Conduct of the Negroes Comparatively Peaceable—Elections in the County.

In June, 1865, Col. Willard Warner, with the 180th Ohio regiment, took charge of the city of Charlotte, and Capts. N. Haight and Andrew Smith were appointed provost marshals. July 1, Gov. Holden appointed Dr. H. M. Pritchard mayor. These summary changes of government were without even a semblance of justification, and the good spirit in which they were received was sufficient evidence of their uselessness. A few days later, Brigadier-General Thomas succeeded Major-General Ruger in command of the Twenty-third corps of the First division with headquarters in Charlotte, and he reviewed the troops, which numbered four thousand.

General Thomas was popular and preserved good order. The sale of liquor was prohibited, and a request was made that all crimes should be promptly reported to the military authorities. All men doing business of any kind were required to take the iron-clad oath. This resulted in the suspension of all industries, as no one who had aided the Confederacy could take the oath. Another obnoxious order was that all arms and ammunition should be surrendered to the Federal authorities. There was, of course, much miscellaneous stealing and petty misdemeanors, but there was no clash between the citizens and soldiers nor between the citizens and the idle negroes. There was said to be in the county a regular band of thieves, who stole horses, cows, and anything else which they could secure. The band was composed chiefly of negroes, but was led by white men.

Some of the stealing was attributed to the soldiers, but not proved.

Col. Warner, who was afterwards a United States Senator from Alabama, was succeeded as commander of the post by Col. J. C. McQuiston with the 123d Indiana regiment, and in August he was succeeded by Col. C. S. Parrish who issued an order that no citizen's clothing should be given or sold to the Federal troops. In January, 1866, S. A. Harris was elected mayor of Charlotte, but he was under the supervision of the military commander. July 4, 1865, was appropriately celebrated. Col. Packard, of the 128th Indiana regiment, delivered a very proper address, Gen. Thomas read the Declaration of Independence, and the military band played Yankee Doodle and Dixie.

In the election in November, 1865, the Democrats, or Conservatives, carried Mecklenburg county by a vote of 534 to 353, and Charlotte by a vote of 277 to 120. Prof. A. McIver and T. N. Alexander were elected delegates to the constitutional convention. Most of the troops had been removed from the city at that time, and Capt. Frank M. Henton, with one company, was in command in December. Christmas day, Editor R. P. Waring, of the Charlotte *Daily Times,* was arrested and taken to Raleigh on a charge of treason, which consisted in vigorous editorial denunciation of the "carpet baggers." He was tried by court-martial and was fined $300. The vote on the constitution, which was submitted to the people in August, 1866, was 277 to 114 in the county, and 20 to 51 in the city, in favor of ratification. In the October following, Worth, the Democratic candidate for Governor, carried the county by a vote of 334 to 11.

Captain H. M. Lazelle commanded the troops in Charlotte from April to December 18, 1867, at which time the troops left the city. On the occasion of their departure, Mayor Harris presented the captain with a resolution adopted by the board of aldermen, thanking the soldiers for good behavior and expressing regret at their leaving.

The captain acknowledged the courteous act with a pleasant note in which he declared his gratitude for the hospitality of the people of Mecklenburg. Sergeant Bates, of the United States army, on his trip from Washington to Vicksburg as a test that he could carry the national flag through the South without molestation, passed through Charlotte March 26, 1868, and was met by officials, escorted into the city in a procession, and cordially entertained during his short visit.

Negroes in the county were generally idle, and it was not unusual for five hundred to congregate in the town. Out of such a condition arose many crimes of small degree, and a few of the vilest nature, but there was no open disturbance or disorder. Hangings were unusually frequent, but there were not more than ten in the ten years following the close of the war. Some criminals were summarily punished, but both the hangings and lynchings were regardless of race, color or previous condition of servitude. The Union League was organized and parades were common, but the white people ignored such things. Negroes manifested interest in politics for a while, but quit it when they found they would not get the "forty acres and a mule." Two of the three delegates to the Republican State convention in 1867 were negroes. At the subsequent election, an old colored man came into town to vote, but when he was unable to get anything for it, he refused to vote at all, and said he was going back home to work. The Ku-Klux played no part in Mecklenburg affairs, and though there were a few members in this section, there was not an organization in the county.

For the election of delegates to the constitutional convention, November, 1867, the registration in the county was 1,668 whites and 1,645 blacks; in the city, 566 whites and 726 blacks. Of the 1,645 blacks in the county, only 764 were listed for taxation. The vote was in favor of a convention by a majority of 1,538, and the Republican candidates, E. Fullings and S. N. Stillwell, were elected by a vote of 790 to 520, which was the only time during the period that the county went Republican. April 16, 1868, on the eve of election, Major H. M. Lazelle and a company of troops arrived in Charlotte very unexpectedly. The election resulted in a majority of 220 against the "Canby" constitution, and in favor of the Democratic candidates, J. W. Osborne for the Senate and R. D. Whitley and W. W. Grier for the House of Representatives. The Legislature, in which the Mecklenburg representatives and their Democratic friends were in a hopeless minority, assembled July 1, 1868, and during the session made appropriations amounting to $26,970,000.

In July, 1868, Governor Holden, without explanation, appointed a mayor and board of aldermen for Charlotte. E. H. Bissell was mayor during August, and he was succeeded by Pritchard and he by Bissell again December 1. January 4, 1869, Major C. Dowd was elected mayor by 228 majority out of 738 votes. He held the office for two years, after which John A. Young was mayor two years, W. F. Davidson succeeding him in 1873, and being himself succeeded in May, 1875, by William Johnston. There were, during those years, eight policemen, of whom two or three were usually negroes, and several of the twelve aldermen were negroes. In the November election of 1868, the county went Democratic by 200 majority, and Charlotte was Republican by 200 majority. The election was peaceable and the negroes behaved well. A company of troops was in the city for a few days. Col. H. C. Jones was elected State Senator in September, to succeed Hon. James W. Osborne, who died August 11.

Col. Jones was re-elected to the Senate in 1870, and J. S. Reid and R. P. Waring were elected representatives. This Legislature, November 29, elected Vance to the United States Senate, but he was not allowed to take the seat. William M. Shipp, of Mecklenburg, was at the same election chosen Attorney General of North Carolina. Mecklenburg voted against the proposed convention in August, 1871, by 63 majority. In 1872, the county and city were Democratic by 200 and 100 majority respectively, and in August, 1873, a small majority was returned against the constitutional amendments. In 1874, R. P. Waring was elected Senator and J. S. Reid and J. E. Jetton representatives.

This county escaped the worst evils of those times. There was some trouble with Judge Logan who was plainly incompetent, and the lawyers of the 9th judicial district met in Charlotte June 2, 1871, and united in signing a petition to the Legislature stating their views clearly. The action was approved by a public mass meeting in the court house on the first day of the following January, but no action was taken and the judge served out his term. In September, 1871, the authorities discovered a plot among some trifling negroes to burn the city, and seven negroes were arrested and one convicted. There were many small fires and one large one November 17, 1870, and another exactly one year later, most of them believed to have been of incendiary origin. The last of the Federal troops left Charlotte in the early Spring of 1872. During this whole period, there was only one disturbance of any consequence, and that occurred in the afternoon of Christmas, 1875. A drunken white man from the country engaged in a quarrel with a large crowd of negroes at the intersection of Trade and College streets. Policeman Joe Orr arrested the white man and then the negroes attacked them with stones; other whites interfered and a general fight resulted, extending up Trade street to the square, and lasting half an hour. About thirty shots were fired, and one negro was killed and ten were wounded, while many others, white and black, were injured by rocks and sticks.

The campaign of 1876 closed the era of reconstruction. The color line was sharply drawn, and the negro voters in Mecklenburg were outnumbered by 375 majority, though Charlotte township was 300 majority the other way. Z. B. Vance was nominated for Governor in Raleigh June 14, and was given a hearty reception when he returned to Charlotte the next day. He and Settle spoke in the city September 21, to a crowd of 4,000 people, and though it was Vance's home, his opponent was treated with all kindness and respect. In November, Vance and the new constitution carried the county by a vote of 3,428 to 2,588, and the city by 1,166 to 1,038. Dr. T. J. Moore was elected to the Senate and W. E. Ardrey and R. A. Shotwell to the House of Representatives.

Authority:—County Records and Newspapers.

CHAPTER XXX.

FIRST DECADE WITHOUT SLAVERY. (1865 to 1875.)

County Affairs in War Times—Emancipation Forced White Men to Work—Attention Diverted to New Things—This Section an Inviting Field for Investors—Reasons for the Progress Made. Death of a Woman Who Remembered May 20, 1775.

War did not cause the cessation of all industries in Mecklenburg county. Most of the able-bodied men were in the armies, and the people did less trading, but the men who remained at home found plenty to do in providing for the soldiers in the field. The families made everything possible on their farms, and not only supported themselves, but sent quantities of clothing to the armies. There was much suffering and poverty, but this immediate section fared better than many others, because it was in good condition when war began and it escaped the blight of invaders. More annoyance was caused by the difficulty of procuring household necessities, such as salt and sugar, than by the impossibility of obtaining luxuries, for the minds of all were upon war and bare existence, and every energy was exerted to sustain life and to encourage the brave troops who were fighting against overwhelming disadvantages.

Taxes in 1863 were 40 cents on the $100 valuation of property and $1.20 on the poll, and this increased considerably during the next two years; in 1864, it was $1.20 and $3.60 respectively. The total sum raised in the county by taxation in 1863, was $129,044; $91,000 was invested in liquor and $40,000 in cotton and woolen factories. The North Carolina powder mill was located at Tuckaseege Ford, twelve miles from Charlotte. This mill was blown up and five men were killed by the explosion May 23, 1863, and in August of the following year, three men were killed by another explosion. S. W. Davis was president and manager of the property. January 7, 1864, the Charlotte depots and warehouses, containing vast amounts of Confederate supplies, were completely destroyed by fire at a loss estimated at ten million dollars.

One of the noticeable features of the times was the lack of trouble with the slaves. They staid at their work without bothering about the war which was being waged with their freedom as an issue. Slaves who sold for a thousand dollars in 1861, were worth three thousand dollars in 1864, and the highest price recorded in that year was $6,100. There were but few sales after 1864, as it was apparent that the end of the war was a question of a few months. Depreciation of Confederate currency became so rapid that trade almost ceased in the last year of the war. There was no political strife, and Mecklenburg people were inclined to palliate errors and faults rather than to criticise. In the gubernatorial election of 1864, the vote of the county was 1,690 for Vance and 112 for Holden, and the city of Charlotte voted 700 to 1.

The effect of emancipation upon all phases of industrial life was immediate and revolutionary. The population of the county was 17,374 in 1860, about 15,000 in 1865, and 24,298 in 1870. Charlotte contained a population or 1,366 in 1860, and 2,212 in 1870. This refers to the population inside the corporate limits. The population of the city, with the suburbs, was about 2,000 in 1860, 1,500 in 1865, and 5,000 in 1870. Under the system of slavery, the population of the county and city did not increase from 1825 to 1860, and wealth and prosperity were in the same condition. The rapid increase in population and wealth after the war was accelerated by several things in addition to the revival of interest in manufactures caused by the abolition of slavery. Charlotte was a central point for a large section of good territory, the railroad advantages were good, and the county enjoyed a better condition of government than those around it. Hence, the people from the more turbulent sections moved into Mecklenburg. At the close of the war, the county contained about four thousand white men and nearly as many negro men; the whites were not accustomed to farm work and could not hire the negroes to work, and the result was that the attention was diverted to something else.

In June, 1866, there were sixty-six stores in the county. In the first six months of 1867, twelve stores and seventy-five other buildings were erected in Charlotte, and a thousand structures of various kinds were built in the city in the five years following the war—almost one a day. New life and progress were at work everywhere. Northern capitalists opened the gold mines, and the money put in circulation enlivened all branches of trade. In 1867, three banks were in operation—the First National, Dewey's Bank, and the Bank of Charlotte. To these was added the Merchants' and Farmers' National Bank in 1871. The Rock Island Woolen Mill, which had been established on the Catawba in 1847, was moved to Charlotte after the war, and was said to be the greatest establishment of the kind in the South. John A. Young was president and John Wilkes was treasurer, and the mill employed one hundred hands. January 15, 1870, it was sold at auction for a mortgage, and was purchased for $29,000 by J. H. Wilson.

Cotton commanded high prices. In February, 1868, it sold for 27 cents a pound, and the first bale of the season in September, 1869, brought 35 cents a pound. There were a number of cotton dealers in the city, and their trade of 1868 in Charlotte amounted to nearly two million dollars. The total tax in that year was 30 cents on the $100 and $1.50 on the poll, and the total receipts of the county amounted to $26,749, which more than paid the expenses. The county debt was $82,000. The tax in 1871, was $1.16 and $2.00 for county and State purposes, and 75 cents and $3.00 for the city. At this time, there were only six postoffices in the county, and the number was not increased until 1870.

This section was an inviting field for those whose homes had been destroyed and who were seeking a favorable location. In the latter part of 1867, three generals (D. H. Hill,

Rufus Barringer and R. D. Johnston), were citizens of Charlotte, and besides them were Ex-Governor Vance, six colonels, two lieutenant colonels, six majors, twenty-four captains and twenty-six lieutenants, all of whom were active in rebuilding the properties of the country. Gen. R. E. Lee was in Charlotte March 31, 1870, and Jefferson Davis was here May 25, 1871. Both were cordially welcomed.

April 16, 1870, a public meeting was held in the court house to consider the question of issuing bonds to aid the railroads. At the election held May 19, the county voted to subscribe $200,000 to the Atlanta road and $100,000 to rebuild the Statesville road, which had not been in operation since the close of the war. The Charlotte Board of Trade, which has been an important factor in the progress of the county and city, was organized July 25, 1870, with J. Y. Bryce as president. In June of the same year, Charlotte voted $3,000 to aid the Mecklenburg Agricultural Society, and annual fairs have been held since that time with more or less irregularity. Among the business establishments then in the city were Wilkes' Iron Foundry, Charlotte Hotel, Mansion House which became the Central Hotel in January, 1873; W. F. Cook's farming implements factory, five drug stores, marble works, three book stores, three carriage shops, two harness makers, several wholesale merchandising stores, one distillery and four retail liquor dealers, J. W. Wadsworth's livery, and about fifty miscellaneous stores and shops.

The market house at the corner of College and Trade streets was completed and occupied in the latter part of 1871. A new jail was built in 1874, at a cost of $20,398. Sample & Alexander were then running a shoe factory in Charlotte, and D. R. Leak and J. Heineman were operating tobacco factories. B. S. Guion and E. H. Woods established a spoke and handle factory in 1872; an ice factory was in operation in 1874, and in July of the same year, a new opera house, with a seating capacity of one thousand, was completed.

April 7, 1873, Mrs. Catherine Williams, aged 113, died

at the residence of John D. Hunter, in Mallard creek township. She was well and in full possession of her mental strength until two weeks before her death. In her youth, she was a near neighbor of John McKnitt Alexander, and she remembered well the events of May 20, 1775.

In 1873, the expenses of the county government were $54,368 and the receipts $60,012. The county debt was $373,530, and the city debt was $45,840. These debts were contracted mainly in the issuance of railroad bonds. The first passenger train from Charlotte to Spartanburg was run March 31, 1873, and the occasion was celebrated, as was also the running of the first train to Greenville April 28. December 15, 1874, passenger trains began running between Wilmington and Charlotte. Until that time, a regular stage line was kept up between Charlotte and Wadesboro. Stock law went into effect in the city January 1, 1876.

At the election August 5, 1874, there were 1,540 votes cast in Charlotte township and 4,180 in the whole county, and in the municipal election in May, 1875, there were 1,157 votes cast. A local census in February, 1876, showed that there were in Charlotte 1,730 buildings and eight thousand inhabitants. *During the last thirty-five years of slavery, the county and city made no appreciable advance in wealth and population. During the first decade after emancipation, both wealth and population doubled in the county and trebled in the city.*

Authority:—Same as Previous Chapter.

CHAPTER XXXI.

INDEPENDENCE CENTENNIAL CELEBRATION. (May 20, 1875.)

Preparations and Committees for the Event—Great Men Present.
—Marshals Were Confederate Generals—Immense Crowd in
Charlotte—The Proceedings and Interesting Incidents.

Anniversaries of the Mecklenburg Declaration of Independence were regularly celebrated in Charlotte and at other places in the county after the war, and preparations for the centennial anniversary began nearly a year before the event occurred. January 4, 1875, a joint meeting of the Charlotte board of aldermen and the county commissioners was held to take official action. The public meeting held on the same day resulted in the formation of an organization of which Mayor W. F. Davidson was chairman and J. P. Caldwell was secretary.

A general executive committee of ten members was appointed at a subsequent meeting, and Dr. Joseph Graham was made chairman. The committee on orators included Gov. Z. B. Vance, Hon. W. M. Shipp and Gen. D. H. Hill. The other chairmen were: Gen. J. A. Young, of the committee on subscriptions; J. H. Wilson, on finance; W. J. Yates, on the press; J. H. Orr, on fire and military companies; Col. Thomas H. Brem, on artillery and fire-works; and Col. H. C. Jones, on county affairs. In addition to these was one auxiliary committee in each township in the county. The committees met often and discussed the situation and perfected plans for the centennial day.

Wednesday, May 19, 1875, dawned bright and fair as was the day one hundred years before, but the contrast between the two occasions was wonderful, even though they were so close together in patriotism and sympathy. Then a few determined men assembled in a little log court house in a straggling village and severed the cord that bound them to their only hope other than themselves; today, in a city of eight thousand inhabitants, with the buildings clothed in flags and every heart full to overflowing with patriotic pride, amid the booming of cannon and the stirring strains of martial music, men, women and children gathered from all parts of the re-united nation to do honor to the men who were first to evince the courage of their convictions.

At noon a large crowd collected in the square to witness the raising of the "stars and bars" to the top of the pole which had been prepared for it. As the emblem rose higher and higher and began to flutter in the breeze, the Citizens' Band, of Newbern, played "The Old North State," and the crowd joined in the words of the song:

> " Carolina, Carolina, Heaven's blessing attend her ;
> " While we live, we will cherish, protect and defend her."

Flags waved on all sides and shouts of enthusiasm rent the air.

Seated on the stand which had been erected under the flag were Governor C. H. Brogden, Mayor William Johnston and Dr. Joseph Graham. When the music ceased and the noise subsided, Mayor Johnston delivered the address of welcome in behalf of the city of Charlotte. He reviewed the thrilling scenes of the Revolution in which Mecklenburg was most concerned, regretted that no monument commemorated the Declaration, extended a cordial welcome to all, and introduced the Governor of North Carolina. Governor Brogden congratulated the people of the county on the success of the occasion, mentioned the deep patriotism of Mecklenburg, the progress of the State and the county, and, as Governor, welcomed the visitors. The Newbern band then played the "Mecklenburg Polka," which was composed for the occasion and which was highly complimented. At the conclusion of the speaking, the Raleigh Light Artillery, under the command of Captain A. B. Stronach, fired thirty-eight guns, one for each State in the Union.

Thursday, May 20, was ushered in by the firing at daybreak of one hundred guns by the Raleigh artillery, and the Richmond Howitzers, commanded by Captain Bidgood. By sunrise, the streets were crowded, and from that time until midday, trains brought vast crowds, and wagons and equipages of all kinds brought in the people from the country, and by 7 o'clock the whole city was packed with one moving mass of humanity. The total number present was variously estimated at from 25,000 to 40,000, but the conservative estimate was about 30,000. Six fire companies arrived on an early train, and were met by the Charlotte companies and welcomed by Captain J. C. Mills.

At 9 o'clock, Gen. W. R. Cox, the chief marshal, began to form the procession. His aides were Gen. Bryan Grimes, of Tarboro; Gen. Johnson Hagood, of South Carolina; Gen. Bradley T. Johnston, of Richmond; Gen. Thomas F. Drayton, of Charlotte; Major Charles Haigh, of Fayetteville; Dr. C. Mills, of Cabarrus county, and Dr. T. J. Moore, of Charlotte. With the marshals galloping through the crowded streets, the eager thousands shouting and singing, ladies leaning from windows and balconies, flags waving on all sides, bands playing and cannon booming, the scene was one to inspire every soul present and to be remembered until death. It was nearly noon when the procession, including eighteen fire companies and twelve military companies, began the march to the fair ground, where the exercises were held.

The proceedings of the day were opened by Ex-Governor William Graham, who announced that Rev. A. W. Miller, D. D., would invoke the divine blessing. After the prayer, the band played "The Old North State," and then Gov. Graham, in a few words, introduced Major Seaton Gales, of Raleigh, who read the Declaration adopted May 20, 1775. Hon. John Kerr was the next speaker, and he was followed by Hon. John M. Bright, a member of Congress from Tennessee. At night, there was speaking from the stand in Independence square, the orators being Judge Davidson, of Tennessee; Gov. Chamberlain, of South Carolina; Gov.

Hendricks, of Indiana; Gov. Vance; Ex-Governor Walker, of Virginia; Col. Thomas Polk, of Tennessee; Generals Cox and Clingman, and Mayor William Johnston. At the conclusion of the speeches, Mr. E. P. Jones, of Greensboro, seconded by Capt. Smith, of Georgia, moved that the thanks of the visitors be tendered to the people of Charlotte for the kindness and hospitality which had been extended to all, and the motion was accepted with cheers.

One of the most pleasing incidents of the day was the cordial greeting on all sides to Gov. Hendricks, of Indiana, who made a pleasant impression upon everyone. Several accidents occurred in the discharge of firearms and fireworks, though no one was killed. Among those on the speaker's stand was James Belk, of Union county, who was born February 4, 1765, and was consequently one hundred and ten years old. Senator Merrimon, Col. John H. Wheeler and many other distinguished men were present. Col. Wheeler delivered a lecture on Mecklenburg history in the court house May 24, being introduced by Gov. Vance. The Mecklenburg Monumental Association was organized June 25, with Z. B. Vance, president; Dr. Joseph Graham and J. H. Wilson, vice presidents, and T. W. Dewey, secretary and treasurer. The Mecklenburg Historical Society was organized May 7, 1875, with the following officers: President, C. Dowd; vice presidents, Z. B. Vance and D. H. Hill; secretaries, T. J. Moore and W. W. Fleming.

Authority:—Charlotte Newspapers of 1875.

CHAPTER XXXII.

LAST QUARTER OF THE CENTURY. (1875 to 1900.)

Public Improvements—Public Buildings—Medical Society—Law Association—Newspapers—Farms.

The history of Mecklenburg and Charlotte during the last quarter of the nineteenth century is chiefly an account of the growth of the manufacturing industries. As manufactures grew, agriculture and the trades were developed to supply the increased demands, and as the city grew, public buildings were erected and improvements made for the benefit of the public.

January 1, 1899, the city purchased the water works plant from the Charlotte Water Works Company, for $226,000. The plant was established in 1882. Two hundred hydrants afford protection from fire, and water is supplied free to the charitable institutions. The water is filtered by the best known mechanical process, and since the city assumed control of the management, the cost has been reduced one-half.

Gas lights have been in operation in Charlotte since 1857, and electric lights were introduced in 1887. Street cars were running in 1887, and the electric power was substituted for horse power in 1893. In 1883, the Southern Bell Telephone Company was granted permission by the board of aldermen to erect their poles in the city, with the provision that the city could place the fire alarm boxes on the poles. The first ordinance prohibiting the sale of tobacco on Sunday was enacted August 20, 1877. The county chain gang was organized in 1868, the new cemetery was first used in 1867, the sewerage system was established in 1881, and the crematory for the disposal of city refuse was established in 1896.

The new city hall was built in 1891. It is made of North Carolina brown-stone and granite, and cost $40,000. The county court house was built in 1896, of terra cotta and brick, at a cost of $50,000. The United States Federal building, containing the postoffice, was erected in 1891, at a cost of $85,000.

In 1890, the Legislature chartered the Charlotte Consolidated Construction Company, which has come to be known as the "4 C's." It was organized with a capital stock of $200,000, and with E. D. Latta as president and J. L. Chambers as secretary and treasurer. The company has since purchased the Charlotte Electric Company, Charlotte Street Railway Company and Charlotte Gas Light Company, and the three were combined under a new charter as the Charlotte Electric Railway, Light and Power Company. The "4 C's" engineered the building of Dilworth, and owns a considerable portion of the property.

There were nine physicians in Charlotte at the close of the war. There are now about fifty in the county, among them being some of the most prominent in the State. The Charlotte Medical Society was organized under an act of the Legislature of January 28, 1897, with R. J. Brevard president and G. W. Pressly secretary and treasurer. The officers now are R. L. Gibbon and J. C. Montgomery. This association has been productive of much good, and only physicians of high standing are allowed to become members of it. The Charlotte *Medical Journal* was begun in 1892 by Dr. E. C. Register and Dr. J. C. Montgomery. The latter withdrew from the management in 1902, and it has since been conducted by Dr. Register alone.

As lawyers devote more time to public affairs than other men, it is but natural they should be the more widely known. Charlotte has for fifty years been distinguished and honored by an able bar, and the reputation increases with each year. In the ten years after the war were such men as A. Burwell, J. W. Osborne, Jones & Johnston, W. M. Shipp, Vance & Dowd, J. H. Wilson and W. P. Bynum. There are now thirty-eight lawyers in the county. The Charlotte Law Association was chartered January 13, 1885. The library of the association, in the Piedmont building, is one of the best to be found in any city of similar size, one of the prominent features of it being the annual Supreme Court reports of every State in the Union.

There have been twenty-five different newspapers and periodicals published in Charlotte since the war, of which only a few survive. The Charlotte *Evening News* was established by Wade H. Harris in 1888, and was continued by him until 1894, when he was succeeded as editor and proprietor by W. C. Dowd. Dr. A. J. McKelway succeeded Mr. Dowd as editor May 23, 1903. The *Daily Carolina Observer* was established in 1869 by Smith, Watson & Co. Francis Justice was editor from January to August, 1870. Mr. Justice was followed by J. W. Wright, J. Jones and C. R. Jones. The latter conducted it until 1883. The *Charlotte Chronicle* was begun in 1887, and in 1892 was sold to D. A. Tompkins and J. P. Caldwell, who changed the name to the *Daily Observer*, and J. P. Caldwell began his duties as editor February 1, 1892. The *Chronicle* was revived as the Charlotte *Evening Chronicle* May 25, 1903, with Howard A. Banks as editor. The first telegraphic news service received in Charlotte was by the old *Observer* in March, 1874. The *Observer* issues a semi-weekly edition, and the *News* also issues a semi-weekly known as the *Times-Democrat*. Besides these are the *Mill News*, the *Peoples' Paper, Southern and Western Textile Excelsior, Carolina Medical Journal, Star of Zion* by and for colored people; *Presbyterian Weekly Standard*, and *Quarterly*, and the publications of the colleges.

It is noticeable that as Mecklenburg has grown richer and more populous, the farms have increased in number and decreased in size. The average number of acres in a farm in the county is seventy-five. There is only one which contains more than a thousand acres, and 64 per cent. of them contain less than one hundred acres. There are 227,995 acres of land, and the 4,190 farms are occupied by 1,226 owners, 290 part owners, 22 owners and tenants, 55 managers, 631 cash paying tenants and 1,966 share tenants.

TRANSITION PERIOD: COUNTY COURT HOUSE, 1888.

TRANSITION PERIOD: COUNTY COURT HOUSE, 1898.

TRANSITION PERIOD: CITY HALL, 1888.

TRANSITION PERIOD: CITY HALL, 1898.

TRANSITION PERIOD: SOUTHERN RAILROAD STATION, 1888.

TRANSITION PERIOD: SOUTHERN RAILROAD STATION, 1898.

TRANSITION PERIOD: AVERAGE ROAD, 1888.

TRANSITION PERIOD: AVERAGE ROAD, 1898.

Sixty per cent. of the farms are occupied by white people, and 40 per cent. by colored people. The number of buildings in the county of all kinds, according to the census of 1900, is 632,922.

Notes:—Information Obtained from County and City Records; Officials of the County, City, 4 C's, Medical and Law Associations; City Code, Newspaper Files and Census Reports.

CHAPTER XXXIII.

THE CHURCHES FROM 1860 TO 1903.

Short Sketches of the Growth of the Principal Congregations of the Leading Denominations in the City and County, and of the Other Religious Organizations.

There are nearly two hundred churches in Mecklenburg county, representing numerous creeds and denominations, and being about evenly divided in number between the white and colored races. In Charlotte and the immediate vicinity are sixty-four houses of worship, of which twenty-seven are for colored people. In 1868, there were only seven churches in the city—Methodist, Presbyterian, Baptist, Episcopal, Lutheran and Catholic. The growth and development of the various religious sects has been in proportion to the growth of the city and county.

St. Peter's Episcopal church was organized in 1844, and the first building was erected in the same year. The present church on North Tryon street was built in 1857, and was rebuilt in 1892. The property is worth about $40,000, and St. Peter's has 325 communicants. St. Mark's, in Long Creek township, was established in 1885. There are four chapels in the county, and the total Episcopal membership is about 450. St. Peter's Hospital, for white people, was established January 1, 1876, and the Good Samaritan Hospital, for colored people, in 1890. Thompson's Orphanage was established in 1887, has property worth $20,000, and regularly cares for about seventy orphans. St. Michael's colored Episcopal church is located on South Mint street, and the pastor also has supversion of St. Michael's Training and Industrial School for colored people.

The First Presbyterian church has occupied its present site since 1821. The old building was many times improved and repaired, and in 1892 and the following year, the beau-

FIRST PRESBYTERIAN CHURCH.

TRYON STREET BAPTIST CHURCH.

tiful edifice now in use was erected at a cost of $31,000. This church has 650 members. The Second Presbyterian church was organized October 22, 1873, in the old court house, with seventeen members, and Dr. W. S. Plumer was stated supply for eighteen months. A building was erected on the present site, at a cost of $10,000, in 1875, and the present church was built in 1892, at a cost of $58,000, and has 1,004 members.

Tenth Avenue Presbyterian church, which was formerly known as Graham Street church, was organized with sixty-two members March 2, 1890. The new building was completed and occupied in November, 1902, and the property is worth $25,000. The membership is more than four hundred.

Westminster congregation was begun in the old graded school building in 1896, by Dr. J. W. Stagg. Atherton Sunday school was combined with it, and in 1897, the building was completed at a cost of $15,000, and the church has eighty members. Most of the bequest of Miss Jennie E. Johnson to the Second church was used in building Westminster church. Besides these prominent churches in the city, the Presbyterians have twenty-six others in the county, with a total membership of 6,600.

The Presbyterian General Assembly of the Confederacy met in Charlotte, May 5, 1864, and the first meeting of the Mecklenburg Presbytery was at Big Steele creek church, April 21, 1870. The *Presbyterian Standard,* official organ of the North Carolina Synod, was moved from Wilmington to Charlotte in 1898, and has since been edited by Dr. A. J. McKelway. The Presbyterian Hospital is practically the city hospital, and the Presbyterians have established a home for aged and helpless women and the Alexander Rescue Home for children.

In 1873, the first church of the Associate Reformed Presbyterians was organized in Charlotte. A new building, at the corner of Tryon and Third streets, was completed in 1890, at a total cost of $20,000. The Second Associate

Reformed Presbyterian church was built in 1899, at a cost of $6,000. The First has 190 members and the Second has 290, and there are five other churches of this denomination in the county.

The First Baptist church in Charlotte was built in 1833, at the corner of Third and College streets. A better building, which cost $1,800, was erected in 1855, at the corner of Seventh and Brevard streets; and the structure now occupied by the First Baptist church was completed in 1884. This church has 500 members. In 1895, the Twelfth Street Baptist church was built, and it has 300 members. There are seventeen Baptist churches in the county.

Tryon Street Methodist Episcopal church is the largest of the nineteen congregations of that denomination in the county. A building was erected on Sixth and Tryon streets in 1859, and it was worked over after the war, and was rebuilt in 1891. The property is valued at $31,000, and the church has 650 members. Trinity Methodist Episcopal church was organized and built in 1896; has 500 members and property worth $40,000. Brevard and Calvary churches have 350 members each, and Hoskins has 300, and the total membership in the county is about 4,000, divided among nineteen churches.

St. Mark's Lutheran church was organized in 1859. The first building was at the corner of Seventh and College streets, and the present building on North Tryon street was built in 1885, at a cost of $18,000, and the church has 175 members. Morning Star Lutheran church, in the southeastern part of the county, is the only other of this denomination in Mecklenburg. The Catholic church was built in 1851, and the new building in 1893, and has a membership of 500. The Jewish population have a congregation known as "Shaaray Israel," but they have no synagogue.

There are about seventy-five colored churches in Mecklenburg, nearly all of which have been built since the war. The Zion Methodist is the leading colored denomination, having fifty churches, and issuing a religious paper from the

TRYON STREET M. E. CHURCH, SOUTH.

CATHOLIC CHURCH.

THE CHURCHES FROM 1860 TO 1903.

Zion Publishing House in Charlotte. The Clinton Chapel of the Zion Methodists and the First and Second Baptist churches (colored) each have 300 members.

The Charlotte Ministers' Conference was organized October 14, 1891. The Young Woman's Christian Association was established in 1902. The Young Men's Christian Association, which has 635 members, was organized November 11, 1874, with sixteen active members and seven associate members. The Association has had only five presidents—A. S. Caldwell, Rev. W. M. Hunter, R. N. Littlejohn, W. A. Truslow and George B. Hanna. Prof. Hanna has been president since 1880, except for six months filled by Mr. Truslow in 1885. Rev. P. J. Carraway, pastor of Tryon Street Methodist Episcopal church, was active in the work of organization. The present Y. M. C. A. building, on South Tryon street, was occupied in 1888, and the Association owns property valued at $40,000.

Notes:—The information for this Chapter was obtained from Church Records, Printed Sketches, Newspapers, and Officials of the Various Organizations.

CHAPTER XXXIV.

EDUCATION FROM 1860 TO 1903.

Development of County Public School System—Charlotte Graded Schools First in the State—Presbyterian, Elizabeth, Davidson and Medical Colleges—Charlotte Military Institute—Biddle University and St. Michael's Training and Industrial School.

During the war, the income from the county school tax was donated to the use of the soldiers, but the amount received from the State was used for the support of the schools. In 1863, Mecklenburg public schools cost $3,860.08. There were also a number of academies in the county from 1860 to 1870, the most prominent ones being at Providence, Davidson, Claremont, and Steele creek. The North Carolina Educational Association convened in Charlotte, November 8, 1864, and Rev. R. Burwell was elected president. The Educational Association of the Confederate States was in session here at the same time, and Calvin H. Wiley was elected president. Rev. R. H. Griffith and Armistead Burwell taught a boys' school in Charlotte in 1865; and from 1867 to 1869, Rev. A. G. Stacy, with a strong faculty, conducted the Mecklenburg Female College in the Military Institute, and the school was well patronized.

COUNTY SCHOOLS.

In 1870, the public school system of the State was reorganized, and in that year the schools of Mecklenburg cost $5,650. In 1874, 46 white schools, with 1,702 children, cost $5,346, and 34 colored schools, with 1,814 children, cost $2,948. In 1876, there were 102 schools in the county, and the total cost was $9,914. In those days, the schools were governed by a board of education, and the teachers applied for license to a county examiner. The educational board still exists, but the tendency has been to make the examiner

DAVIDSON COLLEGE CAMPUS.

more and more important, until now, under the title of superintendent of education, he is the real head of the public schools of the county. In 1873, many teachers taught two or three schools in one year, as the terms continued only from two to five months. Teachers were paid $25 or $30 per month; or if the number of pupils was small, one dollar for each one in attendance.

There are now 141 public schools in the county, of which 61 are for colored people, and the total cost in 1902, was $42,512.55. There are 10,869 white school children and 7,927 colored children, and the school terms range from four to eight months, with an average of a little more than five months. The census of 1900 credits Mecklenburg with 10,370 illiterate persons who are more than ten years of age. Of these, 7,861 are negroes. Among the teachers are seventeen male and thirty lady graduates; white male teachers receive from $30.00 to $50.00 a month, with an average of $38.00; the average for white lady teachers is $28.00, and the colored teachers receive $20.00 or $25.00 a month. Ten schools have three teachers each, and thirty have as many as two each. Among the best schools in the county outside of Charlotte are the Belmont Graded School, Bain Academy, Davidson Academy, Matthews High School, Pineville High School, Newell Academy, Zion Academy, Huntersville Academy and the Atherton Graded School.

CHARLOTTE GRADED SCHOOLS.

In the fall of 1873, Rev. J. B. Boone organized in Charlotte the first graded school in North Carolina. The first session was begun October 21, in Miss Hattie Moore's dwelling house, in the rear of the Episcopal church, and was continued for eight months, with an average daily attendance of 175 and at a total expense amounting to $2,901.75; closing June 19. Gen. Rufus Barringer, Major C. Dowd and Capt. John Wilkes composed the school board, and the teachers were Misses M. H. Barber, Hattie Moore, S. C. Miller, F. A. Walsh, and M. N. Lucas, and Mrs. S. E. Waring. Miss

Moore was succeeded in March by Miss A. B. Carr, and she in May by Miss Sue M. Johnston. September 7, 1874, the second session was begun in two houses on opposite sides of Seventh street, next to the railroad, and was continued for eight months lacking one day, closing May 6, because of lack of money. The expense for the second year was $2,674, and the average attendance was 225, the largest enrollment in any one month being 340 in December. The teachers were Misses Barber, Walsh, Lucas, M. S. Griffith, Sallie A. Bethune, S. H. Miller and Mrs. Waring. Pupils of the white school were properly graded, as were also the pupils of the colored school, but the two were not in any way connected.

When the graded school was begun, $1,700 was on hand, and $600 was received from the Peabody Fund the first year and $1,000 the second year. Some voluntary contributions were received, but there was no charge for tuition, and the only other source of income was the county school fund. The apparent lack of funds and public approval of the work, aided by Mr. Boone's efforts, served to begin an agitation for a special tax. A bill providing a special charter and allowing a tax to be levied, was introduced into the General Assembly by Senator R. P. Waring, and was ratified March 22, 1875. Before it should go into effect, it was stipulated that a majority of "those voting" should vote in favor of it. Several elections were held without securing a majority of the registered voters, during which time the school was suspended. On the first Monday in June, 1880, the election resulted in a vote of 815 to 1 in favor of schools. There were 1,679 names on the registration books, and there had been no new registration for the election, but before the result was announced, the aldermen erased 133 names and then declared that the necessary majority had been obtained. A tax-payer carried the matter into court, and the aldermen were sustained by the lower court, and finally by the Supreme Court, in the Fall session of 1881. The eight school commissioners

PRESBYTERIAN COLLEGE.

EDUCATION FROM 1860 TO 1903.   169

met June 10, 1880, and organized and elected Capt. Fred Nash treasurer, which position he held until 1901.

The school opened September 11, 1882, with 480 white and 253 colored pupils—the white school in the Military Institute building, and the colored school in the basement of the colored Episcopal church. T. J. Mitchell, of Ohio, was superintendent from the opening until August 9, 1886, when he resigned to become president of the Alabama State Normal School. J. T. Corlew succeeded Mr. Mitchell, and served until January 28, 1888. Alexander Graham has been superintendent since February 7, 1888. During the first session under Superintendent Mitchell, there were twelve white teachers and six colored teachers, the local tax was ten cents on the $100 valuation of property and thirty cents on the poll, and there were five hundred white pupils and three hundred colored pupils. The Charlotte Military Institute, which was leased in 1882, was purchased by the schools in 1883, and the North Graded School building was erected in 1900. A manual training department was established in 1891, and was very successful, but was discontinued because of lack of room.

During the session of 1901-1902, the total enrollment of pupils was 3,056, of whom 1,978 were white and 1,078 colored. The average daily attendance was 1,456 whites and 632 colored. The income from the city tax of twenty cents on the $100 valuation and sixty cents on the poll, was $16,006.12, and $11,250.00 was received from the county, making a total of $27,256.12. The white teachers were paid $20,806.00, and the colored teachers $5,419.00. The forty-seven white teachers received salaries of $40 or $50 a month, and the sixteen colored teachers were paid from $30 to $40. Miss Sallie Bethune has been teaching in the public schools regularly since the opening day in 1882, and enjoys the distinction of having taught more children to read than any other teacher in the State. There are ten grades, and departments of music and drawing, and the schools continue for nine months each year.

PRESBYTERIAN COLLEGE.

President R. Burwell continued the Charlotte Female Institute during the war. In 1863, he had four assistants, nine in 1868, and eleven in 1872. The school prospered under his administration, and it was much regretted by the patrons that in the last year mentioned the president resigned to assume the control of Peace Institute in Raleigh. Rev. R. H. Chapman, D. D., was president from 1872 to 1875, and he was succeeded by Rev. S. Taylor Martin, of Virginia, who, with seven assistants, remained in charge until 1878. Rev. W. R. Atkinson, who had been teaching in Peace Institute, assumed control in 1878, and continued until he resigned to go to Columbia. The institution was then closed until Miss Lily Long re-opened it as the Presbyterian College in 1895. In 1896, the city of Charlotte released all claim to the property, and it has since been in control of the Presbyteries of Mecklenburg and Concord. Rev. James R. Bridges, D. D., has been president since 1898, and the building has been rebuilt at a cost of $70,000. The college has a faculty of twenty instructors, and during the session of 1901-1902 enrolled one hundred and six in the collegiate department, thirty-eight in the preparatory and forty-three in the primary. It has also departments of music, art and elocution.

MILITARY INSTITUTE.

In February, 1872, the old Military Institute property was sold to S. W. Saunders, J. H. Carson and S. B. Alexander. October 1, 1873, Col. J. P. Thomas was in charge of the school, and continued it until he left Charlotte in 1883, in which year the building was sold to the city graded schools. Capt. W. A. Barrier founded the Macon school in 1870, and conducted it until he died in November, 1890. Capt. J. G. Baird purchased the building and E. L. Reid was principal from 1890 to 1891. Capt. Baird then assumed control of the school and has since conducted it, and in 1894, the name was changed to Charlotte Military Institute. The present building was occupied in 1901. The school has high school

ELIZABETH COLLEGE.

and primary departments, and is highly considered for efficient training. Since its beginning in 1870, it has given instruction to thirty-five hundred boys.

St. Mary's Seminary in Charlotte was established in 1888, and is conducted by the Sisters of Mercy, who also conduct the Academy of the Sacred Heart near Belmont.

MEDICAL COLLEGE.

North Carolina Medical College was established by Dr. J. P. Munroe at Davidson in 1893, and the property is worth $10,000. It had four instructors and eleven students the first year, and in the session of 1902-1903, there were seventeen instructors and sixty-seven students. The institution is controlled by three directors known as the board of control.

ELIZABETH COLLEGE.

Elizabeth Female College was established in 1897 by the United Synod of the South of the Lutheran church. It is beautifully located on a site of twenty acres, and has property worth $250,000. Dr. C. B. King, as president, opened the institution in the Fall of 1897, with sixteen instructors and ninety-four students. In 1903, there were twenty-two instructors and one hundred and twenty students. The course of instruction is thorough and complete, and the college has from its beginning been classed among the best female schools in the country.

The school now known as Biddle University (for colored people) was established in 1867, the principal movers being Revs. S. C. Alexander and W. G. Miller, and Mrs. Mary D. Biddle, of Philadelphia who gave $1,400 for the building. Col. W. C. Myers donated the eight acres of land on which the building is located, and ten thousand dollars was received from the Freedmen's Bureau. The school was established in the present quarters in 1869, during which year Rev. S. Mattoon was elected president, and he served until 1884 when he was succeeded by Rev. W. A. Holliday, who was president a short time, and was followed by Rev. W. F. Johnson. Rev. D. J. Sanders, D. D., the present head of the institution, was elected in 1891. Biddle University is under the care of the Northern Presbyterian church, includes religious, literary and industrial instruction in the curriculum, and enrolled two hundred and forty students in the session of 1902-1903. The president and teachers are colored people.

St. Michael's Training and Industrial School, under the auspices of the Colored Episcopal church, was established in 1891, has property worth $7,000, three instructors, and regularly trains more than a hundred pupils.

DAVIDSON COLLEGE.

Davidson College, under the administration of Dr. J. L. Kirkpatrick, continued its sessions during the war, and at the close the president and three professors were faithfully performing their duties. Dr. Kirkpatrick resigned in 1866, and the presidents since have been Rev. G. W. McPhail, D. D., L. L. D., from 1866 to 1871; Prof. J. R. Blake (chairman of the faculty), from 1871 to 1877; Rev. A. D. Hepburn, D. D., L. L. D., from 1877 to 1885; Rev. Luther McKinnon, D. D., from 1885 to 1888; Rev. J. B. Shearer, D. D., L. L. D., from 1888 to 1901, and Henry Louis Smith, M. A., Ph. D., from 1901 until the present time. The college owns seventeen buildings, which cost, with equipment, $165,000, and the endowment fund amounts to $125,000. The scientific laboratory is equal to any in the South, and the course of instruction, faculty and students rank with the best. During the session of 1902-1903, there were eight professors, eight instructors and assistants, and 225 students.

Authority:—Catalogues and Historical Sketches of the Various Institutions, Officials, County and City Records, and Charlotte Newspapers.

CHAPTER XXXV.

MINING, BANKING AND THE ASSAY OFFICE. (1860 to 1903.)

Use of Improved Mining Machinery After the War—The Miners and the Products—Minerals Found in the County—Receipts of Gold and Silver at the Assay Office—History of the Office.—Charlotte's Leading Banking Institutions.

At the close of the Civil War, there was only one mine in operation in Mecklenburg, and it was the Rudisill. The United States mint was seized by the Confederate authorities in 1861, and held by them until 1865, and for two years thereafter it was occupied by the Federal military authorities. By 1867, the mining and banking interests of Mecklenburg were beginning to take on new life. Investors and speculators from all parts of the world were in this section examining and considering the various natural resources. In that year there were three banks in Charlotte, and the mint was re-opened as an assay office under the supervision of Dr. Isaac W. Jones.

Humphrey Bissell, who was a learned mining engineer, erected the first improved California stamp battery in the county in 1866. The methods of mining were many and various. Forty-eight different processes for the treatment of ore are known to have been tried in the county within the past fifty years, but only two survived the test of time (clorination and smelting), though the cyanide treatment has encouraged hope that ultimately it may be widely applicable. The chief elements in the problem of the extraction of the precious metals from ore are pulverization, concentration, roasting (or expelling the sulphur with incidental oxidization), and the extraction of the gold and the silver.

There are 83 mines in Mecklenburg which have been worked and can again be worked. The Rudisill, near Charlotte, has a shaft 400 feet deep, and has 3,500 feet of levels.

This mine has produced gold amounting to $2,600,000. The St. Catherine, also near the city, has a shaft 450 feet deep. Capp's mine, six miles west of the city, has yielded $2,300,000. Capp's, and the Surface Hill mine, twelve miles from Charlotte, and the Wilson mine, are worked intermittently. The Wilhelmina, in Paw Creek township, is producing considerable gold, and is the only mine in the county operated regularly. The ore in the county assays from $50 to $180 a ton, and some rich veins are occasionally struck, and nuggets are not uncommon.

Silver is found, but there has been no regular mining for it. It is generally in small quantities in the gold ore. Throughout the county are quarries of red, white and gray granite, sandstone, slate, hornblend and leopardite, the latter being a black spotted granite found only in Mecklenburg. Iron, lead, zinc and thirty-three other minerals have been found, but not in sufficient quantities for practical purposes.

The mint, which is really only an assay office, has not done any coinage since before the war. The comparatively small amount which would be done can be done at the Philadelphia mint much cheaper than here. There have been six assayers in charge since Dr. Jones: Calvin Cowles, 1869 to 1885; R. P. Waring, 1885 to 1889; Stuart W. Cramer, 1889 to 1893; W. E. Ardrey, 1893 to 1897; W. S. Clanton, 1897 to 1903, and D. Kirby Pope in 1903.

Though the assay office was opened in the Summer of 1867, no work was done until the following March, and in that year the receipts were $4,851.95. The total receipts from the establishment of the mint up to June 30, 1873, were $5,129,217.28. In 1873-74, $8,763 worth of gold and silver was received; the next year it amounted to $6,690; in 1877 it was $10,382; 1878, $54,345. From that year, the receipts increased annually until 1888, when they amounted to $283,619, which is the highest mark attained. For the year ending June 30, 1902, the receipts were $267,804; and for the last six months of 1902, 152,080. The total receipts at the office up to January 1, 1903, were $10,163,000. Of this, $30,455 was silver, and the yearly receipt of silver now is from $1,000 to $1,500.

There is a practically inexhaustible source of wealth in the mines of Mecklenburg county, and it is a cause for congratulation that new interest is being taken in them. Capitalists are investigating the situation, and the renewal of the work will result in an increased circulation of money and a consequent and natural increase in wealth and prosperity. New banking institutions have been established in Charlotte recently, and there is an abundance of capital available. The Charlotte National Bank was organized February 1, 1897, with a capital of $125,000; Southern Loan and Savings Bank, July 6, 1901, with $25,000 capital; Southern States Trust Company, July 15, 1901, with $100,000 which has been increased to $200,000; and besides these are the three old banks—the First National, Commercial National and Merchants' and Farmers' National; Mechanics Perpetual Building and Loan Association, Mutual Building and Loan Association, and Charlotte Building and Loan Association. These strong financial institutions have combined assets of nearly six million dollars, which is double what it was in 1890.

Authority:—Records of the Mint, Newspapers and Bank Officials.

CHAPTER XXXVI.

ROAD BUILDING FROM 1880 TO 1903.

Influences Which Made Better Roads Necessary—Original Methods and Subsequent Progress—Cost of Roads—Convict Labor Satisfactory—Lessons Taught by Experience.

Development of manufactures, and consequent increase of wealth and population in the city, necessitated a greater trade in country produce, and the more frequent traveling between country and city soon emphasized the manifest importance of a system of good roads. Manufactures render good roads necessary, and at the same time make them more feasible by the increased income from taxes; and wherever and whenever factories are established, the road question immediately begins to command attention.

Agitation for better roads in Mecklenburg began soon after the war, and some desultory work was done on them, but the movement which has resulted in the present excellent highways did not begin until about 1885. January 26, 1881, Gen. John A. Young and T. L. Vail appeared before the board of aldermen in an attempt to get the city to aid the county in improving the public roads. June 2, 1885, Mayor William Johnston recommended an issue of bonds, and this was the first notable move in the right direction. November 8, 1887, under the administration of Mayor F. B. McDowell, who had succeeded Col. Johnston in May, the city voted an issue of $50,000 of bonds for street improvements.

The bonds were sold February 6, 1888, at their par value, and the improvement of the city streets was then begun in earnest. The first plan adopted was to have stone broken by hand, and laid on the streets to a depth of five or six inches, after having made an equivalent excavation. In this way, about five miles of streets were put in fair condition; but after the issue of bonds, machinery for crushing rock was purchased, and the work was thus made both swifter and cheaper. The city now owns a well-equipped rock-crushing plant, and the macadamizing has been continued by successive administrations, with a constant improvement in methods.

As street building in Charlotte progressed, the authorities of Mecklenburg county undertook the task of improving the highways outside the city. In 1884, S. H. Hilton, of the board of county commissioners, was appointed to take charge of the county road building. The Legislature authorized the county commissioners to put to work on the roads the prisoners of the city or county many of whom were thereafter sentenced to a term "on the roads," and to levy a special road tax of from seven to twenty cents on each $100 worth of property. Mr. Hilton, with three prisoners and a $500 team, began work on the Providence road near the present site of the Thompson Orphanage. Mud was so deep in the road that one load of stones would be thrown in and then the laborers would get on the pile and scatter other stones around, and when the mud holes were filled, the stones on top were broken with hammers. Five hundred yards of this kind of work was done there, and then the force, which was being increased, transferred their attention to others of the worst roads in the county. Within that year, a crusher was purchased for $900, and as more prisoners were sent out, and the supervisor—by investigations of similar work elsewhere—familiarized himself with the best methods, the work improved in efficiency and practicability. When Mr. Hilton left the office, in 1893, the county road force consisted of eighty-five convicts and equipment worth about five thousand dollars; and thirty miles of roads had been macadamized. There are now more than one hundred miles of macadam roads in Mecklenburg.

In 1897, the Legislature created the "Mecklenburg Road and Convict Commission," which consisted of three persons, and assumed the authority for road construction hitherto held by the county commissioners. Two years later, the old system was restored, and all that the county is now doing in building, reconstructing and repairing streets and roads is divided into three departments: First, in the city of Charlotte, under direction of the mayor, city council, city engineer and supervisor of streets; second, in the county at large, under direction of the county commissioners, county engineer, and superintendent of convicts; third, in each township, through its board of trustees, are expended for local work in road repairing the proceeds of the road tax raised within the township.

A road outfit costs about $5,000, and consists of a steam roller, crusher, bins, portable engine, road machine, and a screen made of boiler plate perforated to separate the crushed stones into three sizes. The city of Charlotte owns an outfit, Charlotte township owns one, and the county owns two. The first macadam roads built in Mecklenburg cost from $2,700 to $4,000 a mile, according to the amount and kind of grading required. The cost is now from $1,600 to $2,500 a mile. The present county road tax is eighteen cents on the $100, and this raises twenty thousand dollars a year, which is expended in building roads by convict labor. In addition, each township levies a tax ranging from seven cents to fifteen cents on the $100, and the proceeds are expended by the township trustees in improvements and repairs. The county fund is supplemented by special appropriations by the commissioners to the extent of ten or fifteen thousand dollars annually.

The question of good roads is not one of construction alone, but of development and maintenance as well. The trustees of Charlotte township find it necessary to expend $330 a mile every five years for repairs. Three hundred and fifty cubic yards of stone, costing forty cents a yard, are required, $140 being thus expended for stone alone. This stone is purchased of the farmers, who thus get paid for something which would otherwise be worse than useless. There is also the cost of spiking, distributing, rolling, crushing, harrowing and other labor. Careful observation teaches

ROAD MACHINERY.

ROAD BUILDING FROM 1880 TO 1903.

that the use of broad tires in place of narrow ones would reduce this expense to one-third of what it now is.

Convict labor is regarded with great favor. The reports show that the cost of feeding, clothing and guarding the prisoners amounts to about twenty-five cents a day for each one, which is less than the county would pay for their board in the county jail. Formerly, the roads were constructed by rounding up the roadbed, cutting drain ditches on each side, excavating twelve feet in the middle to a depth of nine inches, and then filling in the excavated portion with stone broken by hand. The system has been developed until not only is the stone crushed by steam power and the processes otherwise improved, but the roads are often re-located and graded, becoming practically new roads.

Experience taught the authorities that when the roads are dry, the clay bed is preferable to macadam, because of the less wear and jolting of vehicles and of the better effect on the feet of the horses. The location of the macadam in the middle of the road left either side too narrow for vehicles, so the plan of having the macadam on one side was adopted. On these roads, the macadam is used in winter, and is saved from the wear of the summer traffic, because in summer the clay bed is preferred.

The result of the work here outlined is that Charlotte has been lifted out of the mud and made a city of clean streets and attractive appearance; the country has been benefited by the easier accessibility of markets, besides furnishing pleasant driveways for the people of city and county. All this has been accomplished within a few years, without imposing any burdens upon the people in a section where, from the earliest times, the roadbeds were comparable to the tempering pits of a brickyard.

Authority:—County Records and Road Officials.

CHAPTER XXXVII.

DEVELOPMENT OF MANUFACTURES. (1865 to 1900.)

Iron Substituted for Wood in Machinery as a Result of the Abolition of Cheap Labor—Necessity Forces Improvements—First Cotton Mill Built in 1881 and First Cotton Oil Mill in 1882—Cotton Compresses—Industrial Progress Attendant Upon Manufacturing—Situation in 1900.

The end of the Civil War left the negroes free, but without any of the habits or feelings of free men, and the acquirement of them required the slow process of time. It soon became difficult for farmers to secure enough negro workmen to gin a crop of cotton, so demoralized had the freedmen become. To them the idea of freedom was absolution from work and restraint of all kinds. This difficulty of obtaining labor was augmented by the advent of the system of farming under which the negroes rented small quantities of land and began farming on their own account. Being unable to get as much labor as the old system demanded, the planters began to manifest a spirit of interest in the introduction of mechanical appliances tending to reduce the number of hands necessary for their work.

Wooden cogs and wallowers of gin running gear, used for transmission of power, and similar machinery, wore rapidly and required frequent renewal. When these renewals were made by labor which cost nothing, such machinery was satisfactory, but when the labor had to be paid for in money, a demand immediately arose for cast bevel wheels. This application of cast-iron gearing was probably the first move in the direction of labor-saving devices. Wrought band iron replaced ropes for binding the bales of cotton, both as a matter of economy and for safety from fire.

The "feeder" and the "condenser" were inventions of much importance; the first was a contrivance into which the

COTTON MILL AND COTTON.

seed cotton could be put, and which would, with proper adjustments, feed the gin; the other attachment caught the lint cotton between two skeleton wire-cloth bound rollers, and delivered it from the gin in a continuous "bat," instead of like feathers in a gale. Next came a compact press capable of pressing a bale by the power of two stout laborers. Then the steam power began to be used, and instead of every planter owning his own gin, the larger ones only owned one, and they ginned for the public. Following these adaptations were well-designed modern steam ginneries, equipped with labor-saving appliances. About 1885, exhaust suction fans came into use, and they made possible the unloading of cotton direct from the wagon through a pipe or flue into the gin feeder or into bins partitioned off in the gin house.

These changes may be said to have forced themselves upon the plantation. They were not the result of any exertions on the part of the planter or tenant to find better or cheaper methods, but each feature was introduced as a matter of necessity; not as a preferable way, but as the only way the crop could be prepared for market. Similar innovations and improvements were being made in all kinds of work. The plantation tools of 1870 were the wooden plow stock with a small variety of small iron plow-shares, a weeding hoe, a scythe and a wagon. On the same plantation, ten years later, could have been seen modern reapers, sulky plows, cotton planters, finely made harrows and like implements.

For a few years after the war, when the price of cotton was so high that anyone could live by a small amount of farming, the land was cultivated extensively; but when the cultivation reached its limit, and the price of cotton became lower, the farmers and home capitalists realized that the only way their condition could be bettered was by manufacturing the raw product at home. In 1873, there were thirty-three cotton factories in North Carolina, with a total capital of $1,130,900, and earning a profit of twelve per cent. on the investment. September 15, of that year, a public meeting was held in Charlotte to discuss plans for a mill here, and committees were appointed to investigate and report. March 6, 1874, another meeting was held, and yet another at Davidson College March 31. A company was then formed to built a factory at Spring's Shoals, on the Catawba. The Charlotte Cotton Factory Company met in Charlotte September 24, 1874, and organized with A. B. Davidson president, A. Macaulay vice president, and F. H. Dewey secretary and treasurer. About the same time, the owners of the Rock Island woolen mill organized to convert it into a cotton factory, with R. I. McDowell president, and A. S. Caldwell secretary and treasurer.

Though these movements did not materialize, the agitation consequent upon them did later result in the beginning of cotton manufacturing in the city. The Charlotte cotton mill was the first, and it began operations in the Spring of 1881. It was established by R. M., J. E., D. W. and J. M. Oates, with a capital of $131,500. Only spinning was done in the mill for ten years, and then the weaving department was added. In 1896, there were five cotton mills in Charlotte, and the development since that time has been remarkable. There are now seventeen mills in Charlotte, with a combined capital of three million dollars, nearly three thousand looms, about 125,000 spindles, 6,000 operatives, and a weekly pay roll of $30,000. There is also one cotton mill at Davidson, one at Pineville, one at Huntersville, and one at Cornelius.

Cotton seed, not needed for planting, were formerly scattered over the fields for fertilizer, but as their value for oil and other purposes became known, oil mills were built. The first one in Charlotte was established in 1882, and there are now two in the city and one at Davidson College. There are also two cotton compresses, which together handle about 150,000 bales annually. These compresses were originated because of the importance of having the bales as small as possible, especially for shipment across the sea. Two large warehouses supply good services to farmers who thus have

COTTON MILL OPERATIVES.

an opportunity to secure cash advances on their cotton while holding it for higher prices by paying a small rental fee. The average cotton trade in Charlotte amounts to about $1,200,000 every year.

Within a radius of one hundred miles around Charlotte are nearly 300 cotton mills, operating more than 3,000,000 spindles and 85,000 looms, and having a capital of $100,-000,000, which not only shows that Charlotte is a manufacturing centre, but the remarkable fact that *one-half of the looms and spindles of the South are within one hundred miles of this city.* In Charlotte are companies which build and equip cotton factories and oil mills, and a number of other agencies for miscellaneous supplies and machinery.

While cotton manufacturing is the chief industry of Mecklenburg county, other manufactures have developed along with it, and represent forty per cent. of the total manufacturing capital. The Mecklenburg Iron Works and the Liddell Company are the oldest establishments in the county. There are three other machine shops and foundries, five clothing factories, and a fertilizer factory, and almost every other kind of manufacturing plant on a more or less extensive scale. More than half the manufacturing capital of the county is invested in cotton factories, but the remaining forty per cent. leaves a wide latitude for diversified industries.

Mecklenburg county has 181 factories, with a capital of $5,108,591, and of these Charlotte has 112, with a capital of $4,112,342. In the county, according to the census of 1900, were 3,988 wage earners, of whom 2,210 were men, 1,102 were women and 676 were children under sixteen years of age; and the average yearly earnings were $219. Materials, mill supplies, freight, power and heat cost the factories annually $3,500,000; wages, $875,000; total cost, $4,375,000; value of products, $5,736,000. *From these figures it is found that the gross profit to the county (not to the manufacturer) from manufacturing raw material at home is thirty per cent., and the annual profit on the capital invested is* twenty-six per cent. Mecklenburg, in 1902, produced 28,407 bales of cotton, for which the farmers received about one million dollars. Manufactured into various products, it would be worth from fifteen to forty-five cents a pound, or a total of from two million to six million dollars. Mecklenburg's cotton factories increase the value of the annual cotton product of the county from one million to two million five hundred thousand dollars.

Authority:—County Records, Newspapers and Officials.

WHEAT.

CORN.

CHAPTER XXXVIII.

MECKLENBURG AND CHARLOTTE IN 1903.

Population, Taxable Real Estate, Personal Property, Railroads and Banks—Expenses and Receipts of County and City—Social and Business Organizations—Incorporated Towns—Farm Products.—New Buildings.

The total taxable value of real estate and personal property in Mecklenburg county in 1902 was $11,717,404, and in the city of Charlotte the value was $8,248,660. Considering the fact that Mecklenburg and Charlotte are one hundred and forty-three and one hundred and thirty-five years old, respectively, there is nothing phenomenal in this development. Other sections have grown more rapidly, some cities have sprung up within a year, but few have equaled the record for steady, reliable and lasting growth. The county and city have ever been free from everything akin to a "boom;" genuine work and merit do not depend upon excitement for recognition. An important rule of the business organizations has been the refusal to pay a "bonus" to get any enterprise to enter the city. New industries are welcomed, but not subsidized, and as a result, everything which comes into the county, comes to stay.

General county expenses in 1902 amounted to $92,542, and city expenditures for general purposes amounted to $141,227. The county indebtedness is $300,000; city, $515,000. The county buildings, court house, jail, road machinery, etc., are worth about one hundred thousand dollars. The city owns the city hall, water works, three school buildings, about thirty acres of land, three town lots, latest improved fire alarm system, and two fire departments. The streets are macadamized, and the city owns and keeps up a crematory for the disposal of refuse, and a sewerage system. There are one hundred miles of macadam roads in the county, forty of which are in Charlotte township. These roads cost from $1,500 to $4,000 a mile, with an average cost of $2,000 a mile.

Though vast improvements have been made in city and county, the general taxes have not increased to any considerable extent. County tax is $1.16 2-3 on the $100, and a $3.50 poll tax; the city taxes are $1 and $3 respectively. Taxable real estate and personal property in the county increased in valuation $917,929 between 1900 and 1902; 318,121 acres of land are valued at $3,092,296, and 4,017 town lots at $4,293,761. Six railroads enter the city, and twelve of the fifteen townships of the county have railroads, their total valuation in the county being $1,369,917. The assessments are about sixty per cent. of the true value.

A municipal census, January 7, 1901, ascertained the population of the city to be 27,752. The last government census, taken in 1900, gives the population as 18,091. The latter is of the city inside the corporate limits, while the former census is of the suburbs also. By the 1901 census, the population of each ward was: First, 5,942; Second, 5,242; Third, 4,556; Fourth, 4,162; total in wards, 19,902; number outside of wards, 7,850; grand total, 27,752. Of these, 11,983 were colored people. The census of 1900 gave Mecklenburg a population of 55,261. In 1903, the population of the county is about seventy thousand, and of the city thirty thousand.

The administration of the city government is vested in a mayor, recorder and board of aldermen, and the city owns and conducts the water works and fire departments. There is a health department which takes every possible precaution against the spread of contagion and in the interest of the health of the people. There are in the city three daily newspapers, two semi-weekly papers, three weeklies, two medical monthlies, two religious papers, and two college annuals, and there are five job printing establishments.

Nearly all the well known fraternal and benevolent socie-

GRAPES.

CATTLE.

ties are represented in Charlotte. The Manufacturers' Club is the most noted, and there are also the North State Club, Chamber of Commerce, a literary and library association, a Scotch-Irish association, six musical organizations, a medical society, a law association, historical association, Carnegie Library Association, country club, five military organizations, composed of Hornets' Nest Riflemen, drum corps and artillery; post of the Grand Army of the Republic, camp of Confederate Veterans, and fifteen others.

There are four incorporated towns in the county: Matthews, with a population of 378; Davidson, 904; Huntersville, 533; Pineville, 585. Derita, Newells and Mint Hill are growing unincorporated towns. There are fifty-nine postoffices in the county. The general elevation of Mecklenburg is 700 feet above sea level, and the soil is well adapted to successful farming. Farmers average to the acre thirty to sixty bushels of corn, twenty to fifty of wheat, three hundred of potatoes, three to five tons of hay. Grapes thrive abundantly, and orchards and vineyards are carefully cultivated.

One thing which attests continued growth and promises a bright future, is the building of suburban towns. Charlotte is growing larger as it grows better and richer. There are several hotels in the city, and a number of attractive public buildings. Among them are the postoffice, assay office, court house, city hall, Carnegie Library, colleges and graded schools. The street car and lighting plants are as good as the best, and Latta Park, at the southern extremity of the car line, is a popular pleasure resort. A long distance and two local telephone companies and two telegraph companies afford excellent service. One of the established institutions of the county and city is the Mecklenburg Fair Association, the annual exhibits of which are events of interest.

The Carnegie Library was completed in the latter part of May, 1903, at a cost of $40,000, and will be maintained by the city by an annual appropriation of $2,500. The Vance

Memorial Association of Charlotte was organized in 1902, for the purpose of raising the funds necessary to place a monument of Vance in the library.

During the past four years, the outlay for new buildings has averaged $500,000 a year, and the average for new dwelling houses has been more than 600 annually. The nine financial institutions represent a combined capital of $1,101,-703; total assets, $5,582,519, and have deposits amounting to about three million dollars. Charlotte wholesale merchandise establishments keep on the road two hundered traveling salesmen. The construction of macadam roads, and the system of free rural mail delivery and county telephone lines, connect the whole county directly with the city, and serve to increase the value and attractiveness of the country districts.

Authority:—County and City Records and Personal Investigations.

ANDREW JACKSON.

Cabin Near Waxhaw, (Site now in Union, but Then in Mecklenburg), in Which Andrew Jackson, Seventh President of the United States, Was Born March 15, 1767.

CHAPTER XXXIX.

MECKLENBURG'S GREAT CITIZENS.

Sketches of the Lives of President Andrew Jackson, President James Knox Polk and Senator Zebulon Baird Vance.

Andrew Jackson, seventh President of the United States, was born in the southeastern part of Mecklenburg county, March 15, 1767. The ruins of the cabin are yet to be seen and are about six miles south of Waxhaw and five hundred yards from the South Carolina line, in what is now Union county. There, in the home of George McKemey, whose wife was a sister of Jackson's mother, the child was born. His father, Andrew Jackson, Sr., had died about a month before, and when the boy was three weeks old, his mother moved with her three children to the home of James Crawford, just over the line in South Carolina. There he lived until the invasion by Cornwallis, in 1780, when his brother, Hugh, was killed at the battle of Stono. Andrew and his brother Robert, were one day ordered by some British soldiers to black their boots. Refusing to do so, they were severely injured by the soldiers, and were sent to prison in Camden. They were soon released, but Robert died from the effect of his wounds, and Mrs. Jackson died a few days later. Andrew, left alone in the world, spent the next few years in the old Waxhaw settlement, and part of his time in Charlotte and Charleston. During this period, he attended school for a short time and acquired a rudimentary education. He was strong, healthy, self-reliant and independent. Resolving to be a lawyer, he entered the office of Spruce McKay, in Salisbury, and under the instruction of McKay, who was afterwards a judge, and Colonel John Stokes, he was prepared for the bar. His first practice was in Randolph county, in the old court house at Brown's Cross Roads, which is still standing. He left there after a year, and in 1789, was appointed solicitor of the Western district of North Carolina, and he located in that section which seven years later was made the State of Tennessee. In Nashville, he married Mrs. Robards, with whom he lived happily until her death in 1828. In 1796, Jackson was elected to Congress, and the next year he was appointed to the Senate, but resigned a year later. He was then elected a judge of the Supreme Court of Tennessee, which position he resigned in 1804, and retired to private life until the beginning of the War of 1812. In that war he made a national reputation by winning the battle of New Orleans, January 8, 1815. He was appointed commander-in-chief of the southern division of the army, and, in 1817, he conducted to a successful conclusion the Seminole War in Florida, and became Governor of the new province. In 1824, he was a candidate for President, and led all the other candidates, but the election was thrown into the House of Representatives, and John Quincy Adams was elected. Jackson defeated Adams in 1828, and he was elected for the second term, defeating Henry Clay in 1832. The most important events in his administration were his opposition to the idea of a centralized national bank controlling all government deposits and having the exclusive right of issuing national bank notes, and to nullification. In all things and at all times, he was firm almost to severity, persevering and persistent. He retired to "The Hermitage" in the Spring of 1837, and died there June 8, 1845.

POLK.

James Knox Polk, eleventh President of the United States, was born eleven miles south of Charlotte, near Little Sugar creek church, November 2, 1795. His father, Samuel Polk, who married Jane Knox, was a son of Ezekiel Polk, nephew of Thomas Polk of revolutionary fame, grandson of William Polk, and great-grandson of John Polk, and great-great-grandson of Robert Polk, who came to this country from Ireland in 1735. In 1806, the father of the President-to-be moved with his family to the southeastern part of

JAMES KNOX POLK.

Cabin Near Pineville, Mecklenburg County, in Which James Knox Polk, Eleventh President of the United States, Was Born November 2, 1795.

ZEBULON BAIRD VANCE.

Tennessee. After attending a grammar school, James Knox Polk was sent to the University of North Carolina, from which he was graduated in 1818, in the same class with Rev. R. H. Morrison, Bishop W. M. Green, H. C. Jones, Hugh Waddell, and William D. Mosely who was afterwards Governor of Florida. He did not miss a recitation during his entire college course, and received the highest honors of his class. He read law with Felix Grundy, and was licensed to practice in 1820, and was elected to Congress in 1825, remaining there for fourteen years and being Speaker from 1835 to 1838. In 1839, he was elected Governor of Tennessee, and in 1844 was elected President. In his acceptation of the nomination for President, he declared he would serve only one term, and his administration was one of glory and prosperity, being marked by the war with Mexico, which resulted in the annexation of Texas. He died in Nashville, June 15, 1849, and on his tomb are inscribed these words:

"By his public policy he defended, established, and extended the boundaries of his country. He planted the laws of the American Union on the shores of the Pacific. His influence and his councils tended to organize the National Treasury on the principles of the constitution, and to apply the rule of Freedom to navigation, trade and industry."

VANCE.

Zebulon Baird Vance, grandson of Col. David Vance who was wounded at the battle of King's Mountain, was born in Buncombe county, May 13, 1830. He was educated at Washington College, Tenn., studied law at the University of North Carolina, was admitted to the bar in 1852, and was elected county attorney the same year. Possessing a mind of comprehensive ability and a wonderfully retentive memory, he met with success in the practice of law, but his inclinations early turned his attention to politics. In all his career he was distinguished for sterling honesty, clean methods, fair and open dealing, and a manly, generous and humorous disposition. He was elected to the State Legislature as a Whig in 1854, to Congress in 1857 and in 1859, and at the end of his service in Congress, he entered the Confederate army as a captain in the Fourteenth regiment. His gallantry won the admiration of the soldiers, and in August of 1861, he was elected colonel of the Twenty-sixth regiment. In the trying days in 1860 and 1861, he was conservative and opposed secession, but when his State seceded, he was among the first to volunteer his services. In August, 1862, he was elected Governor, was re-elected in 1864, and continued in the office until the Federal forces seized the government in April, 1865. In August, 1863, he was married to Miss Harriet Epsey, by whom he had four sons. He was in Charlotte with President Davis, April 16, 1865, and then went to join his family in Statesville. He was arrested by Federal authority in May, and spent several months in the Old Capitol Prison, in Washington. He was released near the end of the year, and returned to make his home in Charlotte, and was active in patriotic work in this county for ten years. In 1876, he was nominated by the Democrats for Governor and was elected, and January 1, 1877, he took the oath of office as Governor for the third time. In 1878, he was elected and assumed the duties of United States Senator, which position he held until his death, April 14, 1894.

Notes:—This chapter is founded upon information contained in the popular biographies of the three men, from Wheeler's Reminiscences, Senator Ransom's Eulogy on Vance, Walkup's Pamphlet on the Birthplace of Jackson, and from Personal Investigations of the Birthplace of Jackson and of Polk.

	1790	SOUTHERN AGRICULTURAL DEVELOPMENT	1830	SLAVERY SYSTEM AT ITS LIMIT	1860	INDUSTRIAL DEVELOPMENT	1900
			937,000	5% A YEAR	2,100,000	2.2 % A YEAR	4,700,000
OHIO	45000	40% A YEAR					
N.Y.	340,000	11% A YEAR	1,900,000	3.37% A YEAR	3,900,000	2.5 % A YEAR	7,200,000
KY.	1,029,000	5% A YEAR	1,200,000	5% A YEAR	3,100,000	3.5% A YEAR	7,300,000
ILL. in 1810	26000	57% A YEAR	215,000	7% A YEAR	700,000	2.2% A YEAR	1,300,000
N.C.	393,000	2.1% A YEAR	737,000	1.1% A YEAR	992,000	2.2% A YEAR	1,800,000
VA.	747,000	4.5% A YEAR	1,200,000	1% A YEAR	1,500,000	1% A YEAR	1,800,000
S.C.	249,000	4.1% A YEAR	681,000	1% A YEAR	703,000	2.2% A YEAR	1,300,000
MECK.	11,000	2.5% A YEAR	20,000	NO INCREASE	17,000	5.5% A YEAR	55,000

Diagram Representing the Increase of Population in Mecklenburg and North Carolina in Four Distinct Periods in Comparison with Typical States.

CHAPTER XL.

SUMMARY.

Explanation of the Growth and Development of Mecklenburg and Charlotte Under Diverse Conditions in Different Periods, in Comparison With the United States and North Carolina.

From the time of the first Federal census, in 1790, until the twelfth, in 1900, the population of Mecklenburg county increased from 11,395 to 55,268, being a total of 385 per cent., and an annual average of 3.5 per cent. During the same period, the yearly average for the United States was 16.8 per cent., and for North Carolina, 3.4 per cent. So that though the county has not grown nearly so rapidly as the nation, its average is almost identical with that of the State, and hence its record fairly represents the result of the conditions which have existed in North Carolina. The population of the State and nation has steadily increased every year, though at times not so fast as at other times, while the population of Mecklenburg has fluctuated from 3.2 per cent. decrease to 3.9 per cent. increase. The earliest census report of the city of Charlotte was in 1860, when the population was given as 1,366. The total increase from then until 1900 was 1,225 per cent., with an annual average of 30.6 per cent. From 1870 to 1900, the increase in Charlotte averaged 24 per cent. a year; in Mecklenburg, 7 per cent.; in North Carolina, 2.5 per cent., and in the United States, 3 per cent.

Previous to the census of 1790, all sections of the country were being continuously developed. By that year, the country was well settled, and had an organized and efficient government. In the last decade of the eighteenth century, Mecklenburg's population decreased from 11,395 to 10,439. This was caused by the creation of Cabarrus, in 1792, which took about 4,000 people from Mecklenburg, but this number was almost regained within the following eight years, so that in 1800 there were only 956 less than in 1790.

By 1800, the simultaneous introduction of slavery and cotton planting had been accomplished. The invention of the cotton gin, in 1796, has been recorded as the greatest of all blessings to the South, and ultimately it may be so, but before 1860 it was nearer anything else than a blessing. It was primarily responsible for the system of slavery, which reached its limit in the South Atlantic States by 1830, and then retarded all growth until it was abolished. Cotton is now deemed a necessity, and in its manufacture it is the life of the South, but we could probably have done as well without it until we began to manufacture it.

The decade between 1800 and 1810 was the most prosperous in the county before the Civil War, the rate of increase in population being 2.5 per cent. a year. This was the result of the beginning of the cotton industry, and within that short space of time nearly all the land in the county was divided into large plantations, and there was no more room for growth. During the next twenty years, the rate of increase was 1.9 per cent. a year, and in 1830, population began to decrease, and continued to decrease one per cent. a year until 1840, and between 1840 and 1850 the annual decrease was 3.2 per cent. When the downward movement began, it was precipitated by a great emigration to the northwest and southwest, which was attributable to the desire of the people either to go where they could have more land for the operation of slavery or to escape the evils dependent upon it, which were even then being realized.

The rapid fall between 1840 and 1850 was caused by the creation of Union county in 1842, which took about 5,000 of Mecklenburg's population. The extent of emigration is shown by the facts that between 1830 and 1840, the State of Alabama increased 90 per cent. in population; Arkansas increased 221 per cent.; Illinois increased 202 per cent.; Indiana, 99 per cent.; Louisiana, 63 per cent.; Michigan, 570 per cent., and Mississippi and Missouri, 175 per cent.

each. During the same ten years, Virginia and South Carolina increased 2.3 per cent. each, and North Carolina only 2.1 per cent., thus showing quite plainly from what sections came the settlers of the northwest and southwest.

The emigration movement ended about 1850, and the thoughtful men at home, who had fully realized the futility of cotton planting as a source of wealth and prosperity, began to turn their attention to other things. Public highways and waterways were improved, canals were worked on, factories were being planned, and the revival of the long dormant interest in important phases of industry served to turn the tide of emigration. In the ten years before the war, the population increased from 13,914 to 17,374, being an annual increase of 2.5 per cent. Then came the war, which paralyzed all progress for five years, and left the county poorer in wealth and population in 1865 than it was in 1860. The increase in the State from 1840 to 1860 was at the rate of 15 per cent. every ten years.

Immediately after the war there was a revival of industrial life. Mecklenburg was favored by home seekers, because of the settled and peaceable state of affairs prevailing here, while all around was turmoil and strife. Investors and speculators and capitalists considered it an inviting field for commercial development at first, and later for industrial development. The natural resources, mines and rich soil, and the healthfulness of the climate, were attractive features. Between 1860 and 1870, the population of the county increased from 17,374 to 24,299, or 39 per cent., while the city population increased from 1,366 to 2,212, or 62 per cent., and all this increase was between 1865 and 1870, as there was no growth during the war. In the same decade, the population of the United States increased 22.6 per cent., and of North Carolina, 7.9 per cent. The growth was greater from 1870 to 1880, being 44 per cent. in the county, 32 in the city, 30.7 in the state, and 30.1 in the United States. This decade between 1870 and 1880, was the most prosperous in the history of the county, as calculated from the average annual increase of population. This growth was caused by the complete change in all phases of life, as the result of emancipation, by the stirring up of new ideas and the beginning of new things, by Charlotte's becoming a market for the exchange and distribution of all kinds of produce for wide territory which was taking on new life, and by the interest manifested in gold mining in the county which put money into circulation and built a large machinery trade in the city.

Cotton manufacturing was begun in Charlotte in 1881, and the first cotton oil mill was established in 1882. From 1880 to 1890, the increase in population was 24.9 per cent. in the United States, 15.6 in North Carolina, 24 in Mecklenburg and 62 in Charlotte. During this period, manufacturing became the chief object of interest in the development of the county and city. In the following decade, from 1890 to 1900, the manufacture of cotton assumed such proportions as to be considered the life of the community, but other manufacturing plants were being built and the manufactories were being diversified. The manufacture of clothing was developed to a degree of considerable importance, as were also the manufactures of cotton oil and machinery. The population increased in this time 20.7 per cent. in the nation, 17.1 in the State, 29 in the county and 56 in the city.

It is not difficult to comprehend the causes actuating the variability in the rate of increase in the nation, State, county and city. In order that they should be similiar, it would be necessary that at all times there should be perfect uniformity in the birth rate, death rate and immigration, which condition is obviously inconceivable. The increase in the nation is the balancing of the sundry conditions prevailing in the separate states, and it has never varied from the average more than one per cent. a year. North Carolina has varied as much as one and one-half per cent. a year, Mecklenburg county as much as two per cent., and Charlotte as much as thirty per cent. This is plainly accounted for by the fact that the conditions causing the abnormal fluctuations affect only a small section, and the smaller the section the greater is the fluctuation.

Since the first Federal census in 1790, there have been three general influences exerted. From 1790 to 1830 was the period of development in the South under the system of slavery, and the increase during the forty years averaged yearly 7.5 per cent. in the United States, and 2½ per cent. in North Carolina and in Mecklenburg county. From 1830 to 1860 was the period of retarded growth attendant upon the slavery system having reached the limit of usefulness, and the average annual increase was 8 per cent. in the nation, 1.1 in the State and less than one per cent. in the county, after having allowed for the decrease caused by the creation of Union county. It is noticeable that during this period, under the domination of slavery, the nation prospered more than during the preceding period, while the growth of the South was barely perceptible. When slavery attained to the greatest possible production of agricultural products, the North was prospering and the South was almost at a standstill. The third movement was the industrial expansion which grew from the business revival in the years following the war. Between 1880 and 1900, the increase was at the rate of 1.6 per cent. a year in the State, 2.3 in the nation, 2.9 in the county and 5.6 in the city. The fact that during this later period, the city grew faster than did the nation or State or county, is evidence of the superb natural advantages of Charlotte as a center of manufacturing industries, and is an encouraging forecast of greater things yet to come.

Note:—The statistics included in this Chapter were obtained from the Census Reports.

INDEX I

ADAMS, John Quincy 190
ALEXANDER, 38 152 Abraham
  29 31 33 46 51 73 Adam 51
  56-57 Charles 51 Cyrus 83
  Daniel 127 Elijah 72 Ezra 51
  61 George A 56 Hezekiah 56-
  57 86 Isaac 33 81 90 108 J R
  112 J W 132 James 75 James
  R 81 Jesse A 57 Joab 128
  John Mcknitt 24 46 51-52 54-
  55 91 153 Joseph 72 77
  Joseph Mcknitt 83 Moses 24
  30 36 39 75 85 Mr 53 Nathan
  90 Nathaniel 29 91 S B 170 S
  C 171 S P 131 T N 144
  Thomas 90-91 William 49 61
  Wm J 66
ALLEN, David J 108 George 32
  36
ALLISON, David 87 J J 108
  Robert G 112 114 William 91-
  92 119
ANDREWS, E H 123
ANSON, Admiral 28
ARCHIBALD, Robert 77-78
ARDREY, W E 148 174
ARGALL, Capt 3
ARMON, Andrew 70
ASBURY, D 120 Daniel 131
ASHBY, Dr 142

ASHE, John 29 Samuel 66
ATKINSON, W R 170
AVERY, Thomas A 114
  Waightstill 51 54 56-57 66
  124
BACON, 5
BADGER, J L 120
BAIRD, J G 170
BAKER, 129 Evangelist 108
BALCH, H J 77 Hezekiah 48
  Hezekiah J 47 51
BALTIMORE, Lord 3
BANCROFT, 6
BANKNIGHT, C 126
BANKS, A 160
BARBER, M H 167 Miss 168
BARNES, Rev 107 Rev Mr 109
BARNETT, William 59 80
BARR, Rev 78
BARRIER, W A 170
BARRINGER, D M 132 Matthias
  20 Paul 29 Rufus 21 152 167
  V C 114 119
BARRY, Richard 24 29 32 51 64
  Robert 89
BARTH, W 121
BATES, Mr 141 Sgt 145
BEATTY, John 90 William 89
BELK, James 157
BELL, 135

BERKELEY, Gov 4
BERKHEIM, G D 109
BETHUNE, Sallie 169 Sallie A 168
BIDDLE, Mary D 171
BIDGOOD, Capt 156
BIGHAM, John 66
BISSELL, 129 E H 146 Humphrey 173 J Humphrey 130 Z H 127
BITTLE, Rev 109
BLACK, John 90
BLACKSOCKS, William 78
BLACKWELDER, Catherine 81
BLACKWOOD, J J 131
BLAKE, J R 172
BOONE, J B 167 Mr 168
BOOTH, 48
BOWMAN, Andrew 24
BOYCE, John 109
BOYD, J D 114
BOYES, Jonah 121
BRANDON, Miss 112
BRECKINRIDGE, 135
BREM, T H 131 142 Thomas H 140 154
BREVARD, A F 119 Dr 53 Ephraim 47 51 57 80-81 R J 159
BRIDGES, James R 170
BRIGHT, John M 156
BRITTON, E H 121
BROGDEN, C H 155
BROWN, Daniel 66 John E 136
BROWNFIELD, Robert 73
BRYCE, J Y 138 152
BUCHANAN, 134
BUFORD, Col 60
BURKE, Edmund 43
BURTON, Robert 115
BURWELL, A 159 J B 115 R 166

BURWELL (cont) 170 Robert 114
BUTLER, Gen 59
BYNUM, 114 W P 159
CABOT, John 1 Sebastian 1
CALDWELL, 72 A S 165 182 D F 122 David 75 Dr 93 G W 122 132 134 Green W 132 Harper 108 J M 112 J P 154 160 P C 122 S C 107 110
CAMPBELL, 26 Col 63
CANNON, James 87
CANTZON, Doctor 80
CARLYLE, 17
CARR, A B 168
CARRAWAY, P J 165
CARROLL, Nathan B 107
CARRUTH, J 49
CARSON, J H 170 William 91 108
CARTER, James 8
CARTIER, Jacques 1
CASWELL, 61 Col 57 Gov 59 Richard 42 William 60
CATHEY, Archibald 85 George 27 85 Jean 27 Josiah 85
CHAMBERLAIN, Gov 156 Miss 112
CHAMBERS, J L 159 Maxwell 116
CHAPMAN, R H 170
CHARLES, Ii 3 Ix 4
CHARLOTTE, Queen Of England 28
CLANTON, W S 174
CLAPP, 64
CLARK, John 8 Johnston 85
CLAY, Henry 190
CLEVELAND, Col 63
CLINGMAN, Gen 157
COLUMBUS, Christopher 1

COOK, John 89 W F 152
COPPLES, W 68
CORLEW, J T 169
CORNWALLIS, 62 64 73 189
  Lord 61 63
COWAN, David 90-91 R C 119
COWLES, Calvin 174
COX, Gen 157 W R 156
CRAIGE, Burton 118
CRAIGHEAD, 76-77 Alexander 25 75
CRAMER, Stuart W 174
CRAWFORD, James 189 James Lewis 92 Samuel C 120
CRITTENDEN, J A 115
CRONER, Frederick 83
CULPEPPER, 5 John 109 John M M 108
CUMMINS, Alexander 82 Elizabeth 72
CUNNINGHAM, H B 122
DARE, Virginia 2
DAVIDSON, A B 182 E C 122 Ephraim B 68 Gen 61 64 George 56 J M 123 John 33 42 51 56-57 Judge 156 Margaret 91 Sarah 114 W F 135 146 154 William 57 90-91 93 116 119 William Lee 115 119 128
DAVIE, 61-62 64 113 William R 59 Wm R 66
DAVIS, Jefferson 152 President 141 192 S W 135-136 149
DAYTON, Mary 114
DEGRAFFENREID, Baron 5
DELLINGER, Valentine 80
DENNY, J C 112
DEWEY, F H 182 T W 157 Thomas W 131
DICKENS, 26

DIEHL, Patricia S 13
DOBBS, Arthur 29 Gov 10-12 16 20 70 75 84
DONNELL, Thomas 82
DOUGLASS, 135
DOWD, 159 C 146 157 167 W C 160
DOWNS, Henry 51
DOYLE, Maj 62-63
DRAYTON, Thomas F 156
DUNLAP, D R 108 114 Samuel C 83
DUNN, 48
DURANT, 5 Elder 108
DYSART, Dr 81
ELIZABETH, Queen Of England 2
ELLIS, Gov 136 J W 121 135 John W 126
EMBERSON, Henry 90
EPSEY, Harriet 192
ESTILL, C P 114
EVVETTE, Adolphus 112
FAIRES, Joseph 91
FANNING, Edmund 38 72 77
FANOLI, 130
FERGUSON, Moses 70 Patrick 63
FEW, James 39
FLEMING, W W 157
FLENNEGIN, James 36 John 51
FLOYD, Matthew 29
FORD, John 51 87
FOSTER, Henry 29
FOX, C J 122 James A 122
FRAZIER, 140
FREEMAN, 92 J F W 108 J W F 112 114
FREW, Mary Ann 112
FROHOCK, John 31 36
FRONTIS, Stephen 115
FROUDE, Mr 16
FULLINGS, E 145

FULTON, James 120
FURMAN, Rev 107
GAGNEY, Col 64
GAITHER, B S 132
GALES, Seaton 156
GATES, Gen 58 61
GEORGE III, King Of England 28
GIBBON, John H 132 R L 159
   Robert 122
GILBERT, Humphrey 2
GLENN, Gideon 132
GOLDSDEN, Ex-president 126
GOULD, Miss 112
GRAHAM, 64 A 119 Alexander
   169 Col 57 Ex-gov 114 George
   49 56 62 90 H G 111 Joseph
   61-62 64 92 122 154-155 157
   Maj 62 William 156 William A
   122
GRANT, 13
GRANVILLE, Lord 6
GREEN, Gen 58 W M 191
GREENE, Gen 95
GRIER, Isaac 110 119 Margaret
   111 W W 146
GRIFFITH, M S 168 R H 166
GRIMES, Bryan 156
GRUNDY, Felix 191
GUION, B S 152
HAGLER, 9-10 King 8
HAGOOD, Johnson 156
HAIGH, Charles 156
HAIGHT, N 143
HALL, James 72
HAMBRIGHT, Col 63
HAMPTON, George 91 J W 120
HANGER, Maj 62
HANNA, George B 165
HAPPOLDT, J M 123
HARNETT, Cornelius 54 56
HARRINGTON, J W 114

HARRIS, Charles 82 Dr 83 J B S
   131 James 51 Maj 75 Mayor
   144 Richard 51 Robert 29-30
   S A 144 Samuel A 134
   Thomas 67 Wade H 160
   William S 121
HARRISON, J K 122 John 131
HARVEY, John 42
HASELL, Chief Justice 27 James
   29
HEINEMAN, J 152
HENDERSON, Archibald 92 Dr
   83 Kerns 72 Richard 66
   Samuel 130 Thomas 80-81
HENDRICKS, Gov 157
HENRY, Patrick 18 29
HENTON, Frank M 144
HEPBURN, A D 172
HERRICK, J E 135
HEWES, Joseph 42
HILL, Col 140 D H 114 139 151
   154 157
HILTON, S H 177
HOGG, Thomas J 131
HOLDEN, 150 Gov 143 146
HOLLIDAY, W A 171
HOLMES, 96 98 Hodgen 95
HOLTON, 120
HOOD, Robert 91 T 87
HOOPER, William 42 44
HOUSTON, James 54
HOWE, Col 56
HUNTER, Humphrey 46 110
   John 109 John D 153 W M
   165
HUSBANDS, 39 Herman 38
HUTCHINS, Anthony 29
HUTCHISON, S D Nye 114 S Nye
   122
IREDELL, James 44
IRWIN, Hugh 66 85 J F 119 John

IRWIN (cont)
119 Robert 51 55 64 S W 112
JACK, Capt 49 James 48
JACKSON, 190 Andrew 60 68 92
189 Andrew Sr 189 Hugh 189
Mrs 60 189 Robert 189
JAMES I, King Of England And
Scotland 17
JEFFERSON, Thomas 18 44
JENKINS, Rev Mr 108
JETTON, J E 147
JOHNSON, Jennie E 163 W F
172 William 136 138
JOHNSTON, 159 Bradley T 156
Cyrus 108 114 121 M D 116 R
D 152 Sue M 168 W D 114
William 119 146 155 157 176
Wm 141
JONATHAN, James 79
JONES, 159 C R 160 Col 146 Dr
174 E P 157 H C 146 154 191
Hamilton C 140 Isaac W 173 J
160
JUSTICE, Francis 160
KEAHEY, W J 119
KENNEDY, F M 142 Joseph 54
80 Samuel 87
KENNON, Col 48 William 47 51
56
KERR, J B 119 John 156
Josephine C 114 W 136
William 83
KING, C B 171
KIRKPATRICK, J L 172 T M 111
KNOX, James 69 Jane 190 John
16-17
KOCH, R H A 112
LANE, Drury 116 J H 140 James
H 139 Jas H 114
LATTA, E D 159
LAZELLE, H M 144 146

LEAK, D R 152
LEAVENWORTH, A J 107-108
113-114
LEE, 64 C C 114 140 Charles C
139 Gen 141 Lieut 136 R E
152
LEWIS, Alexander 29
LINCOLN, 135-136 142 President
138 141
LITTLEJOHN, R N 165
LOCKE, Francis 60 91 George 62
LOGAN, Judge 147
LONG, Lily 170
LOUIS XVI, 19
LOWRIE, S J 119 136 Samuel 90
LUCAS, M N 167 Miss 168 W A
131
LUTHER, 20
LYTTLETON, Gov 12
MACAULAY, A 182
MADISON, James 133
MAGINNIS, John 109 112
MARSHALL, 114
MARTIN, 53 68 Col 57 Gov 33
42-44 49 73 Josiah 41 63
Judge 52 S Taylor 170 Samuel
54
MASON, Winfield 91
MATHISON, 112
MATTOON, S 171
MCADEN, 76 Hugh 16 75
MCCAFFERTY, Jeremiah 24 33
68
MCCAULE, Thomas H 77
MCCLENAHAN, Robert 29
MCCORKLE, Dr 72
MCCULLOH, 27 36 Henry 6
Henry Eustace 31 35
MCDOUGAL, 127
MCDOWELL, Col 63 F B 176 F H
119 R I 182

MCEWEN, John 73
MCGINTY, Alexander 68
MCILWAINE, Dr 122
MCINTYRE, 62
MCIVER, A 144
MCKAY, Spruce 66 189
MCKELWAY, A J 160 163
MCKEMEY, George 189
MCKENZIE, Dr 93
MCKINNEY, R M 114 140
MCKINNON, Luther 172
MCKNIGHT, James 109
MCLURE, Matthew 51
MCOMB, Samuel 129
MCPHAIL, G W 172
MCQUISTON, J C 144
MCREE, James 77 Rev 78
MCWHORTER, Dr 73
MERRIMON, Sen 157
MILES, Pliny 112
MILLER, A W 108 156 J M 140 Robert 29 S C 167 S H 168 W G 171
MILLS, C 156 Daniel 79 J C 156
MITCHELL, T J 169
MONTGOMERY, J C 159
MOORE, Andrew 108 Charles 70 Col 56 Hattie 167 Miss 168 T J 148 156-157
MORGAN, John H 141
MORRISON, Neil 51 R H 107 110 115-116 191 W 131 William 9 83
MOSELY, William D 191
MUNROE, J P 171
MYERS, W C 171 W R 131
NASH, Fred 169 Gov 63
NEEL, James 89 W H 127
NEGRO, Ben 87 Jack 91
NEWMAN, Dr 80
NICHOLAS, Col 3

NICHOLSON, Joseph 67
NORMAN, A A 122
NORRIS, James 36
O'CONNELL, J J 109
O'REILLY, M 122
OATES, Brawley 108 D W 182 J E 182 J M 182 R M 182
OCHILTREE, 68 Duncan 67
OGLETHORPE, John Newman 80
ORR, J H 154 Joe 147
OSBORNE, Adlai 66 Adlai L 91 Alexander 8 Edwin Jay 90 J W 122 146 159 James W 118-119 126 132 136 146
OWEN, H C 132
OWENS, Thomas 108 William A 140
PACKARD, Col 144
PALMER, J D 127 President 126
PARHAM, William 122
PARKER, Eliza 111 Rev Mr 109
PARKEY, John B 111
PARKS, D 131 David 107-108 Sarah J 111 Wilson 127
PARRISH, C S 144
PASS, E A 139
PATTERSON, John 71 92 William 33
PATTON, Benjamin 42 51 56 James 29 William L 121
PENMAN, Thomas 131
PENN, William 3
PEOPLES, Hugh 121
PHARR, S C 110
PHIFER, 39 John 51 54-57 115 Martin 29-33 42 57 73 William 141
PIERCE, Franklin 134
PINCKNEY, W D 127
PITT, Felix 80
PLUMER, W S 163

POLK, 38-39 64 68 Charles 57
Col 46 48 Ezekiel 56 69 190
James 72 James Knox 69 122
190-191 Jane 190 John 190
Leonidas 141 Robert 190
Samuel 69 190 Thomas 24 29
31-33 36 42 44-45 51 54 56-
57 67 72-73 77 141 157 190
Thomas G 93 128 Thomas Jr
58 William 56-58 190
POMEROY, T C 114
POPE, D Kirby 174
POTTS, J W 135 James 90
POWERS, A G 112
PRESSLY, G W 159 W B 111
PRICE, Henry 90
PRITCHARD, 122 146 H M 120
135 143
PROBST, Henry 81
PROSSER, Mr 121
PYLE, 64
RALIEGH, Walter 2
RAMSEY, Joseph 83 Robert 29
RANSON, Alexander 109
RAWDON, Gen 60
RAY, John 91
RAYMOND, 121
REED, Allen 66 Conrad 129
REESE, David 51 Rev 77
REGISTER, E C 159
REID, 134 E L 170 J S 146-147
RICHARDSON, Gen 57
RICHMOND, Charles 91
RIVAFANOLI, Chevalier 129
ROBARDS, Mrs 190
ROBINSON, D C 122 Dr 72
James 29 James B 136 John
115
ROSS, E A 140
RUDISILL, J C 122 Susan 111
RUGER, Maj-gen 143

RUTHERFORD, Col 57 Gen 20
60-61 64
SAMPLE, 152 John 86 Joseph 72
SANDERS, D J 172
SAUNDERS, S W 170
SAVERS, P 127
SELWYN, 35-36 Augustus 31
SEMMES, Raphael 141
SETTLE, 147
SEVIER, Col 63
SHANNON, Dr 121
SHARPE, John 90
SHEARER, J B 172
SHELBY, Col 63
SHERMAN, 141
SHIPP, W M 154 159 William M
146
SHOTWELL, R A 148
SIBLEY, John 83
SINCLAIR, Alexander 108
SLAVE, Alpheus 87 Ben 87
Charlotte 87 Daphne 87 Dice
87 Dinah 87 Ephraim 91
Farrabo 87 Hannah 87 Jack
87 Jacob 87 Joe 87 Joseph 87
Josiah 87 Julius 87 Juno 87
Moses 91 Phebe 87 Plumb 87
Prince 87 Prudence 87
Romulus 87 Sam 87 Simon 87
Sylvia 87 Terah 87 Titus 87
Weyer 87 Will 87
SMITH, 113 160 Andrew 143
Capt 157 F L 119 Henry Louis
172 William 93 Wm 66
SPARROW, P J 115-116
SPEARS, J C 119
SPENCER, Gustavus 115 Samuel
66
SPRATT, Joseph 91
SPRINGS, Leroy 114 134
STACY, A G 166

STAGG, J W 163
STEELE, A C 131
STEVENSON, Andrew 53
STEWART, Andrew 17
STILLWELL, S N 145
STOCKTON, Commodore 131
STOKES, John 189 Joseph 109
STRAIN, William 82
STRONACH, A B 155
SUMMERS, James 91
SUMNER, 61 Gen 63
TARLETON, Lieut-col 60
TAYLOR, 122 R F 111 Zachary 134
THOM, 26
THOMAS, Brig-gen 143 Gen 144 J P 170 John 29
THOMPSON, James 62 John 75
TOMPKINS, D A 160
TOOLE, Matthew 8
TRICE, Archibald 91
TRUSLOW, W A 165
TRYON, Gov 34 36 38-39 43 72 William 37
VAIL, T L 176
VANCE, 146 148 150 159 David 191 Ex-gov 152 Gov 141 Harriet 192 Z B 147 154 157 Zebulon Baird 191
VANE, Gov 141 John 121
VESPUCIUS, Americus 1
WADDELL, 13 Gen 39 Hugh 11-12 36 38 191
WADSWORTH, J W 152
WAHAB, Capt 61
WAINE, Edward 68
WAIT, Rev 109
WALKER, Ex-gov 157 John 135
WALKUP, James 87

WALLACE, M L 136 M W 135
WALLIS, James 78 110-111
WALSH, F A 167 Miss 168
WALTERS, James 72
WARING, 121 Mrs 168 R P 120 144 146-147 168 174 S E 167
WARNER, Col 144 Willard 143
WASHINGTON, 59 Col 64 Gen 18 43 49 58 George 69
WATSON, 160 Samuel 56
WATT, 77-78
WEBSTER, 113
WHARTON, S D 112
WHEELER, John H 132 157
WHITE, Henry 75 J H 134 W E 134
WHITFIELD, 76
WHITLEY, R D 146
WHITNEY, 96 98 Eli 95
WILEY, Calvin H 166
WILKES, Adm 131 John 151 167
WILLIAMS, Catherine 152 Col 63 H B 131 L S 139
WILLIAMSON, A C 120 136 D R 122 Hugh 52 John 110 Samuel 115-116
WILSON, David 58 64 Dr 72 E 113 J H 122 131 136 151 154 157 159 James H 119 John 87 John Kemey 72 Samuel Sr 64 Zaccheus 51
WINSTON, Col 63 W L 119
WOODS, E H 152
WORTH, 144
WRIGHT, J W 160
YATES, E A 139 W J 154 William J 135
YOUNG, Gen 136 J A 154 John A 126 146 151 176 Joseph 115

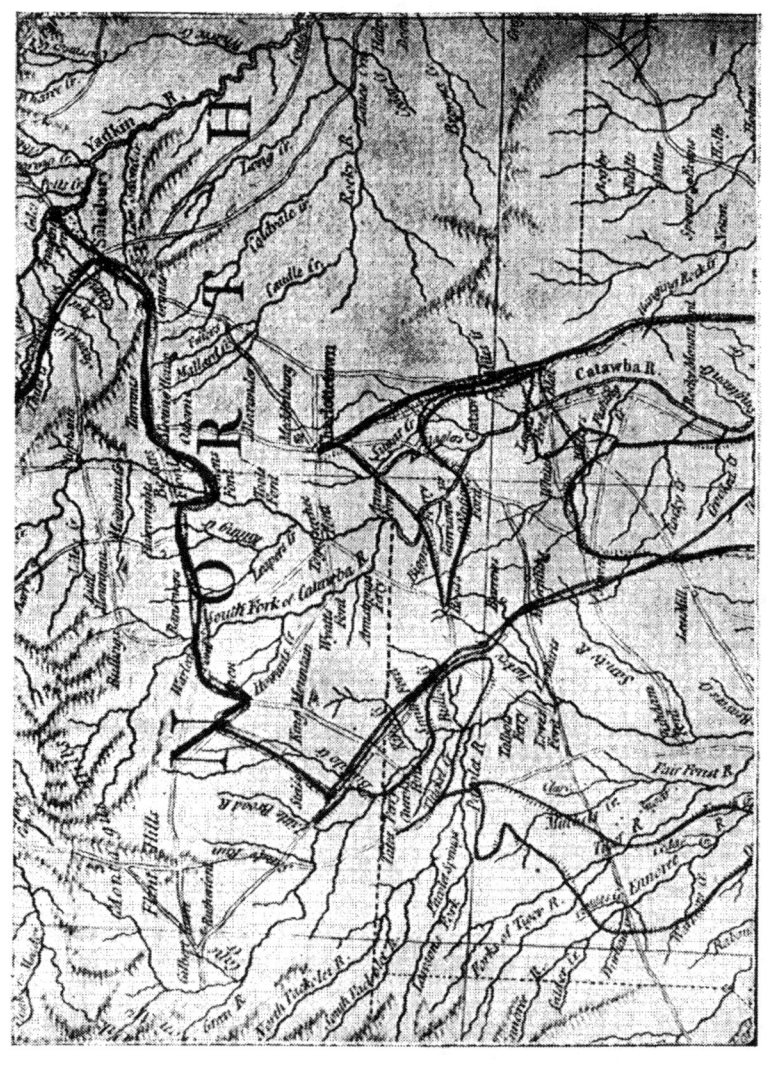

BRITISH MAP OF MECKLENBURG IN 1780.

History of Mecklenburg County

AND

The City of Charlotte

From 1740 to 1903.

BY D. A. TOMPKINS,

Author of COTTON AND COTTON OIL; COTTON MILL, COMMERCIAL FEATURES; COTTON VALUES IN TEXTILE FABRICS; COTTON MILL, PROCESSES AND CALCULATIONS; *and* AMERICAN COMMERCE, ITS EXPANSION.

CHARLOTTE, N. C., 1903.

VOLUME TWO—APPENDIX.

CHARLOTTE, N. C.:
OBSERVER PRINTING HOUSE.
1903.

COPYRIGHT, 1904.
BY
D. A. TOMPKINS.

EXPLANATION.

This history is published in two volumes. The first volume contains the simple narrative, and the second is in the nature of an appendix, containing ample discussions of important events, a collection of biographies and many official documents justifying and verifying the statements in this volume. At the end of each chapter is given the sources of the information therein contained, and at the end of each volume is an index.

PREFACE.

One of the rarest exceptions in literature is a production devoid of personal feeling. Few indeed are the men, who, realizing that the responsibility for their writings will be for them alone to bear, will not utilize the advantage for the promulgation of things as they would like them to be. Many of the works of the Ancients fail to stand the test of modern historical criticism because the advancing conception of historical labors is getting farther and farther from discursive analysis and closer and closer to the presentation of plain, unvarnished facts.

"History is philosophy teaching by example," says Dionysins, and it is obvious that if we are to "judge the future by the past," that the main requisite is a complete record. "To study history," says Wilmot, "is to study literature. The biography of a nation contains all its works. No trifle is to be neglected. A mouldering medal is a letter of twenty centuries. Antiquities which have been beautifully called history defaced, composed its fullest commentary."

Parton, in the preface to his Life of Jackson, gives an apt illustration of the true historian's duty. A young clergyman, fresh from the university, became rector of one of the oldest of English parishes. Examining his church, he found that a crust was falling from the walls. The wardens suggested whitewash, but the new rector discovered that whitewash had been applied too many times already, and that it was these surplus coats which were falling.

Thereupon, he resolved that instead of applying more, he would remove that already on the walls. When this was done, the beautiful frescoes which had been obscured for many years were exposed to the view. These paintings, some of them by the world's greatest artists, had been hidden in order that the cracks might be filled. The true beauty of the structure had been sacrificed to hide the natural results of man's imperfect work. After the restoration, the defects marred the glory of the decorations, yet it left a subject for study even if not for unqualified admiration. And above all, those viewing it could be possessed of the consciousness that they were beholding the truth—displeasing though it might be—yet unquestionably and plainly the truth.

It is not for the writer of history to decide what shall and what shall not be recorded, any more than it is justifiable for a church-member to accept certain articles of his religion and repudiate the others; each must be all-inclusive or of no importance. As a consequence, it is not within the proper bounds of historical endeavor to be argumentative. The person who investigates and accumulates facts for the purpose of strengthening his pre-conceived opinions is not a historian. History's worst enemy is the writer who distorts facts to bolster prejudice. Histories should not be intended to convince, but to enlighten. The true historian's duty is to uncover the naked truth, and though this be a disagreeable task, it is duty nevertheless. In the words of Lord Bacon, the reader should "Reade not to Contradict, and Confute; Nor to Beleeve and Take for granter; Nor to Finde Talke and Discourse; But to Weigh and Consider."

In this History of Mecklenburg County, the author has endeavored to present an historical record, not an historical discussion. "Facts are stubborn," and when they are all in hand, it is well to let them speak for themselves.

D. A. TOMPKINS.

December 1, 1903.

CONTENTS.

Page.

CHAPTER I. 1
MECKLENBURG DECLARATION CONTROVERSY.

Brief Outline of the Discussion—Extract from Wheeler's History.—Charlotte *Democrat* of July 8, 1873—Preface to Martin's History of North Carolina—Correspondence Between Adams and Jefferson—Extracts from the Raleigh *Register*—Certificates of Men who Knew of the Convention—Instructions to Mecklenburg Delegates—Three Copies of the Declaration and the Resolves of May 31—Hitherto Unpublished Correspondence Between John Vaughn, Hon. Peter Force, Gov. D. L. Swain and Hon. George Bancroft—References and List of Publications on the Subject.

CHAPTER II. 57
MECKLENBURG INDEPENDENCE MONUMENT.

Unveiling in Charlotte in 1898 Attended with Impressive Ceremonies.—Hon. Adlai E. Stevenson was Orator of the Occasion.—First Monument Association Incorporated in 1842.—Declaration Poem by Rev. W. W. Moore, of Virginia.

CHAPTER III. 60
"BLACK BOYS" OF CABARRUS.

Young Men Destroyed Ammunition and Supplies Intended for Use Against the Regulators.—Gov. Tryon's Proclamation of Pardon Excepted Them.—Leading Citizens Later Petitioned in Their Behalf and Secured the Pardon.—Col. Moses Alexander Presented the Petition.

CHAPTER IV. 64
BIOGRAPHICAL SKETCHES.

Condensed Items of Interest in the Lives of Persons Prominent in Mecklenburg History.—Brief Biographies Alphabetically Arranged.

CHAPTER V. 84
ANDREW JACKSON'S BIRTHPLACE.

Born in that Part of Mecklenburg Which was Made Into Union in 1842.—Moved Over Into South Carolina When a Few Weeks Old.—Evidence of Those Who Were Present at His Birth.—Col. E. H. Walkup's Publication.

HISTORY OF MECKLENBURG COUNTY.

CHAPTER VI. 87
CUSTOMS OF THE PIONEERS.
Amusements of the Settlers of Mecklenburg.—County Muster and Assemblies.—Horse Racing and Betting.—Liquor Used Freely at Home and at Public Places.—The Old Taverns and Their Uses.

CHAPTER VII...................................92
EIGHTEENTH CENTURY MONEY. (1762 to 1800.)
First Settlers Used Pennsylvania and Virginia Currency.—Paper Money Discounted Nearly One-third.—Many Kinds of Coins Used.—Federal Currency Established in 1792.

CHAPTER VIII..................................96
NOTES ON THE REGULATION.
Miscellaneous Information Summarized in Paragraphs.—The March of Mecklenburg Troops to Hillsboro.—Governor Tryon's Visit in the County.—Sentiment Pertaining to the Regulators and the Governor.

CHAPTER IX...................................100
NOTES ON CHAPTER II. (The Indians.)
Items Regarding Important Events.—Very Few Relics Found in Mecklenburg.—Correspondence Between Governors of North Carolina and South Carolina Respecting the Catawba.

CHAPTER X....................................104
NOTES ON CHAPTER XV. (Religion.)
Coming of Rev. Hugh McAden.—Rev. Alexander Craighead Withdraws from the Presbyterian Synod and Comes to North Carolina.—Established Church of England Met With Much Discouragement in Mecklenburg.

CHAPTER XI...................................109
HISTORY OF MINING IN MECKLENBURG.
Historic Anticipations—Discoveries in Florida—First Find in the County—Geology of Mecklenburg—Development of Mining—Statistics of the Branch Mint in Charlotte.

CONTENTS. VII

CHAPTER XII..............................132

MECKLENBURG COUNTY REPRESENTATIVES.

Complete List of the Members of the General Assembly From This County From 1764 to 1903.—Martin Phifer and Richard Barry Were the First.

CHAPTER XIII.............................135

MECKLENBURG TROOPS IN THE WAR OF 1812.

Five Companies Sent From This County to the War with England Caused by the Searching of American Vessels for British Sailors.—A Total of Four Hundred and Thirty-Three Enlisted Men.*

CHAPTER XIV..............................142

CIVIL WAR TROOPS.

Roster of Officers and Men of the Twenty-one Companies Sent From This County.—2,735 Soldiers and Only 2,021 Voters.—Number Killed, Wounded or Died.*—List of Promotions.

CHAPTER XV...............................180

MECKLENBURG'S PART IN THE MEXICAN WAR.

Roster of the Troops in the Company Organized in Charlotte in April of 1847.*—Green W. Caldwell was Captain and He and the Lieutenants Were Honored by Seats in the General Assembly After the End of the War.—The Total Number of the Soldiers was Seventy-nine, and Eleven of Them Died in the Service.

CHAPTER XVI..............................183

THE SPANISH-AMERICAN WAR.

Account of the Service Rendered by Mecklenburg Troops.—Rosters of the Three White Companies and the Colored Company.*—Charlotte Soldiers Among the First Americans to Land in Havana.

VIII   HISTORY OF MECKLENBURG COUNTY.

CHAPTER XVII 192

LIST OF MINISTERS.

Names of the Preachers who have Served the Leading Churches of Charlotte, With the Number of Years of Service of Each.

CHAPTER XVIII 195

DAVIDSON.

A Brief Sketch of the Progressive Town Which Has Grown up Around the College.—Has Macadam Streets and Factories, and a Large Business is Done.—The Corporation Dates From 1879.

CHAPTER XIX 198

PINEVILLE.

Brief Sketch of the Growth of the Town Which was Built Where President Polk was Born.—In Fifty Years it has Developed Into a Prosperous Community With Factories and a Population of Seven Hundred.—Creditable Churches and Schools, and Names of Some Prominent Families.

CHAPTER XX 200

MISCELLANEOUS PAPERS.

Characteristics of the Mecklenburg Negro.—Comparative Effects of Slavery and Freedom on the Increase of Population.—Tribute to the Memory of Major Ross.—Important Dates in Mecklenburg History.—List of Mayors of Charlotte.—Acts of the General Assembly Creating Mecklenburg, Establishing Charlotte and Permanently Locating the Court House.—County Road Legislation.

INDEX TO ILLUSTRATIONS.

British Map of Mecklenburg in 1780	Frontispiece
Claremont Academy	1
Sugar Creek Church	1
Signatures of Prominent Characters in Mecklenburg History	16-33
Coat of Arms of the Phifer family, 1760	44
Proclamation Money	44
Receipt, 1773	56
Receipt Signed by Thos. Polk in 1773	56
Monument Commemorating the McIntyre Skirmish, Oct. 3, 1780	60
Mrs. Rachel Holton	64
Thos. J. Holton, Editor of the Charlotte Journal	64
James W. Osborne	67
William Davidson	69
Henry Bartlett Williams	71
W. E. Phifer	72
General Hugh Waddell	74
General Joseph Graham	76
David Parks	78
Lieutenant E. C. Davidson	81
W. F. Davidson	82
Map of Vicinity of Jackson's Birthplace	84
Old Wilson Place	86
Alexander Rock House	86
Extracts from Copy Books in use in Mecklenburg County Schools in 1850	88
Note Given in 1767	90
Bill for Teaching, 1822	90
Sale Notice, 1838	92
Contract, 1767	94
Confederate Currency, 1864	96
North Carolina Currency, 1866	100
Itemized Bill for "Learning," 1798	102
United States Bank Note	104
Revolutionary Currency	112
Revolutionary State Money	132
Tomb of Thomas Polk	135
Receipt, 1783	135
Bill of Account, 1767	140

INDEX TO ILLUSTRATIONS.

Bill for Subscription, 1792	144
Stage Line Way-Bill, 1846	160
United States Currency	180
State Currency	184
Contract Dated in 1737	192
Revolutionary Currency	196
Contract, 1765	197
Negro Passes	199
Bill of Sale, 1747	204
Arab-African	208
Saracen-African	208
Dinka-Negro	209
Guinea-Negro	209

CLAREMONT ACADEMY.
(Volume I., Page 166.)

SUGAR CREEK CHURCH.
(See Index to Volume I.)

CHAPTER I.

MECKLENBURG DECLARATION CONTROVERSY.

Brief Outline of the Discussion—Extract from Wheeler's History.—Charlotte *Democrat* of July 8, 1873—Preface to Martin's History of North Carolina—Correspondence Between Adams and Jefferson—Extracts from the Raleigh *Register*—Certificates of Men who Knew of the Convention—Instructions to Mecklenburg Delegates—Three Copies of the Declaration and the Resolves of May 31—Hitherto Unpublished Correspondence Between John Vaughn, Hon. Peter Force, Gov. D. L. Swain and Hon. George Bancroft—References and List of Publications on the Subject.

The controversy regarding the Mecklenburg Declaration of Independence has occupied the time and attention of many of America's most profound thinkers and writers. Some of them contend that the evidence is sufficient, while others maintain that it is not sufficient and that the actual Declaration of Independence was not made as is claimed.

Conclusive proof of a historical proposition depends upon contemporaneous records, personal testimony of reliable persons acquainted with the facts, and traditions. Now, suppose at this late date, some one should question the authenticity of the National Declaration of Independence, made in Philadelphia, July 4, 1776. First would be shown a verbatim copy of the real original which was signed July 4, 1776, and in the days following as new delegates arrived. Then there would be the contemporaneous periodicals, personal correspondence and the known trend of public sentiment toward independence. In proof of the Mecklenburg Declaration, we have all this and in addition, the specific statements of a dozen men who were present and participated in the proceedings. Why is it, then, that there was ever any doubt regarding the action of the people of Mecklenburg?

In the first place, at the time the Mecklenburg Declaration was made, each part of the country was too busy with home affairs to pay much attention to outside matters. There were but few newspapers in this section, yet the *Cape Fear Mercury* and the Charleston *Gazette and Country Journal* mentioned the proceedings. The men of the county were busy with preparations for war, and as every one concerned knew of the action, there was naturally no reason to make superfluous records. The official papers were burned in the fire which destroyed John McKnitt Alexander's house in 1800. The National Declaration was made fourteen months after the Mecklenburg Declaration and, of course, overshadowed the action of the latter until long after the smoke of battle had cleared away. Consequently, there was but little contemporaneous evidence, and when the Mecklenburg Declaration became of national interest in 1819, most of the antagonism to it was based on the false belief that the trend of sentiment in North Carolina was not so strong in 1775 as to render probable a declaration of independence, and not until the publication of the Colonial Records, in recent years, was the falsity of that belief established. These records show, by correspondence and other official documents, that Thomas Jefferson was conservative in his statement to John Adams that "No State was more fixed or forward than North Carolina."* The people of the State, acting independently, convened a congress at New Bern in August, 1774. Gov. Martin left the State and royal authority ended in North Carolina in June, 1775. The Battle of Moore's Creek Bridge was fought February 27, 1776, and the Fourth Provincial Congress, held at Halifax in April, 1776, declared for independence. So it appears not only natural that Mecklenburg should declare her independence, but that she *was* independent and with a government of her own from May 20, 1775. It is to be remembered also, that Mecklenburg then was about five times the present size, and that the proceedings of the convention were participated in by represen-

---

*Correspondence, July 9, 1819.

tative men from other sections, so that while the Declaration could not be construed as a State document, yet it unquestionably represented the attitude of the entire State. All North Carolina was independent, but only Mecklenburg made an official declaration of the fact.

In the latter part of the year 1818, the subject was under discussion among the North Carolina representatives in Congress, and Nathaniel Macon, William Davidson and others corresponded with representative men of this section, the correspondence being published in the Raleigh *Register* in 1819, and in the Essex (Mass.) *Register* of June 5, 1819, and in other papers. The Essex *Register* fell into the hands of John Adams and resulted in the letters regarding the subject between Adams and Jefferson. Jefferson's Writings and Martin's History of North Carolina were published in 1829, and the discussion was reopened. In 1831, the State issued a pamphlet under direction of a legislative committee, which was designed to forever settle all dispute regarding the declaration.

With the people of Mecklenburg, there had never been any doubt, as the old traditions were firmly and generally established. In 1809, nearly ten years before the controversy began, the Raleigh *Minerva* published the declamation of a school boy, William Wallace, at Sugar Creek Academy, delivered June 1, 1809. The teacher was Rev. Samuel C. Caldwell, a son-in-law of John McKnitt Alexander. The declamation began: "On the 19th of May, a day sacredly exulting to every Mecklenburg bosom, two delegates duly authorized from each militia company met in Charlotte. After a cool and deliberate investigation of the causes and extent of our differences with Great Britain, and taking a review of probable results, pledging their all in support of its rights and liberties, they solemnly entered into and published a full and determined Declaration of Independence, renouncing forever all allegiance, dependence, or connection with Great Britain, dissolved all judicial and military establishments emanating from the British Crown, and established others on principles corresponding with their declaration, which went into immediate operation, all of which was transmitted to Congress by express, and probably expedited the general Declaration of Independence. May we ever act worthy of such predecessors!"

On December 18, 1838, Colonel Peter Force, a distinguished antiquarian, found in the New York *Journal* of June 29, 1775, a portion of certain resolves by the people of Mecklenburg, made in May, 1775. He found a second copy in the Massachusetts *Spy* of July 12, 1775. William Kelby, assistant librarian of the New York Historical Society, found that the New York *Journal* had copied the resolves from a Charleston paper. The Northern papers had copied the first four resolves, with the preamble, and had summarized the others. At the instance of Gov. Swain, Dr. Joseph Johnston found in the Charleston library a copy of the South Carolina *Gazette and Country Journal* of Tuesday, June 13, 1775. About the same time, Mr. Bancroft, then American minister to Great Britain, discovered the same number of the South Carolina *Gazette,* which had been forwarded to the British government by the Governor of Georgia, accompanied by the following letter: "By the enclosed paper, your Lordship will see the extraordinary resolves of the people of Charlotte-town, in Mecklenburg county, and I should not be surprised if the same should be done everywhere else."

The original copy was destroyed in the fire which burned the house of John McKnitt Alexander. A copy of the original was sent before the burning of the house to the historian, Williamson, in New York, and it, together with the other sources of his history, were destroyed by a fire in that city. John McKnitt Alexander wrote the Declaration from memory, and with the exception of some superfluous adjectives, it is presumed to be a fairly accurate copy. This was sent to Gen. William R. Davie and recovered after his death, and is now in the library at Chapel Hill. It is known as the Davie copy. The Martin copy is so called from its publication in Martin's History of North Carolina. This book was published in 1829, but it was prepared, in final form, before 1809. A third copy, called the Garden copy, was published in 1828 by Alexander Garden'* of Lee's Legion, and this is almost exactly identical with the Martin copy, which is regarded as the authentic copy. Garden could not have gotten it from Martin's History, which was published a year later, and Martin testifies to Dr. Hawkes that he did not get his copy from Garden, and did not know that Garden had a copy. Garden was an intimate friend and associate of Dr. William Read, of Charleston, who was a surgeon-general of Greene's army, and was stationed in Charlotte during the Revolution, and who attended Dr. Ephraim Brevard in his last sickness at the house of John McKnitt Alexander. Garden had, therefore, ample opportunity for obtaining at first hand the sources of information for his chapter on the Mecklenburg Declaration, in which Dr. Read is mentioned as the source of his information.

While Martin's history was published in 1829, the author testifies in the preface that he had gathered the materials for this history before 1809, when he was sent to the Mississippi Territory by President Madison. And that being warned by an attack of sickness, that he might not live to publish the history, he determined "to put the work immediately to press in the condition it was in when it reached New Orleans." The references he makes are to "Records, Magazines, Gazettes." No one can read the Colonial Records, lately published, and then read the digest of them in Martin's History, without being struck with the accuracy and impartiality of his story. As to this particular document of the Mecklenburg Declaration, Martin testified in a conversation with Rev. F. L. Hawkes, D. D., that he had obtained it "in the western part of the State prior to the year 1800."** Judge Francis Xavier Martin, LL. D., was an eminent jurist and

---

*Garden's Anecdotes of the Revolution.
**"The Mecklenburg Declaration of Independence," an Address by Dr. Hawks in New York, December 16, 1852. Published in "Revolutionary History of North Carolina," 1853.

scholar who emigrated from France to America in 1782, and settled in New Bern. By a resolution of the Assembly, he was employed to compile and edit the "British Statutes" of North Carolina, and devoted the years 1791-92 to that work. He was engaged by the Legislature, in 1794, and again in 1803, to edit the private acts of the Assembly. All this time he was gathering materials for his history of North Carolina, and must have known those members of the Assembly from Mecklenburg who were participants in the scenes of the 19th and 20th of May, such as Robert Irwin, James Harris, William Polk, George Graham, and Joseph Graham. In 1806-7, he was a member of the Legislature and again associated with George Graham, and Nathaniel Alexander, Mecklenburg's first occupant of the Governor's seat, who was a son-in-law of Col. Thomas Polk. Martin had the opportunity for securing original documents, the habit of historical investigation, the tastes and judgment of a scholar, and the judicial temperament which weighs evidence and rejects that which is false. His testimony alone would be sufficient to establish the fact that the committee of Mecklenburg citizens passed the resolutions which he prints in full, on the 20th day of May, 1776.

In the year 1793, Dr. Hugh Williamson, who had announced his purpose to write a history of North Carolina, secured a copy of the Declaration from Mr. Alexander, which copy was seen by Gov. Stokes in Fayetteville in 1793, in the well-known handwriting of John McKnitt Alexander, as Gov. Stokes testifies.* In the year 1800, the Alexander residence, with the original copy of the Declaration and all the other proceedings of the Mecklenburg committee, were destroyed by fire.

The following was affixed to the Davie copy in the handwriting of John McKnitt Alexander: "It may be worthy of notice here to observe that the foregoing statement, though fundamentally correct, may not literally correspond

---

*Dr. Hawks' Address. (See Page 8.)

with the original record of the transactions of said delegation and court of enquiry, as all those records and papers were burnt with the house on April 6, 1800; but previous to that time of 1800, a full copy of said records, at the request of Dr. Hugh Williamson, then of New York, but formerly a representative in Congress from this State, was forwarded to him by Col. William Polk, in order that those early transactions might fill their proper place in a history of this State then writing by said Dr. Williamson, in New York.

"Certified to the best of my recollection and belief, this 3d day of September, 1800."

The Davie copy is a free version of the Martin copy. It begins with the past tense, "Whosoever abetted," showing the act of memory involved. There is a superfluity of adjectives, "unchartered and dangerous," "inherent and inalienable," which may be an echo of the National Declaration, though "rights inalienably ours" is an expression found in the articles of association adopted by Congress in 1774. "Americans" becomes "American patriots" in the old man's memory. A preamble is put to the fourth resolution, "as we now acknowledge the existence and control of no law or legal officer, civil or military"—"all and each" becomes "all, each and every." Instead of "be entitled to exercise the same powers and authorities as heretofore," Mr. Alexander gives as the substance of it, "is hereby reinstated in his former command an authority." "According to law" is changed to "according to said adopted laws," and "the love of liberty and of country" is recalled as "the love of country and the fire of freedom." The resolution about carrying the copy to Philadelphia is omitted in Mr. Alexander's account. Otherwise the copies agree.

It is impossible to believe that in writing down his recollection of the resolutions adopted, Mr. Alexander should have certified that the copy was fundamentally correct, and at the same time have appealed to an exact copy for proof of the fundamental correctness, the exact copy to be published, as he thought, to the world, unless he was confident that his recollection was reliable. When the fire destroyed the original, he remarked that the declaration was safe, as Dr. Williamson had a copy.

Dr. Williamson did not complete his history as projected, stopping with the year 1771. When the missing copy was sought for, it was found that his papers also had been destroyed by a fire in New York. The papers from which Martin compiled his history were sent to France and have disappeared. The data collected for Garden's Anecdotes has also been lost, and no copy of the *Cape Fear Mercury* of June, 1775, has ever come to light except the copy which Gov. Martin sent to London and which Mr. Stevenson, of Virginia, borrowed and did not return.*

They who undertook the task of proving that the Mecklenburg Declaration was not made, chose as their ground for argument that some "Resolves" were adopted May 31, and that these "Resolves" did not go so far as the Declaration. They proved beyond all doubt that the Resolves were made, while their opponents in the discussion proved that the Declaration was made. Hence, we were given conclusive evidence of two meetings, one of which completed the work of the other. Some writers have lost the whole question in a hazy attempt to merge the two sets of resolutions and the two conventions into one, and hence have not noted the fact that the Declaration of May 20 declared the independence of Mecklenburg county, and that the Resolves of May 31 proclaimed the independence of the United Colonies.

*(Rev. Francis L. Hawks, D. D., LL. D.)***

No less than seven witnesses of most unexceptionable character swear positively that there was a meeting of the people of Mecklenburg at Charlotte, on the 19th and 20th days of May, 1775; that certain declarations distinctly declaring independence of Great Britain were then and there prepared by a committee, read publicly to the

---

*Record in the British Museum.
**In an Address. (See Note, Page 5.)

people by Col. Thomas Polk, and adopted by acclamation; that they were present and took part in the proceedings themselves, and that John McKnitt Alexander was a Secretary of the meeting. These seven swear positively to the date, the 19th and 20th days of May, 1775. * * * Now as to the paper sent to Williamson, Hon. Montfort Stokes was Governor of North Carolina in the year 1831; while he occupied that high position, he testified that in the year 1793, (mark the date), he saw in the possession of Dr. Williamson a copy of the documents of the 20th of May, 1775, in the handwriting of John McKnitt Alexander, together with a letter to Williamson from Alexander, and that he conversed with Williamson on the subject.

(*Wheeler's History of North Carolina, Page* 258.)

The first American manifesto against the encroachments of power, the elective franchise, and the unwise interference of trade, was made in North Carolina as early as 1678, and nearly two hundred years before our independence was declared. Thus were sown, deep and broad, the seeds of liberty among her people with a liberal hand. * * * That the people of North Carolina should always have been.

"Men who knew their rights, and knowing dared maintain,"

is evident from every page of her history. But, that her sons should, on the 20th day of May, 1775, assemble at Charlotte, at a period of doubt, of darkness, and of danger, without concert with other States, without assurance of support from any quarter, and there "dissolve the political bands which connected them with the mother country," and there "declare themselves a free and independent people, and of right, ought to be soverign and self governing," is a subject full of moral sublimity, and a source of elevating State pride.

(*Charlotte Democrat, July* 8, 1873.)*

A highly intelligent gentleman, who has lived in Charlotte over fifty years, told us the other day that at a celebration in Charlotte on the 20th of May, 1835, he saw in procession seventy-five persons who were present when the Declaration was made on the 20th of May, 1775; and who testified that the meeting of the 31st of May was an adjourned one from the 20th.

(*Preface to Martin's History of North Carolina.*)

The writer imagined he had collected sufficient materials to justify the hope of producing a history of North Carolina worth

---
*Carnegie Free Library, of Charlotte.

the attention of his fellow citizens, and he had *arranged* all those that related to transactions, anterior to the Declaration of Independence, when, in 1809, Mr. Madison thought his services were wanted, first in the Mississippi territory and afterwards in that of New Orleans; and when the latter territory became a State, the new government thought proper to retain him.

He had entertained the hope that the time would arrive when disengaged from public duties, he might resume the work he had commenced in Carolina; but years have rolled away without bringing on this period; and a shock his health lately received during the year of his great climacteric, has warned him that the moment is arrived when his intended work must engage his immediate attention, or be absolutely abandoned.

A circumstance, for some time, recommended the latter alternative. The public prints stated, that a gentleman of known industry and great talents, who has filled a very high office in North Carolina, was engaged in a similar work; but several years have elapsed since, and nothing favors the belief, that the hopes which he had excited will soon be realized.

This gentleman had made application for the materials not published and they would have been forwarded to him, if they had been in a condition of being useful to any but him who had collected them. In their circuitous way from Newbern to New York and New Orleans, the sea water found its way to them: since their arrival, the mice, worms and the variety of insects of a humid and warm climate, have made great ravages among them. The ink of several very ancient documents has grown so pale as to render them nearly illegible, and notes hastily taken on a journey are in so cramped a hand that they are not to be deciphered by any person but him who made them.

The determination has been taken to put the work immediately to the press, in the condition it was when it reached New Orleans: this has prevented any use being made of Williamson's History of North Carolina, a copy of which did not reach the writer's hands till after his arrival in Louisiana.

The expectation is cherished, that the people of North Carolina will receive with indulgence a work ushered to light under circumstances so untoward.

Very ample notes and materials are ready for a volume, relating to the events of the Revolutionary War, and another, detailing subsequent transactions, till the writer's departure from Newbern, in 1809. If God yield him life and health, and his fellow citizens in

North Carolina appear desirous these should follow the two volumes now presented to them, it is not improbable they will appear.

FRANCIS XAVIER MARTIN.

Gentilly, near New Orleans, July 20, 1829.

(John Adams to Thomas Jefferson.) *

"QUINCY, 22D JUNE, 1819.

"DEAR SIR,

"May I enclose you one of the greatest curiosities, and one of the deepest mysteries that ever occurred to me; it is in the *Esssex Register* of June the 5th, 1819. It is entitled, from the *Raleigh Register*, 'Declaration of Independence.' How is it possible that this paper should have been concealed from me to this day. Had it been communicated to me in the time of it, I know, if you do not know, that it would have been printed in every Whig newspaper upon the continent. You know, that if I had possessed it, I would have made the Hall of Congress echo and re-echo with it fifteen months before your Declaration of Independence. What a poor ignorant, malicious, short-sighted, crapulous mass is Tom Paine's Common Sense in comparison with this paper. Had I known it I would have commented upon it from the day you entered Congress till the fourth of July, 1776.

"The genuine sense of America at that moment was never so well expressed before nor since. Richard Caswell, William Hooper, and Joseph Hewes, the then Representatives of North Carolina in Congress, you know as well as I; and you know that the unanimity of the States finally depended on the vote of Joseph Hewes, and was finally determined by him; and yet history is to ascribe the American Revolution to Thomas Paine. *Sat Verbum sapienti.*

"I am, dear sir, your invariable friend,

"JOHN ADAMS.

"PRESIDENT JEFFERSON."

(Thomas Jefferson to John Adams.) **

This letter is published in the furtherance of the author's desire to give all the evidence. Mr. Jefferson's misinformation and mistakes are numerous. He expresses doubt as to the publication in the Raleigh *Register* and to the exist-

---

*Jones' Defence of the Revolutionary History of North Carolina. Page 296.

**State Pamphlet, 1831.

ence of J. McKnitt (Alexander). He mentions "a copy sent to the dead Caswell," when in truth the copy was sent to William R. Davie who was living at the time Jefferson was writing. He refers to "historians of the adjacent States" and to his own and Patrick Henry's biographers as though he did not know they would be the last of all to acknowledge that the Revolution began in North Carolina.

He speaks of "Williamson, whose memory did not recollect in the history he has written of North Carolina, this gigantic step of its county of Mecklenburg;" and Williamson's history reached only to the year 1771. And worst of all, he speaks disparagingly of Hooper and Hewes, who advocated independence long before he did. (See Volume I., page 44.)

"MONTICELLO, July 9, 1819.

"DEAR SIR,—I am in debt to you for your letters of May the 21st, 27th, and June the 22nd. The first, delivered me by Mr. Greenwood, gave me the gratification of his acquaintance; and a gratification it always is, to be made acquainted with gentlemen of candor, worth, and information, as I found Mr. Greenwood to be. That on the subject of Mr. Samuel Adams Wells, shall not be forgotten in time and place, when it can be used to his advantage.

"But what has attracted my peculiar notice, is the paper from Mecklenburg county, of North Carolina, published in the Essex *Register*, which you were so kind as to enclose in your last, of June the 22nd. And you seem to think it genuine. I believe it spurious. I deem it to be a very unjustifiable quiz, like that of the volcano, so minutely related to us having broken out in North Carolina, some half dozen years ago, in that part of the country, and perhaps in that very county of Mecklenburg, for I do not remember its precise locality.** If this paper be really taken from the Raleigh *Register*, as quoted, I wonder it should have escaped Ritchie, who culls what is good from every paper, as the bee from every flower; and the *National Intelligencer*, too, which is edited by a North Carolinian; and that the fire should blaze out all at once in Essex, one thousand miles from where the spark is said to have fallen. But if really taken from the Raleigh *Register*, who is the narrator, and is the name subscribed real, or is it as fictitious as the paper itself? It appeals, too, to an original book, which is burnt, to Mr. Alexander, who is dead, to a joint letter from Caswell, Hewes, and Hooper, all

---

**The story was of a volcano in Buncombe county.—D. A. T.

dead, to a copy sent to the dead Caswell, and another sent to Doctor Williamson, now probably dead, whose memory did not recollect, in the history he has written of North Carolina, this gigantic step of its county of Mecklenburg. Horry, too, is silent in his history of Marion, whose scene of action was the country bordering cn Mecklenburg. Ramsay, Marshall, Jones, Girardin, Wirt, historians of the adjacent States, all silent. When Mr. Henry's resolutions, far short of independence, flew like lightning through every paper and kindled both sides of the Atlantic, this flaming declaration of the same date, of the independence of Mecklenburg county, of North Carolina, absolving it from the British allegiance, and abjuring all political connection with that nation, although sent to Congress, too, is never heard of. It is not known even a twelve-month after, when a similar proposition is first made in that body. Armed with this bold example, would not you have addressed our timid brethren in peals of thunder, on their tardy fears? Would not every advocate of independence have rung the glories of Mecklenburg county, in North Carolina, in the ears of the doubting Dickinson and others, who hung so heavily on us? Yet the example of independent Mecklenburg county, in North Carolina, was never once quoted. The paper speaks, too, of the continued exertions of their delegation (Caswell, Hooper, Hewes,) 'in the cause of liberty and independence.' Now, you remember as well as I do, that we had not a greater tory in Congress than Hooper;* that Hewes was very wavering, sometimes firm, sometimes feeble, according as the day was clear or cloudy; that Caswell, indeed, was a good Whig, and kept these gentlemen to the notch, while he was present; but that he left us soon, and their line of conduct became then uncertain until Penn came, who fixed Hewes, and the vote of the State. I must not be understood as suggesting any doubtfulness in the State of North Carolina. No State was more fixed or forward. Nor do I affirm, positively, that this paper is a fabrication, because the proof of a negative can only be presumptive. But I shall believe it such until positive and solemn proof of its authenticity shall be produced. And if the name of McKnitt be real, and not a part of the fabrication, it needs a vindication by the production of such proof. For the present, I must be an unbeliever in the apocryphal gospel.

"I am glad to learn that Mr. Ticknor has safely returned to his friends; but should have been much more pleased had he accepted the Professorship in our University, which we should have offered him in form. Mr. Bowditch, too, refuses us; so fascinating is the

---

*These Reflections on Hooper and Hewes are Disproven by Jones' Defence of the Revolutionary History of North Carolina.—D. A. T.

vinculum of the *dulce natale solum.* Our wish is to procure natives, where they can be found, like these gentlemen, of the first order of acquirement in their respective lines; but preferring foreigners of the first order to natives of the second, we shall certainly have to go, for several of our Professors, to countries more advanced in science than we are.

"I set out within three or four days for my other home, the distance of which, and its cross mails, are great impediments to epistolary communications. I shall remain there about two months; and there, here, and everywhere, I am and shall always be affectionately and respectfully yours,

"TH: JEFFERSON."

(*Raleigh Register, April* 30, 1819.)*

It is not, probably, known to many of our readers, that the citizens of Mecklenburg county, in this State, made a Declaration of Independence more than a year before Congress made theirs. The following document on the subject has lately come to the hands of the Editor from unquestionable authority, and is published that it may go down to posterity.

NORTH CAROLINA, MECKLENBURG COUNTY,
May 20, 1775.

In the spring of 1775, the leading characters of Mecklenburg county, stimulated by that enthusiastic patriotism which elevates the mind above considerations of individual aggrandizement, and scorning to shelter themselves from the impending storm by submission to lawless power, etc., etc., held several detached meetings, in each of which the individual sentiments were, "that the cause of Boston was the cause of all; that their destinies were indissolubly connected with those of their Eastern fellow citizens—and that they must either submit to all the impositions which an unprincipled, and to them an unrepresented, Parliament might impose—or support their brethren who were doomed to sustain the first shock of that power, which, if successful there, would ultimately overwhelm all in the common calamity." Conformably to these principles, Colonel T. Polk, through solicitation, issued an order to each Captain's company in the county of Mecklenburg, (then comprising the present county of Cabarrus,) directing each militia company to elect two persons, and delegate to them ample power to devise ways and means to aid and assist their suffering brethren in Boston, and also generally to adopt measures to extricate themselves from the impending storm, and to secure unimpaired their

---

*State Pamphlet, 1831.

inalienable rights, privileges and liberties, from the dominant grasp of British imposition and tyranny.

In conformity to said order, on the 19th of May, 1775, the said delegation met in Charlotte, vested with unlimited powers; at which time official news, by express, arrived of the battle of Lexington on that day of the preceding month. Every delegate felt the value and importance of the prize, and the awful and solemn crisis which had arrived—every bosom swelled with indignation at the malice, inveteracy, and insatiable revenge, developed in the late attack at Lexington. The universal sentiment was: let us not flatter ourselves that popular harangues, or resolves; that popular vapour will avert the storm, or vanquish our common enemy—let us deliberate—let us calculate the issue—the probable result; and then let us act with energy, as brethren leagued to preserve our property—our lives— and what is still more endearing, the liberties of America. *Abraham Alexander* was then elected Chairman, and *John M'Knitt Alexander*, Clerk. After a free and full discussion of the various objects for which the delegation had been convened, it was unanimously ordained.

(Here follows the Declaration.)

A number of by-laws were also added, merely to protect the association from confusion, and to regulate their general conduct as citizens. After sitting in the Court House all night, neither sleepy, hungry, nor fatigued, and after discussing every paragraph, they were all passed, sanctioned, and decreed, *unanimously*, about 2 o'clock a. m., May 20, In a few days, a deputation of said delegation convened, when Capt. *James Jack*, of Charlotte, was deputed as express to the Congress at Philadelphia, with a copy of said Resolves and Proceedings, together with a letter addressed to our three representatives there, viz., *Richard Caswell, William Hooper and Joseph Hewes*—under express injunction, personally, and through the State representation, to use all possible means to have said proceedings sanctioned and approved by the General Congress. On the return of Captain Jack, the delegation learned that their proceedings were individually approved by the members of Congress, but that it was deemed premature to lay them before the House. A joint letter from said three Members of Congress was also received, complimentary of the zeal in the common cause, and recommending perseverance, order and energy.*

The subsequent harmony, unanimity, and exertion in the cause of liberty and independence, evidently resulting from these regula-

---

*This letter was burned with the original Copy of the Declaration.—D. A. T.

tions and the continued exertion of said delegation, apparently tranquilized this section of the State, and met with the concurrence and high approbation of the Council of Safety, who held their sessions at Newbern and Wilmington, alternately, and who confirmed the nomination and acts of the delegation in their official capacity.

From this delegation originated the Court of Enquiry of this county, who constituted and held their first session in Charlotte—they then held their meetings regularly at Charlotte, at Col. James Harris's, and at Col. Phifer's, alternately, one week at each place. It was a Civil Court founded on military process. Before this Judicature, all suspicious persons were made to appear, who were formally tried and banished, or continued under guard. Its jurisdiction was as unlimited as toryism, and i 3 decrees as final as the confidence and patriotism of the country. Several were arrested and brought before them from Lincoln, Rowan and the adjacent counties.

[The foregoing is a true copy of the papers on the above subject, left in my hands by John McKnitt Alexander, deceased. I find it mentioned on file that the original book was burned April, 1800. That a copy of the proceedings was sent to Hugh Williamson, in New York, then writing a History of North Carolina, and that a copy was sent to Gen. W. R. Davie.   J. McKnitt.]*

*(Raleigh Register, February 18, 1820.)***

MECKLENBURG DECLARATION OF INDEPENDENCE.

When this Declaration was first published in April last, some doubts were expressed in the Eastern papers as to its authenticity, (none of the Histories of the Revolution having noticed the circumstance.) Col. William Polk, of this city, (who, though a mere youth at the time, was present at the meeting which made the Declaration, and whose father, being Colonel of the county, appears to have acted a conspicuous part on the occasion,) observing this, assured us of the correctness of the facts generally, though he thought there were errors as to the name of the Secretary, etc., and said that he should probably be able to correct these, and throw some further light on the subject, by inquiries amongst some of his old friends in Mecklenburg county. He has accordingly made inquiries, and communicated to us the following Documents as the result, which, we presume, will do away all doubts on the subject.

---

*Dr. Joseph McKnitt Alexander, son of John McKnitt Alexander.—D. A. T.
**State Pamphlet, 1831.

SIGNATURES OF PROMINENT CHARACTERS IN MECKLENBURG HISTORY.

MECKLENBURG DECLARATION CONTROVERSY.

(*Certificate of Samuel Henderson.*)*
STATE OF NORTH CAROLINA,
MECKLENBURG COUNTY.

I, Samuel Henderson, do hereby certify, that the paper annexed was obtained by me from Maj. William Davie in its present situation, soon after the death of his father, Gen. William R. Davie, and given to Doct. Joseph McKnitt by me. In searching for some particular paper, I came across this, and, knowing the handwriting of John McKnitt Alexander, took it up, and examined it. Maj. Davie said to me (when asked how it became torn) his sisters had torn it, not knowing what it was.

Given under my hand, this 25th November, 1830.
SAM. HENDERSON.

[NOTE.—To this certificate of Doct. Henderson is annexed the copy of the paper A, originally deposited by John McKnitt Alexander in the hands of *Gen. Davie,* whose name seems to have been mistaken by Mr. Jefferson for that of *Gov. Caswell.* See preface, pages 5 and 6. This paper is somewhat torn, but is entirely legible, and constitutes the "solemn and positive proof of authenticity" which Mr. Jefferson required, and which would doubtless have been satisfactory, had it been submitted to him.]

(*Captain Jack's Certificate.*)*

Having seen in the newspapers some pieces respecting the Declaration of Independence by the people of Mecklenburg county, in the State of North Carolina, in May, 1775, and being solicited to state what I know of that transaction; I would observe, that for some time previous to, and at the time those resolutions were agreed upon, I resided in the town of Charlotte, Mecklenburg county; was privy to a number of meetings of some of the most influential and leading characters of that county on the subject, before the final adoption of the resolutions—and at the time they were adopted; among those who appeared to take the lead, may be mentioned Hezekiah Alexander, who generally acted as chairman; John McKnitt Alexander, as secretary; Abraham Alexander, Adam Alexander, Maj. John Davidson, Maj. (afterwards Gen.) Wm. Davidson, Col. Thomas Polk, Ezekiel Polk, Dr. Ephraim Brevard, Samuel Martin, Duncan Ochletree, William Willson, Robert Irvin.

When the resolutions were finally agreed on, they were publicly proclaimed from the Court-house door in the town of Charlotte, and received with every demonstration of joy by the inhabitants.

I was then solicited to be the bearer of the proceedings to Con-

---
*State Pamphlet, 1831.

gress. I set out the following month, say June, and in passing through Salisbury, the General Court was sitting—at the request of the court I handed a copy of the resolutions to Col. Kennon, an Attorney, and they were read aloud in open court. Major William Davidson, and Mr. Avery, an attorney, called on me at my lodgings the evening after, and observed, they had heard of but one person, (a Mr. Beard) but approved of them.

I then proceeded on to Philadelphia, and delivered the Mecklenburg Declaration of Independence of May, 1775, to Richard Caswell and William Hooper, the delegates to Congress from the State of North Carolina.

I am now in the eighty-eighth year of my age, residing in the county of Elbert, in the State of Georgia. I was in the Revolutionary War, from the commencement to the close. I would further observe, that the Rev. Francis Cummins, a Presbyterian clergyman, of Greene county, in this State, was a student in the town of Charlotte at the time of the adoption of the resolutions, and is as well, or perhaps better acquainted with the proceedings at that time, than any man now living.

Col. William Polk, of Raleigh, in North Carolina, was living with his father Thomas, in Charlotte, at the time I have been speaking of, and although then too young to be forward in the business, yet the leading circumstances I have related cannot have escaped his recollection.

JAMES JACK.

Signed this 7th Dec., 1819, in presence of
  JOB WESTON, C. C. O.
  JAMES OLIVER, Atto. at Law.

(*The Alexander Certificate.*)*

NORTH CAROLINA,
CABARRUS COUNTY, Nov. 29, 1830.

We, the undersigned, do hereby certify that we have frequently heard William S. Alexander, deceased, say that he, the said Wm. S. Alexander, was at Philadelphia, on mercantile business, in the early part of the summer of 1775, say in June; and that on the day that Gen. Washington left Philadelphia to take command of the Northern army,** he, the said Wm. S. Alexander, met with Capt. James Jack, who informed him, the said Wm. S. Alexander, that he, the said James Jack, was there as the agent or bearer of the Declaration of Independence made in Charlotte, on the twentieth day of May, sev-

---

*State Pamphlet, 1831.
**June 23.—D. A. T.

enteen hundred and seventy-five, by the citizens of Mecklenburg, then including Cabarrus, with instructions to present the same to the Delegates from North Carolina, and by them to be laid before Congress, and which he said he had done; in which Declaration the aforesaid citizens of Mecklenburg renounced their allegiance to the crown of Great Britain, and set up a government for themselves, under the title of The Committee of Safety.

Given under our hands the date above written.

ALPHONSO ALEXANDER,
AMOS ALEXANDER,
J. MCKNITT.

(*Francis Cummins' Certificate.*)*

LEXINGTON, GA., November 10, 1819.

DEAR SIR:—The bearer, the Hon. Thomas W. Cobb, has suggested to me that you had a desire to know something particularly of the proceedings of the citizens of Mecklenburg county, in North Carolina, about the beginning of our Revolutionary War.

Previous to my becoming more particular, I will suppose you remember the Regulation business, which took its rise in or before the year 1770, and issued and ended in a battle between the Regulators and Governor Tryon, in the spring of 1771. Some of the Regulators were killed, and the whole dispersed. The Regulators' conduct "was a *rudis indigestaque moles*," as Ovid says, about the beginning of creation; but the embryotic principles of the Revolution were in their temper and views. They wanted strength, consistency, a Congress and a Washington at their head. Tryon sent his officers and minions through the State, and imposed the oath of allegiance upon the people, even as far up as Mecklenburg county. In the year 1775, after our Revolution began, the principal characters of Mecklenburg county met on two sundry days, in Queen's Museum in Charlotte, to digest Articles for a State Constitution, in anticipation that the Province would proceed to do so. In this business the leading characters were, the Rev. Hezekiah James Balch, a graduate of Princeton College, an elegant scholar; Waightstill Avery, Esq., Attorney at Law; Hezekiah and John McKnitt Alexander, Esq's., Col. Thomas Polk, etc., etc.

Many men, and young men, (myself one,) before magistrates, abjured allegiance to George III., or any other foreign power. At length, in the same year, 1775, I think, at least positively before July 4, 1776, the males generally of that county met on a certain day in Charlotte, and from the head of the Court-house stairs pro-

---

*State Pamphlet, 1831.

claimed Independence on English Government, by their herald Col.
Thomas Polk. I was present, and saw and heard it, and as a young
man, and then a student in Queen's Museum, was an agent in these
things. I did not then take and keep the dates, and cannot, as to
date, be so particular as I could wish. Capt. James Jack, then of
Charlotte, but now of Elbert county, in Georgia, was sent with the
account of these proceedings to Congress, then in Philadelphia—and
brought back to the county, the thanks of Congress for their zeal—
and the advice of Congress to be a little more patient, until Congress
should take the measures thought to be best.

I would suppose, sir, that some minutes of these things must
be found among the records of the first Congress, that would perfectly settle their dates. I am perfectly sure, being present at the
whole of them, they were before our National Declaration of Independence.

Hon. Sir, if the above few things can afford you any gratification,
it will add to the happiness of your friend and humble servant.

FRANCIS CUMMINS.

Hon. Nathaniel Macon.

(*Joseph Graham's Certificate.*)*
VESUVIUS FURNACE, 4th October, 1830.

DEAR SIR:—Agreeably to your request, I will give you the details
of the Mecklenburg Declaration of Independence on the 20th of May,
1775, as well as I can recollect after a lapse of fifty-five years. I
was then a lad about half grown, was present on that occasion (a
looker on).

During the Winter and Spring preceding that event, several popular meetings of the people were held in Charlotte; two of which I
attended.—Papers were read, grievances stated, and public measures
discussed. As printing was not then common in the South, the
papers were mostly manuscript; one or more of which was from the
pen of the Reverend Doctor Reese, (then of Mecklenburg), which
met with general approbation, and copies of it circulated. It is to
be regretted that those and other papers published at that period,
and the journal of their proceedings, are lost. They would show
much of the spirit and tone of thinking which prepared them for the
measures they afterwards adopted.

On the 20th of May, 1775, besides the two persons elected from
each militia company, (usually called Committee-men), a much
larger number of citizens attended in Charlotte than at any former
meeting—perhaps half the men in the county. The news of the
battle of Lexington, the 19th of April preceding, had arrived. There

---

*State Pamphlet, 1831.

appeared among the people much excitement. The committee were organized in the Court-house by appointing Abraham Alexander, Esq., Chairman, and John McKnitt Alexander, Esq., Clerk or Secretary to the meeting.

After reading a number of papers as usual, and much animated discussion, the question was taken and they resolved to declare themselves independent. One among other reasons offered, that the King or Ministry had, by proclamation or some edict, declared the Colonies out of the protection of the British Crown; they ought, therefore, to declare themselves out of his protection, and resolve on independence. That their proceedings might be in due form, a subcommittee, consisting of Dr. Ephraim Brevard, a Mr. Kennon, an attorney, and a third person, whom I do not recollect, were appointed to draft their Declaration. They retired from the Court-house for some time; but the committee continued in session in it. One circumstance occurred I distinctly remember: A member of the committee, who had said but little before, addressed the Chairman as follows: "If you resolve on independence, how shall we all be absolved from the obligations of the oath we took to be true to King George the III. about four years ago, after the Regulation battle, when we were sworn whole militia companies together. I should be glad to know how gentlemen can clear their consciences after taking that oath." This speech produced confusion. The Chairman could scarcely preserve order, so many wished to reply. There appeared great indignation and contempt at the speech of the member. Some said it was nonsense; others that allegiance and protection were reciprocal; when protection was withdrawn, allegiance ceased; that the oath was only binding while the King protected us in the enjoyment of our rights and liberties as they existed at the time it was taken; which he had not done, but now declared us out of his protection; therefore was not binding. Any man who would interpret it otherwise, was a fool. By way of illustration, (pointing to a green tree near the Court-house), stated, if he was sworn to do anything as long as the leaves continued on that tree, it was so long binding; but when the leaves fell, he was discharged from its obligation. This was said to be certainly applicable in the present case. Out of respect for a worthy citizen, long since deceased, and his respectable connections, I forbear to mention names; for, though he was a friend to the cause, a suspicion rested on him in the public mind for some time after.

The sub-committee appointed to draft the resolutions returned, and Dr. Ephraim Brevard read their report, as near as I can recollect, in the very words we have since seen them several times in print. It was unanimously adopted, and shortly after it was moved and seconded to have proclamation made and the people collected, that the proceedings be read at the Court-house door, in order that all might hear them. It was done, and they were received with enthusiasm. It was then proposed by some one aloud to give three cheers and throw up their hats. It was immediately adopted, and the hats thrown. Several of them lit on the Court-house roof. The owners had some difficulty to reclaim them.

The foregoing is all from personal knowledge. I understood afterwards that Captain James Jack, then of Charlotte, undertook, on the request of the committee, to carry a copy of their proceedings to Congress, which then sat in Philadelphia; and on his way, at Salisbury, the time of court, Mr. Kennon, who was one of the committee who assisted in drawing the Declaration, prevailed on Captain Jack to get his papers, and have them read publicly; which was done, and the proceedings met with general approbation. But two of the lawyers, John Dunn and a Mr. Booth, dissented, and asserted they were treasonable, and endeavored to have Captain Jack detained. He drew his pistols, and threatened to kill the first man who would interrupt him, and passed on. The news of this reached Charlotte in a short time after, and the executive of the committee, whom they had invested with suitable powers, ordered a party of ten or twelve armed horsemen to bring said lawyers from Salisbury; when they were brought, and the case investigated before the committee. Dunn, on giving security and making fair promises, was permitted to return, and Booth was sentenced to go to Camden, in South Carolina, out of the sphere of his influence. My brother George Graham and the late Col. John Carruth were of the party that went to Salisbury; and it is distinctly remembered that when in Charlotte they came home at night, in order to provide for their trip to Camden; and that they and two others of the party took Booth to that place. This was the first military expedition from Mecklenburg in the Revolutionary war, and believed to be the first anywhere to the South.

Yours respectfully,
J. GRAHAM.

Dr. Jos. M'Kt. Alexander, Mecklenburg, N. Carolina.

Certificate (Graham, Hutchison, Clark, Robinson.)*

STATE OF NORTH CAROLINA,
MECKLENBURG COUNTY.

At the request of Col. William Polk, of Raleigh, made to Major-General George Graham, soliciting him to procure all the information that could be obtained at this late period, of the transactions

---

*State Pamphlet, 1831.

which took place in the county of Mecklenburg, in the year 1775, as it respected the people of that county having declared Independence; of the time when the Declaration was made; who were the principal movers and leaders, and the members who composed the body of Patriots who made the Declaration, and signed the same.

We, the undersigned citizens of the said county, and of the several ages set forth opposite to each of our names, do certify, and on our honor declare, that we were present in the town of Charlotte, in the said county of Mecklenburg, on the 19th day of May, 1775, when two persons elected from each Captain's Company in said county, appeared as delegates, to take into consideration the state of the country, and to adopt such measures as to them seemed best, to secure their lives, liberty, and property, from the storm which was gathering, and had burst upon their fellow-citizens to the Eastward, by a British army, under the authority of the British King and Parliament.

The order for the election of Delegates was given by Col. Thomas Polk, the commanding officer of the militia of the county, with a request that their powers should be ample, touching any measure that should be proposed.

We do further certify and declare, that to the best of our recollection and belief, the delegation was complete from every company, and that the meeting took place in the Court-house, about 12 o'clock on the said 19th day of May, 1775, when *Abraham Alexander* was chosen Chairman, and Dr. *Ephraim Brevard* Secretary. That the Delegates continued in session until in the night of that day; that on the 20th they again met, when a committee, under the direction of the Delegates, had formed several resolves, which were read, and which went to declare themselves, and the people of Mecklenburg county, Free and Independent of the King and Parliament of Great Britain—and that, from that day thenceforth, all allegiance and political relation was absolved between the good people of Mecklenburg and the King of Great Britain; which Declaration was signed by every member of the Delegation, under the shouts and huzzas of a very large assembly of the people of the county, who had come to know the issue of the meeting. We further believe, that the Declaration of Independence was drawn up by the Secretary, Dr. Ephraim Brevard, and that it was conceived and brought about through the instrumentality and popularity of Col. Thomas Polk, Abraham Alexander, John McKnitt Alexander, Adam Alexander, Ephraim Brevard, John Phifer, and Hezekiah Alexander, with some others.

We do further certify and declare, that in a few days after the Delegates adjourned, Captain James Jack, of the town of Charlotte, was engaged to carry the resolves to the President of Congress, and to our Representatives—one copy for each; and that his expenses were paid by a voluntary subscription. And we do know that Captain Jack executed the trust, and returned with answers, both from the President and our Delegates in Congress, expressive of their entire approbation of the course that had been adopted, recommending a continuance in the same; and that the time would soon be, when the whole Continent would follow our example.

We further certify and declare, that the measures which were adopted at the time before mentioned, had a general influence on the people of this county to unite them in the cause of liberty and the country, at that time; that the same unanimity and patriotism continued unimpaired to the close of the war; and that the resolutions had considerable effect in harmonizing the people in two or three adjoining counties.

That a committee of Safety for the county were elected, who were clothed with civil and military power, and under their authority several disaffected persons in Rowan, and Tryon (now Lincoln county), were sent for, examined, and conveyed (after it was satisfactorily proven they were inimical) to Camden, in South Carolina, for safe keeping.

We do further certify, that the acts passed by the committee of Safety, were received as the Civil Law of the land in many cases, and that Courts of Justice for the decision of controversies between the people were held, and we have no recollection that dissatisfaction existed in any instance with regard to the judgments of said courts.

We are not, at this late period, able to give the names of all the Delegation who formed the Declaration of Independence; but can safely declare as to the following persons being of the number, viz.: Thomas Polk, Abraham Alexander, John McKnitt Alexander, Adam Alexander, Ephraim Brevard, John Phifer, Hezekiah James Balch, Benjamin Patton, Hezekiah Alexander, Richard Barry, William Graham, Matthew M'Clure, Robert Irwin, Zachias Wilson, Neil Morrison, John Flennegen, John Queary, Ezra Alexander.

In testimony of all and every part herein set forth, we have hereunto set our hands.

                        GEO. GRAHAM, aged 61, near 62.
                        WM. HUTCHISON, " 68.
                        JONAS CLARK, " 61.
                        ROB'T ROBINSON, " 68.

(John Simeson to Col. William Polk.)*

PROVIDENCE, January 20, 1820.

DEAR SIR:—After considerable delay, occasioned partly to obtain what information I could, in addition to my own knowledge of the facts in relation to our Declaration of Independence, and partly by a precarious, feeble old age, I now write to you in answer to yours of the 24th ult.

I have conversed with many of my old friends and others, and all agree in the point, but few can state the particulars; for although our country is renowned for general intelligence, we have still some that don't read the public prints. You know, in the language of the day, every Province had its Congress, and Mecklenburg had its county Congress, as legally chosen as any other, and assumed an attitude until then without a precedent; but, alas those worthies who conceived and executed that bold measure, are no more; and one reason why so little new light can be thrown on an old truth, may be this—and I appeal to yourself for the correctness of the remark—we who are now called Revolutionary men, were then thoughtless, precipitate youths; we cared not who conceived the bold act, our business was to adopt and support it. Yourself, sir, in your eighteenth year and on the spot, your worthy father, the most popular and influential character in the county, and yet you cannot state much from recollection. Your father, as commanding officer of the county, issued orders to the captains to appoint two men from each company to represent them in the committee. It was done. Neill Morrison, John Flennegen, from this company; Charles Alexander, John McKnitt Alexander, Hezekiah Alexander, Abraham Alexander, Esq., John Phifer, David Reese, Adam Alexander, Dickey Barry, John Queary, with others, whose names I cannot obtain. As to the names of those who drew up the Declaration, I am inclined to think Dr. Brevard was the principal, from his known talents in composition. It was, however, in substance and form, like that great national act agreed on thirteen months after. Ours was towards the close of May, 1775. In addition to what I have said, the same committee appointed three men to secure all the military stores for the country's use—Thomas Polk, John Phifer, and Joseph Kennedy. I was under arms near the head of the line, near Col. Polk, and heard him distinctly read a long string of Grievances, the Declaration and Military Order above. I likewise heard Col. Polk have two warm disputes with two men of the county, who said the measures were rash and unnecessary. He was applauded and they silenced. I was then in my 22d year, an enemy to usurpation and

---

*State Pamphlet, 1831.

tyranny of every kind, with a retentive memory, and fond of liberty, that had a doubt arisen in my mind that the act would be controverted, proof would not have been wanting; but I comfort myself that none but the self-important peace-party and blue-lights of the East, will have the assurance to oppose it any further. The biographer of Patrick Henry (Mr. Wirt) says he first suggested Independence in the Virginia Convention; but it is known they did not reduce it to action—so that it will pass for nothing. The Courts likewise acted independently. I myself heard a dispute take place on the bench, and an acting magistrate was actually taken and sent to prison by an order of the Chairman.

Thus, sir, have I thrown together all that I can at this time. I am too blind to write fair, and too old to write much sense—but if my deposition before the Supreme Court of the United States would add more weight to a truth so well known here, it would be at the service of my fellow-citizens of the country and State generally.

I am, sir, your friend and humble servant,

JOHN SIMESON, Sen.

P. S.—I will give you a short anecdote. An aged man near me, on being asked if he knew anything of this affair, replied, "*Och, aye, Tam Polk declared Independence long before anybody else.*" This old man is 81.

(*Certificate of Isaac Alexander.*)*

I hereby certify that I was present in Charlotte on the 19th and 20th days of May, 1775, when a regular deputation from all the Captains' companies of militia in the county of Mecklenburg, to-wit: Col. Thomas Polk, Adam Alexander, Lieut. Col. Abram Alexander, John McKnitt Alexander, Hezekiah Alexander, Ephraim Brevard, and a number of others, who met to consult and take measures for the peace and tranquility of the citizens of said county, and who appointed Abraham Alexander their Chairman, and Doctor Ephraim Brevard Secretary; who, after due consultation, declared themselves absolved from their allegiance to the King of Great Britain, and drew up a Declaration of their Independence, which was unanimously adopted; and employed Capt. James Jack to carry copies thereof to Congress, who accordingly went. These are a part of the transactions that took place at that time, as far as my recollection serves me.

ISAAC ALEXANDER.

October 8, 1830.

---

*State Pamphlet, 1831.

MECKLENBURG DECLARATION CONTROVERSY.

(*Certificate of Samuel Wilson.*)*

STATE OF NORTH CAROLINA,
MECKLENBURG COUNTY.

I do hereby certify, that in May, 1775, a committee or delegation from the different militia companies in this county met in Charlotte; and after consulting together, they publicly declared their independence on Great Britain, and on her Government. This was done before a large collection of people, who highly approved of it. I was then and there present, and heard it read from the Court-house door. Certified by me.　　　　　　　　　　SAMUEL WILSON.

(*Certificate of John Davidson.*)*

BEAVER DAM, October 5, 1830.

DEAR SIR:—I received your note of the 25th of last month, requiring information relative to the Mecklenburg Declaration of Independence. As I am, perhaps, the only person living, who was a member of that Convention, and being far advanced in years, and not having my mind frequently directed to that circumstance for some years, I can give you but a very succinct history of that transaction. There were two men chosen from each captain's company, to meet in Charlotte, to take the subject into consideration. John McKnitt Alexander and myself were chosen from one company; and many other members were there that I now recollect, whose names I deem unnecessary to mention. When the members met, and were perfectly organized for business, a motion was made to declare ourselves independent of the Crown of Great Britain, which was carried by a large majority. Dr. Ephraim Brevard was then appointed to give us a sketch of the Declaration of Independence, which he did. James Jack was appointed to take it on to the American Congress, then sitting in Philadelphia, with particular instructions to deliver it to the North Carolina Delegation in Congress, (Hooper and Caswell). When Jack returned, he stated that the Declaration was presented to Congress, and the reply was, that they highly esteemed the patriotism of the citizens of Mecklenburg; but they thought the measure too premature.

I am confident that the Declaration of Independence by the people of Mecklenburg was made public at least twelve months before that of the Congress of the United States.

I do certify that the foregoing statement, relative to the Mecklenburg Independence is correct, and which I am willing to be qualified to, should it be required.　　Yours respectfully,

Doct. J. M. Alexander.　　　　　　　　　　JOHN DAVIDSON.

---

*State Pamphlet, 1831.

NOTE.—The following is a copy of an original paper furnished by the writer of the foregoing certificate, from which it would seem, that, from the period of the Mecklenburg Declaration, every individual friendly to the American cause was furnished by the *Chairman of that meeting, Abraham Alexander*, with testimonials of the character he had assumed; and in this point of view the paper affords strong collateral testimony of the correctness of many of the foregoing certificates.

NORTH CAROLINA,
MECKLENBURG COUNTY,
November 28, 1775.

These may certify to all whom may concern, that the bearer hereof, William Henderson, is allowed here to be a true friend to liberty, and signed the Association.

Certified by   ABR'M ALEXANDER,
Chairman of the Committee of P. S.

(Letter From J. G. M. Ramsey.) *

MECKLENBURG, T. Oct. 1, 1830.

DEAR SIR:—Yours of 21st ultimo was duly received. In answer I have only to say, that little is in my possession on the subject alluded to which you have not already seen. Subjoined are the certificates of two gentlemen of this county, whose respectability and veracity are attested by their acquaintances here, as well as by the accompanying testimonials of the magistrates in whose neighborhood they reside. With this you will also receive extracts from letters on the same subject from gentlemen well known to you, and to the country at large.

I am, very respectfully yours, etc.,
J. G. M. RAMSEY.

(Certificate of James Johnson.) *

I, James Johnson, now of Knox county, Tennessee, but formerly of Mecklenburg county, North Carolina, do hereby certify, that to the best of my recollection, in the month of May, 1775, there were several meetings in Charlotte concerning the impending war. Being young, I was not called on to take an active part in the same; but one thing I do positively remember, that she (Mecklenburg county) did meet and hold a Convention, declared independence, and sent a man to Philadelphia with the proceedings. And I do further certify, that I am well acquainted with several of the men who formed or constituted said Convention, viz.: John McKnitt Alexander, Hez-

---

*State Pamphlet, 1831.

ekiah Alexander, Abraham Alexander, Adam Alexander, Robert Irwin, Neill Morrison, John Flennegen, John Queary.
Certified by me this 11th day of October, 1827.

JAMES JOHNSON,
In my seventy-third year.

*(Certificate of Elijah Johnson and James Wilhite.)**

We, Elijah Johnson and James Wilhite, acting Justices of the Peace for the county of Knox, do certify, that we have been a long time well acquainted with Samuel Montgomery and James Johnson, both residents of Knox county; and that they are entitled to full credit, and any statement they may make to implicit confidence.

Given under our hands and seals this 4th day of October, 1830.

ELIJAH JOHNSON, [Seal.]
JAMES WILHITE, [Seal.]
Justices of the Peace for Knox County.

NOTE.—Mr. Montgomery's certificate does not purport to state the facts as having come under his own personal observation. It is therefore omitted in this publication.

*Instructions Given to Mecklenburg Representatives to the Provincial Congress, September 1, 1776.***

1. You are instructed to vote that the late province of North Carolina is and of right ought to be, a free and independent State, invested with all the power of Legislation, capable of making Laws to regulate all its internal policy, subject only in its external connections and foreign commerce, to a negative of a continental Senate.

2. You are instructed to vote for the Execution of a civil Government under the authority of the People for the future security of all the Rights, Privileges and Prerogatives of the State, and the private, natural and unalienable Rights of the constituting members thereof, either as Men or Christians. If this should not be confirmed in Congress or Convention—protest.

3. You are instructed to vote that an equal Representation be established, and that the qualifications required to enable any person or persons to have a voice in Legislation, may not be secured too high, but that every Freeman who shall be called upon to support Government either in person or property, may be admitted thereto. If this should not be confirmed, protest and remonstrate.

*State Pamphlet, 1831.
**Wheeler's History, page 260. Date according to Governor Swain.

4. You are instructed to vote that Legislation be not a divided right, and that no man, or body of men be invested with a negative on the voice of the People duly collected, and that no honors or dignities be conferred, for life, or made hereditary, on any person or persons, either legislative or executive. If this should not be confirmed—protest and remonstrate.

5. You are instructed to vote that all and every person or persons, seized or possessed of any estate, real or personal, agreeable to the last establishment, be confirmed in their seizure and possession, to all intents and purposes in law, who have not forfeited their right to the protection of the State by their criminal practices towards the same. If this should not be confirmed—protest.

6. You are instructed to vote that Deputies to represent this State in a Continental Congress be appointed in and by the supreme Legislative body of the State, the form of nomination to be submitted to, if free, and also that all officers the influence of whose office is equally to extend to every part of the State, be appointed in the same manner and form—likewise give your consent to the establishing the old political divisions, if it should be voted in convention, or to new ones if similar. On such establishments taking place you are instructed to vote, in the general, that all officers, who are to exercise their authority in any of the said districts, be recommended to the trust only by the freemen of said division—to be subject, however, to the general laws and regulations of the State. If this should not be substantially confirmed—protest.

7. You are instructed to move and insist that the people you immediately represent be acknowledged to be a distinct county of this State as formerly of the late province, with the additional privilege of annually electing in their own officers both civil and military, together with the election of Clerks and Sheriffs, by the freemen of the same. The choice to be confirmed by sovereign authority of the State, and the officers so invested to be under the jurisdiction of the State and liable to its cognizance and inflictions, in case of malpractice. If this should not be confirmed, protest and remonstrate.

8. You are instructed to vote that no chief justice, no secretary of State, no auditor-general, no surveyor-general, no practicing lawyer, no clerk of any court of record, no sheriff, and no person holding a military office in this State, shall be a representative of the people in Congress or Convention. If this should not be confirmed—contend for it.

9. You are instructed to vote that all claims against the public, except such as accrue upon attendance of Congress or Convention, be first submitted to the inspection of a committee of nine or more

men, inhabitants of the county where said claimant is a resident, and without the approbation of said committee, it shall not be accepted by the public, for which purpose you are to move and insist that a law be enacted to impower the freemen of each county to choose a committee of not less than nine men, of whom none are to be military officers. If this should not be confirmed—protest and remonstrate.

10. You are instructed to refuse to enter into any combinations of secrecy as members of Congress or Convention, and also to refuse to subscribe any ensnaring jests binding you to an unlimited subjection to the determination of Congress or Convention.

11. You are instructed to move and insist that the public accounts fairly stated shall be regularly kept in proper books, open to the inspection of all persons whom it may concern. If this should not be confirmed—contend for it.

12. You are instructed to move and insist that the power of County Courts be much more extensive than under the former constitution, both with respect to matters of property and breaches of the peace. If not confirmed—contend for it.

13. You are instructed to assent and consent to the establishment of the Christian Religion as contained in the scriptures of the Old and New Testaments, and more briefly comprised in the 39 Articles of the Church of England, excluding the 37th Article, together with all the Articles excepted and not to be imposed on dissenters by the act of toleration; and clearly held forth in the confession of faith compiled by the assembly of divines at Westminster, to be the Religion of the State, to the utter exclusion forever of all and every other (falsely so called) Religion, whether Pagan or Papal, and that the full, free and peaceable enjoyment thereof be secured to all and every constituent member of the State as their unalienable right as Freemen, without the imposition of rites and ceremonies, whether claiming civil or ecclesiastical power for their source, and that a confession and profession of the Religion so established shall be necessary in qualifying any person for public trust in the State. If this should not be confirmed—protest and remonstrate.

14. You are instructed to oppose to the utmost any particular church or set of clergymen being invested with power to decree rites and ceremonies and to decide in controversies of faith to be submitted to under the influence of penal laws—you are also to oppose the establishment of any mode of worship to be supported to the opposition of the rights of conscience, together with the destruction of private property. You are to understand that under modes of worship are comprehended the different forms of swearing by law required. You are moreover to oppose the establishing

an ecclesiastical supremacy in the sovereign authority of the State. You are to oppose the toleration of the popish idolatrous worship. If this should not be confirmed—protest and remonstrate.

15. You are instructed to move and insist that not less than four-fifths of the body of which you are members, shall, in voting, be deemed a majority. If this should not be confirmed—contend for it.

16. You are instructed to give your voices to and for every motion and bill made or brought into the Congress or Convention, where they appear to be for public utility and in no ways repugnant to the above instructions.

17. Gentlemen, the foregoing instructions, you are not only to look on as instructions, but as charges, to which you are desired to take special heed as the general rule of your conduct as our Representatives, and we expect you will exert yourselves to the utmost of your ability to obtain the purposes given you in charge, and wherein you fail either in obtaining or opposing, you are hereby ordered to enter your protest against the vote of the Congress or Convention as is pointed out to you in the above instructions.

THREE COPIES OF THE DECLARATION.

As some writers were confused by the difference between the Resolves and the Declaration, so they were also by three different alleged copies of the latter. The first, or Martin copy, is given in the ninth chapter of the first volume, and was secured by Judge Martin, as he says, in Western North Carolina prior to 1800. As it would have been virtually impossible for an incorrect copy to have co-existed with the original, which was destroyed in 1800, this is obviously a genuine reproduction.

Following is the Davie copy, which was written from memory by John McKnitt Alexander soon after the burning of his house and the official papers:

1st. *Resolved*, That whosoever directly or indirectly abbetted or in any way or form countenanced the unchartered and dangerous invasion of our rights as claimed by Great Britain, is an enemy to this country, to America, and to the inherent and inalienable rights of man.

2d. *Resolved*, That we, the citizens of Mecklenburg county, do hereby dissolve the political bands which have connected us to the

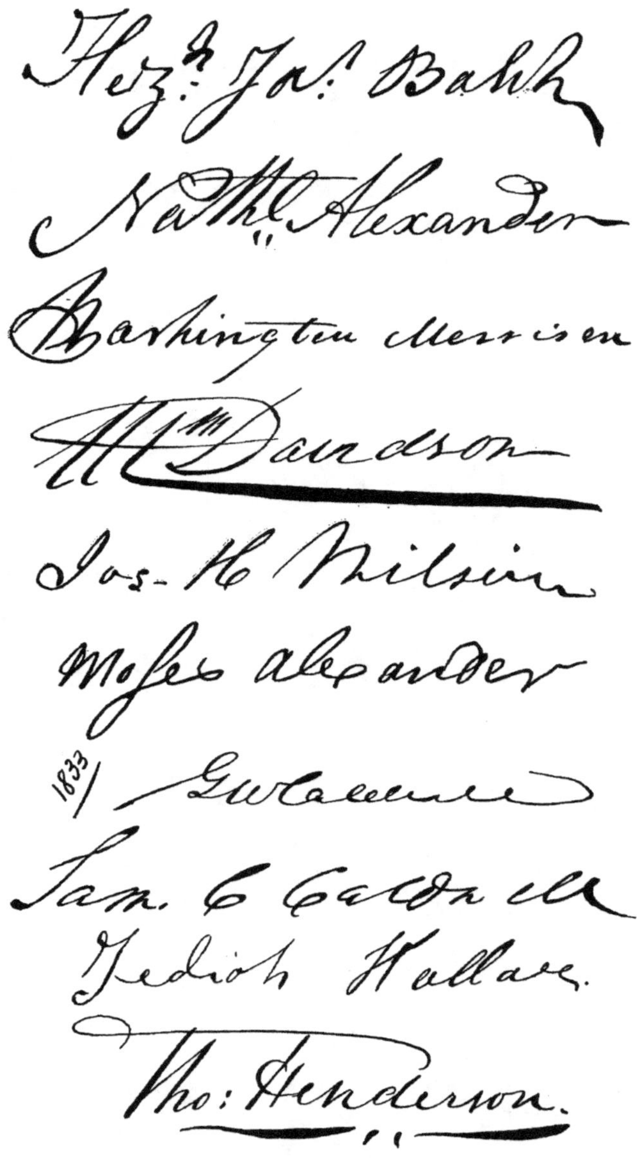

Hez.ᵈ Jaˢ Balch

Nathˡ Alexander

Harhington Merrison

Wᵐ Davidson

Jos. H. Wilson

Moses Alexander

1833 / G W Caldwell

Sam. C Caldwell

Jediah Wallace

Thoˢ Henderson

SIGNATURES OF PROMINENT CHARACTERS IN MECKLENBURG HISTORY.

mother country, and hereby absolve ourselves from all allegiance to the British Crown, and abjure all political connection, contract or association, with that nation who have wantonly trampled on our rights and liberties, and inhumanly shed the blood of American patriots at Lexington.

3d. *Resolved*, That we do hereby declare ourselves a free and inpendent people; are and of right ought to be a sovereign and self-governing association, under the control of no other power but that of our God and the general government of the Congress; to the maintenance of which independence, we solemnly pledge to each other our mutual co-operation, our lives, our fortunes, and our most sacred honour.

4th. *Resolved*, That as we now acknowledge the existence and control of no law or legal officer, civil or military, within this county, we do hereby ordain and adopt as a rule of life, all, each and every of our former laws, wherein, nevertheless, the crown of Great Britain never can be considered as holding rights, privileges, immunities, or authority therein.

5th. *Resolved*, That it is further decreed, that all, each and every military officer in this county is hereby reinstated in his former command and authority, he acting conformably to these regulations. And that every member present of this delegation, shall henceforth be a civil officer, viz: a Justice of the Peace, in the character of a "Committeeman," to issue process, hear and determine all matters of controversy according to said adopted laws, and to preserve peace, union and harmony in said county; and to use every exertion to spread the love of country and the fire of freedom throughout America, until a more general and organized government be established in this province.

The Garden copy, which is almost exactly similar to the Martin copy, was published in Garden's Anecdotes of the Revolution, in 1828, one year before the publication of Martin's history. Alexander Garden acknowledges as his source of information Dr. William Read, who attended Dr. Ephraim Brevard in his last illness in 1777, at the home of John McKnitt Alexander. Both the Garden and Martin copies are undoubtedly genuine reproductions of the original; the first was published in 1828 and the other in 1829, and Garden and Martin both stated that they did not know of the existence of the other copy until both had appeared in print. The Garden copy is as follows:

Resolved, That whoever directly or indirectly abets, or in any way, form, or manner, countenances the invasion of our rights, as attempted by the Parliament of Great Britain, is an enemy to his country, to America, and to the Rights of Man.

Resolved, That we, the citizens of Mecklenburg county, do hereby dissolve the political bonds which have connected us with the Mother Country, and absolve ourselves from all allegiance to the British Crown, abjuring all political connection with a nation that has wantonly trampled on our right and liberties, and inhumanly shed the blood of Americans at Lexington.

Resolved, That we do hereby declare ourselves a free and independent people, that we are and of right ought to be a sovereign and self-governing people, under the power of God and the General Congress, to the maintenance of which independence we solemnly pledge to each other our mutual co-operation—our lives—our fortunes—and our sacred honours.

Resolved, That we do hereby ordain and adopt, as rules of conduct, all and each of our former laws, and the Crown of Great Britain cannot be considered, hereafter, as holding any rights, privileges or immunities among us.

Resolved, That all officers, both civil and military, in this County, be entitled to exercise the same powers and authorities as heretofore—that every member of this delegation shall henceforth be a civil officer, and exercise the powers of a Justice of the Peace, issue process, hear and determine controversies, according to law, preserve peace, union and harmony in the county, and use every exertion to spread the love of liberty and of country, until a more general and better organized system of governmnet be established.

Resolved, That a copy of these Resolutions be transmitted by express to the President of the Continental Congress, assembled at Philadelphia, to be laid before that body.

Resolves of May 31, 1775, Copied from the South Carolina Gazette and Country Journal of June 13, 1775, No. 498—Printed at Charleston by Charles Crouch, on the Bay, Corner of Elliott Street.*

CHARLOTTE-TOWN, Mecklenburg County, May 31, 1775.

This day the Committee of this county met, and passed the following Resolves:

WHEREAS, By an Address presented to His Majesty by both Houses of Parliament, in February last, the American colonies are declared

---

*Copies of this paper are now on file in Charleston, S. C., and London, England.

to be in a state of actual rebellion, we conceive, that all laws and commissions confirmed by, or derived from the authority of the King or Parliament, are annulled and vacated, and the former civil constitution of these colonies, for the present, wholly suspended. To provide, in some degree, for the exigencies of this county, in the present alarming period, we deem it proper and necessary to pass the following Resolves, viz.:

I. That all commissions, civil and military, heretofore granted by the Crown, to be exercised in these colonies, are null and void, and the constitution of each particular colony wholly suspended.

II. That the Provincial Congress of each province, under the direction of the great Continental Congress, is invested with all legislative and executive powers within their respective provinces, and that no other legislative or executive power, does, or can exist, at this time, in any of these colonies.

III. As all former laws are now suspended in this province, and the Congress have not yet provided others, we judge it necessary, for the better preservation of good order, to form certain rules and regulations for the internal government of this county, until laws shall be provided for us by the Congress.

IV. That the inhabitants of this county do meet on a certain day appointed by this Committee, and having formed themselves into nine companies (to-wit), eight in the county, and one in the town of Charlotte, do chuse a Colonel and other military officers, who shall hold and exercise their several powers by virtue of this choice, and independent of the Crown of Great Britain, and former constitution of this province.

V. That for the better preservation of the peace and administration of justice, each of those companies do chuse from their own body, two discreet freeholders, who shall be empowered, each by himself and singly, to decide and determine all matters of controversy, arising within said company, under the sum of twenty shillings; and jointly and together, all controversies under the sum of forty shillings; yet so as that their decisions may admit of appeal to the Convention of the Select-Men of the county; and also that any one of these men shall have power to examine and commit to confinement persons accused of petit larceny.

VI. That those two Select-Men, thus chosen, do jointly and together chuse from the body of their particular company, two persons properly qualified to act as Constables, who may assist them in the execution of their office.

VII. That upon the complaint of any persons to either of these Select-Men, he do issue his warrant, directed to the Constable, commanding him to bring the aggressor before him or them, to answer said complaint.

VIII. That these eighteen Select-Men, thus appointed, do meet every third Thursday in January, April, July, and October, at the Court-House, in Charlotte, to hear and determine all matters of controversy, for sums exceeding forty shillings, also appeals; and in cases of felony, to commit the person or persons convicted thereof to close confinement, until the Provincial Congress shall provide and establish laws and modes of proceeding in all such cases.

IX. That these eighteen Select-Men, thus convened, do chuse a Clerk to record the transactions of said Convention, and that said Clerk, upon the application of any person or persons aggrieved, do issue his warrant to one of the Constables of the company to which the offender belongs, directing said Constable to summons and warn said offender to appear before the Convention, at their next meeting, to answer the aforesaid complaint.

X. That any person making complaint upon oath, to the Clerk, or any member of the Convention, that he has reason to suspect, that any person or persons indebted to him, in a sum above forty shillings, intend clandestinely to withdraw from the county, without paying such debt, the Clerk or such member shall issue his warrant to the Constable, commanding him to take said person or persons into safe custody, until the next sitting of the Convention.

XI. That when a debtor for a sum below forty shillings shall abscond and leave the county, the warrant granted as aforesaid, shall extend to any goods or chattels of said debtor, as may be found, and such goods or chattels be seized and held in custody by the Constable, for the space of thirty days; in which time, if the debtor fail to return and discharge the debt, the Constable shall return the warrant to one of the Select-Men of the company, where the goods are found, who shall issue orders to the Constable to sell such a part of said goods as shall amount to the sum due; That when the debt exceeds forty shillings, the return shall be made to the Convention, who shall issue orders for sale.

XII. That all receivers and collectors of quit-rents, public and county taxes, do pay the same into the hands of the chairman of this Committee, to be by them disbursed as the public exigencies may require; and that such receivers and collectors proceed no further in their office, until they be approved of by, and have given to, this Committee, good and sufficient security, for a faithful return of such monies when collected.

XIII. That the Committee be accountable to the county for the application of all monies received from such public officers.

XIV. That all these officers hold their commissions during the pleasure of their several constituents.

XV. That this committee will sustain all damages that ever hereafter may accrue to all or any of these officers thus appointed, and thus acting, on account of their obedience and conformity to these Resolves.

XVI. That whatever person shall hereafter receive a commission from the Crown, or attempt to exercise any such commission heretofore received, shall be deemed an enemy to his country, and upon information being being made to the Captain of the company in which he resides, the said company shall cause him to be apprehended, and conveyed before the two Select-Men of the said company, who, upon proof of the fact, shall commit him, the said offender, to safe custody, until the next sitting of the Committee, who shall deal with him as prudence may direct.

XVII. That any person refusing to yield obedience to the above Resolves, shall be considered equally criminal, and liable to the same punishment, as the offenders above last mentioned.

XVIII. That these Resolves be in full force and virtue, until instructions from the Provincial Congress, regulating the jurisprudence of the province, shall provide otherwise, or the legislative body of Great Britain, resigns its unjust and arbitrary pretentions with respect to America.

XIX. That the eight militia companies in the county, provide themselves with proper arms and accoutrements, and hold themselves in readiness to execute the commands and directions of the General Congress of this province and this Committee.

XX. That the Committee appoint Colonel Thomas Polk, and Doctor Joseph Kenedy, to purchase 300 lb. of powder, 600 lb. of lead, 1,000 flints, for the use of the militia of this county, and deposit the same in such place as the Committee may hereafter direct.

Signed by order of the Committee.

Eph. Brevard,
Clerk of the Committee.

CORRESPONDENCE BETWEEN JOHN VAUGHN AND COLONEL PETER FORCE.

The following letters were secured many years ago through the kindness of William L. Force, of Washington, D. C., and are here published for the first time.* John Vaughn, whose inquiry elicited the valuable reply from Col. Force, was born in England in 1756, was a brother of

---

*Preserved in manuscript by Lyman J. Draper.

38   HISTORY OF MECKLENBURG COUNTY.

Benjamin Vaughn, the friend and correspondent of Franklin, came to America in 1776, and became acquainted with Washington, Jefferson, Franklin, Adams and others; was president of the American Philosophical Society and a man of extensive learning and strong character, and died in Philadelphia in 1841.

Colonel Peter Force, historian, was born at Passaic Falls, New Jersey, November 26, 1790. His father, William Force, was a soldier in the Revolution, and moved to New York city in 1793, and his son there learned the printer's trade and was president of the Typographical Society in 1812. In 1815, he moved to Washington City, where he published an annual called the National Calendar, from 1820 to 1836; in 1823, he established the *National Journal* in support of Adams for the presidency; was councilman and alderman; mayor from 1836 to 1840; rose to the rank of major-general of militia; and was president of the National Institute. He published several volumes of importance, the greatest of them being the American Archives, in nine volumes. Gen. Force died in Washington January 23, 1868, leaving two sons, William L. Force and Manning F. Force, the latter having been a general in the Civil War, and afterwards becoming a judge in Ohio.

In reading these letters, it is to be remembered that they were written in 1841, and it is obvious that neither of the writers had read even all the literature on the subject which was then obtainable. Col. Force recognizes the overwhelming evidence in support of the authenticity of the Mecklenburg Declaration, and for want of a better explanation of the difference between the Declaration and the Resolves, endeavors as others have done, to account for it on the assumption that there was but one meeting of the committee and that one or the other of the two documents was incorrect. Not until the publication of the Colonial Records, nearly half a century later, was it known that these meetings were frequent not only in Mecklenburg, but in other counties in North Carolina, and then it was made known that the Resolves were adopted at a meeting of the Mecklenburg Committee held eleven days after the convention, and that they were amended and added to at similar meetings convened subsequently.

(From John Vaughn to Col. Force.)

PHILADELPHIA, Nov. 26, 1841.

Peter Force, Esq., Washington:

DR. SIR:—Mr. Jefferson has been accused of borrowing from the Mecklenburg, N. C., Declaration sundry expressions which he made use of in his draught of the Declaration of Independence, and the question was discussed at a meeting of our Historical Society, when a paragraph was produced from a newspaper stating that you had found a North Carolina paper in which the Mecklenburg Declaration was published soon after the resolutions were adopted, which did not contain the expressions said to be borrowed by Mr. Jefferson. Knowing your correctness, they were desirous of learning whether you had authorized such information. Oblige me by informing me when the Mecklenburg Declaration was made, and what was the date of the newspaper and its title, and whether the expressions alluded to were not found in the original Declaration, and in the published one, and, if not, when probably they were introduced in future publications and at what time.

It is desirable to put this question to rights whilst it can be done, and no evidence can be more conclusive than yours.

I remain yours truly,

JNO. VAUGHN.

(From Col. Force to John Vaughn.)

WASHINGTON, Dec. 11, 1841.

DEAR SIR:—I avail myself of the earliest opportunity in my power to reply to your letter of the 26th of November. The Mecklenburg Resolutions, commonly called "The Mecklenburg Declaration of Independence," were adopted in May, 1775. There are two papers which are said to be copies of these Resolutions, one is in manuscript (A), where the Resolutions are dated May 20th; the other is printed (B), where they are dated May 31st* of that year. You ask if certain expressions are not found in the original Declaration, and in the published one. By "the original Declaration" I suppose you mean

---

*A, was the Declaration; B, was the Resolves.—D. A. T.

the manuscript copy; for of the existence of the original at this time nothing is known. We are told that the original book, that is, the book in which the Resolutions were originally entered, was burned in April, 1800. It is not pretended that the manuscript now in the executive office at Raleigh is the original Declaration—there it purports to be nothing more than a mere copy, and is incorporated into a notice of the transactions of that period, drawn up some time afterwards, apparently for publication. When it was written is not stated, but it bears evidence on the face of it that it was written after the 4th of July, 1776.* It was first published in the Raleigh *Register* of April 30, 1819. "The expressions Mr. Jefferson has been accused of borrowing for his draft of the Declaration of Independence," are found in this copy.

That the Resolutions were published soon after its date, Governor Martin's Proclamation of the 8th of August, 1775, furnishes evidence. The Governor says: "And whereas, I have also seen a most infamous publication in the Cape Fear *Mercury*, importing to be the Resolves of a set of people styling themselves a committee for the county of Mecklenburg, most traitoriously declaring the entire dissolution of the Laws, Government and Constitution of their county, and setting up a system of Rule and Regulation repugnant to the Laws, and subversive of His Majesty's Government." After a careful research and extensive inquiry, I have not been so fortunate as to find a copy of this newspaper, and, of course, have never said that I had found a North Carolina newspaper in which the Mecklenburg Declaration was published soon after the Resolutions were adopted.

But, I have two of the early printed copies of the Mecklenburg Resolutions. One is in the New York *Journal* of the 29th of June, the other in the Massachusetts *Spy* of the 12th of July, 1775. The Resolutions, then dated May 31st, do not contain the expressions you refer to. They were printed in New York more than a year before the Declaration of Independence, in less than a month after their date, within a week of the time when the messenger by whom they were transmitted to the Continental Congress was in Philadelphia, and at the very time when the publication of a forged or false copy must have been followed by instant detection and exposure. They were then received as genuine, and I believe their authority has not, to this day, been disputed. With regard to the date, it is possible that in transcribing or printing a figure (3) may have been substituted* for a (2), and then made May 31st instead

---

*The copy referred to was the Davie copy, made in 1800.—D. A. T.

of May 21st. This is altogether possible;* but it does not change the character or affect the genuineness of the paper. It is proper to call your attention to the fact that though the printed copy contains the Resolutions which form the Declaration of Independence, it does not give all the Resolves adopted at the same time by the Committee. This remark applies also to the manuscript copy; but there is this difference between the two copies—the writer of the manuscript takes no notice of any omitted resolutions; he gives five (numbering the Preamble as one of them), as all that were "unanimously ordained," leaving every one to believe, and such has been the universal belief, that he had given the whole. The printed copy of the 29th of June, after the Preamble and four Resolutions, gives the substance of the succeeding eleven, and then the sixteenth Resolve at length.* The eleven omitted Resolutions relate exclusively to the county of Mecklenburg, or to the province of North Carolina, and from the *"System of Rule and Regulation,"* for the temporary government of that county or the province mentioned in Gov. Martin's Proclamation. As these eleven Resolutions apply only to the local affairs of the county or province, we can readily account for the omission by a printer in New York; but it is not easy to imagine why the same Resolutions (that is, the Resolutions containing the Rules and Regulations), were omitted by the writer of the manuscript, if they were in his possession when he drew up his narrative, unless we suppose he intended to cover the omission by his 5th resolution.

The two copies differ very widely in another respect. The manuscript does not "declare the *entire dissolution* of the Laws, Government and Constitution of this country." It applies to Mecklenburg county alone; that county only is declared independent—"a sovereign and self-governing association" by itself, separated alike from the Crown and the province, and leaving North Carolina and all the

---

*The subsequent discovery of the full series of resolves in the South Carolina *Gazette and Country Journal* confirmed the correctness of the date (May 31), when they were adopted. For reasons unknown, the Declaration of May 20th was not submitted for publication.—D. A. T.

---

*The entire set of Resolves of the 31st of May had not at this period been discovered, and hence Col. Force was not aware that they really numbered twenty beside the Preamble. It is also to be borne in mind that he was endeavoring to construe the Resolves as the Declaration, when in fact they were merely supplementary.—D. A. T.

other colonies in subjection to the Crown. The Declaration in the printed copy is of an entirely different character. It does declare "the entire dissolution" in that the whole country is declared independent.* The Declaration is not for one county of one colony; it is for all the colonies.

It is a Declaration of the independence of the United Colonies, and made by men who saw far into the future—whose patriotism was not limited by the boundaries of their own county. At that early day the men of Mecklenburg marked out the true course to be pursued by the whole continent for a redress of grievances; this was afterwards found to be the only course. When they took their ground they stood alone—their own province of North Carolina did not join them. They did not ask their fellow subjects to unite with them in so daring an enterprise without first encountering the peril themselves. They did not wait for others to take the first step—they did not stand at ease until the whole were prepared to advance in line; but they boldly and fearlessly marched out to the front, inviting by their example all the rest to follow. These men were the first to declare that the authority of the King and Parliament over "their colonies" was annulled and vacated. They were the first to declare "that the Provincial Congress of each province, under the direction of the great Continental Congress, is invested with all legislative and executive power, within their respective provinces, and that *no* other legislative or executive power does, or can at this time exist in any of these colonies." They were the first to incur the responsibility, whatever it might be, of making such a declaration, and publishing it to the world.

The Resolutoins were immediately forwarded by an express to the Continental Congress. I need not ask which of the two Declarations, the "manuscript" or the "printed" would be the most appropriate for such a special communication—that which related to the separation of a single county from a province, then represented by three delegates in that body; or that which in substance and in terms was a full and complete Declaration of Independence of all the colonies? With one, the Congress had nothing to do, while North Carolina was firm (and North Carolina was never otherwise than firm) in her support of the Continental measures. The other presented for consideration a question which no other body of men on the continent was competent to decide. What was the result of

---

*The convention of May 20th declared the independence of "the citizens of Mecklenburg county," while the Resolves of May 31st "conceive" the suspension of *"the former civil constitution of these colonies."*—D. A. T.

the mission? The Congress, as will be seen by their Declaration of the 6th of July,* believed it inexpedient at the time to declare independence. The people of Mecklenburg acquiesced in this decision, and fell back into line; their delegates in the next Provincial Congress, held at Hillsboro, in August, 1775, united with the other members in all their proceedings, and we find subscribed to the "Test," adopted and signed on the 23d of August, which begins with these words: "We, the subscribers, professing our allegiance to the King, and acknowledging the constitutional executive power of government"—the names of Thomas Polk, John McKnitt Alexander, John Phifer, Waightstill Avery, with one hundred and eighty others, members of that Congress.

It has been suggested that there were two sets of Resolves adopted —two separate and distinct Declarations made on two different days—one by a convention, another by a committee of Mecklenburg county, and that the manuscript copy is the record of the proceedings of one of these meetings, the printed copy of the other meeting. But this is a mere assumption not supported by a particle of evidence. The writer of the manuscript mentions but one. None of the survivors in 1830 of those who were inhabitants of Mecklenburg county in May, 1775, and present when the resolutions were adopted, speak of two Declarations.** But one messenger was sent by the Committee to the Continental Congress with "The Declaration." Gov. Martin alluded to one only, which had then been printed, and we find one printed six weeks before the date of his Proclamation corresponding so exactly with his description of it as to leave no room for doubt that it is the identical paper he denounces as "the *Resolves* of a set of people styling themselves *a committee for the county of Mecklenburg*, declaring *the entire dissolution* of the Laws, Government and Constitution of *this country*, and setting up *a system of Rule and Regulation*," etc.

In answering your letter, my dear sir, I have endeavoured to be as brief as possible to notice such points only as were necessary, and to avoid everything that had not a direct bearing upon your questions; yet I am conscious that I have extended mine to an unreasonable length. But upon looking it over, I see nothing that

---

*6th of July, 1775.—D. A. T.

**They were called upon to certify specifically that the Declaration was made and they did so. There was only one Declaration, and there was no occasion for remarks about the Resolves of May 31. Meetings were held at intervals during the entire year, but were not mentioned in a discussion wholly concerned with the Convention of May 20.—D. A. T.

strikes me as proper to be omitted, so I send it all, trusting to your patience and good nature to find a suitable excuse for me. If I have succeeded in establishing a single truth, or in removing a single doubt—if I have cleared away one of the many clouds of error, that for twenty years have thrown so much darkness around this brilliant star in our history, I shall be entirely satisfied. For the convenience, I add copies of the two papers marked A and B, I have referred to so often.

Very respectfully, etc.,
[Signed.]   PETER FORCE.

John Vaughn, Esq., Philadelphia.

GOV. SWAIN'S LETTERS.

David Lowry Swain, son of George Swain, was born near Asheville, Buncombe county, North Carolina, January 4, 1801. He was educated in Asheville, attended the State University for a short while, studied law under the direction of Judge John L. Taylor in Raleigh, served as member of the General Assembly, Solicitor of the Edenton district, member of the State Board of Internal Improvements, trustee of the University, Judge of the Superior Court, and was elected Governor in 1832, being then only thirty-one years of age. He was elected president of the University in 1835, and served in that capacity until his death, August 27, 1868. He organized the historical society of the University in 1844, and in 1855, he was appointed State Historical Agent. In this position he did work of great and lasting value in securing and preserving documents of importance. His generosity in assisting Bancroft, Lossing, Hawks, Wheeler, Randall and other historians without reward in any form, attests the sterling character of the man.

Governor Swain probably devoted more time to the study of the Mecklenburg Declaration of Independence and the involved questions than did any other man. He examined carefully all the available testimony in a spirit in which even his unswerving patriotism and love for his native State could not influence him in his search for truth. Of the authority of the Declaration, he had no doubts, but he could not satisfy himself as to the details. It matters not to

COAT OF ARMS OF THE PHIFER FAMILY, 1760.

PROCLAMATION MONEY.

us to-day whether the Declaration was made May 20 or May 31, but to Governor Swain, it was a matter of importance to accurately and positively determine every item of historical importance. No one has ever disputed the account of the resolves of May 31, which were published at the time, and when the discussion arose, the forthcoming evidence proved the facts of the convention of May 20. Then some writers undertook to reconcile the two or prove there was but one, but there were the two sets of resolutions and all finally came to the same conclusion as did Governor Swain, as is shown in the following correspondence.

(*Gov. Swain to Hon. Benson J. Lossing.*)*

CHAPEL HILL, Dec. 20, 1851.

MY DEAR SIR:—Your letter of the 14th was received this morning. In reply to your enquiries about the Mecklenburg Declaration, I find myself constrained to say several things which might be much more satisfactorily communicated if I had you before me in the midst of the books and documents to which I must necessarily refer.

The preface to the State Pamphlet, of which you speak, was written by me for Gov. Stokes. The report of the committee (p. 9) was drawn by Mr. Badger, of the United States Senate, the brother-in-law of Gen. J. G. Polk, Chairman, and the son-in-law of Colonel Wm. Polk. The latter was the only surviving field officer of the North Carolina line, a shrewd observer, and of unquestioned truthfulness, and it was he who first called attention to the subject by the publication which produced the correspondence between Adams and Jefferson.

Neither Gov. Martin's Proclamation, nor the five Resolutions in the American Archives (Vol. XI., p. 855), had then been disinterred by Col. Force, and it is not very surprising that in the then state of facts I should have yielded to the force of my own argument. (Gov. Stoke's preface.)

The entire series of Resolutions adopted 31st of May (2d Wheeler, p. 255), was first discovered in the Charleston Library by Dr. Joseph Johnson, after repeated searches made at my instance, was copied

---

*Benson John Lossing, born in New York, February 12, 1813, author of the Pictoral Field Book of the Revolution, Life of Washington, and other books. Died near Dover Plains, New Jersey, June 3, 1891.—D. A. T.

and communicated to me, and by me sent to Mr. Bancroft, at London. He had found it there before my letter reached him, but not until after Dr. Johnson had sent it to me.

All the original papers which were copied in the State Pamphlet are now in my possession. I have examined Dr. Smyth's pamphlet, Mr. Tucker's life of Jefferson, and probably all that has been written, and worth reading upon the subject. There may have been a meeting of the Committee on the 20th, and resolutions may have been adopted; but there is no evidence satisfactory to my mind if it be so, that the papers purporting to be Mecklenburg Declaration are true copies of the original record. If they be, where were they made and by whom?

The Davie paper, as we call it, (State Pamphlet, pp. 14, 15, 16), shown to be in the handwriting of John McKnitt Alexander, in whose house the original was burned in April, 1800, was written in September, 1800, about five months after the destruction of the record. It was not taken from the record, it is not shown to be the copy of a copy, or that there was a copy extant in September, 1800.* In form it appears to be a narrative of past events, not a record of present proceedings. Compare it with the copy in second Martin's History of North Carolina, page 574, and the discrepancies are numerous and remarkable. The former consists of five, the latter of six resolutions. The former speaks in tne past, the latter in the present time ; and in fine the latter is not merely an enlarged, but an improved edition.* I wrote to Judge Martin in 1842, requesting to be informed when and by whom his copy was furnished, but I did not succeed in extracting a reply.**

Without entering farther into the enquiry than to call attention to the two facts which follow, I feel free to say that I regard the paper of the 31st as the better, supposing both to be genuine.

1. You will perceive from the editorial copied from the Raleigh *Register* (p. 23), that previous to February, 1820, Col. Polk, who was present at the meeting held, "thought there were errors as to the

---

*The "Davie paper" was written from memory by John McKnitt Alexander, and the fact that its variance from the genuine (Martin's) copy is no greater, is evidence that John McKnitt Alexander was thoroughly acquainted with the original document. See his certificate.—D. A. T.

**Martin testified to Dr. Hawks that he secured the copy before 1800 from some one (not an Alexander) in Western North Carolina, but that at that late date, he did not remember the name of the person.—D. A. T.

names of the secretary, etc." There was but one clerk on the 31st, Eph. Brevard. Is it probable that a committee organized under the articles of the American Association would have had two clerks at any time?*

2. How is it to be accounted for that the Resolutions of the 31st make no reference to the proceedings of the 20th, if the former were not merely more important than but the foundation of the latter?

Dr. Brevard died in a short time, and was no doubt succeeded in his office as clerk of the committee by J. McK. Alexander. Mr. Alexander's house was burned in April, 1800, and with it, as was supposed, the only written memorial of a most interesting and important historical event. The narrative sent to Gen. Davie was probably the most accurate account of the great transaction which his memory enabled him to furnish. Be this as it may, the evidence that the paper published in the Cape Fear *Mercury* and denounced by Gov. Martin; that transmitted by Gov. Wright to Lord Dartmouth, and the official dispatch forwarded by Capt. Jack to the Continental Congress are identical with the copy discovered in Charleston, is exceeding strong, if not conclusive.

The evidence of Gen. Graham on the point to which you refer, goes very far towards identifying the Resolutions of the 31st as those discussed in his hearing. The statement of John Simeson (p. 25), which seems not to have attracted your attention, appears to me to strip the enquiry almost of reasonable doubt. At the distance of fifty years the memory of no man can be relied upon as to dates and precise form of expression, while there are substantial facts so remarkable that no man can forget them.

"As to the names of those who drew up the Declaration, I am inclined to think Dr. Brevard was the principal, from his known talents in composition. * * *

"It was *towards the close of* May, 1775. In addition to which I have said the same committee appointed three men to secure all the military stores for the county's use. Thomas Polk, John Phifer and Joseph Kennedy. I was under arms near the head of the line near Col. Polk, and heard him distinctly read a long string of grievances, the Declaration and military order above." Apply this statement of Mr. Simeson to the last of the series of the Resolutions of the 31st of May. "That the Committee appoint Col. Thomas Polk and Dr. Joseph Kennedy to purchase 300 lbs. of powder, 600 pounds of lead, 1,000 flints for the use of the county and deposit the same in such places as the Committee may hereafter direct.

---

*There was but one Secretary May 20.—D. A. T.

"Signed by order of the Committee, Ephraim Brevard, Clerk of the Committee."

There is something potential in this closing resolution decidedly Cromwellian, and in unison with the character of the sturdy Scotch-Irish Presbyterian from whom it emanated:

> "Then put your trust in God, my boys,
> And keep your powder dry."

Queen's College was the Faneuil Hall of the South. Are you familiar with its history? Previous to its establishment there were but two chartered seminaries of learning in the province—Edenton and New Bern Academies. None but a member of the Established Church was eligible to the office of trustee or instructor, and the latter even appointed by the Governor. The Presbyterians applied to the Colonial Assembly for an unrestricted charter for a college in a county named in compliment to the King and Queen, Mecklenburg (Strelitz), the native place of the latter, in a town bearing the name of his consort, for an institution to be known by the titular distinction. The bill passed the Commons, of course; the Council did not choose to breast the storm of popular indignation, which a rejection would have excited. Gov. Tryon had not the firmness to disallow it;" but the triple compliment to royalty availed little on the other side of the Atlantic, and a year afterwards, 1771, the charter was "repealed by a royal proclamation." It continued to exist nevertheless, and the first Legislature under the State Constitution, in 1777, gave it a charter by the name of Liberty Hall Academy. In accordance with the instruction of the people of Mecklenburg, the Constitution of 1776 made the creation of a University imperative upon the Legislature and declared that no preference should be given to one religious denomination over another. So far as Mecklenburg was concerned, the war of the Revolution was a war waged mainly for religious liberty, and this was the seminal principle which made it, "the most rebellious county in America." The instructions, etc., (2d Wheeler, p. 260) should bear date in September, 1776, instead 1775. I have the original papers before me. You are probably aware that Foote and others, regarding it as dated in 1775, rely upon it as giving collateral support to the Declaration of the 20th.

It is proper that I should apprise you that Dr. Smyth, of Charleston; Gov. Graham and Judge Cameron, and many others, concur with Dr. Hawks in the opinion that the authenticity of the latter paper cannot be controverted.

While I have never assumed to speak excathedra upon this subject, I have never concealed my opinion from my friends. Wheeler and Wiley were fully apprised of them, and the former persisted in maintaining the authenticity of the paper despite of assurances from me that none of the gentlemen* to whom his book is dedicated would sustain him. If you publish the sketch of Gov. Caswell, sent you sometime since, please strike out the words "in conjunction with Col. Lillington." The statement implying a divided command was first made by Jones and followed by Wheeler, in entire disregard or ignorance of all the evidence, traditionary and written on the subject and in the teeth of records of uncontrovertable verity. The very Assembly, which in April, 1776, gave Caswell a vote of thanks and promoted him to the office of Brigadier General of the New Berne District, appointed John Ashe Brigadier General of the Wilmington District, over the head of Lillington. I sat down without any intention of writing so long a letter. The day is very cold and my fingers very numb, and I have written in unavoidable haste. You will read, however, if you succeeded in deciphering it at all, with unavoidable deliberation. You may show it to Mr. Bancroft if you choose.

Yours very truly,

D. L. SWAIN.

You must not infer from what I have said that I do not consider Col. Lillington to have been a meritorious officer. Very far from it. I mean simply to say, that at Moore's Creek he acted, and was regarded universally, as a subordinate.

(Governor Swain to Hon. George Bancroft.)**

CHAPEL HILL, 6th March, 1858.

MY DEAR SIR:—Your note of the 1st was received yesterday. The

---

*"To George Bancroft, LL. D., whose writings have marked the age in which he lives, and the only historian who has done justice to North Carolina; to Peter Force, of Washington City, whose patient labors and indefatigable research have proved his early patriotism; and to David L. Swain, LL. D., whose native worth, whose services and whose talents are alike her pride and ornament."—Wheeler's Dedication.

**George Bancroft, born in Worcester, Massachusetts, October 3, 1800, graduated at Harvard in 1817, studied in Europe until 1822, Secretary of the Navy in Polk's Cabinet, Minister to England from 1846 to 1849, Minister to Germany from 1867 to 1874. First notable work, "History of the Colonization of the United States," published in 1834. Greatest work, History of the United States in ten volumes. Died in Washington, January 17, 1891.—D. A. T.

copy of my report, to which you refer, is, as you perceive from the date, a corrected reprint of the one sent you a year ago.* The reply of Lord Shaftebury, a copy of which you were so kind as to send me, was not received until after my report to the General Assembly was published. I wish very much it was in my power to have a personal conference with you in relation to the Mecklenburg Resolutions, and other events in our Revolutionary history. I have held very free and full discussion with Dr. Hawks after a minute examination of all the papers at my command, and we understand each other better, and are more nearly together in opinion than we were at the time we appeared before your Historical Society. I would like very much to go over the same ground with you. He never saw the evidence on which I rely as conclusive until his arrival here in June last, after the delivery of his lecture in Charlotte. At the close of the examination I gave him a paper copied below. and expressed the opinion that every fact set forth might be embodied in a *special verdict*, and established by the evidence before us, if an issue were made up and submitted to a jury.

"The documentary evidence in my possession satisfies me that there was a meeting of the Citizens of Mecklenburg, at Charlotte, on the 19th and 20th of May, 1775, and that resolutions in relation to independence were discussed and adopted. I entertain no doubt that the record of the proceedings of the Mecklenburg Committee was burned in the home of John McKnitt Alexander, in the month of April, 1800, and that the Davie paper contains what Gen. Graham, Col. Wm. Polk, and other gentlemen of high character, whose certificates appear in the State Pamphlet, believed to be a true narrative of the transactions of these two days. I have seen no paper purporting to be a copy of the resolutions, which I suppose to be of earlier date than September, 1800.

"I entertain the opinion that the resolutions of the 31st May were the resolutions published in the *Cape Fear Mercury*, and referred to in the Proclamation of Governor Martin, and that there was no contemporaneous publication of the proceedings of the 19 and 20 of May. That a copy of the record of these events was placed in the hands of Dr. Williamson, with the intent that they should find a place in history of North Carolina, I believe to be incontrovertable."

I send you by the present mail a copy of the *University Magazine* for November. The leading article on the battle of Moore's Creek is worthy of your attention. In addition to the authorities relied upon by Prof. Hubbard, the article Caswell, in Roger's Biographical Dictionary, and more especially a note in 2d Williamson, N. C., pp.

---

*Refers to his report as State Historical Agent.—D. A. T.

277-78, which escaped the research of Prof. H., supply direct and positive evidence of the accuracy of Prof H.'s conclusions. Williamson was at the head of the medical staff of our Revolutionary Army, was not merely contemporary with Caswell, but knew him familiarly during the most interesting period of his life, and survived him many years. But for Caswell's resignation he would have been his colleague in the Convention that formed the Federal Constitution in 1787.

Yours very truly,

D. L. SWAIN.

Hon. George Bancroft.

Who was Col. Grey of the Loyal Militia of S. C., whose MS. you placed in the possession of Prof. Riven, of Columbia? Sabine makes no mention of him. May I publish the MS.?*

(Governor Swain to Hon. George Bancroft.)

CHAPEL HILL, 18th March, 1858.

MY DEAR SIR:—I avail myself of the earliest opportunity to reply to your note of the 11th, which arrived during my absence of a few days in attendance upon a meeting of the Green Mountain Association at Greensborough.

There is no document which fixes with certainty the date of the first meeting in Mecklenburg; nor, with the exception of a series of doggerel verses which have recently come into my possession, is there any paper containing a direct reference to the subject, which I suppose to be of earlier date than September, 1800. The conclusion at which I have arrived is founded upon a chain of facts and inferences which I could very readily present to your consideration, if we were together with the papers before us, but which I cannot very readily explain in writing.

The inquiry, indeed, seems to be, at present, of little importance, since it is concluded (conceded) on all sides that the resolutions of the 31st May were the resolves published in the *Cape Fear Mercury*, and transmitted by Gov. Martin to the English Government. The last paragraph on p. 12 of the State Pamphlet, states that at the close of the proceedings on 20th May "a select committee was appointed to draw a more full and definite statement of grievances." It is not reasonable to suppose that the committee met on

---

*Col. Robt. Grey commanded a company in the regiment of South Carolina Loyalists, and his interesting narrative of Whig and Tory warfare in South Carolina in 1780-81 was published in the North Carolina University Magazine for November, 1858.—D. A. T.

the 31st without preconcert and preliminary arrangement, adopted a series of resolutions and adjourned. There can be no doubt that independent of the committee there was a numerous meeting of citizens, called by a summons from Col. Polk. This meeting probably agreed upon some general principles which the committee was expected to embody in proper form and present to the Continental Congress. The Davie Paper is simply the narrative of these events, according to the recollection of John McKnitt Alexander, drawn up after the destruction of the original record.

A note on page 5 of the State Pamphlet gives us the assurance of Gov. Stokes that in 1793 he saw in the hands of Dr. Williamson, in Fayetteville, a copy of this record, together with a letter from J. McKnitt Alexander in relation to it. I wrote the note myself under the direction of Gov. Stokes; and though I know he had an exceedingly retentive memory, did not at the time attach much importance to it. I have now before me a letter from Israel Pickens, whom I knew familiarly from my boyhood until the period of his death. He represented my native district in Congress during the War of 1812, and was the first Governor of the State of Alabama. He died in Cuba, after his election to the Senate of the United States. I know no living man whose testimony is entitled to higher consideration than that of Gov. Davie, Judge Cameron and Gov. Pickens. Gov. Picken's letter is addressed to his father-in-law, Gen. William Lewis, and is dated 23d March, 1823.

"Agreeably to your request, I have made from my best recollection a statement of the proceedings of the Mecklenburg Convention of 1775, as related to me many years ago by John McKnitt Alexander, Esq., formerly and until his death a resident of that county. The relation of that transaction by that remarkable old man made a strong impression on my mind, as well as it formed a curious part of the history of my native county, and because my informant himself was a member of the Convention and proverbial for his scrupulous accuracy in recollecting and detailing events. The following is concisely the substance of his narrative:

"Understanding that Davie or Hugh Williamson was about to write a history of N. Carolina some twelve years ago, I apprised him of the circumstances of the Convention of Mecklenburg. He informed me that he had many years previously been informed of it by Gen. Steele and others, but compared their acts of anticipation of the American Independence to that whereby Virginia had claimed the title of the *Ancient Dominion* on account of having declared in favor of Charles the Second sometime before the restoration took place in England, both events being expected long before.

"Whatever credit this small revolution may reflect on its author for patriotism, or whatever discredit for imprudence, or as a historical fact, the relation here given is believed to be derived from a correct source and faithfully detailed.

Yours most obt.,
ISRAEL PICKENS.

The poem to which I refer above bears date 18th March, 1777, extends thro' 260 lines, and is of unquestionable authenticity. It opens as follows:

"THE MECKLENBURG CENSOR.

"When Mecklenburg's fantastic rabble,
Renowned for censure, scold and gabble,
In Charlotte met in giddy council,
To lay the Constitution's ground sill,
By choosing men both learned and wise,
Who clearly could with half-shut eyes,
See mill-stones through, or spy a plot,
Whether existed such or not;
Who always could at noon define
Whether the sun or moon did shine,
And by philosophy tell whether
It was dark or sunny weather;
And sometimes, when their wits were nice,
Could well distinguish men from mice.
First to withdraw from British trust,
In Congress they, the very first,
They their independence did declare."

I am ashamed to send you this very hasty and almost illegible communication. I must either do so, however, or loose a "mail," and under your injuction of haste do not feel at liberty to delay my reply for trivial causes.

Yours very truly,
D. L. SWAIN.

Hon. George Bancroft.

(Governor Swain to Hon. H. S. Randall.)**

CHAPEL HILL, 6th April, 1858.

DEAR SIR:—Your letter of the 31st ult. was received by yester-

---

**Henry S. Randall, born in New York in 1811, graduated at Union College, and studied law, but never practiced, Secretary of the State of New York in 1851; member of the General Assembly in 1871; published several volumes of his writings; author of Life of Thomas Jefferson (1758); died in Cortland, New York, in August, 1876.

day's mail. By turning to the 18th page of my Report as Historical Agent to the General Assembly of North Carolina, a copy of which I send you, you will find a letter from Dr. Hawks, in which he assures me that he will put no portion of his forthcoming History to press without submitting it to my examination. That assurance has since been repeated orally and in writing, and I am in daily expectation of his arrival here with the MS. of his second volume** in order to afford the fairest opportunity for joint personal revision. Under these circumstances, I do not feel myself at liberty to anticipate or forestall him by any authorized publication of my views with respect to the Mecklenburg Resolutions.

My letters to Mr. Bancroft were hastily written, and in their present shape, are unworthy of incorporation in such a work as yours. They contain, nevertheless, nothing which I do not believe to be true and susceptible of proof from evidence in my possession. The facts and inferences are entirely at your service and may be used at your discretion, in the composition of your narrative.

You remark that the main question, so far *as Mr. Jefferson is concerned*, is this: "Is the Alexander copy of the Mecklenburg Resolutions *genuine?*" The paper *is* unquestionably *genuine*. I have it before me, in the well-known hand-writing of John McKnitt Alexander. But what is it? It is not the record of the Mecklenburg Committee that perished in the fire which consumed Mr. Alexander's home in April, 1800; and this paper bears date in the following September. It is not a transcript, therefore, of the original record, If it be the copy of a copy, the inquiry presents itself, of that copy: How authenticated? where, when and by whom taken? Does it purport to be a copy, or is it simply upon the face of it the most accurate narrative which Mr. Alexander's memory could supply of the transactions to which it relates?

Regretting, for the reasons suggested, which I am certain will be satisfactory, that I cannot, with propriety, enter at present upon the preparation of such a paper as you desire, I remain,

Very respectfully yours,

D. L. SWAIN.

H. L. *Randall, Esq.*

Literature Discussing or Referring to the Mecklenburg Declaration,

in Addition to that Contained in this Book.

Raleigh Minerva, 1809.
North American Review, January, 1821.

**Dr. Hawks' History of North Carolina, in two volumes, published in 1859, only covered the period from 1584 to 1729.—D. A. T.

Nile's Principles and Acts of the Revolution, 1821.
Dr. M. W. Alexander's Address at Hopewell, July 5, 1824.
Catawba Journal (of Charlotte), October 19, 1824.
Garden's Anecdotes of the Revolution, 1828.
Martin's History of North Carolina, 1829.
Memoirs of Thomas Jefferson, by Thomas G. Randall, 1829.
Jones' Defense of North Carolina, 1834.
Life of Jefferson, by George Tucker, 1837.
New York Review, March, 1837, containing an article by Dr. Francis L. Hawks.
Pamphlet, by Prof. George Tucker, replying to Dr. Hawks' article, Feburary, 1838.
Southern Literary Messenger, April, 1838.
Southern Literary Messenger, August, 1838, containing an article by Dr. C. L. Hunter, son of Rev. Humphrey Hunter.
National Intelligencer, December 18, 1838.
Nile's Register, May 25, 1839.
Southern Literary Messenger, November, 1839, containing an article by Dr. C. L. Hunter.
Southern Literary Messenger, June, 1839.

Force's American Archives, 1839.
History of Virginia, by Charles Campbell, 1847.
Raleigh Register, February 14, 1847.
Southern Presbyterian Review, March, 1848.
Wheeler's History of North Carolina, 1851.
Correspondence between Force, Bancroft and Swain, 1841 to 1858.
Lossing's Field Book of the Revolution, 1852.
North Carolina University Magazine, May, 1853.
Nassau Literary Magazine (Princeton, N. J.), September, 1853, containing an article by Samuel S. Force.
Annals of Tennessee to the End of the Eighteenth Century, 1853, by Dr. J. G. M. Ramsey.
Revolutionary History of North Carolina, 1853; addresses by Hawks, Swain and Graham.
The Virginia Convention of 1776; an address by Hugh Blair Grigsby at William and Mary College, July 3, 1853.
National Intelligencer, September, 1856.
Address by Dr. Francis L. Hawks, in Charlotte, May 20, 1857, published in the Charlotte Democrat; Carolina Watchman (Salisbury), May 26; North Carolina Whig (of Charlotte), May 26; Raleigh Register, May 27.
National Intelligencer, August 13, 1857.
National Intelligencer, November 6, 1857.
Raleigh Sentinel, Charlotte Democrat and Wilmington Journal,

June 18 to September 6, 1874, containing articles by Daniel R. Goodloe, Major C. Dowd and John H. Wheeler.

North American Review, April, 1874.

American Historical Record, May, 1874, containing an article by Benjamin J. Lossing, LL. D.

New York Herald, May 14 and 20, 1875, containing letters from Gov. Graham and others.

Southern Home (of Charlotte), May 10, 1875.

Address by Hon. Wm. A. Graham, February 4, 1875.

Sketches of Western North Carolina, by Dr. C. Hunter, 1877.

Wheeler's Reminiscences of North Carolina, 1884.

Bancroft's History, 1884.

Foote's Sketches of North Carolina.

Memoirs and Reminiscences of Rev. Humphrey Hunter.

Pitkin's Political and Civil History of the United States.

RECEIPT, 1773.

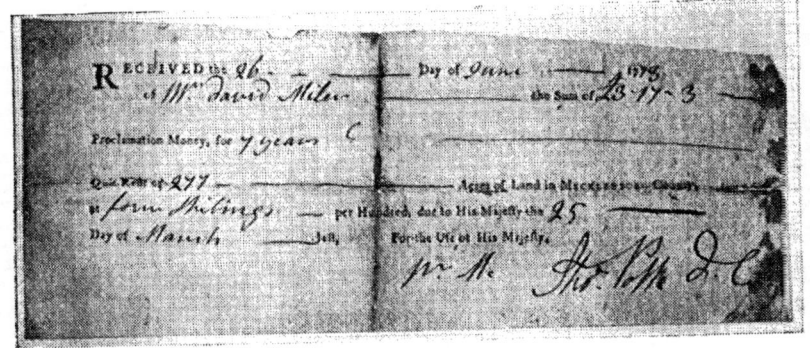

RECEIPT SIGNED BY THOS. POLK IN 1773.

CHAPTER II.

MECKLENBURG INDEPENDENCE MONUMENT.

Unveiling in Charlotte in 1898 Attended with Impressive Ceremonies.—Hon. Adlai E. Stevenson was Orator of the Occasion.—First Monument Association Incorporated in 1842.—Declaration Poem by Rev. W. W. Moore, of Virginia.

May 20, 1898, the one hundred and twenty-third anniversary of the Mecklenburg Declaration of Independence, a monument to the memory of the signers was unveiled in Charlotte. The handsome granite shaft, bearing appropriate inscriptions on bronze tablets, stands in front of the Mecklenburg County Court House, which was built on the site of the building in which was conducted the school known successively as Queen's College, Queen's Museum and Liberty Hall Academy.

The State Legislature, in 1842, passed an Act incorporating the Mecklenburg Monument Association. May 20, 1844, the first effort to raise money for the purpose was made, a supper being given in Charlotte in honor of the Revolutionary soldiers. There was a good attendance and a considerable sum was contributed. Judge Osborne, who made the address of the occasion started the subscription with a twenty-dollar gold piece.

During the Centennial celebration in May, 1775, new interest was awakened in the projected building of the monument. June 25, 1775, an organization was perfected, with Z. B. Vance, president; Dr. Joseph Graham and J. H. Wilson, vice-presidents, and T. W. Dewey, secretary and treasurer. A total of $5,000 was secured but was afterwards lost in the failure of the bank in which it was deposited.

In 1890, the Monument Association was again formed, with Mr. F. B. McDowell as president, and under his management the final and successful effort was made. For some years there was but little progress, and in the Fall of 1897, the leaders of the movement resolved that the work should be culminated by the following anniversary. In a short time the amount of money on hand justified them in contracting for the monument and announcing that it would be unveiled May 20, 1898.

The celebration on the day of the unveiling was one of the greatest ever witnessed in Charlotte. Speeches were made by Hon. Adlai E. Stevenson, Mr. F. B. McDowell, Mr. J. P. Caldwell, Governor Atkinson, of Georgia, and Col. Julian S. Carr. Rev. J. R. Howerton, D. D, led in prayer, and the Declaration of Independence was read by Capt. A. F. Brevard. Mr. McDowell stated that the *Charlotte Observer* had offered a prize for the best poem on the Mecklenburg Declaration. Col. H. C. Jones then announced that the winner was Rev. Walter S. Moore, D. D., of Hampden Sydney, Va., and he read the poem as follows:

To Piedmont Carolina, where virgin prairie soil
Bespoke abundant harvests to reward the tiller's toil,
From homes beyond the ocean there came in days of old
A band of sturdy heroes, a race of yeomen bold.

On all Catawba's uplands—for there they found their rest,
Those woods and wide savannas fulfilled their longing quest—
They reared their modest dwellings, they built their kirk and school,
For well they knew how danger grew from skeptic and from fool.

Behind the walls of Derry, their father's faith in God
Had filled their souls with courage to defy the tyrant's rod;
'Twere folly then to fancy that sons of sires like these
Would bear a yoke of bondage, or obey unjust decrees.

Their heirloom was a volume which taught the rights of man,
And made the least a king and priest free from despotic ban;
The people are the sovereigns, with rights inalienate.
The people make the government, the people are the State.

This truth was taught by Craighead, thus Mecklenburg believed,
And when oppressive measures passed, her sons were not deceived;
While others talked of redress as subjects of the crown,
They boldly broke the tyrant's yoke, and flung the gauntlet down.

From seven congregations in which they preached and prayed,
From woodlands and plantations, in homespun garb arrayed,
These yeomen rode to Charlotte, these man of mien sedate,
While high empires shone in their eyes—they came to found a State.

And there these dauntless statesmen, in ringing words and high,
Declared their Independence—"We'll win it or we'll die;
With lives and sacred honor, with fortunes great or small,
We will serve the cause of freedom, we will break the Briton's thrall."

Next year the Nation followed where Mecklenburg had led,
To all the world, with flag unfurled, her high resolve she read:
"No more shall sons of freemen endure the tyrant's rod,
This land shall be as Freedom, or we forsworn to God."

Through flaming broil of battle where Britain's bravest stood,
On field and flood, by blade and blood, they made their pledges good.
And now, where'er their banner floats over land and sea,
With grateful lays the people praise the men who made us free.

Then up with granite column, inscribed with lofty phrase,
Let Mecklenburg's achievement resound through endless days;
Her sons were first to utter the disenthralling word,
Let men proclaim their deathless name till all the world has heard.

CHAPTER III.

"BLACK BOYS" OF CABARRUS.

Young Men Destroyed Ammunition and Supplies Intended for Use Against the Regulators.—Gov. Tryon's Proclamation of Pardon Excepted Them.—Leading Citizens Later Petitioned in Their Behalf and Secured the Pardon.—Col. Moses Alexander Presented the Petition.

March, 17, 1771, Governor Tryon wrote to Colonel Moses Alexander, of Mecklenburg this letter:

"As I have come to a resolution by consent of my Council to March a Body of Troops from the Regiments of Militia of this Government, it will be necessary that several Commissaries should be appointed for the service, and as you acquitted yourself in that Department very much to my approbation in the late Hillsborough Expedition, I am induced to make you the offer of being Commissary to the Mecklenburg, Rowan and Tryon Detachments to supply the same with Ammunition, Provisions and about fifty camp kettles, at the same time observing that it would be very agreeable to me could you make it so to yourself that Captain Polk should be equally interested and concerned with you in the undertaking. From Col. Harris you will learn the orders that are to be observed by the Mecklenburg Detachment which I expect to see greatly animated by the zealous and spirited conduct of the several officers of the Corps in so necessary and essential a service."

Colonel Alexander immediately set about to procure the ammunition and supplies needed, at Charleston, South Carolina. While the supplies of powder and camp kettles were being carried through that part of Mecklenburg, which is now Cabarrus, James Ashmore, James White, John White, Jr., William White, Robert Caruthers, Robert Davis, Benjamin Cochran, Joshua Hadley and "William White, son of the Widow White," all disguised as Indians, went to Captain John Phifer's "old muster ground, where they found and stopped the wagons and enquired for the powder that was being carried to General Waddell; and in the wagon belonging to Colonel Alexander, they found the pow-

MONUMENT COMMEMORATING THE McINTYRE SKIRMISH, OCTOBER 3, 1780. (See Vol. I., Page 62.)

This monument is seven miles from Charlotte, on the Beatty's Ford road, and near by is the oldest house in Mecklenburg County, and in the house are imbedded some of the bullets fired in the skirmish. The inscription is: "In Commemoration of the McIntyre Skirmish, October 3, 1780. Erected by Mecklenburg Chapter Daughters of the American Revolution, 1901."

der and took it out of the wagons, broke open the hogsheads and kegs that contained the powder and set the same on fire, and destroyed some blankets, leggins, kettles and other things, and then dispersed soon after." This is the account of the transaction as sworn to by James Ashmore, before Capt. Thomas Polk, June 22, 1771, Ashmore says, in regard to the incipiency, that he with a number of others, were together at Andrew Logan's "old plantation in consequence of an advertisement (set up by one James McCaul, as it was said), when and where he was accosted by one James White Jr., to know whether he (Ashmore) thought it any harm to burn the powder," and they forthwith made and carried out the plan.

When Governor Tryon issued his amnesty proclamation, June 11, 1771, he excepted those unknown persons who had blown up the ammunition at Phifer's Hill. Colonel Moses Alexander and the law officers of this county began diligently to ascertain who had perpetrated this offense, and they were soon rewarded with success, Ashmore confessing and disclosing the names, under oath. When the authorities ascertained who the offenders were and under what circumstances the crime had been committed, they relented and began to take measures to secure their pardon at the hands of Governor Tryon, and with success. The representation of the following facts, to the Governor and his Council to secure the pardon of the offenders, was made by "a number of the Distressed Inhabitants of Rocky River and Coddle Creek Settlement," and carried to Newbern in November, 1771, by Col. Moses Alexander, whose property it was that had been destroyed.

The representation is as follows:

"That whereas a certain number of young men, ignorant of their Duty to our Sovereign Lord the King, riotously Assembled in a wicked manner, Combined against Government, without the least Knowledge, Advice, or Consent of Any Parent, friend, and some of them even Demented by Spirituous Liquors, did, about the first of May last, rashly and inconsiderately Destroy the ammunition of General Waddell and Sundrys, the Property of Colo. Moses Alexander; for which wicked deed, their parents and Friends are Drowned in Sorrows and the Unhappy Perpetrators truly and Deeply Afflicted. Permit us, Yr Excellency's most humble petitioners, to assure your Excellency that these Miserable persons were, prior to this Fact, esteemed faithful and loyal Subjects. We cannot but most tenderly Compassionate the Desolate and Distressed, and Even take part of their affliction, and Having learned of your exceeding Humanity and that benign Temper of mind which you are so Eminently Possessed of, we therefore beg with expectation, Cannot but Solicit and most earnestly and importunately pray, that your Excellency would be Graciously pleased to extend to these unhappy, though unworthy Subjects, his Majesties most free and gracious Pardon. That Your Excellency may see Loyalty to the best of Sovereigns and Fidelity to our noble Constitution, flourishing among us; and the Reigns of Government easy and Delightfull to yourself, shall be the Sincere Prayer of your Excellency's most humble and Dutifull Petitioners."

The petition for pardon, which was granted, was signed by Moses Shelby, Samuel Loftain, Matthew Stewart, John Morrison, David Slough, Samuel Harris, James Morrison, Robert McMurray, William White, John Davis, John Russell, Robert Russell, James Russell, William Scott, Robert Campbell, William Blair, Thomas Hall, Thomas Smith, William Adden, George Davys, Robert McCallan, James Callwall, James Harris, William Sper, John Callwall, Oliver Wiley, James Harris, David Caldwell.

This petition was presented to the Governor in Newbern by Colonel Alexander, in November, 1771. The Council recommended the pardon of the offenders and Governor Tryon issued the pardon. Some of the "black boys" were faithful soldiers in the Revolution.

James Ashmore's Testimony.

June 22, 1771.—James Ashmore swears before Thos. Polk as follows:
"NORTH CAROLINA, Mecklenburg County.
"The Deposition of James Ashmore, of full age, who being voluntarily sworn on the holy Evangelists of Almighty God, voluntarily deposeth and saith that he, this deponent, with a number of other persons, was convened at Andrew Logan's old plantation in conse-

quence of an advertisement (set up by one James McCaul as it was said), when and where this Deponent was accosted by one James White, Junior, to know whether this Deponent thought it any harm to burn the powder then carrying through the County aforesaid, to the army then under the command of General Hugh Waddell, to which this deponent made answer that according to the Reports passing of the Governor and his officers, that he did not think the bare burning of the powder any Harm, and that then this deponent went Home and the Day following, between the Hours of ten and eleven o'clock, in the forenoon, this deponent quit work on his plantation and went to look for his Horses. When about three-quarters of a mile from his House this Deponent was met by six men, disguised, in the Road, who in appearance resembled Indians, but after some persuasion, consented in part and then went Home with his Horses, and after returned with Joshua Hadley to a place about half a mile from this Deponent's House, where were assembled with himself nine persons, to-wit., James White, Junior, John White, Junior, William White, Robert Caruthers, Robert Davis, Benjamin Cochran, Joshua Hadley and William White, son of the Widow White, who all went thence disguised to Capt. Phifer's old muster Ground where they found and stopped the waggons and enquired for the powder that was carrying to Gen. Waddell. When in the waggon belonging to Col. Alexander they found the powder and took it out of the waggons, broke open the Hogsheads and kegs that contained the powder, and set the same on Fire and destroyed some blankets, leggins, kettles and other things, and then dispersed soon after, having at this Deponent first joining of them sworn him to secrecy as they informed who they all before, and further this Deponent sayeth not.

JAMES ASHMORE.

NOTE.—All these papers are verbatim copies from the Colonial Records.

CHAPTER IV.

BIOGRAPHICAL SKETCHES.

Condensed Items of Interest in the Lives of Persons Prominent in Mecklenburg History.—Brief Biographies Alphabetically Arranged.

Alexander, Abraham, born in Maryland in 1718, moved to Mecklenburg and settled near the Catawba River, member and chairman of the County Court for many years; in the Legislature in 1771; presided at the Convention of May 20, 1775; died April 23, 1786, leaving a widow and five sons and one daughter. Was buried at Sugar Creek.

Alexander, Adam, signer of the Mecklenburg Declaration of Independence, was born in Maryland in 1728; moved to the Clear Creek section of Mecklenburg, prominent magistrate of the county; became a colonel in the Revolution; died in 1798. He married Miss Shelby and had four sons— Evan, Isaac, Adam, Charles— and one daughter who married John Springs.

Alexander, Ezra, signer of the Mecklenburg Declaration of Independence, was born in 1720; was a Captain in the Revolutionary War, and in 1880 fought the Tories in Lincoln County. He died in 1790 and is buried in the Sharon church yard.

Alexander, Hezekiah, signer of the Mecklenburg Declaration of Independence, was born in Pennsylvania January 13, 1722; was a member of the District Committee of Safety in 1775, of the State Council in 1776; member of Provincial Constitutional Convention in 1777; lived four miles from Charlotte; died in 1801, and is buried in the Sugar Creek church-yard.

Alexander, Isaac, son of Adam Alexander, born in 1756; entered the army in 1775, and served throughout the war; married a daughter of David Reece, elected Clerk of the Court in 1790, and served until his death in 1833.

Alexander, John McKnitt, signer of the Declaration and

MRS. RACHEL HOLTON.
First Newspaper Woman in North Carolina; Editor of the Charlotte Journal in 1861.

THOMAS J. HOLTON, EDITOR OF THE CHARLOTTE **JOURNAL,**
1829.

secretary of the Convention, was born in Pennsylvania in 1733, and came to North Carolina in 1754. He was elected to the Provincial Assembly in 1772; was a delegate to the Assembly at Hillsboro in August 1775, and to the Halifax Assembly in April, 1776; and was the first member of the State Senate from Mecklenburg, elected under the Constitution, in 1777. He died July 10, 1817, and is buried at Hopewell. He left two sons—Joseph McKnitt Alexander and William Baine Alexander. The former was born in 1774, and died October 18, 1841; and the latter was born May 3, 1798, and died February 27, 1845.

Alexander, Governor Nathaniel, born in Mecklenburg in 1756; married Margaret Polk Brevard (a daughter of Dr. Ephraim Brevard and grand-daughter of Thomas Polk); was graduated from Princeton University in 1776; studied medicine, and entered the army; member of the General Assembly in 1797, 1801 and 1802, elected to Congress in 1802; elected Governor in 1803, and served two years; died in Charlotte November 8, 1808.

Ardrey, Dr. William A., son of William and Mary Ardrey, who emigrated to this country from Ireland in 1776, was born in York County, S. C., April 19, 1798; studied medicine, and located in the lower part of Mecklenburg; married Mrs. Lydia L. Cureton, daughter of John Potts, by whom he had seven children. Capt. James P. Was killed in the Civil War; Capt. W. E., of Providence township; J. W. of Fort Mill, S. C.; Dr. J. A., of Pineville; Mrs. Mary J. Bell, of Providence; Mrs. Margaret R. Potts, and Mrs. S. H. Elliott.

Alexander, William Julius, born in Salisbury in March, 1797; educated at Poplar Tent, by Rev. Dr. Robinson; was graduated from the University in 1816; studied law under Archibald Henderson, and was admitted to the bar in 1818. He married Catherine, daughter of Joseph Wilson; was elected to the Legislature from Mecklenburg in 1826, and re-elected until 1830, when he succeeded Joseph Wilson as Solicitor; was appointed Superintendent of the Charlotte Mint in 1846.

Avery, Waightstill, signer of the Mecklenburg Declaration of Independence, tenth child of Humphrey Avery, was born in Connecticut, May 3, 1743; was graduated from Princeton in 1766; studied law with Littleton Dennis, of Maryland, and came to North Carolina and was admitted to the bar in 1769. He lived with the family of Hezekiah Alexander; was a member of the Hillsboro Provincial Congress of August, 1775, and of the Halifax Congress in April, 1776. In the latter Avery, who was a learned scholar, rendered important service in forming the Constitution and Statutes of the State. He was a member of the Legislature in 1777, and was elected Attorney General in 1778. He moved to Burke County in 1781 and died there in 1821.

Balch, Rev. Hezekiah James, signer of the Mecklenburg Declaration of Independence, was born in Harford County, Maryland in 1748; was graduated from Princeton in 1766, in the same class with Waightstill Avery, He studied for the ministry and was apppointed a missionary to North Carolina by the Synods of New York and Philadelphia. He was the first pastor of Rocky River and Poplar Tent churches, and served those congregations until his death in 1776, and is buried in the church-yard at the latter place.

Barringer, John Paul, born in Germany in 1721, arrived in Philadelphia, in 1743; married Ann Eliza Iseman in Pennsylvania, in 1750; after the death of his first wife, married Catherine Blackwelder; Captain of the militia; exerted great influence in having Cabarrus County created; died in 1807. His brother, George, emigrated to this country and settled at Gold Hill; Matthias, another brother, settled in Lincoln, and was killed by the Indians. Three sisters also came; Catherine married Christian Overstein; Dolly married Nicholas Cook, and Elizabeth married Christian Barnhardt.

Barringer, General Paul, son of John Paul and Catherine, was born in 1778 in what is now Cabarrus County; a prominent and influential citizen; commissioned Brigadier-General of the North Carolina troops in 1812; member of the Legis-

JAMES W. OSBORNE.

lature from Cabarrus from 1806 to 1815, and of the State Senate in 1828; died at Lincolnton June 20, 1844, and was buried at Concord. He married Elizabeth, daughter of Matthew Brandon in 1805, and their children were as follows; D. M., member of Congress, Minister to Spain; Paul, of Mississippi; Rev. William, of Greensboro; Gen. Rufus Barringer, of Charlotte; Major Victor C. Barringer, First North Carolina Cavalry and Judge of International Court of Appeals in Egypt, 1874 to 1894; Margaret married John Boyd, and after his death married Andrew Grier; Mary, married Charles Harris, M. D.; Elizabeth, married Edwin Harris; and Catherine married W. G. Means.

Barringer, General Rufus, born at Poplar Grove, Cabarrus County, December 2, 1821; educated at Sugar Creek and at the State University, from which he was graduated in 1842; studied law under his brother, D. M. Barringer, and later under Judge Pearson, was a member of the Legislature from Cabarrus in 1848, and of the Senate in 1849; was a Bell and Everett elector in 1860; commissioned as Captain of Company F of the First Cavalry Regiment in May, 1861; Major in August, 1863; Lt. Colonel in October, 1863; Brigadier-General in June, 1864; located in Charlotte after the war; was influential in the establishment of the graded school and the public library; died February 3, 1895. He married, first, Eugenia, daughter of Dr. R. H. Morrison, and they had two children: Anna, who died young, and Dr. Paul Brandon Barringer, now of the University of Virginia; second, Rosalie Chunn, of Asheville, who had one son, Rufus; third, Margaret Long, of Hillsboro, who had one son, Osmond L. Barringer.

Barry, Richard, signer of the Mecklenburg Declaration of Independence, was born in Pennsylvania in 1726; married Anne Price, of Maryland; moved to Mecklenburg in 1760, and settled twelve miles northeast of Charlotte; member of the County Court; served in the militia, and was with Gen. Davidson at Cowan's Ford; died August 21, 1801.

Brevard, Dr. Ephraim, signer of the Mecklenburg Declaration of Independence, son of John Brevard, who married Jane McWhirter, was born in Maryland in 1744, and his parents moved with their family to North Carolina in 1747; was graduated from Princeton University in 1768; studied medicine in Maryland, and began practice in Charlotte; was a tutor in Queen's Museum; married a daughter of Thomas Polk, by whom he had one daughter; was captured at the surrender of Charleston in 1780, while serving as a surgeon; was taken sick in prison and was released; returned home, and lived only a few months, dying in 1781, at the age of 37 years.

Caldwell, Dr. D. T., son of Rev. S. C. Caldwell, and grandson of John McKnitt Alexander, was born in 1796; Educated by his father at Sugar Creek Church and at the State University; studied medicine under McKenzie and in Philadelphia; was a leading physician for many years; married Harriet, daughter of William Davidson, by whom he had four children; died December 25, 1861.

Caldwell, Green Washington, born in Gaston County, near Tuckaseege Ford, April 13, 1811; was educated by John Dobson; studied medicine with Dr. Doherty, near Beattie's Ford, and practiced for sometime, but finally abandoned it for the practice of law; elected to the Legislature from Mecklenburg in 1836 and 1838, and to Congress in 1841; appointed Superintendent of the Charlotte Mint in 1844; declined the nomination of his party for Governor in 1846; volunteered for the Mexican War and served as a Captain; was elected to the State Senate in 1849, with his brother officers (J. K. Harrison and E. C. Davidson) as members of the Legislature.

Caldwell, Rev. Samuel Craig, son of Dr. David Caldwell, of Guilford, and grandson of Rev. Alexander Craighead; began preaching in 1792, and continued until the year of his death, 1829; married twice and had eleven children, five of whom became ministers.

Clark, Jonas, born in Pennsylvania, May 16, 1759, came with his parents to Mecklenburg in 1771; entered the army in 1779, and served in Georgia, South Carolina and North

WILLIAM DAVIDSON.

Carolina, and in the battles at Hanging Rock, Eutaw Springs, Guilford Court House and Cowan's Ford. He lived in Mecklenburg until 1830, when he removed to Madison County, Tenn., where he died February, 28, 1846.

Cummings, Rev. Francis, D. D., born in Pennsylvania in 1752; moved to Mecklenburg in 1771; was in Charlotte May 20 1775; taught school during the Revolution; licensed to preach, and served congregations in North Carolina, South Carolina and Georgia; was a member of the South Carolina Constitutional Convention in 1788; died February 2, 1832.

Davidson, Adam Brevard, son of Jack Davidson, whose wife was Sally Brevard, was born March 19, 1808, and died July 4, 1896. He married a daughter of John Springs of South Carolina. He was a wealthy planter and leading citizen for many years; moved from his farm to Charlotte in 1876 and lived there until his death.

Davidson, John, signer of the Mecklenburg Declaration of Independence, was born in Chester County, Pennsylvania, December 15, 1735. His father was Robert Davidson. He was a member of the Colonial Assembly in 1771; was a Major in the army in 1776, and served under General Rutherford in the campaign against the Cherokee Indians. He was with General Sumter in 1780 at the battles of Hanging Rock and Rocky Mount; with Joseph Graham and Alexander Brevard, he established Vesuvius Furnace, Terza Forge, and other iron works in Lincoln County. He died January 10, 1832, in his 97th year, at the house of his son-in-law, William Lee Davidson, who was a son of Gen. William Davidson.

Davidson, William, State Senator from 1813 to 1817; Congressman from 1818 to 1821; State Senator from 1827 to 1829; a prominent and influential citizen for many years.

Davidson, General William Lee, was born in Lancaster County, Pennsylvania, in 1746. He was the youngest son of George Davidson, who moved to North Carolina and settled in Rowan County in 1750. William Lee Davidson was educated in Charlotte, and when the Revolutionary War began, he was commissioned a Major in the Fourth Regiment, of which Thomas Polk was Colonel. He rapidly rose to the rank of General and was killed at Cowan's Ford, on the Catawba, February 1, 1781. He was active in the defense of Mecklenburg against the British invaders. He is buried at Hopewell, and a monument to his memory has been erected at Guilford Battle Ground. He married Jane Brevard, daughter of John Brevard, and sister of Ephraim Brevard, and left seven children: George, William Lee, John, Ephraim, Jane, Parmela and Margaret.

Davidson, William Lee, Jr., born in 1777; lived near Davidson College, which was located on his land; moved to Alabama in 1850; married, but died in 1865, leaving no children.

Davie, William Richardson, son of Archibald Davie, was born at Egremont, England, June 20, 1756; was brought to the Waxhaw settlement (in South Carolina) in 1763; educated in Charlotte and in Princeton University; entered the army in 1776; Lieutenant of Cavalry in 1779; Captain and Major in the same year; participated in the battle of Stono; Commissary-General in 1781; commanded in the battle at Hanging Rock; active in the fighting around Charlotte; present at the battle at Guilford Court House; began the practice of law in 1783, married Miss Sarah Jones, of Northampton, and settled at Halifax; member of the Federal Constitutional Convention in 1787; elected Governor in 1798; Special Envoy to France in 1799; moved to near Landsford, S. C., in 1805; died November 18, 1820, and was buried in the old Waxhaw cemetery.

Downs, Henry, signer of the Mecklenburg Declaration of Independence, was born in Pennsylvania in 1728; moved to the Providence section of Mecklenburg in 1746; died October 8, 1798, and was buried at Providence.

Dunlap, Dr. David R., grandson of Rev. Alexander Craighead, whose daughter, Jane, married Mr. Dunlap, of Anson County, was born in Anson in 1781, moved to Charlotte in 1805, and practiced his profession until 1845; was Clerk of the Court of Equity; died in 1865. He married,

HENRY BARTLETT WILLIAMS.

first Miss Jenkins, of Anson County, by whom he had one son; and, second, her sister. This being contrary to Presbyterian doctrine, he withdrew from the Church and became one of the pioneer leaders in Methodism in the county. After the death of his second wife, he married Miss Polly Lowrie, a daughter of Judge Lowrie, by whom he had one daughter, who married Dr. Edmund Jones, of Morganton, and after his death, married Col. T. H. Brem, of Charlotte.

Erwin, John Randolph, son of William L. Erwin, born in York County, S. C., August 1, 1838; moved to Steele Creek, in Mecklenburg, in 1851; engaged in merchandising until 1859, when he went to Texas, where he remained until 1861; enlisted as a private in a Mecklenburg company and was soon elected a Lieutenant; elected Captain of a Cavalry company in 1862, and served through the war; married Miss Jennie Grier, daughter of Major Z. A. Grier, of Steele Creek, in 1867; lived at Steele Creek from 1868 to 1873; returned to Charlotte; elected chief of police in 1873; Clerk of the Court from 1875 to 1887; went back to Steele Creek; Chairman of the County Finance Committee from 1893 to 1895; chairman of County Commissioners (living in Charlotte) from 1895 until his death, March 19, 1901. After the death of his first wife, he married Miss Sallie Grier, daughter of Col. Wm. M. Grier.

Flennegin, John, signer of the Mecklenburg Declaration of Independence, was born in Pennsylvania March 7, 1744; moved to Mecklenburg in 1761, and located near McAlpin's Creek; member of the County Court for several years; died in 1815. His brother David was born in 1748; served in the war; was wounded at Hanging Rock, and died in 1826. Each of the brothers left several children.

Ford, John, signer of the Mecklenburg Declaration of Independence, was born in Maryland in 1740; moved to Mecklenburg in 1768; was a magistrate and member of the County Court; served the county militia during the war, and died in 1800.

Gibbon, Dr. Robert, born in Philadelphia in 1823; was educated at Yale and the Jefferson Medical College; moved to Charlotte to practice his profession in 1849; served as a surgeon in the Confederate service throughout the war; was a brother of the Federal General, John Gibbon, returned to Charlotte in 1865; married Miss Mary Rodger, of Charleston, and had two children—Dr. Robert Gibbon, Jr., of Charlotte, and Dr. John Gibbon, of Philadelphia. After the death of his first wife, he married Miss Corrina Harris. Dr. Gibbon died in 1900.

Graham, George, was born in Pennsylvania in 1758, and came to Mecklenburg with his widowed mother in 1769. He was educated in Charlotte, and proved himself a zealous patriot before the beginning of the war. He was leader of the attack on the British at McIntyre's, October 3, 1780; was for many years Clerk of the Mecklenburg Court, and several times a member of the Legislature; died March 29, 1826, in his 68th year, and is buried in Charlotte.

Graham, Joseph, born in Pennsylvania in 1759, moved to the vicinity of Charlotte in 1769; was educated in Charlotte; present at the Convention of May 20, 1775; enlisted in the Fourth Regiment in 1778; Adjutant in 1780; opposed Cornwallis' entrance into Charlotte, with General Davidson at Cowan's Ford; died in 1836.

Graham, William, signer of the Mecklenburg Declaration of Independence, was born in 1746; raised a regiment in Lincoln County in 1776, and marched against the Scovilites in South Carolina, and later marched to Charleston. His command was at the battle of King's Mountain, under Colonel Dixon. He died near Hopewell in 1815.

Grier, Calvin Eli, son of William M. Grier, born in Steele Creek township December 30, 1845; attended the Military Institute in Charlotte; enlisted as a private in 1861; served through the war and rose to the rank of Captain; studied law, and located in Charlotte in 1868; moved back to Steele Creek in 1872, but returned to Charlotte in 1876; married Miss Addie Ramseur, daughter of General Ramseur, in 1828; died May 1, 1889, and was buried at Steele Creek.

Harris, Charles, M. D. was born in what is now Cabarrus County in 1762; engaged in the fighting around Charlotte;

W. E. PHIFER.

was educated in Charlotte and at Clio Academy, in Iredell: studied Medicine in Camden, S. C., and in Philadelphia; located in Salisbury and later moved to Cabarrus, where he remained. He died September 21, 1825, leaving two sons: William Shakespeare Harris and Charles J. Harris.

Harris, James, born in Pennsylvania in 1739; moved to Mecklenburg in 1750, served in the war and rose to the rank of Colonel; member of the State Senate in 1785; died September 27, 1797.

Harris, Robert, signer of the Mecklenburg Declaration of Independence, was born in Pennsylvania in 1741; moved to Mecklenburg in 1750.

Hill, General D. H., was born in York County, S. C., in 1821; was graduated from West Point in 1841, served with distinction in the Mexican War, rising to the rank of Major, and receiving a sword as a token of esteem of his native State; professor in Washington College, Va., from 1849 to 1854; professor in Davidson College from 1854 to 1859; Superintendent of the North Carolina Military Institute, in Charlotte, from 1859 to 1861; Colonel of the First North Carolina (Bethel) Regiment in 1861; rose to the rank of Lieutenant-General by gallant service; returned to Charlotte in 1865; published "The Land We Love," and "The Southern Home;" went to Arkansas in 1876 to accept the presidency of the State University; President of the Georgia Agricultural College in 1887; returned to Charlotte in poor health in 1889, and died there a few months later. He was buried at Davidson College. He married Miss Isabella, daughter of Dr. R. H. Morrison, who, with several children, survived him.

Holton, Rachel Regina Jones, born in Richmond May 28, 1813; married Thomas J. Holton, of Charlotte, in 1834; edited the North Carolina Whig for two years, from the time of her husband's death, in December of 1860.

Holton, Thomas Jefferson, son of Thomas Holton, born in Richmond, Va., August 25, 1802; located in Salisbury to work as a printer in 1823; went from there to Fayetteville, and moved from Fayetteville to Charlotte in 1828 and established the *Journal* in the same year. The name of the paper was changed to the *Whig* in 1852, and Holton continued as editor until his death, December 27, 1860. He was married to Miss Rachel Regina Jones, of Richmond, June 24, 1834. They had eleven children: Mrs. Sarah Deaton, of Charlotte; Mrs. Mary S. Sprinkle, deceased: Virginia W. Holton, deceased; Harrison Holton, of Charleston; Henry C. Holton, deceased; Leopold Holton, deceased; Charles S. Holton, of Charlotte; Harriet C. Holton, of Charlotte; Margaret Q. Holton, deceased; Mrs. J. C. Crisp.

Hunter, Rev. Humphrey, born May 14, 1755, in north of Ireland; landed at Charleston with his widowed mother in 1759, and proceeded at once to Mecklenburg and located in the Poplar Tent neighborhood; was present at the Convention, May, 20, 1775; educated by Rev. James Hall; Lieutenant in General Rutherford's campaign against the Cherokees; licensed to preach in 1789; preached in York County, S. C., and at Steele Creek, where he died in 1827.

Hunter, Rev. John, son of Thomas Hunter, born November 13, 1814; educated at Jefferson, Pa.; licensed to preach in 1843; preached in Mecklenburg except from 1855 to 1858, when he was in Alleghany County; died May 16, 1890; married, first, to Miss Isabella Peoples in 1843; second, to Mrs. Martha Bell, in 1861; third, to Miss Mary McDill in 1866.

Hunter, Robert Boston, born in 1818; married Rebecca Wilson Jones in 1845; died July 17, 1902.

Hunter, Rev. Wm. May, son of R. B. Hunter, born February 1, 1850; educated at Due West, S. C.; licensed in 1874; preached three years in Charlottte, one in Georgia, ten in Iredell County, ten in Mecklenburg, and then at Lebanon, W. Va.

Hutchinson, William, born in Augusta County, Va., in 1750; removed to Mecklenburg in 1774, served as Commissary in Colonel Polk's Regiment in the Snow campaign, in 1775; was a Lieutenant in Rutherford's Brigade in 1778; Captain in Colonel William Polk's Regiment in 1781; was a

GENERAL HUGH WADDELL.

good citizen and well known in the county, and died November 23, 1833.

Irwin, Robert, son of William Irwin, signer of the Mecklenburg Declaration of Independence, was born in Pennsylvania August 26, 1740; moved to Mecklenburg in 1763, and settled near Steele Creek; married Mary, daughter of Zebulon Alexander; member of the Provincial Congresses in 1776; participated in the Cherokee campaign of the same year; General of the State Militia; member of the General Assembly at intervals from 1778 to 1800; died December 23, 1800, leaving seven children.

Jack, Captain James, born in Pennsylvania in 1739; moved to Charlotte in 1766; participated in the Snow campaign and Cherokee campaign and the Hornets' Nest; moved to Georgia in 1783, and settled in Wilkes County, where he died.

Jackson, Andrew, Sr., born in Carrickfergus, Ireland, in 1720; married Miss Elizabeth Hutchison, emigrated to America in 1765; landed at Charleston, and settled on Twelve-Mile Creek, near the present town of Monroe, North Carolina. He died in February, 1767, and was buried in the old Waxhaw cemetery, near Landsford, S. C. He was the father of President Andrew Jackson, and Hugh and Robert Jackson. The two latter died young.

Jackson, President Andrew. See Chapter XXXIX., Volume I.

Johnston, Colonel William, born in Lincoln County, March 5, 1817; educated at the State University; studied law under Judge R. M. Pearson; admitted to the bar and located in Charlotte in 1842; president of the Charlotte and South Carolina Railroad in 1856; was the chief mover in the building of the Atlantic, Tennessee & Ohio Railroad, work on which was interrupted by the war; an ardent advocate of secession; delegate to the Secession Convention; Commissary General of the State in 1861; engaged in railroad construction after the war; Mayor of Charlotte 1875, 1876, 1877, 1885; married in 1846 to Miss Anna Eliza Graham, daughter of Dr. George Graham, and to them were born Julia M., wife of Col. A. B. Andrews; Frank G.; Cora J., wife of Capt. T. R. Robinson; and W. R. Mrs. Johnston died in 1881, and Colonel Johnston in 1896.

Kennon, William, signer of the Mecklenburg Declaration of Independence, was chairman of the Rowan Committee of Safety in 1774; resided in Salisbury; was a prominent lawyer; member of the first Provincial Congress, and was appointed Commissary to the First Regiment in 1776.

Lowrie, Samuel, son of Robert Lowrie, was born in Newcastle County, Delaware, May 12, 1756, and came with his family to Rowan County in 1760. He was educated by Rev. James Hall, at Clio Academy, studied law in Camden, S. C., and was elected to the Legislature from Mecklenburg in 1804. He was elected a judge of the Superior Court in 1806, and held the position until his death, December 22, 1818. He was married twice: First, to Margaret, daughter of Robert Alexander; second, to Mary, daughter of Robert Norfleet, of Bertie County.

Martin, Samuel, son of Hugh Martin, who emigrated from Ireland to New Jersey in 1721 and brother of Governor Alexander Martin, of North Carolina, was born in New Jersey in 1746; came to North Carolina with his brother in 1768, and he settled in Mecklenburg, while his brother located in Guilford; elected Clerk of the Court in 1774; delegate to the Provincial Congress in August, 1775; served as a soldier in the war, being a Captain in the battle at Eutaw Springs; served as Clerk until his death in 1789. He married a widow Caldwell, of South Carolina, and left two children: Samuel A. and Jane C.

McClure, Matthew, signer of the Mecklenburg Declaration of Independence, was born in Ireland in 1745; came to Mecklenburg in 1760; settled six miles south of Davidson College, and died in 1808.

Maxwell, William, born seven miles east of Charlotte, September 9, 1809, third son of Guy Maxwell, who emigrated from Ireland in 1795. He was for many years a member of the County Court, and was apppointed Clerk in 1862, and he continued in the office for six years; Register

GENERAL JOSEPH GRAHAM.

of Deeds from 1868 to 1888, and died October 26, 1890. His first wife was Mrs. Mary E. Johnston, who died a year after being married. His second wife was Miss Nancy A. Morris, by whom he had three children; D. G. Maxwell, W. C. Maxwell and Miss Carrie Maxwell.

McLeary, Michael, born in 1762; served through the war; represented Mecklenburg in the General Assembly from 1819 to 1826, and died in 1828.

Morris, Colonel Zebulon, son of William Morris and grandson of John Ford who was one of the signers of the Mecklenburg Declaration of Independence, was born ten miles east of Charlotte, April 23, 1789; married Martha, daughter of John Rae, in 1814, was a prominent planter and slave owner; died May 1, 1872.

Morrison, Neal, signer of the Mecklenburg Declaration of Independence, son of James Morrison, was born in Philadelphia in 1728; moved to Mecklenburg in 1770; Captain in the Cherokee campaign of 1776; magistrate and member of the County Court; died in 1784, and was buried at Providence. His son, William, served in the war, became a prominent physician; member of the General Assembly in 1796, and died in 1806. Alexander, another son was a member of the General Assembly in 1801, 1802 and 1803. His daughter married Thomas Alexander.

Morrison, Washington, State Senator in 1833.

Neal, General Wm. H., born in the south-western part of the county in 1799; General of the Militia before the war; County Commissioner; married Miss Hannah Alexander, by whom he had the following children: S. W. Neal, who moved to the Indian Territory and died there; Dr. Z. C. Neal, who practiced medicine in Mecklenburg and died in 1901; Susan Neal, who married Rev. Walter W. Pharr; Mary Neal, who married Capt. N. H. Peoples; Nancy Neal, who married R. W. McDowell; W. B. Neal; Louisa Neal, who married Rev. J. B. Watt, and P. A. Neal, who lives in Rock Hill, S. C. After the death of his first wife, he married Mrs. Martha D. Williamson. He died in 1889.

Oates, Brawley, born in Cleveland County; moved to

Mecklenburg in 1830; Clerk of the Court from 1836 to 1842, and from 1845 to 1854; married Miss Lillie Lowrie, daughter of Judge Lowrie, and had three children: Margaret married C. E. Spratt; Mary married Mr. Agnew; and Dr. David Oates, who served through the war and then emigrated to Alabama. He died in 1872.

Osborne, Adlai, was born June 4, 1744; was graduated from Princeton University in 1768; studied law; Clerk of the Rowan Court from 1770 to 1809; member of the first Board of Trustees of the State University; married Margaret Lloyd in 1771; lived in Salisbury, and died in 1815, leaving a large family.

Osborne, Alexander, born in 1709; settled in Rowan County in 1755; was a Colonel in the Militia in 1768; member of the Rowan Committee of Safety in 1775; married Agnes, daughter of Rev. Alexander McWhirter; died in 1776, leaving one son, Adlai, and four daughters: Rebecca married Nathaniel Ewing; Mary married John Nesbit; Jean married Moses Winslow; and Margaret married John Robinson.

Osborne, James W., son of Edwin J. Osborne, was born in Salisbury December 25, 1811; was graduated from the State University in 1830; studied law in Salisbury with Hon. Wm. A. Graham; admitted to the bar in Charlotte in 1833; was active in the public improvements, the establishment of the Mint and agitator for railroads; twice elector for the State at large; Superintendent of the Charlotte Mint from 1849 to 1853; appointed to a vacant judgeship by Governor Ellis in 1859, and confirmed by the General Assembly in November, 1860; member of the State Senate in 1868, and member-elect at the time of his death, August 11, 1869. He married Mrs. Mary A. Moore, daughter of John Irwin, of Charlotte, April 5, 1842, and left three sons and four daughters: R. D. Osborne, a soldier in the Civil War, died young; Frank Irwin Osborne, lawyer, solicitor of the Sixth District, and now Judge of the Court of Private Land Claims, and James W. Osborne, a prominent lawyer of New York City.

DAVID PARKS.
Ordained Elder of the First Presbyterian Church of Charlotte, in August, 1833.

Patton, Benjamin, signer of the Mecklenburg Declaration of Independence, born in Ireland in 1838; settled in the Poplar Tent section of Mecklenburg in 1863; was an active church member and prominent in county affairs; represented the county in the First Provincial Congress, held at Newbern in August, 1774; member of the Salisbury District Committee of Safety in 1775; collector of taxes for Mecklenburg in 1782; died and was buried near Concord in 1817. When he went to Newbern in 1774, he was unable to secure a horse, and walked there and back.

Phifer, Caleb, was born at Cold Water, April 8, 1749; in the Legislature, representing Mecklenburg, from 1778 to 1792; State Senator from Cabarrus 1793 to 1801; Colonel in the Revolution; married Barbara Fulenwider; died July 3, 1811, leaving eight children.

Phifer, John, signer of the Mecklenburg Declaration of Independence, was born at Cold Water March 22, 1747; married, in 1768, Catherine, daughter of Paul Barringer; was a member of the Provincial Assembly at Hillsboro in August, 1775, and at Halifax in April, 1776, and of the Constitutional Convention of November, 1776; commissioned Lieutenant-Colonel in Colonel Griffith Rutherford's Regiment, December 21, 1776; served in the campaign against the Scovilites and the Cherokee Indians; and died at "Red Hill" in 1778, leaving two children: Paul, who married Jane Alexander, and died in 1801, and Margaret, who married John Simianer, and died in 1806.

Phifer, Martin, born October 18, 1720; was a native of Switzerland, emigrated to Pennsylvania in 1738, and later to North Carolina. He settled in the Rocky River section of Mecklenburg, which was made into Cabarrus in 1792. He was prominent in county affairs before and during the Revolution; was a member of the Legislature in 1777; married Margaret Blackwelder, and died in 1789, leaving three sons: John, Caleb and Martin.

Phifer, Martin, Jr., born at Cold Water, March 25, 1756; married Elizabeth Locke; was Colonel of a Regiment of

Cavalry on duty at Philadelphia; was a large land owner; died November 12, 1837, leaving five children.

Phifer, William Fullenwider, descendant of Martin Phifer, born in Cabarrus County February 15, 1809; moved to Charlotte in 1850 and died there.

Polk, Ezekiel, son of William Polk, brother of Thomas Polk, and grandfather of President James Knox Polk, born in Pennsylvania December 7, 1747; moved to North Carolina in 1754; Clerk of the Court in Tryon County in 1769; moved to Mecklenburg in 1778; was active in the Revolution but counseled peace.

Polk, James Knox. See Chapter XXXIX, Volume I.

Polk, Thomas, signer of the Mecklenburg Declaration of Independence, born in Somerset County, Maryland, in 1730. He was a son of William Polk, who was a son of John Polk, who emigrated from Ireland in 1685, and great uncle of James Knox Polk; moved to Mecklenburg in 1754; was prominent in the events of the county in those times, and founded the city of Charlotte; was a surveyor, represented Mecklenburg in the General Assembly in 1770; Colonel of the Militia; issued the call for the Convention of May 20, 1775; member of the Provincial Assembly during the Revolution, Colonel of the Fourth Regiment in 1776; Commissary-General for General Greene's Army in 1781; owned mills and stores after the war; died in 1773 and is buried in the old cemetery. He married Susannah Spratt of Charlotte, and had several children: Ezekiel, Charles, William, James, and Margaret who married Dr. Ephaim Brevard.

Polk, William, son of Thomas Polk, born July 8, 1757, educated in Charlotte, was present at the convention of May 20, 1775, served as a lieutenant in Snow Camp campaign in 1775; appointed Major of the Ninth Regiment November 26, 1776, participated in the battles of Brandywine and Germantown after having served in South Carolina, spent the winter at Valley Forge, served with Sumter at Hanging Rock and as Lieutenant-Colonel in South Carolina in 1781, was with Davie at the fight at Wahab's, represented Mecklenburg in the General Assembly in 1787, 1790, and 1791,

LIEUTENANT E. C. DAVIDSON.

moved to Raleigh and became president of a bank and died there January 14, 1834.

Queary, John, signer of the Mecklenburg Declaration of Independence, was born in Scotland in 1743; migrated first to Pennsylvania, and to Mecklenburg in 1767, lived and died near Rocky river and was buried in what is now Union county.

Reese, David, signer of the Mecklenburg Declaration of Independence, born in Wales in 1710, came to America in 1725; married Susan Polk, of Pennsylvania, moved to Mecklenburg in 1750, acted as commissary during the war, lived near Poplar Tent and died in 1787.

Robinson, Rev. John, born near Sugar Creek in 1768, educated in Charlotte, preached in Mecklenburg for more than half a century, and died December 15, 1843.

Robinson, Robert, born in Lancaster county, Pa., in 1751; moved to Mecklenburg while very young, served in the army and in the battles at Hanging Rock, Ramsour's Mill, Charlotte and "McIntyres." Was well known and highly esteemed and died August 26, 1839.

Ross, Major E. A. See tribute in Chapter 20, Vol. 2.

Shipp, W. M., was born in Lincoln county November 19, 1819, was graduated from the State University in 1840, admitted to the bar in 1842 and began practice in Lincoln county, served as Captain in the Civil War until he was elected Judge, elected Attorney General of North Carolina in 1870, practiced law in Charlotte from 1872 to 1881, appointed judge by Governor Jarvis in 1881 and elected for a term of eight years in 1882, died in 1890. He was married twice—first to Miss Catherine Cameron, second to Miss Margaret Iredell. He was a son of Bartlett Shipp.

Strong, John Mason, M. D., son of Rev. Charles Strong, born in Newberry county, S. C., September 1, 1818; educated at Jefferson College, Pa., studied medicine with Dr. John Harris, of Steele Creek, and in Charleston and in Jefferson Medical College, was a surgeon in the Civil War, lived at Steele Creek and died March 22, 1897. He was married first to Miss Rachel Harris, by whom he had five children, and second to Miss Nancy Grier.

Walker, John, born in 1801; member of the General Assembly from 1840 to 1848, 1854, 1869, chairman of the County Court, lived eight miles east of Charlotte and died September 8, 1876, leaving one son, Rev. James Walker.

Waring, R. P., born in Virginia, moved to Charlotte in 1850 and began the practice of law, began publishing the Charlotte *Democrat* in 1852, elected County Attorney in 1855 and 1859, elector in the Buchanan campaign in 1856, appointed Consul to the Danish West Indies in 1859 and served there until the beginning of the Civil War, served throughout the war as Captain, returned after the war and edited the *Times*, arrested for treason in 1870 because of his denunciation of carpet baggers and military outrages and fined $300; elector in 1876, chairman of the County Court from 1877 to 1884, member of the General Assembly from 1870 to 1875; assayer in charge of the Charlotte mint from 1885 to 1889, and shortly thereafter retired to private life.

Watson, Samuel Brown, M. D.; born in York county, S. C., December 17, 1805; graduated from the Charleston Medical College in 1828 and located in Charlotte where he practiced until his death, August 24, 1895.

Williams, Henry Bartlett, born July 1, 1811, for many years a leading citizen, died August 12, 1885.

Wilson, Rev. John McKemey, D. D., son of John Wilson and grand-son of George McKemey, whose wife, Margaret, was a sister of Andrew Jackson's mother; born six miles east of Charlotte in 1769, educated at Liberty Hall, in Charlotte, and at Hampden Sidney, Va., prepared for the ministry by Rev. James Hall, licensed in 1793, served as itinerant missionary and in Burke county until 1801, in Mecklenburg from 1801 until his death in 1831; married Miss Mary Erwin, of Burke county, taught a classical school for many years; died in 1831, leaving several children.

Wilson, Joseph, educated by Rev. David Caldwell, licensed to practice law in 1804, elected to the Legislature from Stokes county in 1810, elected Solicitor of the Mountain

W. F. DAVIDSON.

Circuit in 1812, and served in that capacity until his death in August, 1829.

Wilson, Zaccheus, signer of the Mecklenburg Declaration of Independence, was born in Pennsylvania in 1735, moved to Mecklenburg in 1750, and settled in what is now Cabarrus county, member of the Provincial Congress in 1776 and of the Constitutional Convention of 1788, moved to Tennessee in 1796 and died in 1824.

Yates, W. J., born in Fayetteville in 1827, began newspaper work in his youth, became proprietor of the Fayetteville *North Carolinian,* moved to Charlotte in 1856 and bought the *Democrat,* the *Southern Home* and *Democrat* were consolidated as the *Home-Democrat* in 1881, was president of the directors of the Morganton Asylum, trustee of the State University, declined all political honors, and died October 28, 1888.

CHAPTER V.

ANDREW JACKSON'S BIRTHPLACE.

Born in that Part of Mecklenburg Which was Made Into Union in 1842.—Moved Over Into South Carolina When a Few Weeks Old.—Evidence of Those Who Were Present at His Birth.—Col. E. H. Walkup's Publication.

Andrew Jackson, seventh President of the United States, was born in Mecklenburg County, North Carolina, March 15, 1767. The ruins of the McKemey cabin, in which he was born, are on the land belonging to Mr. J. L. Rodman, of Waxhaw, and are in Union County, which was cut off from Mecklenburg in 1842. The site is six miles south from Waxhaw, near the Charlotte and Lancaster road, and four hundred and eighty yards from the South Carolina line.

In 1858, Colonel S. H. Walkup, of Union County, undertook the task of gathering testimony as to the time and place of Jackson's birth. He spent a great deal of time in the work, and accumulated conclusive evidence that Jackson was born in George McKemey's cabin, in the "Waxhaws," March 15, 1767. The affidavits were published in the *North Carolina Argus*, of Wadesboro, September 23, 1858, and were later printed in pamphlet form, and in Parton's Biography of Jackson. The Charlotte and Lancaster papers of 1858 engaged in a controversy over the questions involved, but all finally acquiesced in the completeness of Colonel Walkup's presentation of the facts.

Fourteen affidavits were secured. They were made by persons, in several instances unknown to each other, yet they corroborate with uniformity every important detail. The substance of them is as follows: Six sisters—Misses Hutchison—married and emigrated with their husbands to this country, and settled in the "Waxhaws." Margaret married George McKemey, and settled on Waxhaw Creek, in North Carolina; Jane married James Crawford and settled on Waxhaw Creek in South Carolina; Elizabeth married

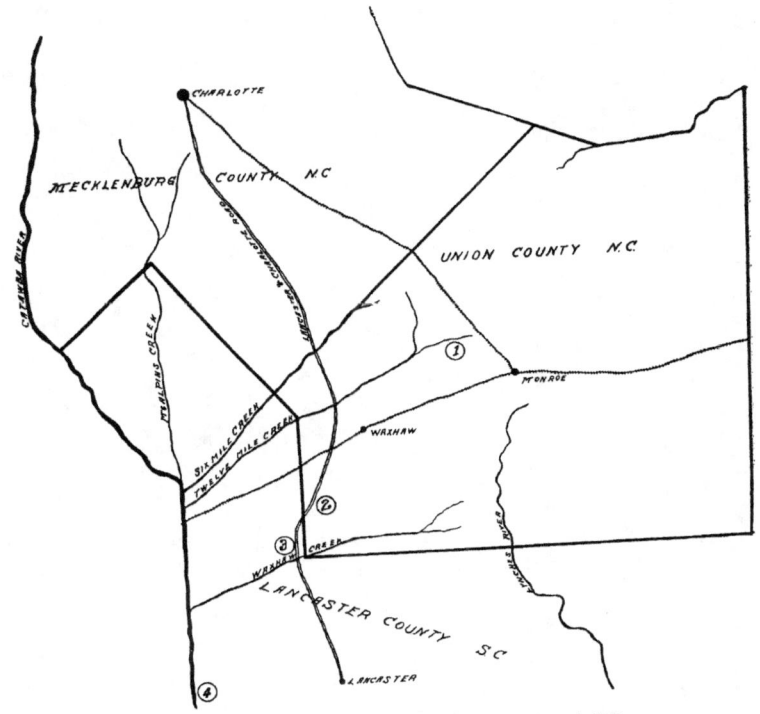

VICINITY OF JACKSON'S BIRTHPLACE.
1.—Where Andrew Jackson, Sr., Died.
2.—Where President Jackson was Born.
3.—Where President Jackson was Raised.
4.—Where Andrew Jackson, Sr., was Buried.

Andrew Jackson, Sr., and located near the present site of Pleasant Grove camp-ground, in North Carolina; Sarah married Samuel Leslie and settled near George McKemey's; Grace married James Crow and settled near Landsford, S. C. Andrew Jackson, Sr., built his cabin about nine miles from South Carolina, and the site of it is known to this day. There, in February, 1767, he died, leaving a widow and two sons—Hugh and Robert. His body was interred in the old Waxhaw cemetery, near Landsford. Mrs. Jackson, soon after the death of her husband, started to the home of her sister, in South Carolina. On the way she stopped to visit Mrs. George McKemey, another sister, and in her home, in the night of March 15, 1767, Andrew Jackson was born. So soon as Mrs. Jackson recovered sufficient strength, she went with her three boys, to the home of James Crawford, in South Carolina, and there Andrew lived for thirteen years. The Crawford place was two and one-half miles from the McKemey place.

In the affidavits, Benjamin Massey, John Carnes, John Lathan, James Faulkner and Thomas Faulkner (the three latter being second cousins of Jackson), all declare that Mrs. Sarah Leslie and Mrs. Sarah Lathan (aunt and cousin of Jackson, respectively) often asserted that Jackson was born at George McKemey's and that they were present at his birth; that Mrs. Leslie "was sent for on the night of his birth, and she took her daughter, Mrs. Lathan, and recollected well of walking the near way through the fields in the night time." In addition is the testimony of Mrs. Elizabeth McWhirter and her son George, and Mrs. Mary Cousar, who state that they were "near neighbors and present on the night of the birth of General Jackson, at the house of George McKemey, in North Carolina," March 15, 1767, which testimony rests upon the statements of Samuel McWhirter, grandson of Mrs. Elizabeth McWhirter, and Thomas Cureton and Jeremiah Cureton, who heard the old persons speak often and positively of the facts.

For many years it was not known in which state the McKemey cabin was located, but the records of land titles in the Mecklenburg County court house established the fact that the site of the cabin has always been in North Carolina. In a deed given by McKemey to Crawford in 1792, it is described as being "north of Waxhaw Creek." The McKemey tract of land was surveyed in 1757, for John McKemey, and was patented in 1761, was sold by John McKemey to Repentance Townsend in 1761, and by Townsend to George McKemey in 1766. McKemey sold it to Thomas Crawford (son of James Crawford) in 1792; Crawford to Jeremiah Cureton in 1796; from him, it passed to his son, William J. Cureton, from whose estate it was purchased by Mr. J. L. Rodman, the present owner. The records of the transactions, prior to 1842 are in the Mecklenburg County court house; after that year in Union County.

Thus we have the sworn testimony of fourteen persons, whose irreproachable character will be vouched for by persons now living, many of them unknown to each other and all agreeing in reporting the settled family traditions, that Andrew Jackson was born in the McKemey cabin, March 15, 1767; and the incontrovertible testimony of the county records, that the McKemey place is and always has been in North Carolina.

Authority and References:—Governor Swain's Tucker Hall Address; Parton's Biography of Jackson; Appleton's Encyclopedia; The North Carolina Argus of September 23, 1858; Register's Book XIV, page 202, and Book XI, page 38. The name "McKemey" was spelled in various ways; the spelling here adopted is that on his tombstone and is the version accepted by Parton. George McKemey could not write, and consequently his name was spelled variously in his depositions.

OLD WILSON PLACE.
Where Andrew Jackson Lived for a Short Time in 1780, With the Family of John Wilson who Married Margaret McKemey, a Cousin of Jackson, and was the Father of Rev. John McKemey Wilson. This House is Six Miles East of Charlotte.

ALEXANDER ROCK HOUSE, ONE OF THE OLDEST BUILDINGS IN THE COUNTY, FIVE MILES EAST OF CHARLOTTE.

CHAPTER VI.

CUSTOMS OF THE PIONEERS.

Amusements of the Settlers of Mecklenburg.—County Muster and Assemblies.—Horse Racing and Betting.—Liquor Used Freely at Home and at Public Places.—The Old Taverns and Their Uses.

The amusements of the first people who lived in this county differed in many respects from those of the present generation. The women and the children were, perhaps, the most destitute part of the population in this respect. The men, at least the great majority of them, would attend the neighborhood musters of their companies and the county musters of their regiment, which assemblies were, during the first years of our history, composed almost wholly of men. In later years, the women and children sometimes attended these assemblies, but the custom developed at a comparatively late date.

The muster of the early days was nominally a military assembly, but it also had its social and political aspects. The small number of churches, as well as the infrequent meetings for worship, tended to make the muster days almost the only days the greater part of the population had for social intercourse and the discussion of political questions. During the first years of our history, such questions as the McCulloh land question, the boundary dispute, the vestry and marriage acts, the regulation, and other questions of Colonial politics, were discussed at these meetings.. Besides affording the people a means of social and political discussion, from the nature of existing conditions, the musters served to supply the absence of the newspaper, there being no local newspaper in this county for the first fifty years of its history.

County courts and the annual election for members of the Provincial Assembly, all held at the county seat, also served to bring the leading men of the county together for the exchange of ideas and for purposes of social intercourse. The several musters, county courts and elections, together with the occasional meetings held in all parts of the county for public worship, afforded our ancestors opportunities for knowing each other which many of this day do not enjoy. Add to all these, too, the frequent visits of many of the people to Charleston, Philadelphia, and other markets, and the bringing back to this section of the best newspapers and other publications of that day, and we find that the people who lived here more than a hundred years ago are not to be pitied so very much on the plea that they were isolated from the rest of the world. Even the older boys occasionally went to Charleston, which was an event long to be remembered. Some of them, too, attended the meetings, while all the children generally received some months of "schooling" for two or three years of their early youth. But the early times were such that nature and necessity were the school masters that were ever present in this section, to develop the latent powers in every boy and girl.

The diversions of the men partook somewhat of the rude nature of their surroundings. Horse-racing, long bullets, shooting matches, and like sports engaged the attention of the majority. "Long bullets" was a game played with a large iron ball. There were two goals. The work of those near one goal was to prevent the ball rolled in their direction from passing their goal, the winning side being that one which could succeed in rolling the ball with enough force to pass the adversary's line. One of the first ordinances of Charlotte prohibited this game from being played in the streets of the town.

But one of the old customs which has long since passed away here, but which still exists in parts of Scotland, was the custom of having "liquor at the funeral." The life of this custom was prolonged in this section by the fact that the people were settled far apart, and an excuse for refreshments at the graveyard, after the funeral, could be made on the ground that the friends had gathered from long distances and should be sent away only after having been re-

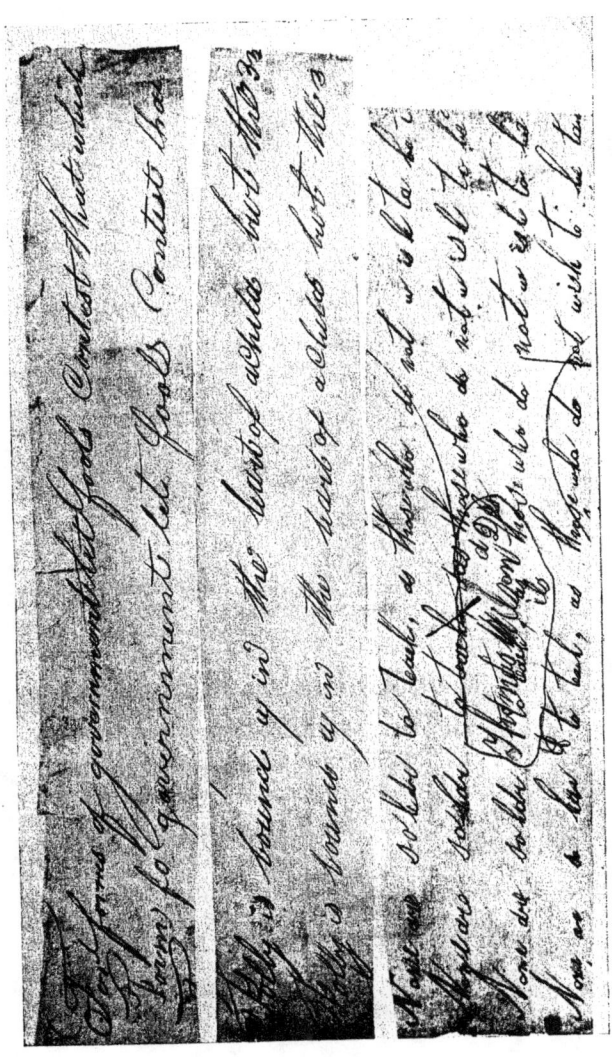

EXTRACTS FROM COPY BOOKS IN USE IN MECKLENBURG COUNTY SCHOOLS IN 1850.

freshed. The prevalence of this custom of having "liquor at the funeral" may be inferred when it is stated that almost every estate settled in this country up to, and for sometime after, 1800, contained an item for funeral whiskey, paid out of the assets of the estate in the same way as other funeral expenses are now paid.

"Liquor at the funeral" was not necessarily the liquor drank by those who kept watch over the dead body before it was buried, but the spirits consumed at a dinner which was spread at the church or graveyard after the funeral ceremonies were over, consisting of cakes, bread, cheese, wine, whiskey or rum. The amount of whiskey consumed varied according to circumstances. As early as 1767, seven gallons and more were consumed on one funeral occasion, costing five shillings per gallon. Wine was more expensive, costing ten shillings per gallon. Sometimes rum instead of whiskey and wine was used, indicating that the dead man was in his lifetime in more comfortable circumstances than one whose funeral dinner was set with only corn whiskey as a beverage.

Another occasion for the consumption of whiskey was the "vendue," or sale of a dead man's estate. "Whiskey for the vendue" was as necessary a part of the expenses of an administrator in settling an estate as was the funeral whiskey. Here, again, the amount consumed depended on circumstances. If the amount of property sold was large, the whiskey bill was large accordingly. If little property was sold, only a small crowd being attracted hither, then the bill for spirits was small in proportion.

While horse-racing and long bullets seem to have been indulged in by only a part of the population, whiskey drinking was a general custom before 1800. Rev. Alexander had his punch bowl and glasses among the effects sold at his sale. Nearly every teacher, of which any record now remains, was sometime or other charged with whiskey by some one of those who patronized his school. But whiskey drinking and intemperance were not then synonymous terms to the extent they are now.

Betting at horse races was the custom. And while betting and gambling were permitted, there is evidence that profanity was criminal, being frequently punished by the county courts. The meagreness of the court records before 1774 prevents a statement as to the punishment accorded such offenses before that time, but after that time there are numbers of instances where men were fined various amounts for "swearing profanely." An interesting feature of such records is that they always state the number of oaths the culprit was charged with "swearing profanely," the gravity of the offense seeming to be measured by the number.

The making and sale of spirituous liquors was, of course, as general as their consumption. They who hired whiskey made in the early days paid the distiller six pence per gallon. Nearly every leading man in the county owned a distillery. Such an institution was almost as much a part of the equipment of a plantation as the plows and other farming implements. There seems never to have been, in the early days, an excise duty on the sale of whiskey at the place of it's manufacture, but there was such a duty on all those who kept taverns, ordinaries, and places of amusement.

But there was a reason for the existence of a distillery on almost every farm during the first period of our history, which, leaving out of all consideration other reasons, fully accounts for the phenomenon, viz: the distance people were situated from markets for their simple products of corn, rye and fruit. It was much more convenient to market the surplus products in liquid form than in bulk, and the returns were larger and surer.

No picture of the social life of the first period of our history would be complete without some reference to the taverns which were kept in all parts of the country from the earliest days of its history. These institutions sprang up along all the public roads, and in the town of Charlotte after 1768. The number of persons always passing through this section to the South must have been considerable, even as early as 1760. The tavern was a place where such travelers could

NOTE GIVEN IN 1767.

BILL FOR TEACHING, 1822.

be provided for over night. "A public house," or a tavern, also meant a place where spirituous liquors were sold. If we are to judge by the bills these tavern-keepers rendered their customers, we shall gain an adequate idea of the kind of entertainment furnished, as well as the cost of it. In all of these houses the punch bowl was an ever present institution. Such drinks as "Stued wine," "toddy," rum "slings," and the like, were served. In compounding these drinks the tavern-keepers used whiskey of local manufacture, as well as West India rum, Continental rum, claret, Madeira and Teneriffe wine, domestic and imported beer, and domestic and imported cider..

CHAPTER VII.

EIGHTEENTH CENTURY MONEY. (1762 to 1800.)

First Settlers Used Pennsylvania and Virginia Currency.—Paper Money Discounted Nearly One-third.—Many Kinds of Coins Used.—Federal Currency Established in 1792.

The first settlers of this county came from Virginia and Pennsylvania and, of course, brought the currency of those States with them, which was, no doubt, the first paper money in circulation in this section. But some of these settlers brought gold and silver as well as the paper currency. The "hard money" of that day, as it was called, consisted of English and Spanish and German coins, and in rare instances coins of French mintage. In 1763, George Cathey, who first lived in Pennsylvania and then in Maryland and afterwards came to North Carolina, loaned Jean Cathey "ten silver dollars," valued at four pounds English money, and "one Dubloone in gold," valued at six pounds of the same currency. At Henry Eisenhart's sale, in 1764, one "half Johannes" was valued at two pounds and seven shillings, as money was then reckoned in this province.

After the settlers found their way to the markets of Charleston, South Carolina, currency became somewhat common in this section, especially about the year 1770. But even with the progress of the trade with Charleston, the volume of money was not sufficient for the needs of the growing popuplation. Chief Justice Hasell, who held Salisbury court in the Spring of 1766, said that there was "scarce any specie circulating among the people of this section, not enough to pay the stamp duties, should that odious act be enforced."

The value of the North Carolina proclamation, or paper currency, varied in value at different times prior to 1776. In 1767, it was valued at two-thirds its face value in sterling. It seems that this money never decreased much below thirty-three and one-third per cent. during the period that this

SALE NOTICE, 1838.

county was under the royal authority, except in 1773, when it decreased almost fifty per cent. The inadequate currency was a matter of much concern to our local politicians before 1776, and they often introduced bills in the Colonial Assembly to make taxes payable in certain commodities, thereby hoping to lighten the burdens of the poorer class and render the collection of taxes more easy. But no such bill ever became a law of the Province.

Before January, 1772, James Wylie, who had been sheriff of this county died. The inventory of his estate showed that he had in his possession fifty-six "half Joes" Johanneses), each valued at sixty-four shillings in currency; eight guineas, each valued at thirty-six shillings; six "pistoles," valued at twenty-eight shillings; two "chickeens," valued at fourteen shillings; one "Maidon," valued at forty-six shillings; and four "Doublo:n ." each valued at one hundred and twelve shillings. The total value of this "hard money" was £266 16s., "Total of gold as the same passes here January, 1772." The administrator of the estate of Solomon Elliott, in 1775, returned cash on hand as follows: Forty-nine half Johanneses, seven and one-half guineas, three pistoles, one "maidon," one "Caroline," one hundred and three dollars, or £38 12s. 6d., and £206 11s. Pennsylvania currency, or £698 16s. 9d. North Carolina Currency. Elliott was a merchant who lived somewhere within the bounds of New Providence congregation.

With the change of the government from King to people, 1777, the old proclamation money was made legal tender for a definite period, and hence that currency remained here and many people paid debts with it until as late as 1780. All through the years 1775 and 1776, notes were drawn payable in that money. By the inventory of Samuel Gingles returned to the county court in January, 1777, it appears that this man left in cash £25 South Carolina currency, £40 Continental currency, £82 North Carolina currency, one "Doubloone," and five Spanish milled dollars. In July, 1781, Robert McDowell's personal estate was valued at £179 19s. in hard money and 1715 paper dollars." When this estate was finally settled in 1790, it took eight hundred dollars to make one of "hard money," which indicates how worthless our National and State paper currrency had become.

During the period from 1780 to 1783, the money lenders in this county most always drew their notes payable in "hard money" or in "gold or silver." In 1783, several payments were confessed before John McKnitt Alexander, in which "half Johannes were to Rente at three pound five shillings; dollars at eight shillings." Beginning in 1782, and continuing until 1793, it was the usual custom to reckon twelve and one-half cents as a shilling, eight shillings to the dollar. So when pounds are spoken of during that period, it must be remembered that one pound was two dollars, and not the old sterling value of something like five dollars.

But English money did not cease to be a part of our currency with the close of the Revolution. Many of the people of this section still used the money of the mother country long after that conflict had ended. In 1785, John McCutcheon gave his note for sixty-one pounds "sterling," guineas to be reckoned at twenty-one shillings and nine pence, dollars at four shillings eight pence, the whole to be paid in "hard money." In the same year McCutcheon, who was a merchant, gave another note payable in "half Joes," at three pounds four shillings each, indicating that the old currency silver and gold still circulated in this county at that time.

In 1768, $3,870 in Continental currency was valued in returning the value of an estate to the county court at only three pounds, or about six dollars in gold. In 1794, the executors of Edward Erwin said they had in their possession "a Bill of Virginia money of twelve hundred dollars, which we have not been able to dispose of." In 1791, Matthew Walker exchanged a "gold guinea" with David Flow in some business transaction. In October, 1792, Robert Irwin bought 1,084 Continental dollars at the sale of Wm. Whitsett, who lived in the town of Charlotte, paying three pounds nineteen shillings for the same. In the same year John

KNOW ALL MEN BY THESE PRESENTS, That I John Taylor of Alfred Hallman County, in the Province of NORTH-CAROLINA, _____ am held and firmly bound unto Henry Euftace McCulloh, of Chowan County, in the Province aforefaid, Efquire, in the full and juft Sum of One Hundred and forty eight pounds fifteen shillings ____

Proclamation Money, to be paid unto the faid Henry Euftace McCulloh, his certain Attorney, Heirs, Executors, Administrators, and Affigns: For the which Payment well and truly to be made and done, I bind myfelf, my Heirs, Executors, and Administrators, and each and every of them, jointly and feverally, firmly by thefe Prefents. Sealed with my Seal, and dated this Ninth Day of January 1767.

THE CONDITION of the above Obligation is fuch, That if the above bounden John Taylor his _____ or theirs, or any of their Heirs, Executors, or Administrators, do and fhall well and truly pay, or caufe to be paid, unto the faid Henry Euftace McCulloh, or his certain Attorney, Heirs, Executors, Administrators, or Affigns, the full and juft Sum of Seventy four pounds seven shillings and eight pence proclamation money _____ and Interest, to commence for the fame from the Date hereof, in Manner following, that is to fay, £25 ___ ____ on the 9th Jany 1768, other £25 ___ ____ on the 9th Jany 1769 ____ and £24.7.8 ____ on the 9th Jany 1770 ____ _____

And in Cafe Default fhall happen in the payment of _____ the faid Sum and Intereft, then I the faid John Taylor _____ do impower William Hooper _____ Attorney at Law, or any other practifing Attorney in this Province, or elfewhere, to appear for me in any Suit or Suits to be brought againft me _____ for the fame, and to receive a Declaration, and confefs Judgment, by Nil dicit, or otherwife, hereby releafing all Errors; and for fo doing this fhall be your, or any of your fufficient Warrant. GIVEN under my Hands and Seals as aforefaid, the Day and Year firft above-faid.

Signed, Sealed and Delivered,
in the Prefence of us ____

John Taylor

John Hancock
Thomas ____

CONTRACT, 1767.

CHAPTER VIII.

NOTES ON THE REGULATION.

Miscellaneous Information Summarized in Paragraphs.—The March of Mecklenburg Troops to Hillsboro.—Governor Tryon's Visit in the County.—Sentiment Pertaining to the Regulators and the Governor.

1. On Sunday, September 25th, Rev. Mr. Suter and Rev. Henry Patillo preached to the Rowan and Mecklenburg battalions in camp at Hillsboro.

2. On September 28th, " the officers and soldiers of the Rowan and Mecklenburg Brigade wrote to Adjutant General and Major of Brigade, desiring them in their behalf to wait on His Excellency, and in the most dutiful and respectful terms to express their happiness and entire satisfaction in having this day His Excellency's thanks for their behavior since they have been employed on this service, adding their most ardent wishes for His Excellency's speedy recovery."

3. The march of the Mecklenburg and Rowan battalions from Hillsboro back to Salisbury was made under the command of Colonel Osborne. Colonel Osborne carried back with him a pardon for the insurgents, which he read at the head of the brigade when it arrived at Salisbury, and posted a copy of it on the court house door. The conditions of the pardon were that the insurgents were to give bond and security to pay all their taxes by a certain day and agree not in the future to obstruct any public officer in the execution of his office. The principal insurgents, however, were not to be pardoned, but tried in the courts for their offenses.

4. At a council of war, held at Hillsboro on September 22, 1768, Colonel Robt. Harris, Lieutenant-Colonel Moses Alexander, Major John Phifer and Captain Thomas Polk, Mecklenburg's member of the Assembly, were present.

5. The Mecklenburg battalion, which began the march

CONFEDERATE CURRENCY, 1864.

to Hillsboro, from Major Phifer's, on September 12, 1768, consisted of one colonel, one lieutentant-colonel, one major, seven captains, eight lieutenants, eight ensigns, one adjutant, one quartermaster, fifteen sergeants, seven corporals, seven drummers, and two hundred and fifty-three privates, making a total force of three hundred and ten men. The total expenses of the Mecklenburg battalion were £1854 9s. 6d., of which sum Colonel Moses Alexander was paid £608 23. 6d., proclamation money.

6. Mecklenburg furnished for the 1768 expedition against the Regulators, a force of three hundred and ten men, out of a total of 1461, raised to quell the disturbance. The total expenses of the expedition were £4844 19s. 3d., proclamation money.

7. On Sunday, August 21, 1768, while Governor Tryon was the guest of Major John Phifer, he and Mr. Phifer attended a church where divine services were conducted by Rev. Mr. Suter, a "Swiss or Dutch minister." The discourse enjoined all to obey the laws of the country.

8. The North Carolina Assembly of November, 1768, expressed its conviction of the necessity of the action of Tryon in assembling soldiers at Hillsboro in September of that year, expressed its detestation of the proceedings of the insurgents, extending its thanks to Gov. Tryon for quelling the insurrection, and promised as soon as the finances would permit, to pay the expenses of those soldiers who had marched against the insurgents.

9. The powder burned at Phifer's Hill was not powder that Gov. Tryon had procured in Charleston, but powder that Colonel Moses Alexander had bought there, as Commissary of the Mecklenburg and Rowan Volunteers.

10. David Caldwell was one of the leading men in the Rocky River section and an elder at Rocky River Presbyterian Church. Many of the other names signed to the request for the pardon of the "black boys of Cabarrus" will be recognized as the names of men who at one time or another have played a considerable part in the history of the county.

Their statement of the facts about this episode, leaving out their "obsequious loyalty," ought to commend itself to all lovers of truth as an authentic presentation of the matter.

11. To show that the Regulation did not gain any appreciable headway in this county, it may be remembered that the sheriffs of Rowan and Anson were at a later date empowered, on account of the Regulation troubles, to collect back taxes for the year 1770. No Mecklenburg sheriff ever asked for the passage of such an act of relief. Hence, it is to be presumed that whatever taxes were not collected here were not collected for causes others than those attending the Regulation troubles.

12. As the name of Edmund Fanning is connected with Mecklenburg history, in connection with Queen's College, and that connection may be thought strange, in view of all that has been said about him in North Carolina histories, it may be interesting to note here that the Assembly proceedings of January 25, 1771, Vol. VIII., page 461, of the Colonial Records, recites that Fanning had been charged with many things injurious to his character. It is said that the House had inquired into those charges and after the strictest examination found the several accusations to be "false, wretched and malicious, arising from the malevolence of a set of insurgents, who style themselves Regulators." Captain Alexander was on the committee that investigated Fanning's conduct.

13. It is well known that the sentiment of many North Carolinians, by the year 1772, had changed in regard to the Regulators. August 30th, 1772, Governor Josiah Martin wrote Lord Hillsborough that he had lately visited Orange, Guilford and Chatham counties, and said that as he went through Guilford County, the Regulators and Hunter, their leader among them, came to him in great penitence and contrition and asked pardon. The Regulators claimed they had no intention of subverting the government and maintained that they had been misled. Martin says these people were barbariously ignorant beyond description, and

that mercenary attorneys and other litttle officers had evidently taken advantage of this ignorance.

14. James McCaul, the Regulator, whose advertisement is said to have been the occasion of the meeting referred to by James Ashmore in his confession, was an Anson County man.

CHAPTER IX.

NOTES ON CHAPTER II. (The Indians.)

Items Regarding Important Events.—Very Few Relics Found in Mecklenburg.—Correspondence Between Governors of North Carolina and South Carolina Respecting the Catawba.

1. The occasion of the Indians going to Salisbury and insulting the Chief Justice and disturbing the court was this: A band of the Catawbas was returning from Virginia, where they had gone to take part in one of the campaigns of the French and Indian war.. These Indians robbed a wagon and tied the wagoner with his own chain. The whites followed the Indians and recovered the stolen goods, which so incensed the Indians that they acted in the manner indicated above.

2. The Indian remains in this section present no special peculiarities, except that there are evidences at one or two points of the work of mound builders. Mr. A. Nixon, of Lincolnton, N. C., has several ornaments like those usually found in localities where these prehistoric peoples are known to have lived. Mr. Nixon has several ornamented pipes and other interesting relics, collected near Hardin, N. C., and Iron Station, N. C., in the territory which lies between the South Fork and the Catawba rivers.

3. Robert Campbell and Thomas Keasey were the two white men wounded at Fort Dobbs in February, 1760. Both of these men were pensioned by the Colonial Assembly, Campbell finally being sent back to England, the Assembly paying his passage.

4. The Catawba Indians had, in 1755, two hundred and forty to three hundred warriors, with King Hagler at their head. In 1760, smallpox reduced the number of warriors to sixty. Governor Dobbs says that besides the sixty warriors, there were left after the smallpox epidemic ended, sixty old men and boys and a "suitable number of women." If these figures are reliable, it will be seen that the Catawba

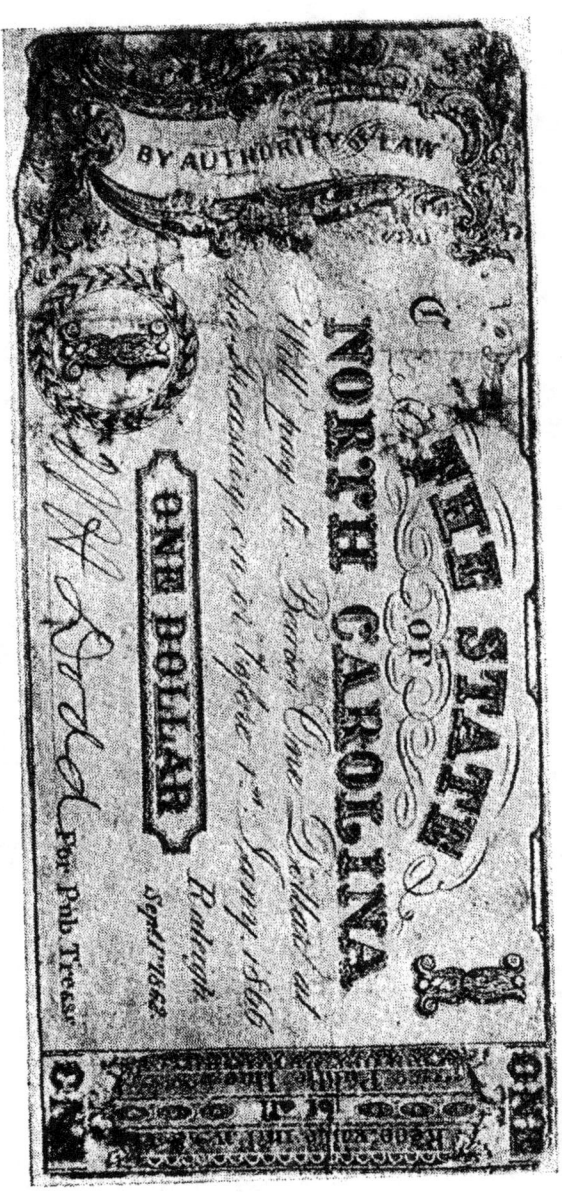

NORTH CAROLINA CURRENCY, 1866.

tribe must have been reduced by disease, in 1760, by about four-fifths its size in 1755. This also accounts for the fact that the Catawbas were not heard of as an Indian power after 1760, and may account, too, for some of their friendliness towards the whites after that date.

5. Governor Dobbs, writing to Governor Boone of South Carolina, July 6, 1762, says: "Mr. Samuel Wily arrived here and informs me he had directions from Mr. Bull to run out lines of the lands alotted for the Catawba Nation, a tract fifteen miles square, commencing at the Southward from 12 mile Creek to the Northward 15 miles from the East to West 7 miles and a half on each side of Catawba River, pursuant, as he says, to an agreement made with the Catawba Nation about a year ago between Mr. Atkins, agent for Indian affairs, with King Hagler, and Hagler, with these Indians have arrived here the same day upon the same account.

"It does not a little surprise me to find that Mr. Atkins should have peremptorily have taken upon him to have fixed so large a tract of land to them without first acquainting me with it, as there is the highest probability that all these lands will be within the province by the parallelled lines which will determine our boundary, without even showing his power to me of determining it, without His Majesty's approbation or consulting the Government of this Province, and still more so in never having communicated his agreement to me since he concluded it.

"And this survey, if perfected would ascertain the Catawbas' claim hereafter and would at present occasion much confusion among those who had taken warrants and patents upon these lands. For upon the Indians' removal from Sugar Creek Town to 12-Mile Creek, many of the lands northward from Sugar Town have been surveyed and some patents isssued, as I appprehended upon their removal, they had chosen and accepted of other lands, more southerly, and more so as to their number of warriors have been reduced in a few years, by Hagler's confession, from three hundred to fifty, and all their males don't exceed one hundred old and young included, as they are now scarce a Nation; the lands alotted to them since their reduction by Mr. Atkin is 144,000 acres.

"As the Catawba's have behaved well, though their numbers are reduced, I would agree to their having a large tract and proportion of land, and would not think it imprudent to advise His Majesty to allow them a tract 12 miles square, which would contain 96,000 acres, a sufficient quantity for so small a number."

"Bounds might be limited between 12-Mile Creek and Sugar Creek on the east side of Catawba and as much more to the westward as shall make up the complement, till His Majesty's approbation is obtained, and therefore at present should advise that the surrounding lines should be suspended and only the distance run from 12-Mile Creek to Sugar Creek, to ascertain that distance, and in the meantime I shall suspend the issuing of any more patents within that limit, and think it reasonable that Captain Steward, who succeeds Mr. Atkins should send me a copy of Mr. Atkins' power, by which he is acting in fixing their limits without His Majesty's approbation or the consent of this Province, and then when the limits are ascertained no private purchase should be allowed, though their numbers should diminish, without the approbation of the Government of the Province, in which the lands may lay, and the General consent of the Catawba Nation."

The above besides being interesting as bearing on the general history of the Catawbas, is especially interesting as mentioning the original town of the Catawbas, on Sugar Creek. Tradition has not even located that original capital of the Indian Nation, and it is perhaps now useless to try to locate it with any degree of certainty. It is enough for us to remember that this town or original capital of the Catawbas was on big Sugar Creek, somewhat nearer the present town of Charlotte, perhaps, than it was distant from the final location of the capital on the southern border of this county.

6. Lawson, in his description of this section in the year 1701, speaks of the "Sugaree" Indians, as well as the Ca-

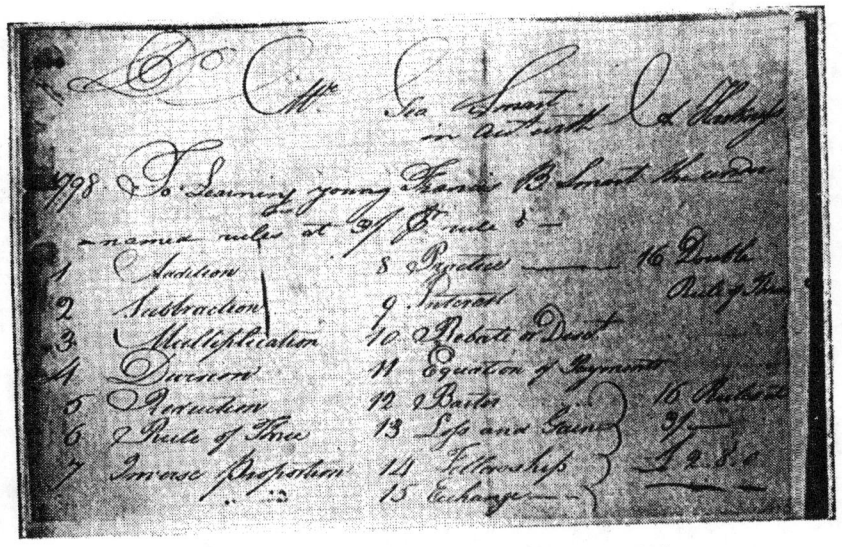

ITEMIZED BILL FOR "LEARNING," 1798.

tawbas. In view of what Governor Dobbs says, in 1762, and in view of the whole history of the Indians of this section, the opinion may be advanced that the Sugarees were a branch of the Catawbas (Kadapaws in Lawson's vernacular), and were finally absorbed by them, the name remaining in the stream on which their principal settlement was situated.

CHAPTER X.

NOTES ON CHAPTER XV. (Religion.)

Coming of Rev. Hugh McAden.—Rev. Alexander Craighead Withdraws from the Presbyterian Synod and Comes to North Carolina.—Established Church of England Met With Much Discouragement in Mecklenburg.

Rev. Hugh McAden began his trip South with Lancaster county, Pennsylvania, as a starting point, June 3, 1755. The second Sunday in June he was at Rock Spring where he met Rev. James Campbell, who the next year came to North Carolina, to the Cape Fear section, and has the distinction of being the first resident Presbyterian minister in the colony, whose name has come down to us. Mr. McAden crossed the Potomac on June 16, went to Winchester and came South through the Shenandoah Valley. He preached at the forks of the James river on the second Sunday in July, and on Wednesday following at the house of a friend, he heard the lamentable story of Braddock's defeat by the Indians and French. The whole country was thrown into confusion, which increased with the stories of Indian murders on the frontier. Braddock's defeat and the danger apparently threatening the people of the Valley, sent many families to the more peaceful sections of North Carolina. Rev. Alexander Craighead, whose congregation on the "Cow Pasture" had probably been entirely scattered from their homes, was one of those who came to North Carolina on this account.

Mr. McAden considered whether he should return to Pennsylvania or should continue his journey. He writes: "I resolved to prosecute my journey, come what will, with some degree of dependence upon the Lord for his divine protection and support, that I might be able to glorify Him in all things, whether in life or death." He preached the first Sunday in August in North Carolina. Soon afterwards he

UNITED STATES BANK NOTE.

preached most acceptably to the people at the Baptist Yearly Meeting, in what is now Granville county.

Rev. Alexander Craighead was one of the charter members of the Presbytery of Hanover, Virginia, formed by the Synod of New York, in 1755. He came of a race of Presbyterian preachers in Scotland and Ireland where the name is an honorable one among the Church archives. He came from the Presbytery of Donegal, in the old country, and joined the Synod of Philadelphia in 1736. In 1746, he was accused of unusual methods in his evangelistic services, but was able to appeal so successfully to the sympathy of the community that the Presbytery could not bring the case to an issue. He withdrew from the Synod with eleven others, in 1841, forming the "New Side" Presbytery of Brunswick. Then he dropped out of the records for a time, being, as is supposed, associated with the great Whitfield in his labors in America.

In 1743, Thomas Cookson, one of His Majesty's justices in Pennsylvania, brought in a complaint to the Synod of a certain paper, attributed to Alexander Craighead, a Presbyterian minister. It will be noted that Mr. Craighead now belonged to the opposite party from the Synod. The Synod set aside all other business to consider the paper, and the following record was made: "The above mentioned paper, with an affidavit concerning it, being read in open Synod, it was unanimously agreed that it was full of treason, sedition and distraction, and grievous perverting of the sacred oracles to the ruin of all society and government, and directly and diametrically opposite to our religious principles; as we have on all occasions declared to the world; and we hereby unanimously and with the greatest sincerity declare that we detest this paper. And if Mr. Alexander Craighead be the author, we know nothing of the matter; and we hereby declare that he hath been no member of this society for some time past, nor do we acknowledge him as such, though we cannot but heartily lament that any man that was ever called a Presbyterian should be guilty of what is in this paper." In addition to this, the moderator, with three leading members, was appointed a committee to draw up an address to the Governor on the occasion.

This seems a little hard on Mr. Craighead. Probably, thirty years afterwards, the members of the same Synod would have considered the paper a most patriotic document, when every Presbyterian minister and almost the whole body of the people were on the side of the colonies as against the crown and were preaching sedition and treason at every opportunity.

July 20, 1766, Rev. Mr. Reed, an Episcopal clergyman, writing from New Bern to the Society for the Propagation of the Gospel, says: "Mr. Morton arrived here about the 18th of last month from the northward and stayed with me to refresh himself a few days, then proceeded to Brunswick to wait upon the Governor and from thence intended to go to Mecklenburg county. But on his arrival at Brunswick, he was very creditably, and, I believe, very truly informed, that the inhabitants of that county evaded the Vestry Act by electing the most rigid dissenters for Vestrymen who would not quaify; that the county abounded with dissenters of various denominations and particularly with Covenanters, Seceders, Anabaptists and New Lights; that he would meet with a very cold, if any reception at all, have few or no hearers and lead a very uneasy life." Governor Tryon took a more charitable and tolerant view of the religious conditions in this county and said to the same Society October 1, 1766: "I intend as a rule to myself to dispose of the ministers as they arrive into those counties where the inhabitants are most willing to receive them. Those of Mecklenburg county are almost all Presbyterians. I have, therefore, sent Mr. Morton, at his own request, to Northampton county." On August 25, 1766, Mr. Morton himself wrote that he "was well informed that the inhabitants of Mecklenburg are entire dissenters of the most rigid kind. That they had a solemn league and covenant teacher settled among them; that they were in general greatly averse to the Church of England, and that they looked upon a law lately enacted in this province for the better establishment of the Church as oppressive as the Stamp Act, and were determined to prevent its taking place there by opposing the settlement of any minister of the Church of England that might be sent among them." In 1766, it was said that Pennsylvania was the breeding place of sects; that that colony sent down to this province all kinds of sects and among the number "gifted brethren," or "New Lights." In 1767, Governor Tryon estimated the white taxables of Mecklenburg at 1,600, "mostly Presbyterians."

It is not very probable that the Rev. Mr. Reed or the Rev. Mr. Morton knew very much about the different classes of dissenters, the terms, Covenanters and Seceders, simply referring to the Scotch antecedents of the Presbyterians, and "New Light," probably denoting the "New Side" branch of the Presbyterian Church, though the Old and New side had by this time been united. Nor is it probable that there were any "Anobaptists" in Mecklenburg in the historical sense of the word. There may have been some Baptists here as there were in other parts of the colony, and they always stood with the Presbyterians in their advocacy of civil and religious liberty.

In January, 1771, the Assembly passed an act which the Governor wisely signed, and which took away one of the long-standing grievances of this section. It was introduced by Edmund Fanning, Thomas Polk being one of the special committee appointed to formulate the statute. It permitted regularly called Presbyterian ministers to solemnize the rites of marriage by publication in their assemblies or by license. Fanning reported that the restrictions put upon Presbyterian ministers worked great hardships, the people having been trained to prefer the ceremony celebrated by a minister to marriage by a justice of the peace.

In 1770 Providence congregation established a church in the Clear Creek section for the convenience of those members who lived in that neighborhood, and this later on became the Philadelphia Church.

There were some members of the Episcopal Church coming in with the English emigrants from the East, as is evident from the mention of the Book of Prayer occasionally at the sale of libraries. In DeRosset's Church History of North Carolina, we find this statement: "Speaking of the marriage of dissenters by dissenting clergymen, Bishop Cheshire says: 'It seems an ungracious provision of this law, meant to be an act of courtesy as well as of justice, to the growing settlements along the Yadkin and the Catawba, that it provided that the Episcopal minister in the parish where the marriage was performed should be entitled to the fee, if he had not refused to perform the service. This, howver, was of less consequence, as there was not a single minister in any parish in the province where a Presbyterian minister resided.'"

Prior to 1767, the Germans of Cabarrus had a pastor at Coldwater, Mr. Suter, who preached there in August, 1768, when Governor Tryon was visiting at John Phifer's. This church on Coldwater was the first Reformed Church founded in North Carolina. About 1760, the Lutherans and Reformed Germans built a log church in the present county of Catawba, near the present town of Newton, which they called St. Paul's. In 1764, this church was served by Mr. Dupert. Paul Anthony and Henry Weidner (Whitner) were the prime movers in this church enterprise, which seems to have been the oldest church erected in Catawba county, in territory then regarded as belonging to Mecklenburg.

On October 26, 1767, Matthew Floyd was granted a tract of land on the waters of the South Fork of the Catawba, joining the lands of Jonathan Potts and Peter Statler, "including a school house." This school house was built by the Lutherans and German Calvinists about 1765, and was also used for church purposes, being one of the oldest churches west of the Catawba river. On this spot are now situated two churches, five miles west of the present town of Lincolnton, the one a Lutheran and the other a Reformed church, which have been erected by the descendants of the pioneer inhabitants of that section which was once a part of Mecklenburg. This original union church was known as "school house" church until after 1819, when its name became Daniel's Church.

CHAPTER XI

HISTORY OF MINING IN MECKLENBURG.

Historic Anticipations—Discoveries in Florida—First Find in the County—Geology of Mecklenburg—Development of Mining—Statistics of the Branch Mint in Charlotte.

By George B. Hanna, E. M.*

From the earliest entrance of the Spaniards into the territory, now known as the United States, the question of the precious metals was always the foremost consideration. The large treasure found in Mexico and in Peru excited the cupidity of this avaricious race, and suggested the existence of other stores in other parts of the New World.

On entering Florida, the first inquiry was concerning gold. Native copper from the shores of Lake Superior, and probably also from the mountains of the Carolinas, as well as mica from this latter region, had been widely scattered to the South, Southwest and Southeast among the natives, the copper being used largely for tools, and the mica for ornaments.

It is now quite certain from the results of modern exhumations in Florida and along the cost of the Gulf States, that nuggets of gold had also traveled thither from what we now call the Southern Appalachian gold region, and were used widely both for barter and for ornaments.

The gold found in the exhumations has been assayed in late years, and found to correspond with the gold from the mountains of Georgia and of the Carolinas, and this indication of origin is confirmed by the physical appearance of the nuggets.

It is not probable that De Soto or his immediate followers ever penetrated the Appalachian mountains, but scattered parties of his followers apparently did, as evidenced by their

---

*Prepared by Prof. Hanna especially for this book

frequent allusions to these mountains and rivers under names variously spelled by the early Spanish chroniclers. The Altamaha river, for instance, became a familiar name as a source of gold. An early traveler even went so far as to picture the rude way which the natives in the region of the Altamaha had in panning, or rather concentrating, the fine particles of gold—a method totally unknown at the present time among our miners—an agitation with air or water in hollow tubes of cane.

The earliest American miners of the nineteenth century have denied that the Indians ever practiced the collection of the fine gold; their extremest skill went no farther than the securing of nuggets and coarse gold, which could be picked out with the fingers.

The vast collections of the Spaniards held the world spellbound, and when the English came to this country, they, too, gave their attention to the possible occurrence of the precious metals, though cupidity was held in subjection to the practical aims of the settlers; gold was only an incidental end. Sir Walter Raleigh, in his assignment of territorial rights, reserved to himself one-fifth of the gold and silver that might be discovered.

The immigrants to the Piedmont section of the Carolinas, as soon as securely settled, began to hunt for gold. Several points are known where prospecting was carried on more than 125 years ago. Among these was the Aborigines shaft at the Brewer mine in Chesterfield county, S. C., and the Oliver mine in Gaston county, near the Catawba river, from which an old German miner was frightened away by the approach of Cornwallis' troops.

FIRST DISCOVERY OF GOLD.

The search was finally rewarded. The little son of Conrad Reed, of Cabarrus county, in 1799, found a large nugget at the Reed mine, and soon thereafter, and continuing till the present time, other nuggets of varying sizes have been mined, and soon after nuggets were found at the locality afterwards known as the Dunn mine, near Rozzel's Ferry, in Mecklenburg county; and as at the Reed mine, the character of the nuggets was not suspected, and they were used by the local gunsmiths for the ignoble purpose of "bushing" rifles.

The spirit of discovery spread, and by 1821 the known producing area in North Carolina was, according to Olmsted, 1,000 square miles in extent, reaching from Montgomery county and Anson (including Union county, not then set off), in the east to Gaston county in the west, and to Guilford county in the north; a distinct race of native professional "gold hunters" had arisen, which steadily enlarged the limits of producing territory.

The date of the opening of the first mine is unknown to the writer, but it is supposed that the McCombs mine was the first. In Professor Mitchell's report in 1826, two mines, the McCombs and the Capps, are indicated on the accompanying map as in full work in Mecklenburg county, and from the description, the McCombs mine seems to have been well equipped for that period. This mine is one mile west of Charlotte, and later was known as the Old Charlotte, and still more recently as the St. Catherine mine.

GEOLOGY OF MECKLENBURG COUNTY.

The eastern part of Mecklenburg county shows argillite or clay slate, and the western, bordering on Gaston, has granite, or more properly speaking, gneiss; the interior part from north to south, is an area of confused material, which may show in a small hand specimen several varieties of rock. Dikes everywhere seam the country, and both dikes and the formation which they penetrate are altered and peroxidized, and softened to a surprising depth. The area, in its longitudinal extension from northeast to southwest, was designated by Professor Emmons as the "Salisbury and Greensboro granite;" it can only be called granite by a very considerable degree of accommodation, for it contains a heavy proportion of hornblende, pyroxene, chlorite and epidote. It is probably among the most primitive rocks on the American continent, and apparently antedated the introduction of the earliest life, as it has not, in the writer's knowledge, shown the smallest fossil. The history of opinion among the geologists of this immediate belt of which Mecklenburg forms a conspicuous part, is extremely curious. Olmsted, Mitchell, and Rothe, all eminent men, early examined it; Olmsted (1821) thought it to be argillite, (clay slate); Rothe (1826) regarded it as granite and gneiss; Mitchell (1826) was more cautious, and fluctuated between the two. Professor Eaton thought it to be talcose slate. Professor Emmons, State Geologist of North Carolina, called it (1856) the igneous or pyrocrystalline formation. Professor Kerr, a most careful observer (Geology of North Carolina, vol. 1, page 123, 1875,) says, "the characteristic and prevalent rocks are syenyte, doleryte, greenstone, amphibolyte, granite, porphyry and trachyte." Other observers, however, place the formation high up in the geological column. Nitze, (Bulletin No. 10, North Carolina Geological Survey, 1897, page 15), designates the rock as "devitrified ancient colcanics, (rhyolite, quartz-porpryry, etc., and pyro-clastic breccias; igneous plutonic rock, granite, diorite, diabase, etc.")

The formation is everywhere pierced by trap dikes, which in weathering have, near the surface, been peroxidized and mingled confusedly with the weathered material of the formation proper, down to a depth in some instances of 100 feet. Becker has aptly called this material "Saprolite," or rotten rock (16 Annual Report United States Geological Survey, part III, 1894-95, pages 289 and 290.)

It is evident that a name at once descriptive and comprehensive is lacking, and probably will be lacking till either the United States or the State Geological Survey takes the matter up, and deals with the material by careful field work, supplemented by the most extensive chemical and microscopical examination in the laboratory.

There is very little true stratification, but some stratification due to dynamic metamorphism.

REVOLUTIONARY CURRENCY.

It may be added that it is not known that a fossil has ever been found in the country. The identification of the formation depends on mineralogical characters, or the stratigraphy, and to some extent on the associations.

MINERALS OF THE COUNTY.

The late Dr. F. A. Genth, a very close observer and an indefatigable student, gives the following list of minerals found in Mecklenburg county:

Malachite, azurite, chalcopyrite, chrysocolla, bornite, copper glance, cuprite, chalcotrichite, barnhardtite, melaconite, native copper, galenite, lead, monazite, diamond, leopardite, rutile, misaeous iron ore, magnetite, chalybite, soapstone, sphalerite, gold, silver, platinum, mica, granite, quartz, amethyst, graphite, arsenic, (mineralized), arsenic, (native), antimony, (mineralized), antimony, (native), cobalt, (mineralized), nickel, (mineralized).

Few of these are of commercial importance. Iron ore has been found sporadically over the entire county. Micaceous iron ore (or specular iron, or red hematite), of high grade and purity are found widely scattered, but in small quantity. Magnetic iron ore is found in Steel Creek township on the plantation of Dr. Strong, near Center A. R. P. church, in several narrow veins, also at Hopewell, and near the old Rock Island Factory, on the Catawba; specular hematite is also found in the north part of the county, near Davidson College. A great deal of labor has been given in prospecting for iron; an occasional vein or rather seam has been found, but ore in commercial quantity is not known. Chalybite occurs very sparingly at most gold mines.

Copper minerals were long dreaded by the gold miners, and especially by the mill men, who thought, and with some reason, that this element prevented the collection of the gold in the amalgamating process. The mining population learning about 1854, of the discovery of workable ores of copper in other parts of the State, especially in Guilford county, prospected most diligently for similar ores in this county. Large workable deposits were not found except in two or three instances; occasionally, as at the Cathey mine, the Rogers, the Crosby, and the Ray mines, pockets of copper have been found rich enough for a separate and a smelting treatment; in every mine the small amounts of auriferous ores mined in regular work, have been sorted out till an accumulation of such material has justified shipment to smelting works, usually to Boston, Baltimore, or Swansea. No further special treatment on a large scale has ever been given to this class of ores, and none are now mined. Lead and silver ores are sometimes found, but never in quantities to attract attention. The gold ores invariably contain a small proportion of silver. Zinc ore (sphalerite) is still more rare.

Arsenic, antimony, and bismuth, tellurium, etc., mineralized arsenic, antimony and bismuth, sometimes occur in the auriferous sulphurets in minute percentages; metallic arsenic and antimony have been reported. The occurrence of tellurets, etc., is doubtful.

Monazite and rutite have been found in placer work concentrated with the gold. Mica is sparingly, but widely distributed wherever granite rocks occur, but it is rarely found in pieces large enough for industrial purposes. Graphite (black lead), is found in small quantities as an accessory in most mines of the county. Amethyst and quartz crystals are frequently met with, but few of notable value have been found.

Cobalt and nickel in very small percentages occur in the McGinn mine; the former occasionally as peach blossom ore (erythrite), and both metals are occasionally found as an accidental constituent of the auriferous sulphurets; their occurrence has hitherto proved of no industrial importance.

Granite and other building minerals and material are found along the Catawba river, and near the Iredell line, and in patches in various parts of the country, but they have rarely found a use out of the immediate neighborhood in which they are found.

Soapstone of an impure variety occurs locally in many

places, and has found an important local use in the construction of fireplaces and chimneys.

Limestone and gypsum in commercial quantity are wanting. Marls and phosphates are unknown.

Leopardite is found near the factory settlement now called Belmont. It extends in a narrow ledge on the lands of Mr. William W. Phifer, a distance of nearly one-third of a mile. It is substantially an orthoclase felspar with veinlets and spots of black oxide of manganese penetrating it as the roots of grass penetrate a soil. The black and white constituents are mingled in most pleasing variety, and have made it a beautiful ornamental stone, but it is so hard and irregular and so abounds in "dry seams" as to be troublesome and uncertain to work. Blocks of more than local interest have been quarried. One of these blocks was sent by the public spirited citizens of Charlotte to the Washington monument. Another block is a part of the foundation of the mint, and still another lies in the pavement in front of Jordan's drug store. As a whole, it has failed to find its expected use. "Float" blocks of leopardite have also been found at Hunter's Calcic Springs, at Derita.

Sandstone for building purposes is absent.

Coal does not exist. In fact these geological formations are not the home of the coal beds.

One diamond was found in the gold sands of Todd's branch in Paw Creek township in 1852; Dr. C. L. Hunter, who was familiar with its history, says: "It weighs about three-fourths of a carat, and is nearly of the first water." This locality, with many others, has been repeatedly examined for this precious stone, but hitherto the result has been negative. If the gold sands had been carefully examined in the palmy days of placer mining, it is highly probable that other specimens of the gem would have been found.

Garnets and zircons are sometimes found in the gold sands, but not in usable quantity.

A few scales of platinum were claimed to have been found in the placer workings in the northeast border of the county, near the Pioneer Mills neighborhood.

Material for brick making is found everywhere; for the most part the altered, weathered, and thoroughly rotted country rock immediately above the bed rock is chosen for brick making. The brick manufactured is strong and durable, but not so sightly as the Philadelphia and Wilmington brick; nevertheless it finds a wide and profitable use.

ECONOMIC MINERALS.

The economic minerals and mine materials are confined to gold (and incidentally silver) ores, copper ores and material for building uses.

The precise year in which gold was found in Mecklenburg county is unknown; by 1821 placer work was practiced somewhat extensively, and as the placers became exhausted, the veins which supplied the placers were searched out. The situation in 1821 was discussed by Professors Olmsted, and Mitchell; in 1830 the mining localities were very numerous. Until the discovery of gold in California in 1847, this county was the seat of a very active industry; a large number of miners and speculators turned away to this new Eldorado, and from this period gold mining lagged, until at the close of the late war only one mine, the Rudisil, was in operation.

The mines of Mecklenburg county are quite widely scattered over its area. In this area of 20 by 30 miles, are nearly 100 mines, which at one or another time have been worked profitably, and gold is more widely diffused than in any other county of the central part of the State.

The ores of these mines are auriferous and sometimes cupriferous; they rarely contain any notable amound of lead, zinc or nickel; the sulphur present is usually combined with iron. Arsenic and antimony are not common; the sulphur, in the form of sulphurets, was formerly greatly dreaded by the mill men as a great hindrance, but now the presence of the sulphurets is accounted an advantage. The vein fissures are from a few inches to 60 feet wide. Most of these fissures are filled with killas (slates), quartz and ores,

History of Mining in Mecklenburg. 117

but in depth the slaty structure is not so evident, or does not exist. The quartz itself shows a tendency to lamination, and there is often a parallelism in the bodies of sulphurets.

The weathering influences have peroxidized the iron constituents of the entire surface to a great depth, sometimes to a depth of 150 feet.

There has been no glacial action, other than a purely local and sedentary one, and the disintegrated surface has remained largely in place. The upper part of the vein has undergone a corresponding change, in which much of the slaty part has "rotted" to "saprolites" and changed to a more or less hydrated "brown ore;" the copper pyrites has altered to malachite (rarely to azurite), chrysocalla, and sometimes to red or black oxide of copper, or occasionally to native copper, and quite often has been leached out from the surface ores, or has been concentrated at lower levels. The brown ore holds not only the gold which was originally in the sulphurets, but it has been further enriched as a result of the alterations, as is shown by the presence of grain and nugget gold, which is found in this zone more abundantly. Such ores are easily won and are treated without expensive machinery, for the process is a mechanical rather than a metallurgical one; ordinarily a relatively large part of the gold is extracted at a small cost.

The permanent water level of the mines is, perhaps, a little below that of the adjacent streams, and is found at a depth of from twenty to sixty feet. The amount of water in the mines is usually large, and a very considerable part of the expense of mining is due to the cost of pumping. At the water level the sulphurets occur with little alteration, and the value of the ores is apt to be smaller, as the sources of the enrichment have been less active than in the gossan part near the surface. Any general statement must necessarily find exceptions, and occasionally the very best ores of a mine have been found at great depths, e. g., the Rudisil mine, where three "chimneys" or "shoots" of great width, (11 feet), and longitudinal extent are found with very exceptionally high grade ores.

The difficulty in dealing with the ores from these levels efficiently and economically was also increased so long as amalgamation was practiced, and the winning of the gold from these complex ores was early shown to be the vexed problem that we know to-day.

The great expense of mining and treating such ores, and the decreased yield led to the abandonment of the larger part of the mines of North Carolina, and most of them still remain closed. Occasionally the ore bodies actually disappear entirely in this zone, through the closing in of the syenite walls, i. e., by the "pinching out" of the ore body.

The veins are too numerous for special description here. To a great extent they are capable of grouping into neighborhoods pre-eminently mineral.

MINING GROUPS.

The vicinity of Charlotte is one of these mineral districts, and around it on all sides are mines, among them the Davidson, Blake, Point, Parks, Clark, St. Catherine, Rudisil, Smith & Palmer, McDonald, Howell, Trotter, Carson, Taylor, Isenhour (Iceyhour), Chinquepin, and many others unknown to the general public, or unnamed.

A second group is three to ten miles west and north west from Charlotte, viz., Summerville, Hayes, McGee, Brawley, Frazer, Hipp, Campbell, Todd, Arlington, Capps, McGinn, Means, S. Wilson, Troutman, Prim, Abernathy, Alexander (Chapman), Dunn, Sloan, McCorkle and Cathey.

A third group is found around the Ferris (Faires), six miles north of Charlotte, the Alexander and the Garris, and to the west of the Ferris, the Henderson, Elwood and the J. P. Hunter.

Another group is found in Providence township, and about Sardis church, some five to ten miles southeast from Charlotte, among others the Hunter mine (two veins), Tredinick, and the Ray (three veins).

The Pioneer Mills group, in Cabarrus county, extends

into the northeast part of Mecklenburg. Specially prominent are the Johnson, Stinson, Maxwell, Black and Harris.

The Davidson Hill mine, (really three mines), one mile west of Charlotte, has been worked to the depth of 160 feet at its north end.

The Rudisil and St. Catherine are respectively the south and north ends of the same mine, being one-half mile to one mile southwest from Charlotte. Both mines have been worked almost from the earliest days of the vein mining of this section, and the former has received more attention than any mine in the county. The strike is N. 30 degrees E. and the dip nearly 45 degrees westerly. At the outset, and to a depth of 100 feet, two bodies of ore (or veins) were exploited—the "back vein" and the "front vein;" the two varied from two to six feet in thickness; at 200 feet the vein appears more consolidated. This mine, for many years, was prosperous, the material being the easily treated familiar brown ores; from 100 to 200 feet the ore was more scattered through the gange; just below the 200 foot level three rich shoots of ore made their appearance, one of which far excelled the gossan in richness; it reached below the 350 foot level, at which depth the vein was apparently "thrown" from its position.

No statistics of production exist, but it is quite certain that the yield has been not less than a half million dollars.

The St. Catherine end of the vein has had a history almost as eventful and has been worked to the vertical depth of 370 feet. The Capps (or Capps Hill) mine is five and one-half miles from Charlotte. It is one of a group of mines closely united, of which two are convergent—the McGinn or Jane gold vein, and the Capps. The former courses with some variations N. 40 to 60 degrees E., and dips S. E.; the Capps courses N. 30 degrees to 35 degrees W., and has a southwest dip. The McGinn mining tract has also some small and less well known veins approximating to the Capps in strike. The Capps is known to be fully 3,000 feet long, and the Jane vein is of equal extent; the former was worked to a depth of 160 feet, and the Jane or McGinn to 150 feet. Both veins have been very productive. Some of the older miners attribute an output of $2,000,000 to the Capps. The record of underground work is in great part lost, but there are abundant indications of very extensive work two generations ago. The Dunn mine, ten miles northwest from Charlotte, was the first discovered mine of the county, not long after the finding of the historic Reed nugget.

Few mines are now worked in Mecklenburg county; the only ones of importance are the Capps, Surface Hill and the Wilhelmina, (Summerville.)

METALLURGICAL TREATMENT OF GOLD ORES.

The early methods practiced in placer work were speedily developed, and in no long time brought to a high degree of efficiency by the native miners working along the old familiar lines. The cradle, the tom and the sluice, with blanket washings, constituted the earliest forms of recovery; quicksilver was early introduced, and greatly assisted the profitable extraction of gold. On account of the comparative flatness of the surface of the county, hydraulic methods found little opportunity for application or development.

About 1825, the rocker, the drag mill and the arrastra, or Chilian mill, were known to be in use. As soon as the hard quartz was discovered there was immediately a necessity for some grinding apparatus; the home-made drag mill was the first step and no more efficient single machine has ever been introduced for saving the gold; its defect is lack of capacity, and this lack finally led to the introduction of the arrastra, which was also made of home material. The arrastra or Chilian mill was copied from South American models, but the models were greatly excelled. The Hungarian bowl and jigs came shortly thereafter. The stamp mill, (the pounding mill, as it was then termed), soon followed; the earliest stamp mill known to the writer was put up at the Haile mine, Lancaster county, S. C., in 1837, by a French-

History of Mining in Mecklenburg.

man named Gugnot; it is claimed that the first stamp mill in Mecklenburg county was erected in 1840, at St. Catherine's mill at the outlet of Bissell's pond, two miles southwest from Charlotte; the remains of this mill were still standing in 1872. This was the work of the late Humphrey Bissell, a co-laborer with Morse on the telegraph, and one of the most skillful and intelligent of the old mining population. This mill was used as one piece in a train of machinery, which accomplished a very thorough extraction, and was used for many years as a custom mill by most of the mine owners of the county within easy reach. This mill merits a brief description, for it was the progenitor of the powerful stamp battery, (the California stamp battery), now so generally used in dealing with gold ores; the frame work was of light timber, and the foundations were weak; the stems were also of wood of square section; the stamps were of cast iron, and the mortar, also of iron, was shallow and narrow. The whole structure was a toy compared with batteries now used.

It is worthy of passing remark that the late Mr. Edward Bissell and Dr. Daniel Asbury both informed the writer that Mr. Humphrey Bissell had also anticipated the modern stamp battery of the Lake Superior copper region in making a mortar with discharges from both faces.

The first improved California stamp battery was erected soon after the Civil War.

Mr. Bissell, with great forethought, had forecast the possibilities of the mining future of this county and section, and had visited Europe and studied the metallurgical methods practiced at Freiberg, Swansea and other metallurgical and mining centers. On returning to Charlotte, in connection with a German engineer, he set up a small experimental smelting plant, which was operated for several campaigns. Dates are wanting. From the papers, which he left, it may be inferred that he smelted for gold directly, and also practiced copper matte smelting. His untimely death terminated his experiments.

Other experimental furnaces were erected by other parties, but trustworthy data of these experiments are not known to the writer.

Very marked progress was made in milling, amalgamating and concentrating, and many of the methods now practiced in the West owed their earliest popularization to the South Appalachian slope. Even the method of dredge mining, now carried out so extensively in the West, in New Zealand and in Georgia, appears to have been early outlined on the borders of Mecklenburg county in the Catawba river.

Dr. J. H. Gibbon, assayer of the mint in Charlotte, as early as 1843 says that a Mr. Gibson took out a patent for a location on the Catawba river, naively remarking that he cared nothing for the water, but for the gravel on its bed; the bottom of the river was scooped out by men on a float, using long handled shovel-like-scoops, and the material was carried ashore and washed for recovering the gold.

Very early in the history of vein mining the South was visited and exploited by every class of foreign miners of all degrees of skill, from the learned and experienced mining engineer to the humblest class of underground laborers; the writer's notes evidence the presence of Mexican, Brazilian, Spanish, French, German, Australian, Hungarian, Italian, Turkish, English, Scotch, Welsh and Irish miners. But the Cornish miners outstayed all others, and formed a very unmerous population, even so late as 40 years ago. Many of the best citizens of Mecklenburg are descended from these old miners: for instance, the Gluyas family, the Chapman family, the Tredinicks, the Groses, the Northeys, Severs, Elwoods, Richards, Lilycrops, Vivians, Fidlers, Hoopers, Moyles, Symons, Treloars, and Venos, show the vigor and worth of the race of early miners from abroad.

The earliest period of speculative mining began about 1830, and was ended by the commercial depression of that decade, and by 1839-40 the excitement had largely subsided. In the forties it commenced again and lasted with some vigor till the discovery of gold in California in 1848, when there was an immediate stampede of the mining population. The war between the States put an end to all operations, and when it closed the Rudisil mine was the only one operated in the county.

Among the noted characters who figured during this period were Mr. Humphrey Bissell, a graduate of Yale College, and a learned and versatile man. The chevalier Vincent de Rivafanoli played a conspicuous part in the early thirties. He has been given the credit of having served under the great Napoleon, and of having enjoyed his confidence. He brought and engaged a large staff, and occupied for his headquarters and residence the house lately occupied by the Yates family, on South Tryon street. His style of living was deemed magnificent for that day, and his organization was run on severely military lines. His chief mines were the Rudisil and the St. Catherine.

Thomas Penman operated many mines over a period of several years. Dr. Daniel Asbury was also a skillful operator, and made several fortunes.

Commodore Stockton and Admiral Wilkes mined successfully for several years.

With the exception just mentioned, the apparatus introduced in this period was grinding and concentrating machinery. The grinding machines were largely the pan—an iron drag mill—and the iron Chilian mill. In the pan the bed sometimes revolved (the Berdan pan), but commonly the revolution was the normal one of the mullers or grinders about a vertical axis with projecting arms. It was generally maintained by careful observers that these iron pans were inferior to mills made of stone—stone grinding on stone—and it is quite certain that the old mill men made a better recovery with their home-made apparatus. The main elements of the metallurgical problem were early perceived, and attacked.

After the war and continuing to the present time, a swarm of speculators and inventors came from the newly developed mining sections of the West. Charlotte has always been the center of their operations. Very little of permanent value has resulted.

Not less than 48 different processes or methods have been first or last introduced within the writer's observation in the Appalachian section, and most of them in Mecklenburg county, of which only two survive as practical, though it is possible that another one, (the cyanide treatment), may ultimately be widely applicable.

The elements of the problem to be solved are: Pulverization, concentration, roasting, (or expelling the sulphur, with incidental oxidation) and the extraction of the gold and silver.

The pulverization has finally been left to the old stone drag mill, the arrastra, and the stamp battery; efforts to supplant these were:

1. Revolving pulverizers on a horizontal axis. (Names and close descriptions of these are omitted on professional grounds..)
2. Pan grinding, i. e., discs revolving in the bed of the pan.
3. Iron mills after the general form of the drag mill, or the arrastra. Of these nine different forms are known.
4. Crushing with Cornish rolls.

The old-fashioned drag mill, arrastra, and stamp battery, (with an occasional use of rolls, and iron arrastras), have outlived the others. In other words, the older forms, in spite of uneconomical use of power and labor, have proved most useful, and in the long run most economical.

CONCENTRATION.

The course followed in concentrating has been: sizing by trommels, and other apparatus, followed by jigging, and supplemented by crushing and concentrating by spitz boxes, by sweeping tables, or by buddles, or by belts. Five different systems have been used.

Sizing, jigging, crushing and (after amalgamation) concentrating on belts have been found to be the best and most generally applicable methods.

ROASTING.

Here the crudest ideas have been exemplified. Generally described the following forms may noted: Magnetic roasting, chloridizing roasting, (two methods), horizontal roasting furnace with vertical axis; shaft roasting, i. e., dropping the pulverized ore from a height against an upward current of hot air; kiln roasting, roasting with carbonaceous matter, as sawdust, roasting the ore while passing through highly heated spiral pipes.

The horizontal roasting furnace with vertical axis is sometimes used even now, but on the whole the old-fashioned reverberatory furnace, with two or three hearths has proved the most applicable to the wants of this section, being at once effective and easily under control, though possibly not the most economical of fuel or of labor.

THE EXTRACTION OF THE GOLD AND SILVER BY AMALGAMATION.

The old methods of amalgamation were grinding the ore in drag mills and in arrastras with the use of mercury at the end of the grinding for collecting the gold liberated, with occasionally a rude concentration of the tailings by rockers, sweeping tables, launders and strakes, mercury frequently being used on or in the extra apparatus; later came the stamp battery with amalgamation in the mortar, and on copper or silvered copper plates, from which the gold was afterwards scraped; the defect of these was the uneconomical use of power and labor, and the inefficient collection of the gold; at least 25 per cent. was lost in the rejected tailings, and perhaps 50 per cent.

More ingenuity has been expended in devising improved methods of amalgamation than in any other department of the metallurgy, and not one of these amalgamation methods has survived, thus leaving the field to the old methods of fifty years ago.

THE CHEMICAL TREATMENT OF THE ORES.

Five methods were used at different times, but all were too costly, as well as ineffective.

One of the most noted was: The Designolle process, consisting of the treatment of the roasted pulp with corrosive sublimate in iron vessels, with the intention of bringing the liberated mercury into touch with each particle of gold.

In the cyanide method, the pulp was treated with a weak solution of cyanide of potassium, which has a strong solvent action on gold, which subsequently was precipitated by zinc, or by electrolysis.

In other countries, (e. g., South Africa), and other parts of the United States, cyaniding has been successful, but in Mecklenburg county and the South in general, it has in the long run been uncertain.

The Plattner Chlorination, though effective in Europe and in California, has not been effective in this section.

Chloridizing, or the roasting of gold ores with the addition of common salt to convert the gold into soluble chlorides, was also uncertain.

Barrell chlorination (two methods) has, after various vicissitudes, been brought to a wide and effective application in the mode known as the "Thies Chlorination Process;" it is cheap, efficient and thorough.

Three methods of electrical treatment were introduced, but the results have not been revealed to the public.

Direct smelting for bullion has been a failure.

Lead smelting, followed by the cupellation of the base lead bullion for the gold and silver contents has been successfully carried out at least twice, and was successful metallurgically, but not economically, as there are no lead ores within easy reach.

Matte smelting, by which roasted and raw ores and concentrates are smelted together and an artificial sulphide of cipper formed, which contains substantially all the copper in the entire mass, with the gold and silver. The concentrated matte is still farther concentrated by a second smelting to black copper, which in turn is treated by electrolysis for its gold and silver, and the copper separated in the form of pure cathode copper.*

THE HUNT AND DOUGLAS (OLD) METHOD.

The ores, after pulverization and roasting, were treated with chloride of iron to dissolve the copper, which in turn as cement copper was precipitated from the solution by scrap iron. The residues were either amalgamated or smelted for the gold contents. The products of the mine were ingot copper and bar gold.

A FEW METHODS DEFY CLASSIFICATION.

The methods which have survived are the older forms of amalgamation chiefly by stamp battery, followed by belt and other concentration, roasting and chlorination, and in another line by the copper matte smelting process.

THE UNITED STATES BRANCH MINT IN CHARLOTTE.

This mint, a branch of the United States mint at Philadelphia, was established by act of March 3, 1835, and by the same act the branch mint at Dahlonega, Ga., and at New Orleans, La. Fifty thousand dollars was appropriated for the Charlotte mint.

Eight lots were purchased on November 25, 1835, by Samuel McCombs, agent and commissioner for the United

---

*Note.—Copper matte smelting, except in its preliminary stages, has not been carried on in Mecklenburg county; neither has the Hunt and Douglas method in its entirety.

States, on Trade street, for $1,500, viz., lots No. 135, 136, 133, 165, 166, 167, 168, and 144.

This legislation by Congress grew out of a long continued agitation on the part of the miners of Anson (and Union), Cabarrus, Rutherford, Davidson, Mecklenburg, and other counties of North and South Carolina, commencing very early after the discovery of gold. In 1830, the demands had grown sufficiently loud to lead the General Assembly of North Carolina to appoint a special committee to investigate the subject under the chairmanship of Gideon Glenn. This report, among other matters, stated that the production of North Carolina was $500,000 annually, at a cost estimated at $150,000. The main conclusion of the report was the propriety of erecting a mint. The disadvantage was for the time obviated by the coinage of $5.00, $2.50 and $1.00 pieces by the Bechtlers at Rutherfordton.

The Charlotte mint was opened for business December 4, 1837, and had for that time a large business immediately. The first depositor was Irwin & Elms.

On July 27, 1844, the mint was burned at mid-day, probably from the carelessness of a tinner repairing the roof.

The question of its re-erection was at once sprung, and was opposed in Congress, and strangely by many people of this section.

The extent of the damage is indicated by the following extract from a letter of the Director of the Mint at Philadelphia to the Secretary of the Treasury of date of December 14, 1844:

"Of the main building it may be assumed that there is nothing left which can be made available, except a portion of the material, and perhaps of the old foundation. The outbuildings are all saved. In the department of the superintendent and treasurer, the coin, bullion, scale beams, furniture, books and papers were saved. In the assay room and in the melting room, but little damage was done. In the separating room the destruction was more considerable; but all the losses of the apparatus and material can be replaced without resort to any new appropriation. In the coiner's department the steam engine was slightly injured. . . . The draw-bench is so much injured that it will be expedient to replace it. . . . Of the cutting presses, one can be repaired, but the other must be replaced. The coining presses are past repair. The milling machine and the rolls are destroyed."

The report recommended the expenditure of $25,000 for a new building, and $10,000 for machinery.

The Hon. D. M. Barringer, who represented this district in Congress in 1844-5, writing in 1875, says: "I succeeded in getting an appropriation to rebuild it. . . . You will find a full report . . . in the Congressional Globe, pages 223, 224, 225, February 21, 1845, second session 28th Congress."

A commendatory local in the *Jeffersonian* April 1, 1845, has the following: "The Superintendent of our mint (Hon. Green W. Caldwell) is a great fellow—a real business man. He received on this day week from the Director of the Mint his instructions for putting up a new building, and on Monday after he made a contract for the whole job at a less cost than the Government appropriated. Our enterprising fellow townsman, H. C. Owens, Esq., took the contract for $20,000, the building to be completed by the 1st of January, next."

The important officials of the institution were:

Col. John H. Wheeler, appointed Superintendent in 1837; Col. Burgess S. Gaither, appointed Superintendent in 1841; Hon. Green Washington Caldwell, appointed Superintendent in 1844, resigned in 1846 and went with the volunteer forces to Mexico; Hon. William Julius Alexander, appointed Superintendent in 1846; Hon. Jas. W. Osborne, appointed superintendent in 1849; Col. Green Washington Caldwell, appointed Superintendent in 1853; Dr. Isaac W. Jones, appointed Assayer in Charge in 1867; Hon. Calvin J. Cowles, appointed Assayer in Charge in 1869; Col. Robt. P. Waring, appointed Assayer in Charge in 1885; Prof. Stuart

W. Cramer, appointed Assayer in Charge in 1889; Captain W. E. Ardrey, appointed Assayer in Charge in 1893; Hon. W. S. Clanton, appointed Assayer in Charge in 1897; D. Kirby Pope, Esq., appointed Assayer in charge in 1903.

Dr. John H. Gibbon was Assayer during the whole period preceding the war, and W. F. Strange Clerk. Other important officials were: Edward Terres, John R. Bolton, Emmor Graham, John Rigler, A. N. Gray, Andrew Erwin, Thomas H. Harmer, Frederick Eckfeldt, George B. Hanna, W. D. Cowles, Josiah D. Cowles, W. C. Wilkinson, Robert P. Chapman.

Operations by the United States were practically terminated May 21, 1861, when the State, which had seceded on the 20th, occupied the building with its troops. Subsequently it was used by the Confederate authorities, especially by the navy office, till the termination of hostilities, when it was seized by the Federal authorities and used by the military officials till the summer of 1867. It was then opened as an assay office, and has so continued till the present time, with a brief interruption from July 1, 1875, to October 16, 1876.

The selection of Charlotte as the mint centre of this section has been abundantly justified, and no better point could have been indicated to accommodate the mining and commercial interests of this region; it draws its patronage most largely from the South Appalachian slope, from Maryland to Alabama, but also in a lesser degree from twenty-one other States, Territories and foreign countries.

Its business during the calendar year 1902 was, at coining rates, $288,985.87.

The total coinage at the Charlotte mint from its organization in 1838, to its suspension in 1861, was $5,059,188.00, all in gold, viz., half eagles, quarter eagles, and dollars. The coins were discriminated by the letter "C."

The following table is official:

[*Coinage of the Mint at Charlotte, N. C., from its Organization, 1838, to its Suspension, 1861.*]

Calendar Year.	GOLD.			Total Value.
	Half Eagles.	Quarter Eagles.	Dollars.	
1838	$ 64,565	$19,770 00	....	$ 84,335 00
1839	117,335	45,432 50	....	162,767 50
1840	95,140	32,095 00	....	127,235 00
1841	107,555	25,742 50	....	133,297 50
1842	137,400	16,842 50	....	154,242 50
1843	221,765	65,240 00	....	287,005 00
1844*	118,155	29,055 00	....	147,210 00
1845	....	....	....	....
1846	64,975	12,020 00	....	76,995 00
1847	420,755	58,065 00	....	478,820 00
1848	322,360	41,970 00	....	364,330 00
1849	324,115	25,550 00	$11,634	361,299 00
1850	317,955	22,870 00	6,966	347,791 00
1851	245,880	37,307 50	41,267	324,454 50
1852	362,870	24,430 00	9,434	396,734 00
1853	327,855	....	11,515	339,370 00
1854	196,455	18,237 50	4	214,696 50
1855	198,940	9,192 50	9,803	217,935 50
1856	142,285	19,782 50	....	162,067 50
1857	156,800	....	13,280	170,080 00
1858	194,280	22,640 00	....	216,920 00
1859	159,235	....	5,235	164,470 00
1860	74,065	18,672 50	....	92,737 50
1861	34,395	....	....	34,395 00
Total	4,405,135	544,915 00	109,138	5,059,188 00

*Mint burned July 27, 1844.

The total deposits at the Charlotte office from its organization to December 31, 1902, amounted to $10,163,666.54, of which possibly $60,000.00 may have been silver contained in the native gold.

GEORGE B. HANNA.

CHAPTER XII.

MECKLENBURG COUNTY REPRESENTATIVES.

Complete List of the Members of the General Assembly From This County From 1764 to 1903.—Martin Phifer and Richard Barry Were the First.

Year.	Senator.	Representative.
1764		Martin Phifer, Richard Barry.
1765		Martin Phifer, Richard Barry.
1766		Martin Phifer, Thomas Polk.
1767		Martin Phifer, Thomas Polk.
1768		Martin Phifer, Thomas Polk.
1769		Thomas Polk, Abraham Alexander.
1770		Thomas Polk, Abraham Alexander.
1771		Thomas Polk, Abraham Alexander.
1772		Martin Phifer, John Davidson.
1773		Martin Phifer, John Davidson.
1774		Thomas Polk, John Davidson.
1775		Thomas Polk, John Phifer, John McKnitt Alexander, Samuel Martin, Waightstill Avery, James Houston.
1776		John Phifer, Robert Irwin, John McKnitt Alexander.
1777	Jno. McKnitt Alexander.	Martin Phifer, Waightstill Avery.
1778	Robert Irwin	Caleb Phifer, David Wilson.
1779	Robert Irwin	Caleb Phifer, David Wilson.
1780	Robert Irwin	Caleb Phifer, David Wilson.
1781	Robert Irwin	Caleb Phifer, David Wilson.
1782	Robert Irwin	Caleb Phifer, David Wilson.
1783	Robert Irwin	Caleb Phifer, David Wilson.
1784	James Harris	Caleb Phifer, David Wilson.
1785	James Harris	Caleb Phifer, George Alexander.
1786	James Mitchell	Caleb Phifer, George Alexander.
1787	Robert Irwin	Caleb Phifer, William Polk.
1788	Joseph Graham	Caleb Phifer, Joseph Douglas.
1789	Joseph Graham	Caleb Phifer, George Alexander.
1790	Joseph Graham	Robert Irwin, William Polk.
1791	Joseph Graham	Caleb Phifer, William Polk.
1792	Joseph Graham	Caleb Phifer, James Harris.
1793	Joseph Graham	Charles Polk, George Graham.
1794	Joseph Graham	Charles Polk, George Graham.
1795	Robert Irwin	Charles Polk, George Graham.
1796	George Graham	David McKee, William Morrison.

REVOLUTIONARY STATE MONEY.

MECKLENBURG COUNTY REPRESENTATIVES.

1797..Robert Irwin..........James Connor, Nathaniel Alexander.
1798..Robert Irwin.........James Connor, Hugh Parker.
1799..Robert Irwin.........James Connor, Sherrod Gray.
1800..Robert Irwin.........Charles Polk, Hugh Parker.
1801..Nathaniel Alexander...Charles Polk, Alexander Morrison.
1802..Nathaniel Alexander..Thos. Henderson, Alexander Morrison.
1803..George Graham.......Thos. Henderson, Alexander Morrison.
1804..George Graham.......Thos. Henderson, Samuel Lowrie.
1805..George Graham.......Geo. W. Smart, Samuel Lowrie.
1806..George Graham.......Thomas Henderson, Samuel Lowrie.
1807..George Graham.......Thomas Henderson, John Harris.
1808..George Graham.......Geo. W. Smart. John Harris.
1809..George Graham.......Thos. Henderson, Hutchins G. Burton.
1810..George Graham.......Thos. Henderson, Hutchins G. Burton.
1811..George Graham.......Jonathan Harris, Henry Massey.
1812..George Graham.......Jonathan Harris, Henry Massey.
1813..William Davidson.....Jonathan Harris, Cunningham Harris.
1814..Jonathan Harris......William Beattie, George Hampton.
1815..William Davidson.....John Ray, Abdon Alexander.
1816..William Davidson.....Joab Alexander, John Wilson.
1817..William Davidson....John Rea, John Wilson.
1818..William L. Davidson..John Rea, John Wilson.
1819..Michael McLeary.....John Rea, Miles J. Robinson.
1820..Michael McLeary.....John Rea, Miles J. Robinson.
1821..Michael McLeary ....John Rea, Samuel McCombs.
1822..Michael McLeary ....John Rea, Matthew Baine.
1823..Michael McLeary ....Thomas G. Polk, Matthew Baine.
1824..Michael McLeary ....Thomas G. Polk, Matthew Baine.
1825..William Davidson....Thomas G. Polk, Matthew Baine.
1826..Michael McLeary.....William J. Alexander, Matthew Baine.
1827..William Davidson.....Wm. J. Alexander, Joseph Blackwood.
1828..William Davidson.....Wm. J. Alexander, Joseph Blackwood.
1829..William Davidson....Wm. J. Alexander, Evan Alexander.
1830..Joseph Blackwood....Wm. J. Alexander, Evan Alexander.
1831..Henry Massey........James Dougherty, John Harte.
1832..Henry Massey ....James Dougherty, John Harte.
1833..Washington Morrison. Wm. J. Alexander, Andrew Grier.
1834..William H. McLeary..Wm. J. Alexander, J. M. Hutchison.
1835..Stephen Fox..........J. A. Dunn, J. M. Hutchison.
1836..Stephen Fox..........G. W. Caldwell, J. A. Dunn, J. M. Hutchison.
1838..Stephen Fox ....G. W. Caldwell, Jas. T. J. Orr, Caleb Irwin.
1840..J. T. J. Orr..........G. W. Caldwell, John Walker, Benjamin Morrow.

1842..John Walker.......... John Kirk, Jas. W. Ross, Caleb Irwin.
1844..John Walker......... John Kirk, J. A. Dunn, Robt. Lemmons.
1846. John Walker.......... John W. Potts, John N. Davis, Robt. Lemmons.
1848..John Walker.......... J. K. Harrison, J. N. Davis, J. J. Williams.
1850..Green W. Caldwell....J. K. Harrison, E. C. Davidson, J. J. Williams.
1852..Green W. Caldwell....W. Black, J. A. Dunn, J. Ingram.
1854..John Walker.......... W. Black, W. R. Myers.
1856..W. R. Myers.......... W. Matthews, W. F. Davidson.
1858..W. F. Davidson ......H. M. Pritchard, W. Wallace.
1860..John Walker.. ....S. W. Davis, J. M. Potts.
1862..John A. Young........ J. L. Brown, E. C. Grier.
1864..W. M. Grier.......... J. L. Brown, E. C. Grier.
1866..J. H. Wilson.......... R. D. Whitley, J. M. Hutchison
1868..Jas. W. Osborne...... R. D. Whitley, W. M. Grier.
1870..H. C. Jones........... R. P. Waring, J. W. Reid.
1872..R. P. Waring........ John E. Brown, S. W. Reid.
1873..R. P. Waring.......... John E. Brown, S. W. Reid.
1874..R. P. Waring......... John E. Brown, S. W. Reid.
1875..R. P. Waring.......... J. L. Jetton, J. W. Reid.
1877..T. J. Moore.......... R. A. Shotwell, W. E. Ardrey.
1879..S. B. Alexander.......J. L. Brown, W. E. Ardrey.
1881..A. Burwell............A. G. Neal, E. H. Walker.
1883..S. B. Alexander...... J. S. Myers, T. T. Sandifer, W. H. Bailey.
1885..S. B. Alexander...... R. P. Waring, W. E. Ardrey, H. D. Stowe.
1887..S. B. Alexander....... J. T. Kell, E. K. P. Osborne, J. W. Moore.
1889..J. S. Reid............ N. Gibbon, J. W. Hood, J. C. Long.
1891..W. E. Ardrey......... R. A. Grier, J. W. Hood, W. D. Mayes.
1893..F. B. McDowell...... J. R. Erwin, H. W. Harris, J. L. Jetton.
1895..W. C. Dowd.......... J. T. Kell, J. D. McCall, J. G. Alexander.
1897..J. B. Alexander.......M. B. Williamson, W. S. Clanton, W. P. Craven.
1899..F. I. Osborne......... Heriot Clarkson, R. M. Ransom, J. E. Henderson.
1901..S. B. Alexander...... C. H. Duls, W. E. Ararey, F. M. Shannonhouse.
1903..H. N. Pharr.......... H. Q. Alexander, Thomas O. Gluyas, R. C. Freeman.

CHAPTER XIII.

MECKLENBURG TROOPS IN THE WAR OF 1812.

Five Companies Sent From This County to the War with England Caused by the Searching of American Vessels for British Sailors.—A Total of Four Hundred and Thirty three Enlisted Men.*

SEVENTH COMPANY, DETACHED FROM THE FIRST MECKLENBURG REGIMENT, APRIL, 1812.

OFFICERS.

Joseph Douglass, Captain.
William M. Kary, Lieutenant.
Hamilton Brevard, First Sergeant.
David Gibony, Second Sergeant.
Samuel Brown, Third Sergeant.
William M. Barrett, Fourth Sergeant.
Thomas Allen, First Corporal.
John Solon, Second Corporal.
Isaac V. Pitt, Third Corporal.
R. Duckword, Fourth Corporal.

Harrison, Adam.
Wiley, Hugh.
Moore, James.
Caldwell, John.
Love, Joseph.
Bingham, Joseph.
Gregg, Hugh.
Hood, Junius.
Alexander, David.
Parker, James.
Wallace, Matthew.
McRae, Thomas.
Phillips, John.
Farr, Henry.
Todd, Hugh.
Elliott, Hugh.
Jimison, Arthur.
Parish, Nicholas.
Walker, Andrew.
Roden, Upton.

Wilson, David B.
Beaty, Isaac.
Sharply, William.
Erwin, Francis.
Mason, Richard.
Darnell, John L.
Hutchison, Samuel J.
Hutchison, James.
Darnell, John.
Moore, Alexander.
Darnell, William.
Cunningham, Jacob I.
Alexander, Eli.
Lucas, Allen.
Graham, Samuel.
Shepherd, Thomas.
Fat, John.
Washam, Alexander.
Sullivan, William.
Henderson, David.

*From the Roster published by the State in 1837.

136 HISTORY OF MECKLENBURG COUNTY.

Robertson, Will.
Solomon, Drury.
McIie, Thomas.
Munteeth, William.
Alexander, Palau.
Elliott, John B.
Camerson, William.
Clark, Joshua.
McLure, John.
Thompson, Benjamin.
Smitn, Alexander.
Darnel, David.
Harris, Hugh.

Johnston, Mitchell.
Downy, William.
Bushbey, Will.
Sloan, Allen.
Lane, Andrew M.
Weir, Howard.
Ferret, John, Sr.
Garretson, Arthur.
Simmimer, James.
Holmes, Hugh.
Stevenson, Hugh.
Scott, Will.

Total, 76.

EIGHTH COMPANY, DETACHED FROM THE SECOND MECKLENBURG REGIMENT, APRIL, 1812.

OFFICERS.

Robert Wood, Captain.
Jacob Shaver, Lieutenant.
Peter Mape, Second Lieutenant.
John Wilson, Ensign.
William Flenigan, First Sergeant.
John Hooker, Second Sergeant.
John Barnes, Third Sergeant.
James Watson, Fourth Sergeant.
John Hummons, First Corporal.
Obed Dafter, Second Corporal.
Will John, Third Corporal.
Charles Hart, Fourth Corporal.
Allen Stewart, Drummer.
John Rice, Fifer.

Bambow, Paten.
Purvins, Antheris.
Crowell, Charles.
Lemmond, William L.
Starns, Jacob.
McLoyd, Daniel.
Walker, James.
Brown, John.
Flenigan, Robert.
Sharp, William.

Flenigan, Elias.
Cheek, Randolph.
Flenigan, Samuel E.
McCallok, Elias.
Stewart, Andrew.
Wiley, Samuel.
John, Ash.
Sharp, Cunningham.
Wiat, John.
Black, John.

TOMB OF THOMAS POLK IN THE CHARLOTTE CEMETERY.

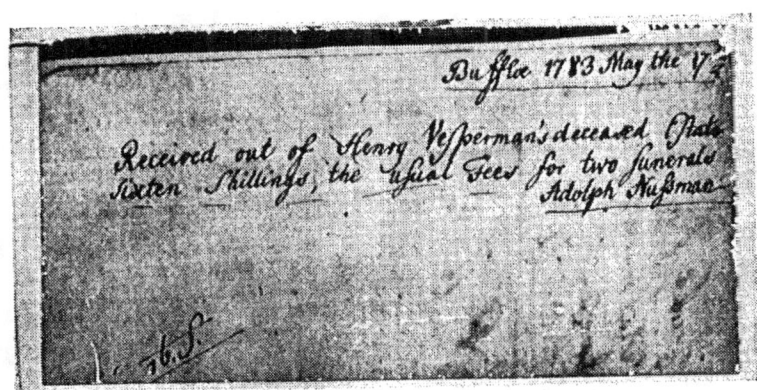

RECEIPT, 1783.

MECKLENBURG TROOPS IN WAR OF 1812. 137

Bryan, Joseph.
Clontz, Henry.
Cathberton, John.
Flow, John.
Boid, Robert.
McReley, Roderick.
Stunford, Moses.
Lancey, Charles.
None, John.

Prifly, Valentine.
Moser, Henry.
Robertson, James.
Yandles, Jesse.
Henley, Thomas.
Fobes, John.
Howard, Lewis.
Irvey, Will U.
Long, John.
Givens, Samuel.

Shannon, Robert.
Morris, Solomon.
Pool, William.
Broom, Allen.
Belk, Brelon.
Holden, Samuel.
Flenigan, Michael.
Coughran, Eli.
Redford, William.
Rea, Will.
Ormond, Samuel.
Ormand, Adam.
McCorkle, John.
Thompson, James.
Miller, Thomas.
Martin, William.
Pirant, William.
Barns, William.

Total, 71.

NINTH COMPANY, DETACHED FROM THE SECOND MECKLENBURG REGIMENT, APRIL, 1812.

OFFICERS.

John Garretson, Captain.
Isaac Wiley, Lieutenant.
Natheil Sims, Ensign.
Archibald Sawyer, First Sergeant.
Ira B. Dixon, Second Sergeant.
William Smith, Third Sergeant.
Joro Kimmons, Fourth Sergeant.
William Mays, First Corporal.
John Holbrooks, Second Corporal.
Frederick Kiser, Third Corporal.
A. M. Grady, Fourth Corporal.
George Kenty, Drummer.
John Jaccour, Fifer.

Irwin, John.
Harris, Samuel H.
Ross, James.
Harris, Houston.
Alexander, John.

Harris, Isaac.
Alexander, Laid.
Carrigan, Robert, Sr.
Carrigan, Robert, Jr.
Gaylor, Theophilus.

138   HISTORY OF MECKLENBURG COUNTY.

Carroll, John.
Hamilton, Joseph.
Houston, David.
Neele, Andrew.
Neele, James.
Flemming, George.
Icehour, Martin.
Dove, George.
Smith, William.
Linker, George.
Smith, Daniel.
Barnhardt, John
Fink, Son.
Carriher, Andrew.
Fink, Philip.
Taylous, John S.
Johnston, John.
Campbell, Cyrus.
Cochran, Robert M.
Morrison, John.
Morrison, Robert C.
McCain, Hugh.
Bost, Daniel
House, Jacob.
Miller, Henry.
Rinehart, Jacob.
Rowe, Henry.
Bost, Matthias.
Owrey, Michael.

Light, John.
Goodnight, John.
Freeze, Adam.
Freeland, John.
Clisk, John.
Chaple, Jesse.
Sneed, Reuben.
Johnston, Rufus.
Black, David H.
Black, John.
Biggers, Johnston N.
Newitt, William.
Right, George.
Gilmore, Josiah.
Martin, Edward.
Kelly, William.
Wines, William.
Keelough, Ebenezer.
Hall, James.
Gaugus, Jacob.
Gooaman, John.
Walter, Charles.
McGraw, James.
Luther, Daniel.
Shank, Martin.
Simmon, Jacob.

Total, 78.

MECKLENBURG FIRST REGIMENT, DETACHED TROOPS,

AUGUST, 1814.

James Wilson, Captain.
Thomas Boyd, Esq., First Lieutenant.
Joseph Blackwood, Second Lieutenant.
Isaac Price, Third Lieutenant.
Charles Hutchinson, Ensign.

Caldwell, Robert.
Caldwell, Robert, Ja.
Carson, William.
Wynens, John.
Garner, Barzilla.

McCombs, James.
Barnett, John.
McKelvia, William.
Hawkins, John.
Barnett, Amos.

MECKLENBURG TROOPS IN WAR OF 1812.

Alexander, Ezekiel.
Shelvey, William.
Garrison, John C.
Means, James.
Hope, Thomas.
Price, John.
Parks, John, Sr.
Johnston, Samuel, Jr.
Parrish, Andrew M.
Dunn, William.
Lewing, Andrew, Jr.
Perry, Francis.
Farra, John.
Lewing, John.
Carothers, James.
Dinkins, James.
Bigham, Robert, Jr.
Johnston, John.
Johnston, William.
Neeley, Samuel.
Reed, David.
Whiteside, Joseph.
Miles, Augustus.
West, Matthew.
Connell, Thomas.
Benhill, William.
McKnight, Robert.
Baker, Michael.
Baker, Abel.
McDowell, Hugh.
Wolles, William, Jr.
Wallis, Matthew, Jr.
Parks, Samuel.
Wynns, Ann.
Sadler, John.
Barnhill, John.
Julin, Jacob.
Henderson, James.
McCracken, Elisha.
Love, Christopher.
Dunn, Robert, Jr.
Brown, John.
Norman, William J.
Baxter, Daniel.
Wilson, Benjamin.
Elliott, Thomas.

Conner, James.
Davis, Daniel.
Elliott, William.
Hartley, Richard.
Duckworth, George.
Meek, James.
Alexander, James.
Jones, Joel.
Morrison, Isaac, Jr.
Sloan, James.
Parker, John.
Williams, Joseph.
Menteith, James.
Prim, Andrew.
Kerr, William.
Hawkins, John.
Baker, Aaron.
Walker, Andrew.
Porter, James.
Beaty, John.
Bigham, Samuel.
Pelt, Simon V.
Beaty, John.
Jackson, Peavon.
Blackburn, John.
Wilson, John, Jr.
Osborne, Robert A.
White, John.
Channels, Michael.
Ferrel, Gabriel.
Irwin, Giles.
Ferrel, John.
Wallis, Joseph.
Hunter, Henry, Jr.
Ferrel, William.
Steele, James.
Gray, Nelson.
Steele, John.
Montgomery, Robert.
Brady, James A.
Peoples, Richard.
McKellerand, Joseph.
Alexander, John D.
Goforth, George.

Total, 105.

MECKLENBURG SECOND REGIMENT, DETACHED TROOPS.
AUGUST, 1814.
OFFICERS.

David Moore, Captain.
John Wilson, First Lieutenant.
Solomon Reed, Second Lieutenant.
William John, Third Lieutenant.
Albertes Alexander, Ensign.

Barfleet, Richard.
McCall, Matthew.
McCall, James.
Thompson, Henry.
Stewart, Alexander.
Cheery, William.
Robertson, James.
Yaudles, Samuel.
Harbeson, James.
Starns, Nathaniel.
Shehorn, Morris.
Yerby, William.
Rone, James.
Belk, John.
Rich, Daniel.
Downs, William.
Shelby, William.
Freeman, Gideon.
Morrison, John.
Allen, John.
Forsythe, John.
Barnes, James.
Purser, Moses.
Barns, Micajah.
Wilkinson, Osborne.
Allen, Robert.
Vinson, Groves.
Helms, William.
Helms, Charles.
Starns, Frederic.
Spravey, Benjamin.
Reed, Joseph.
Kerr, Adam.
Matthews, John.
Parke, George.
Junderbusk, John.
Flowers, Henry.

Yaudles, David B.
Alexander, Salamachus.
Alexander, Abdon.
Smart, Osborn.
Smart, Elisha.
McCullock, John.
Cook, Robert.
Hanson, Stephen.
Craig, Moses.
McCoy, William.
Howood, Robert.
Woodall, William.
Gray, Jacob.
Howie, Aaron.
King, Andrew.
Finsher, Joshua.
Rape, Samuel.
Rener, Samuel.
Hambleton, James.
Vick, Moses.
Phillips, John.
Train, James.
Berns, George.
Fisher, William.
Button, Daniel.
McAlroy, Hugh.
Ivey, Jess.
Hauley, John.
Story, David W.
Fuller, John.
Shaw, James.
Reed, William.
Taylor, Wilson.
Maglauchlin, John.
Maygeehee, William.
Hall, Joseph.
Hargett, Henry.

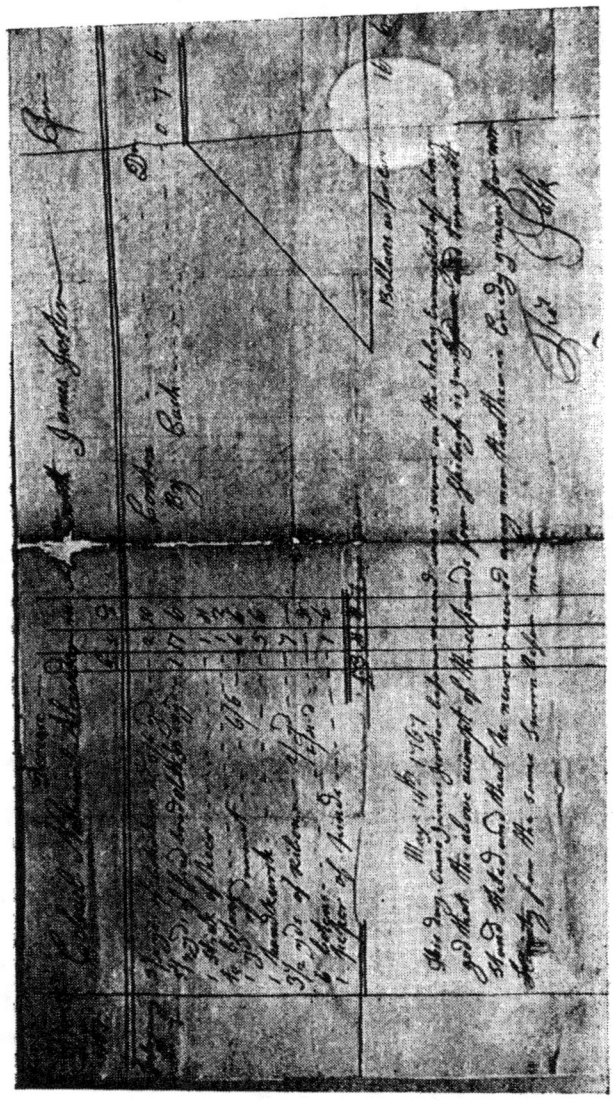

BILL OF ACCOUNT, 1767.

Hargett, William.
Helmer, Joel.
Crowell, John.
Chainey, Peter.
Harkey, David.
Tutor, George.
Stilwell, Elias.
Morrison, James.
Tomberlin, Moses.
Reak, Edward.
Morrison, Neel.
Costley, James.
Cochran, Thomas S.
Houston, William, Jr.
Cochran, Robert.

Wilson, Hugh.
Hood, Reuben.
Dennis, Charles.
Neele, Samuel.
Harkey, John.
Rogers, James.
Harrison, Robert.
Hodge, John.
Lambert, Richard.
Webb, Lewis.
Story, James, Sr.

Total, 103.

Grand total, 433.

CHAPTER XIV.

CIVIL WAR TROOPS.

Roster of Officers and Men of the Twenty-one Companies Sent From This County.—2,735 Soldiers and only 2,021 Voters.—Number Killed, Wounded or Died.*—List of Promotions.

*Abbreviations: W, wounded; K, killed; D, died; W. C., wounded and captured; P, promoted.

COMPANY B (HORNETS' NEST RIFLES), FIRST (OR BETHEL) REGIMENT.

(Enlisted in April, 1861, for Six Months.)

OFFICERS.

L. S. Williams, Captain, commissioned April 18, 1861, Mecklenburg County.

W. A. Owens, Captain, P.

W. A. Owens, First Lieutenant, commissioned April 18, 1861, Mecklenburg County; promoted Major of Thirty-fourth Regiment, k.

Robt. Price, First Lieutenant.

W. P. Hill, Second Lieutenant.

T. D. Gillespie, Third Lieutenant.

NON-COMMISSIONED OFFICERS.

T. D. Gillespie, First Sergeant.
J. H. Wyatt, Second Sergeant.
J. B. French, Fourth Sergeant.
R. B. Davis, First Corporal.
J. J. Alexander, Second Corporal.
W. M. Mattheus, Jr., Third Corporal.
A. M. Rhym, Fourth Corporal.
Phillips, First Sergeant.
Black Davis, Corporal.
Julius Alexander, Sergeant.
Minor Sadler, Druggist.

Anderson, C.
Alexander, J. L.
Alexander, M. E.
Alexander, F. T.
Barnett, William.
Bond, Newton.

CIVIL WAR TROOPS. 143

Boone, J. B. T.
Black, Josiah.
Bourdeaux, A. J.
Biggart, W. S.
Crawford, R. R.
Crowell, E. M.
Caldwell, R. B.
Caldwell, J. E.
Cannedy, Robt.
Davis, J. G. A.
Davis, R. A. G.
Davidson, J. F.
Dorsett, J. F.
Dyer, W. G.
Eagle, A.
Eagle, John.
Frazier, M. L.
Frazier, John.
Fredrick, J. R.
Fullenweider, H.
Fanygen, M. L.
Gray, H. N.
Gray, R. F.
Grier, S. A.
Graham, S. R.
Gillett, J. H.
Griffin, J. H.
Hunter, J. H.
Hollingsworth, B.
Harris, W. L.
Howell, S. A.
Hilton, S. H.
Henderson, W. M.
Howell, E. M.
Jacobs, G. W.
Jones, Milton.
Jaswa, L. R.
Kesiah, Wm.
Kerr, Wm. J.
Landler, Orminer.
Lee, J. M.
McGinnis, R. C.
Lowrie, J. B., k. at Gettysburg.
Lowrie, J. B., k.
Muny, T. N.

McDonald, Allen.
McCorkle, R. B.
Moseley, M.
Means, W. N. M.
Meholers, John.
Nichols, J. S.
Norment, A. A.
Oates, Jas. H.
Oates, Coowy.
Orr, S. H.
Price, R. S.
Phifer, R.
Paredoe, S. M.
Potts, J. W.
Price, Joseph.
Phelps, H. M.
Query, R. W.
Rose, W. C.
Rieler, G. H.
Rea, W. P.
Rozzell, W. F.
Squires, J. B.
Stowe, John.
Sharpe, R. A.
Shaw, L. W. A.
Sadler, Julius.
Smith, J. Perry.
Steel, M. D.
Sheppard, J. W.
Taylor, J. W.
Torrence, George.
Tovam, William.
Tiddy, J. F.
Tiddy, R. A.
Tate, A. H.
Thompson, R.
Vagorer, J. V.
Winale, M. F.
Wiley, W. J.
Williams, W. S.
Williamson, J. W.
Tate, Henry.

Total, 108.

144   HISTORY OF MECKLENBURG COUNTY.

CHARLOTTE GRAYS, COMPANY C, FIRST (OR BETHEL) REGIMENT.

(Enlisted in April, 1861.)

OFFICERS.

E. A. Ross, Captain; Promoted Major of Eleventh North Carolina.
E. B. Cohen, First Lieutenant.
T. B. Trotter, Second Lieutenant.
C. W. Alexander, Second Lieutenant.
C. R. Staley, Orderly Sergeant.
J. P. Elms, Second Sergeant; Promoted Lieutenant Thirty-seventh North Carolina.
J. G. McCorkle, Third Lieutenant.
W. G. Berryhill, Fourth Lieutenant.
D. L. Bringle, Fifth or Ensign.
W. D. Elms, First Corporal; Promoted Captain Thirty-seventh North Carolina.
W. B. Taylor, Second Corporal; Promoted Second Lieutenant Company A, Eleventh North Carolina.
Henry Terris, Third Corporal.
George Wolfe, Fourth Corporal.
Dr. J. B. Boyd, Surgeon.

M. R. Alexander.
T. A. Alexander.
Lindsey Adams.
J. P. Ardery, P. Capt. 49th N. C.
W. E. Ardrey, P. Capt., 30th N. C.
A. H. Brown.
Wm. Brown.
Wm. J. Brown.
Ed. F. Britton
L. Behrends.
Wm. Calder.
J. W. Cathey.
S. P. Caldwell.
J. F. Crawson.
T. B. Cowan.
T. J. Campbell.
J. W. Clendennen.
J. F. Collins.
T. G. Davis.
J. T. Downs, P. Lieut., 30th N. C.

L. W. Downs.
J. P. A. Davidson.
J. R. Dunn.
I. S. A. Frazier.
James Flore.
R. H. Flow.
J. A. Elliott.
S. H. Elliott.
J. A. Ezzell.
M. F. Ezzell.
J. M. Earnheardt.
J. Engel.
R. H. Grier, P. Lieut., 49th N. C.
J. C. Grier, P. Capt., 49th N. C.
J. M. Grier.
D. P. Glenn.
J. R. Gribble.
J. A. Gibson.
N. Gray.
R. L. Gillespie.

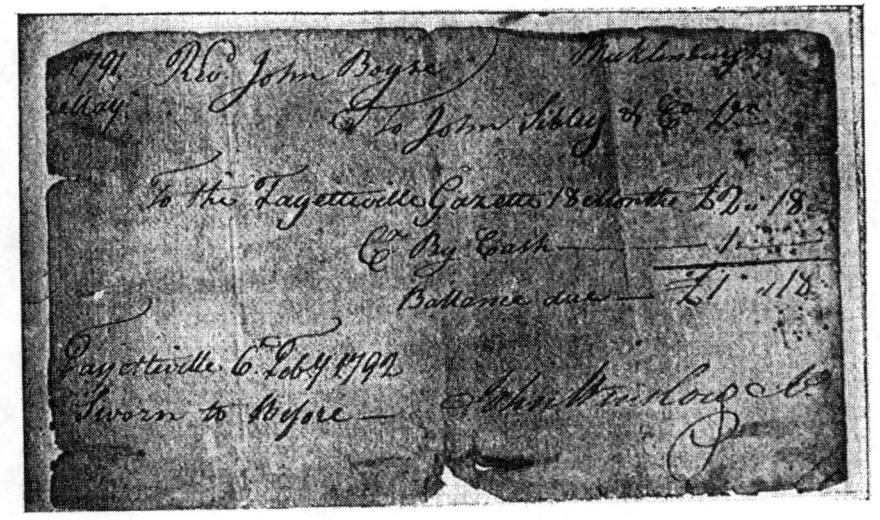

BILL FOR SUBSCRIPTION, 1792.

CIVIL WAR TROOPS.

D. W. Hall.
J. C. Hill.
W. J. Hill.
H. H. Hill.
W. Lee Hand, P. Capt. A, 11th N. C.
Robt. H. Hand, P. Lieut. A, 11th N. C.
R. H. Howard.
Thomas Howard.
Jas. M. Hutchison.
Cynes N. Hutchison.
Tom F. Holton.
Tom M. Harkey.
S. Hymans.
Harper C. Houston.
T. Lindsey Holmes.
Jas. T. Haskell.
W. T. Hanser.
George T. Herron.
Geo. W. Howey.
Jacob Harkey.
L. P. Henderson.
Jack R. Isreal.
Wm. S. Icehower.
E. P. Ingold.
Robt. W. Johnston.
Jacob Katz.
Wm. H. Kistler.
Jack A. Kinsey.
J. H. Knox.
Robt. Keenan.
Louis Leon.
J. C. Levi.
Jacob Leopold.
Henry Moyle.
Thomas F. McGinn.
John McKinley.
Wm. McKeever.
D. Watt McDonald.
John H. McDonald.
Robt. J. Monteith.
Moses O. Monteith.
Sam'l J. McElroy.
Jack Norment.
Isaac Norment.
Wm. B. Neal.
L. M. Neal.

S. R. Neal.
P. A. Neal.
Thos. W. Neely.
S. Oppenheim.
J. T. Orr.
John L. Osborne.
J. E. Orman.
Mack Pettus.
S. A. Phillips.
W. R. Carter.
R. A. Carter.
John G. Potts, P. Lieut., 49th Rgt.
Wm. M. Potts.
Lamson A. Potts, P. Capt., 37th N. C.
Calvin M. Query.
Theo. C. Ruddock.
J. R. Rea.
D. B. Rea.
Wm. D. Stone.
W. Steele.
Jim M. Stowe.
Wm. E. Sizer.
J. Monroe Sims, Q. M. Sergt., 11th N. C.
Richard A. Springs.
C. Ed. Smith.
S. B. Smith.
M. H. Smith.
W. J. B. Smith.
W. H. Saville.
John W. Sample.
David I. Sample.
James M. Saville.
Robt. Frank Simpson.
S. E. Todd.
Wm. Todd.
John W. Treloar.
Hugh A. Tate.
Charles B. Watt.
B. Frank Watt.
C. C. Wingate.
T. D. Wolfe.
T. J. Wolfe
John Wiley.

Total, 143.

COMPANY C, FIRST REGIMENT OF CAVALRY.

OFFICERS.

J. M. Miller, Captain.
M. D. L. McLeod.
R. H. Maxwell, Lieutenant.
J. L. Morrow, Lieutenant, k.
W. B. Field, Lieutenant.
J. F. Johnson, Captain.

NON-COMMISSIONED OFFICERS.

M. Steel.
D. S. Hutchison.
J. P. Alexander.
P. C. Harkey.
J. M. Pugh.
R. H. Cambell.
D. K. Orr, w.
J. Lewellyn.
M. L. Davis.
J. B. Stearns.
J. W. Moore.
J. W. Kizziah.
W. T. Bishop.

Antrice, J. W.
Antrice, W. M., d.
Archey, J. W.
Anderson, L. D.
Ardrey, J. W.
Blake, S. N.
Barris, E. C.
Burris, J. T.
Breffard, W. J.
Ballard, F. A.
Ballard, J. L.
Boyd, P. L.
Butler, J. T.
Black, T. N.
Barnett, T. E., k.
Calloway, J. C., d.
Cobble, J. D.
Connor, T. A., d.
Cottraim, A. W.
Carroll, J. H.
Craig, M. F.
Cruse, M. C.
Crump, R. H.
Cathey, J. W.
Davidson, E. C.
Dulin, J. M., d.
Edleman, T. P.
Edwards, A. J.
Edwards, E., k.
Efird, J. C.
Efird, J. E.
Finley, M. K., w.
Furr, John, d.
Flow, E.
Flow, J. M., w.
Fords, H. H.
Gillespie, S. A.
Gaisesen, W. G.
Graham, J. R.
Goodsen, H. M.

CIVIL WAR TROOPS.   147

Gillespie, A. M.
Hurston, A. W.
Harget, Harrison, d.
Hargett, H. M., d.
Hargett, Osborne.
Harkey, T. B., d.
Helms, J. A.
Helms, J. W.
Helms, H. M., c.
Hopkins, P.
Hudson, J. H.
Holden, E. M., d.
Hilton, S. H.
Henderson, W. M. F.
Hunter, J. W., w.
Hartis, M. A.
Hartis, A. L.
Holbrook, A.
Johnson, W. P.
Jennings, C. J.
Jordan, B. F.
King, R. R.
Lewis, C. J.
Lewis, J. M.
Morris, G. C.
Martin, Edward.
McCall, J. M.
McCarver, Jas.
McNeely, T. N., w.
McLeod, J. M., w.
McCall, J. A.
McGinnis, John.
McDoughall, M.
McCall, Wm.
McCarver, Alex.
Noles, A. T., d.
Noles, W. A.
Orr., J. A., k.
Orr, N. D., w.
Orr, J. J., k.
Parks, J. L., c.
Potts, T. E.
Potts, C. A.
Pholan, J.
Page, E. M.

Peach, H.
Rea, J. M.
Rea, D. B.
Robson, G. M.
Reenhardt, J. F.
Rea, W. A.
Rea, R. R.
Rea, Robt.
Rea, J. L.
Sparrow, J. S.
Smith, J. W.
Stanis, J. B.
Schneider, G.
Sanders, W. H.
Starns, C. R., c.
Steele, W. G.
Stucker, Christian.
Tye, W. B., deserted.
Tomberlen, E. M., w.
Thompson, J. M., d.
Taylor, A. W.
Taylor, Art, deserted.
Taylor, J. C.
Taylor, J. A.
Taylor, J. M.
Tomlin, J.
Taylor, W. F.
Tredermick, W. S., k.
Tredermick, N. P.
Tredermick, J. R.
Thompson, R. G.
Underwood, S. M.
VanPelt, J. N.
Vance, J. C., d.
Ualle, P. O.
Watson, W. A.
White, J. S.
Wilson, John.
Williamson, J. A.
Werner, L.
Wallace, M. L., k.
Williford, T. F.
Walker, J. B.
Wallace, Wm., k.
Williams, J. M.

HISTORY OF MECKLENBURG COUNTY.

Whitaker, H. A., k.
Yardle, W. A.
Yardle, W. H.

Yardle, J. B.

Total, 145; from other counties, 56; 8 wounded; killed, 9.

COMPANY D, SEVENTH REGIMENT.

OFFICERS.

W. L. Davidson, Captain.
T. J. Cahill, Captain.
Wm. J. Kerr, wounded 1862; killed 1863.
Tim P. Mollay.
Lieutenants: I. E. Brown, J. A. Torrance, B. H. Davidson, Thos P. Mollay, P. J. Kirby.

NON-COMMISSIONED OFFICERS.

Jas. M. McLure.
Paul James.
Al. LeLain.
W. G. W. Herbert.
W. Wedlock.
S. N. Jamison.
James Clark.
Thomas Bundle.

Alexander, Wm., d.
Anderson, Richard.
Ayers, A. G., k. '62.
Bynum, Rufus, d.
Buglin, Patrick.
Beard, J. H., d.
Bennett, G. W.
Bennett, J. G.
Berry, Jas.
Bolton, G. B.
Brannan, Patrick.
Brinkle, John, w.
Brinkle, Thomas.
Burnett, J. S., d. '62.
Brown, J. J., w. '63.
Billow, W. H., d. '62.
Brown, Alex.
Brown, Nicholas.
Donovan, Philip.
Donovan, Jeremiah.
Dasinger, Francis.
Dobson, Hiram.
Davidson, J. W.
Davidson, B. W.

Elliott, Wm.
Elmore, J. T., d.
Eller, John.
Edmirton, J. R., k.
Frick, Jacob.
Fogleman, P. L.
Gallagher, Arch., w.
Claywell, J. F., d. '62.
Carricker, Levi, d. '62.
Caskill, Tim. L.
Cable, Lewis.
Conder, Wiley, k. '63.
Colling, John.
Chancy, John.
Calder, Wm., Sr.
Calder, Wm., Jr.
Cashion, W. M., w.
Cashion, Thomas, k.
Carter, F. B., d.
Gallagher, Jas.
Gleason, Jas. W.
Grady, Jas.
Griffin, Thomas.
Goodman, S. C.

Graves, A. C.
Grant, R. W.
Hartsell, J. M., w.
Howell, Jas.
Howell, John.
Howell, David, w.
Harris, Francis, k.
Hicks, T. W., w.
Halshouser, A. R.
Hanna, J. M., d.
Humble, David.
Icenhour, P. E.
Jackson, John.
John, E. Edward, k.
Jones, David, k.
Jannison, R. J., w.
Johnson, Thomas.
Johnson, Rufus.
Jamison, S. N.
Kurtz, P. K.
Kelley, Lawrence, w.
Kanapum, A. E.
Kirby, Patrick, w.
Kisler, Wm.
Kennedy, Jepe.
Lane, A. D.
Mason, Wiley J.
McConnell, Thomas.
McClellan, W. A.
McGarar, Wm. W.
Meredith, Stephen W.
McGuire, John, k.
McGinnis, George.
Munsey, John.
Mulson, Robt.
McBean, John.
Mason, W. B.
McConnell, T. A., d.
McConnell, A. M.
Meredith, J.
Newton, Eli.
Newton, Meredith, d.
Newton, John, k.
Nail, Richmond, k.
Nantz, A. E.

Oliver, Calvin.
Plyler, R. C.
Packard, John.
Petit, Jas.
Patterson, J. E., k.
Quinn, Jas.
Rhodes, Wm.
Rafferty, Thos.
Rogers, Jas.
Rogers, J. C.
Reynolds, John.
Riddick, H. L.
Riddick, J. A.
Rolmer, W. C.
Riggins, Robt.
Sullivan, D. C.
Stephens, M.
Spears, Wm. H.
Stewart, Thos. A.
Sherrill, L. J.
Seagraves, A C.
Sanders, G. W., k.
Sheridan, John, w.
Stanning, Wm.
Stroup, David, k.
Spawl, A. B.
Skinner, S. L.
Sullivan, D. C.
Staly, John.
Staly, W. Y.
Towey, Lewis.
Vincent, Jas. B.
Varker, Wm., w.
Vance, Richard.
Vaughn, H. J.
Weaver, Wm.
Wilson, Lewis.
Woodard, W. L., d.
Williamson, D. J.
Whalon, Roderick, w.
Wilkerson, W.
Wilkerson, J. H.
Winecoff, J. T., k.
Washam, J. B., d.

Total, 154.

COMPANY C, TENTH REGIMENT OF ARTILLERY.
OFFICERS.

T. H. Brem, Captain.
James Graham, Captain.
A. B. Williams, Captain, w.
Adbon Alexander, Lieutenant, w.
T. L. Seigle, Lieutenant, w.
H. A. Albright, Lieutenant.
J. S. Davidson, Sergeant.
Dennis Collins, Sergeant.
J. L. Hoffman, Sergeant.
R. V. Gudger, Sergeant.
J. E. Albright, Sergeant.
R. P. Chapman, Sergeant, w.
J. P. Smith, Sergeant.
Moses Blackwelder, Corporal, d.
D. M. L. Faunt, Corporal.
Patrick Lyons, Corporal.
Mathero Chapman, Corporal.
M. A. Henderson, Corporal.
W. W. Shelby, Corporal.
Wm. S. Williams, Corporal.
Dan W. McLean, Corporal.
J. N. Peoples, Sergeant, d.
James W. Murray, Bugler.
R. R. Peoples, Guidon.
Wm. H. Runfelt.

Abernethy, Jas.
Abernethy, Clem H.
Baldwin, Alfred.
Beatty, Wm.
Beatty, J. W.
Bridgers, W. B.
Burus, Jas.
Brackett, Wm.
Broadway, Whitson.
Buff, Henry.
Baker, J. B.
Bray, Winfield M.
Cannon, Fred.
Cannon, Sid.
Cannon, Joseph, d.
Carroll, Francis, c.
Connell, S. C.
Chapman, A. H.

Chapman, Wm.
Chapman, Peter.
Chapman, A. J., d.
Costener, Jacob.
Carter, Jas.
Canips, John.
Canips, Henry.
Christenburg, A. B., d.
Cannon, Wm. S., c.
Canster, Martin L.
Crane, Madison C.
Carter, Jas. N.
Culer, J. A. J.
Crane, Wm.
Cannell, Jas. H.
Chalkley, W. P.
Christenburg, A. B., d.
Doyle, Bernard.

Dunlap, Sam'l N.
Dobbin, Mark H.
Ellington, Werley P.
Farley, A.
Fite, J. C.
Fite, Robt. D. R.
Fox, W. T.
Faunt, Sam'l.
Faunt, D. L.
Fancy, John.
Dawns, Robt. R., d.
Fullbright, J. K.
Fullbright, D. B., d.
Fullbright, M., k.
Fullbright, K.
Fite, Sam'l, d.
Flowers, Jessie, deserted.
Goodman, John.
Grigg, B. W.
Grier, W. M.
Grier, Marshal.
Grier, C. E.
Heavner, J. J.
Hoover, T. H.
Hoover, J. D.
Hoover, W. G.
Hoover, W. H.
Hoover, J. T.
Howell, Jas.
Hinkle, J. L.
Hawkins, J. A.
Hawkins, J. P.
Hawkins, Albert.
Herrvell, R.
Hoyle, D. R.
Hunter, R. B.
Johnson, Daniel.
Johnson, R. L.
Johnson, Joseph.
Jenkins, Aaron.
Jenkins, Tillman.
Jenkins, Sam'l.
Jenkins, Edward.
Kaloram, Thos.
Knuipe, Henry.

Kean, J. H.
Kean, J. B.
Kean, S. W.
Kean, R. F.
Lattimer, A. M.
Lane, J. D.
Laughlin, D. P.
Ledford, John.
Lindsey, W. G.
Lamb, Mike, deserted.
Lawler, John, deserted.
Lineberger, J. M.
Lawing, A. W.
Lawing, J. W.
Marrable, W. M.
Meaghim, W. H.
Marshal, Jas. H.
McCausland, W. B.
McCorkle, Robt.
McKinney, Sam'l.
Moad, John.
Murphy, Daniel C.
Motz, Mayfield.
Needham, Thos., d.
Morris, J. S., w.
Newton, Robt.
Nantz, R. E.
Nantz, Calvin.
Nantz, R. R.
Potts, Wm. P.
Potts, Jas. A.
Potts, A. W.
Pool, A. W.
Pool, J. T.
Parker, Wm.
Queen, Joseph.
Queen, Laban.
Roberts, J. W.
Richard, J. W.
Rodden, T. B.
Scott, Nelson.
Seagle, G. W.
Shaw, J. G.
Shelby, J. M.
Shaw, Wm.

Sloan, J. W.
Sloan, Sam'l, k.
Sloan, Robt., w.
Sloan, Robt., d.
Smith, J. A.
Smith, Jacob.
Smith, George.
Smith, W. M.
Stillwell, Jacob, k.
Stuly, J. J., c.
Stant, S. G.
Summerville, J. W.
Tallent, Daniel.
Terepaugh, J. H.
Todd, Wm.
Underwood, J. S.

Underwood, J. O.
Underwood, Jas.
Underwood, Reuben.
Underwood, J. R.
Underwood, David.
Veno, Francis.
Watts, C. L.
Watts, Charles.
Walls, A. A.
White, D. W.
White, A. S.
West, Wm. F.
Will, John.

Total, 179.

COMPANY A, ELEVENTH REGIMENT.
OFFICERS.

E. A. Ross, Captain; promoted Major, k.
W. L. Hand, First Lieutenant, w.
C. W. Alexander, Second Lieutenant, retired.
R. H. Hand, Lieutenant, w.
W. B. Taylor, Lieutenant, w.
J. G. McCorkle, Orderly Sergeant; promoted Lieutenant Company E.
S. J. McElroy, Sergeant, w.
R. B. Alexander, Sergeant, w.
J. M. Simms, Quartermaster Sergeant, c.
T. W. Neely, Sergeant, w.
T. C. Ruddock, Corporal, c.
W. S. Icehower, Corporal, k.
J. R. Gribble, Corporal, w.
E. Lewis, Corporal, w.

M. R. Alexander, w.
M. Mc. Alexander, k.
M. A. Alexander, k.
J. G. Alexander, k.
W. S. Alexander.
R. C. Alexander.
J. N. Alexander, w.
H. W. Allen, w.
C. A. Allen.
L. Allen.

P. S. Auten, k.
E. L. S. Barnett.
J. F. Barnett.
J. L. Barnett, k.
M. F. Blakely.
J. J. Blakely, k.
James Byrum.
C. C. Brigman, w.
J. M. Black.
T. J. Black, w.

CIVIL WAR TROOPS. 153

Ezekiel Black.
J. R. Bigham, w.
J. W. Bigham, w.
W. J. Brown, p. sergeant, w.
J. Creasman,
J. F. Cochrane.
M. E. Cheshire.
W. H. Campbell.
H. D. Duckworth, w.
J. A. Duckworth.
J. C. Deaton.
Daniel Dulin, w.
Jack Darnell, w.
J. H. Earnheardt, k.
J. M. Earnheardt, p. to d. s., w.
W. C. Earnheardt.
S. O. Earnheardt.
G. R. Ewing, w.
W. E. Ewing, w.
W. A. Elliott, k.
J. P. Elms, p. Lt., k.
R. H. Flow, w.
I. S. A. Frazier, w.
J. W. Fisher.
W. C. Ford.
J. S. Galloway, k.
W. W. Gray.
J. A. Gibson.
D. P. Glenn, w.
F. C. Glenn.
Joshua Glover, w.
R. A. Groves.
J. S. Garrison, k.
W. J. Goodrum, k.
C. H. Goodrum.
H. H. Hill, w.
Milton Hill.
Miles Hill, w.
Monroe Hovis, w.
A. J. Hand.
I. S. Henderson.
T. M. Henderson.
G. T. Herron, w.
J. H. Hutchison, k.
T. L. Holms, k.

T. H. Hunter.
D. P. Hunter.
M. B. Hunter.
J. M. Herron.
G. T. Hinson, k.
T. M. Howard.
W. C. Harris.
F. Hobbs, w.
N. O. Harris, w.
L. Hutspeth.
Alfred Johnston.
David Jenkins, w.
Jacob Jenkins.
J. D. Kerns.
Wm. Kennedy, w.
Thos. Knipper.
J. A. King.
C. C. King, w.
B. Kinney.
R. J. Monteith.
H. L. D. Monteith.
M. O. Monteith, k.
J. H. McConnell, w.
J. F. McConnell, k.
T. Y. McConnell.
J. H. McWhirter, w.
James McWhirter, k.
R. F. McGinn.
J. A. McCall, w.
J. H. Montgomery, p. Lt., w.
S. A. McGinnis, w.
Isaac Norment, w.
Jack Norment.
G. A. Neal, k.
A. H. Newell.
J. F. Orr.
N. C. N. Orr.
J. E. Orman.
Dan Powell, k.
H. M. Pettus.
J. W. Pettus.
Stephen Pettus.
C. Paysour, w.
Peter Paysour.
T. A. Prim, k.

154   HISTORY OF MECKLENBURG COUNTY.

R. L. Query.
S. F. Query.
B. W. Ruddock, w.
B. M. Ruddock.
Peyton, Roberts, w.
M. B. Rayborn.
R. A. Ross.
E. C. Ratchford.
J. M. Stowe, w.
J. C. Stowe, k.
R. F. Simpson.
J. W. Simpson.
J. S. Smith, k.
R. C. C. Taylor.
H. S. Taylor.

J. Q. Taylor, k.
J. C. Thomason.
Angus Wingate, k.
M. Wingate.
C. C. Wingate.
W. A. Wallace, w.
S. H. Williams.
Taylor Wright, w.
B. A. Withers, w.
J. L. West.
W. M. Wilson.
J. Steele, k.
J. H. Bingham, w.
A. J. Hunter.

Total, 154; killed, 29, wounded 4.

COMPANY E, ELEVENTH REGIMENT.
OFFICERS.

J. S. A. Nicholas, Captain, d.
Wm. J. Kerr, Captain.
J. B. Clanton, Lieutenant.
W. S. Turner, Lieutenant.
W. N. S. Means, Lieutenant, k.
W. F. Rozzell, Lieutenant.
James F. Alexander, Lieutenant.

NON-COMMISSIONED OFFICERS.

D. W. McDonald, w.
J. E. Goodman, k.
J. H. McDonald.
J. S. Means, d.
R. S. Wilson, c.
A. J. Hunter, Sergeant.

Abernethy, E. R.
Alexander, Peter.
Auten, S. W.
Ashley, M.
Adams, H. A.
Baker, Aaron.
Baker, Wm. M.
Ballard, Benj.
Bradshaw, J. T.
Beal, Charles, c.
Beal, John, c.
Bird, W. L., w. and pr.

Bass, Jas. A., w.
Bass, Buston, c.
Beek, Wm. A.
Baker, Joel M.
Bradley, J. L., c.
Beatty, J. W., c.
Bunier, J., w.
Christy, J. H., k.
Clark, J. A., k.
Cathey, W., w. and pr.
Carmick, J.
Campbell, J. W., c.

Culberson, J. W., c.
Clemmons, R. R.
Denton, John.
Dixon, W. W., k.
Edwards, Shepherd.
Edwards, Marshal, c.
Eller, A.
Eller, S. W.
Finger, John, w.
Grier, T. H.
Garrison, Alex., c.
Hartline, Andrew.
Hartline, Adam.
Harris, C. C.
Holdslaw, R.
Hinton, A. J.
Hollingsworth, J. B.
Hartgrue, W. W., w.
Hartgrue, R. D. S., w. and c.
Hill, J. W., w.
Helms, E. T., k.
Hartline, P., w.
Hartline, D. L., w.
Hartline, G. H., d.
Jameson, J. W., c.
Jameson, T. J., w.
Jameson, J. W., c.
Johnston, J. H., c.
Kyles, Fielding, c.
Kyles, Wm.
King, G.
Kestler, P. H.
Kyle, P. H.
Ledwell, David.
Linebarger, Marshall.
Lawson, Hudson.
Loften, Martin.
Lambert, Wm.
Lewis, Lindsey, w.
Lambert, J. M.
McQuay, S., d.
McQuay, W. H., k.
McClure, C. A. w. and c.

McCorkle, H. P., c.
Mitcha, John, c.
Martin, W., w.
Murdock, W. D.
Miller, J. F.
McLure, J., d.
Maddan, G. W.
Munday, O. M.
Mathison, Jas.
Narson, J. G., c.
Null, J. T.
Nesbitt, J. G., d.
Neal, G. A., w. and c.
Ostwalt, Francis, c.
Pucket, T. J., w.
Pucket, W. C., w.
Pool, G. S.
Pennix, J. W.
Pennix, J. A.
Rives, J. R.
Reid, J. C., k.
Rhyne, David, c.
Ruis, W. R., w.
Richley, W. L., k.
Rozzell, J. T.
Stone, A.
Stinson, J. B.
Sherrell, W.
Smith, D. J.
Griffin, G., d.
Turner, J. W.
Wilson, J. R.
Walker, B., k.
Walker, L. L., c.
Walker, J. H., c.
Walker, Jas. H.
Wingate, J. w. and c.
Wingate, T., w.
Williamson, E. Y., c.
Younts, R. C., k.
York, G. W., c.

Total, 121.

COMPANY H, ELEVENTH REGIMENT.

OFFICERS.

W. L. Grier, Captain.
P. J. Lowrie, Lieutenant, d.
C. B. Boyce, d.
J. B. Lowrie, k.
J. M. Saville.
J. M. Knox.
R. B. Lourie.

NON-COMMISSIONED OFFICERS.

R. D. Saville, w.
P. M. Clark, w.
J. S. P. Caldwell.
C. E. Bell.
Aug. Cotchkip, c.
Thos. Campbell, k.
J. T. Smith.

Abernathy, Elig.
Ashby, J. T.
Alexander, J. A.
Andrews, E. M.
Ashley, Wm., c.
Bailey, Wm.
Brown, A. M.
Belk, Wm.
Boyd, J. J.
Boyd, J. A.
Boyd, David.
Brown, J. W.
Blair, S. W.
Black, J. B.
Bigart, Jas.
Barns, Robt.
Bryant, Sydney.
Boyce, Hugh.
Blankenship, J. N.
Blankenship, T. G.
Blankenship, S. P.
Caruthers, J. A.
Caruthers, J. B., d.
Chentenberg, C. E., d.
Coffe, B. M., w.
Cooper, J. M., c.
Crowel, E. M.

Campbell, J. C.
Cobb, C. A.
Clark, W. A., d.
Carpenter, J. C.
Carpenter, W. B.
Cox, Eli.
Clark, P. M.
Drewry, A. G.
Deggarhart, J. V., c.
Deggarhart, J. L.
Dallarhit, J. D., d.
Dixon, Hugh M., d.
Ettres, J. H., d.
Edwards, J. M., c.
Ellis, Dan, c.
Earnhardt, Geo.
Fite, W. J.
Greer, Z. B., d.
Greer, E. S.
Harris, R. H.
Hall, R. B.
Harris, F. C., w.
Harris, J. C.
Harris, J. H.
Hannel, A. R., k.
Harmon, Levi, c.
Hannon, J. N.

Hays, J. B., c.
Hargett, Aleg.
Herron, J. W.
Hill, C. H.
Humphrey, T. L.
Haron, S. L., c.
Hanna, J. W., c.
Hatchup, A., c.
Hall, N. C.
Henry, J. B.
Henry, B. G.
Hedgepath, Geo.
Harris, Morris.
Holland, Robt.
Hainant, Henry, w.
Hoffman, Miles.
Henderson, W. R.
Ingle, Peter. w.
Johnson, J. W.
King, J. A.
Keenan, Peter.
Key, Albert, w.
Kerr, R. O., d.
Knox, W. H., w. and c.
Kilpatrick, W. F.
Lourie, R. B.
Madden, J. P.
McQuaig, James.
Mincel, Willis, w.
Morrison, W. T.
McMillan, J. C.
McQuaise, Jas., c.
Marshburn, J. M., w.
Neely, J. J.
Porter, R. C., w.

Price, J. A., d.
Peppen, John.
Russell, J. C.
Rice, J. S.
Rhine, A. M.
Rachelle, J. B.
Reid, W. M.
Rumell, J. C.
Ross, R. A., d.
Smith, J. W.
Smith, T. J.
Smith, John L.
Smith, A. J.
Sloop, Alex.
Snider, J. A., k.
Snead, Frank.
Squire, J. A.
Sanders, Jacob.
Sumney, J. B.
Sumney, George, c.
Scott, R. S.
Tarbifield, Jas.
Taggart, J. C.
Thuner, E. A., w.
Thuner, J. T., w.
Watt, C. B.
Wingate, R. G.
Wilkerson, W. H.
Wilkerson, Jno.
Warren, T. W., c.
Walker, P. L., w.
Watters, Allen.
Young, J. H., d.

Total, 137; killed, 4; wounded, 14.

COMPANY B, THIRTEENTH REGIMENT.
OFFICERS.

A. A. Erwin, Captain, w.
W. W. Robinson, Captain, w.
J. D. McLean, Lieutenant.
J. R. Erwin, Lieutenant.
Joe Thompson, Lieutenant, k.
R. S. Warren, Lieutenant.
W. A. Presley, Lieutenant.

HISTORY OF MECKLENBURG COUNTY.

W. S. Alexander, Lieutenant.
W. S. M. Hart, Lieutenant, d.
E. Smith, Lieutenant.
H. J. Walker, Lieutenant, w.
J. M. Choat.

NON-COMMISSIONED OFFICERS.

F. C. Youngblood, a.
F. L. Erwin.
J. W. Todd.
R. L. Swann, k.
J. M. Knox, k.
Jas. R. Wingate, k.
Jas. F. Knox, w.

Alexander, Aswold.
Alexander, H. C., k.
Alexander, Ossil.
Alexander, O. S. P., k.
Alexander, M. C.
Alchison, J. C., d.
Adair, Thos.
Adair, Wm.
Brown, Jas. W.
Bailes, G. S., d.
Baker, Green C., k.
Baker, J. C.
Bartlette, W. F., w.
Berryhill, J. J.
Berryhill, Jas. L., d.
Blackwelder, A., w.
Bowden, S. D.
Boyd, Jepe A.
Boyd, John, d.
Boyd, J. G. W., w. and d.
Brimer, Alfred, k.
Brown, C. W., k.
Brown, R. E.
Bryan, T. J.
Bigham, M. S.
Beeman, G. C.
Barnett, R. S.
Bartlett, J. H., w.
Clark, A. A., d.
Crawford, Micajah.
Caruthers, J. K.

Cathey, Henry, w.
Choate, A. D., k.
Choate, R. W., w.
Choate, Wm., w.
Clanton, W. D.
Clark, R. F., d.
Crowell, S. W., c.
Darnall, J. J.
Davis, J. C.
Edwards, M. A., w.
Erwin, A. R.
Erwin, J. C., d.
Erwin, J. M., w.
Ellis, Wm.
Frazier, Richard.
Frazier, W. F.
Frazier, Isaac A.
Frazier, J. T.
Flenekin, J. B., d.
Freeman, W. H., w.
Gallant, J. A., w.
Glover, T. M., d.
Grier, E. C.
Grier, S. M., k.
Grier, Thos. M.
Groves, J. R., c.
Garner, Wm.
Hail, W. H.
Heitman, O. B.
Hawkins, J. P.
Hall, W. H., w.

CIVIL WAR TROOPS.

Hawkins, F. A., w.
Hotchkip, S. A.
...l, W. H.
Jamison, E. A.
Johnson, H. F.
Kerr, John B., w.
Kimball, J. L., k.
Kirkpatrick, J. F., w.
Knox, J. D.
Knox. J. N. k.
Knox, T. N.
Kerr, J. T.
Lee, D. P.
Liberman, C. S., k.
Marks, S. H., w.
Marks, T. H.
McGinn, I. H., w. and c.
McGinn, N. C., w. and c.
McGinn, W. A., w.
McGinn, J. N.
McLean, J. L.
McRumb, S. W.
McRumb, S. J. S., k.
Mulwee, J. W.
Morrison, J. E., d.
Moser, H. S., k.
Maness, J. A.
McConnell, Jas. H.
Neagle, Jas. H., w. and c.
Nicholson, J. R.
Nevins, J. G., w.
Orr., G. B., k.
Okely, C., w.
Parks, D. K.
Parks, G. L., d.

Porter, S. A.
Prather, E. L., k.
Powell, A. T.
Prag, W. J.
Parker, S. S., d.
Reed, J. W.
Sterling, J. W.
Sheffield, J. M.
Sloan, G. W., w.
Smith, D. H.
Smith, Ed.
Smith, J. W.
Sturgan, C. S., w.
Spencer, Clark.
Stowe, R. A.
Torrence, W. B.
Taylor, W. J., w.
Thomburg, F. B., k.
Thomburg, G. J.
Thomburg, H. M.
Thomburg, S. L., d.
Ticer, R. C. S., k.
Tradewice, N. P.
Thompson, W. J.
Todd, J. A. W., d.
Taylor, A. A.
Walker, L. J., w.
White, Wm.
Wilson, J. E., k.
Wingate, N. J., w.
Wolfer, H. F., w.
Wryfield, J. R., w. and d.
Wiley, J. C.
Watt, W. T.
Weaver, G. H.

Total, 152; killed 20; wounded 32.

COMPANY K. THIRTIETH REGIMENT.
OFFICERS.

J. T. Kell, Captain, w.
B. F. Morrow, Captain.
J. G. Witherspoon, Captain, k.
W. E. Ardrey, Captain, w.
C. E. Bell, Lieutenant.
N. D. Orr, Lieutenant.

J. T. Downs, Lieutenant, w.

NON-COMMISSIONED OFFICERS.

J. T. Lee, Sergeant, k.
A. L. DeArmond, w.
A. B. Hood, Sergeant, k.
J. W. McKinney, Corporal.
J. P. Bales, Corporal.
H. T. Cotlharp, Corporal.
A. J. Dunn, Corporal, k.

Adkins, W. H., w.
Adams, Wm.
Alexander, S. D., w.
Alexander, T. P.
Alexander, J. L.
Alexander, J. M., k.
Allen, J. W., d.
Anderson, Wm. d.
Baker, J., k.
Bailey, E. D.
Bailey, J. A.
Bailey, Wm.
Bales, E. M., w.
Bales, J. P.
Barnett, R. C., k.
Barefoot, N. G., w.
Bentley, M. W. H.
Bell, N. J.
Black, J. N., k.
Black, J. S., d.
Black, J. H., k.
Black, T. A., d.
Bradston, V. M.
Brewer, J. H.
Bowman, R.
Boyce, S. T.
Brinkley H.
Bristow, J. C.
Church, Eli.
Church, Martin.
Coffey, A. S.
Crowell, Isreal.
Culp, A. A., w.
Davis, G. W., k.
Downs, W. H.

Dixon, S. L., w.
Duckworth, G. P.
Dunn, Geo., c.
Dunn, A. S.
Dunn, S. W. T., d.
Ezzell, M. F., d.
Gamble, Jas., d.
George, E. P.
George, Prepley, d.
Glover, B. C., w.
Griffin, J. J., w. and d.
Griffith, A. E., k.
Graham, J. W.
Hall, J. F.
Hall, A. G.
Hall, R. B.
Harts, J. H., d.
Hart, W. S., k.
Henderson, W. M., d.
Henderson, W. T., d.
Hood, W. L., w.
Howie, J. H.
Howie, Wm.
Holmes, B., d.
Jennings, G. W., w.
Johnston, D. E.
Johnston, S. A.
Johnston, J. H.
Johnston, G. W.
Kirkpatrick, H. Y., d.
Lee, S. B., d.
Lee, J. A., d.
Lewis, W. H.
Massingale, R. H.
McLean, Thos., w.

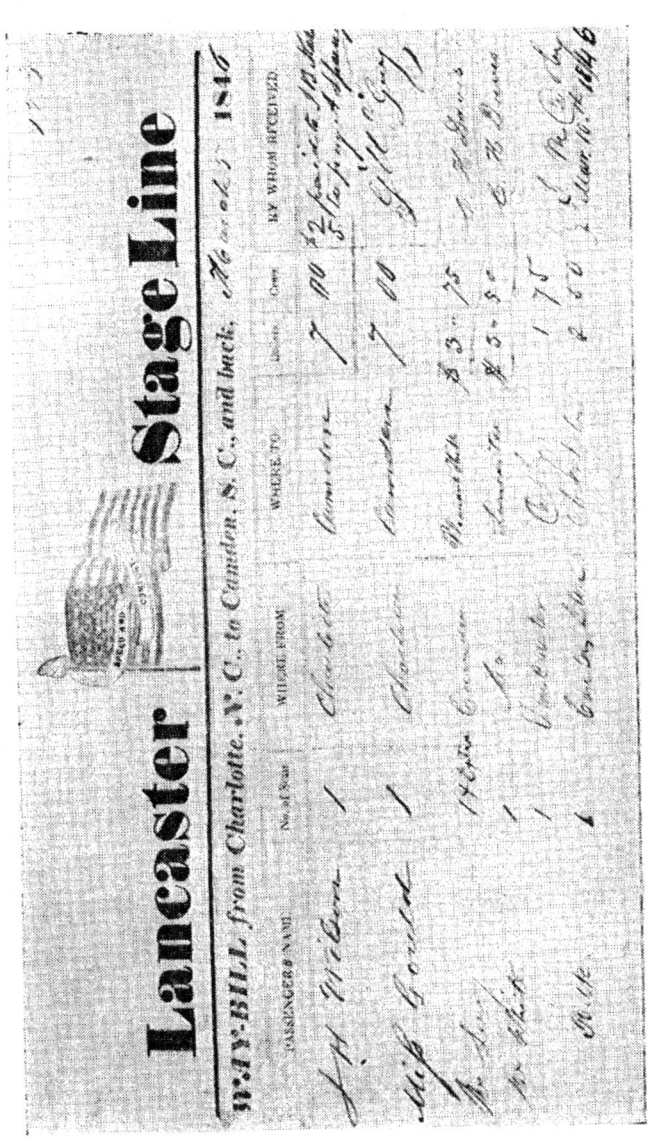

STAGE LINE WAY-BILL, 1846.

CIVIL WAR TROOPS.   161

McCurry. J. A.
McKinney, R. M.
McMallen, J. H., k.
McQuaig, J.
McRea, James, k.
Miller, D. M., w.
Milton, J. G.
Morris, W. T., d.
Morris, J. T., d.
Myers, James.
Nichols, B. G.
Nelson, J. H.
Orr, T. J.
Patterson, M. S.
Pierce, Orren L.
Pierce, J. M.
Pierce J. W.
Pierce, J. R., d.
Rayner, L., k.
Ray, J. M., k.
Richardson, W. W.
Robinson, W. H., m.
Robinson, J. R., k.
Rap, W. J.
Rap, J. N., k.
Russell, W. D.
Saville, J. C.
Sample, Wm.
Shelby, D. H.
Simmons, —.
Smith, W. S.
Smith, S. B., d.
Smith, J. D.
Smith, J. S., w.

Shaw, Alex.
Simpson, M. S.
Simpson, J.
Squires, J. W.
Squires, J. B., k.
Stanford, M. T.
Stancil, A. G.
Steel, A. F., k.
Stephenson, J. R., k.
Tart, Henry.
Tedder, Sid., k.
Thomasson, J. L., k.
Thomas, W. B.
Thompson, L.
Thompson, Lewis.
Thompson, Lee, d.
Thompson, Jas., d.
Trower, T. J.
Walston, S. L., d.
Webb, Wm., d.
West, Wm.
Weeks, R. B., k.
Witherspoon, M. T., k.
Wolf, J. N.
Wolf, R. B.
Wolf, G. D., d.
Williams, W. E.
Yeargan, W.
Young, S. T.
Young, J. A.

Total, 150; killed, 25; **wounded, 16**; died, 23.

COMPANY G, THIRTY-FOURTH REGIMENT.
OFFICERS.

W. R. Myers, Captain.
G. M. Norment, Captain, w.
J. M. Lawing, Lieutenant.
A. A. Cathey, Lieutenant.
A. H. Creswell, Lieutenant.
R. S. Reed, Lieutenant, k.
Jas. C. Todd, Captain, w.
J. N. Abernathy, k.

HISTORY OF MECKLENBURG COUNTY.

NON-COMMISSIONED OFFICERS.

H. C. Lucas, Sergeant.
Joe B. McGhee, Sergeant.
J. L. Todd, Ordnance Sergeant.
J. W. Davenport, Corporal, k.
Geo. L. Campbell, Corporal, d.
Jas. A. Todd, Corporal, k.
T. A. Johnson, w.

Alcorn, A. S., w.
Alexander, J. O. D., k.
Abernethy, C. W., w.
Abernethy, J. N., k.
Anderson, C. J., k.
Asbury, J. R., w.
Bain, J. J., d.
Beatty, A. W., w.
Beatty, Samuel, d.
Beatty, John, w.
Bennett, Thos., w.
Berryhill, J. H., w.
Bailiff, Fred, k.
Brotherton, John, w.
Brotherton, Wm.
Burgwyn, Fred.
Bolton, J. C.
Cathey, J. L., w.
Cathey, W. H., d.
Clark, John, k.
Cathey, Wm. A.
Clark, Almirive, k.
Cox, W. C. L., w.
Carpenter, Jas. k.
Downs, Frank.
Duan, T. J., w.
Duglass, S. A.
Elliott, H. W., k.
Etters, P. P., d.
Etters, H. P., d.
Erving, John.
Faires, G. N., d.
Frazier, I. A.
Garren, Andrew.
Gregg, D. H., d.
Greenhill, Lawson, k.
Hayes, S. L., k.

Hovis, Moses, w.
Hipp, Andrew, d.
Hipp, Pinkney, d.
Hipp, John, d.
Hipp, Wm.
Hipp, J. M.
Hoover, A. B., w.
Hutchison, S. B.
Johnston, D. H., d.
Johnston, F. E., k.
Jarrett, Samuel, k.
King, Thos., w.
King, Ezekiel.
Lawing, J. S., w.
Lawing, J. M., d.
Lynch, Robt.
McGhee, T. J., d.
Mills, W. T.
McGhee, J. T., d.
McCord, W. C., w.
Means, G. W. d.
Means, J. K. P., k.
McCall, Jas., w.
McCall, Alex., c.
McGahey, T. C.
Nicholson, John.
Odell, J. C., d.
Odell, G. W., d.
Puckett, J. H., d.
Parks, George, w.
Pickerell, J. H., w.
Phillips, J. J., k.
Proctor, J. A., m.
Rodden, J. J., w.
Reid, Robt. S., w. and d.
Rosick, G. W.

CIVIL WAR TROOPS. 163

Scott, W. A., k.
Shelby, J. L., k.
Stephens, A. B., d.
Stephens, R. T., w. and d.
Sanford, J. M., k.
Sanford, Jas. O.
Terres, James, w.
Todd, G. F., k.
Todd, G. N., k.
Todd, C. B., w.

Todd, G. C., w.
Todd, J. L., k.
Todd, J. W. S.
Todd, D. S.
Todd, L. N.
Watters, J. G., c.
Winston, C. W.

Total, 100; killed, 26; wounded, 32.

COMPANY H, THIRTY-FIFTH REGIMENT.

D. G. Maxwell, Captain.
H. M. Dixon, Captain.
J. M. Davis, captain.
Alexander, Thos. M., captain, d.
Alexander, J. G., lieut.
Alexander, J. K., w.
Alexander, Leander.
Alexander, C. F.
Alexander, A. P., k.
Alexander, S. W.
Alexander, G. W.
Auten, J. W., w.
Barckley, A. C.
Barckley, H. S.
Brown, J. F.
Brown, J. F., c.
Brown, S. H., w.
Benfield, H. S.
Benfield, J. R.
Blount, J. M.
Blakely, W. J., w.
Blakely, A. C., w.
Burgwyn, W. H. S., lieut.
Benfield, B. E., c.
Baker. J. R.
Biggers, W. A.
Beaver, J. M.
Cheshire, C. M., d.
Cook, R. W., d.
Cook, J. P., k.
Caldwell, G. M., sergt., w.
Caldwell, H. W., k.
Caldwell, J. M., d.

Caldwell, R. N.
Caldwell, D. G., d.
Caldwell, D. P., d.
Caldwell, D. A., lieut.
Campbell, W. H., k.
Cochrane, R. B.
Cochrane, N. R. J., c.
Cochrane, L. J., d.
Campbell, C. M., c.
Cochrane, J. L., sergt.
Cochrane, W. C., sergt., k.
Deaton, L. L., k.
Dulin, D. H., c.
Dulin, John, sergt., k.
Dulin, R. H., d.
Dulin, J. C., d.
Dulin, T. L.
Dulin, Matthias, d.
Dulin. W. W., k.
Davis, W. H.
Dennis, J. T.
Earnhardt, C. D., d.
Earnhardt, S. O.
Farris, M. C., w.
Fesperman, M. W., d.
Foard, J. C., k.
Foard, C. A.
Foard, Henry.
Flow, T. J.
Garrison, R. W., w.

Garrison, J. W., w.
Gibson, J. M., k.
Grier, J. O., w.
Hodges, P. B.
Hodges, C. J.
Hodges, W. G.
Howie, S. E., w.
Hunter, G. S., w.
Hunter, Hugh.
Hunter, A. G., w.
Hunter, J. M.
Hunter, J. M. C., w.
Hunter, Hester, k.
Hunter, J. M. C.
Hunter, R. C., d.
Hunter, S. C., lieut., w.
Hunter, R. H.
Hutchison, J. R., corporal.
Hall, T. M.
Hall, Amzi.
Hooks, Dave.
Hood, J. M.
Hood, J. R.
Hood, W. S., k.
Hucks, D. W.
Hucks, John.
Harris, C. C.
Harris, G. W., k.
Harris, F. R., k.
Herron, Calvin.
Herron, Green, w.
Herron, John.
Houston, G. W., d.
Irwin, G. C., d.
Johnson, J. J.
Jordan, Mc. H.
Kirk, Wm., k.
Kirk, J. C., w.
Keenan, John, w.
Kilough, Ed.
Kerns, T. M. A., d.
McCombs, Jas.
Mason, J. J., w.
Mason, R. C., d.
McCall, C. N.

McCall, D. H.
McCall, R. W., d.
McCall, Josiah F., k.
McGinnis, J. J.
McGinnis, T. M.
McLean, H. W., d.
McLure, James.
McLaughlin, W. J., w.
McLaughlin, J. J., w.
McKay, Robt. W., w.
Miller, H. M. W., d.
Miller, J. M., k.
Miller, S. J., d.
Montgomery, Leander.
Montgomery, J. P. C., d.
Morris, W. G., sergt., d.
Morris, D. W.
McCorkle, T. J., d.
Maxwell, W. M.
Morrison, S. N.
Morrison, D. M.
Morrison, Marshall.
McCewon, J. M.
Morris, J. C., k.
McConnell, T. M.
Neal, W. B.
Noles, John, k.
Newell, D. S.
Nelson, R. A.
Nelson, T. J.
Osborne, Harvey, d.
Orr, Franklin, d.
Petre, Wm.
Puckett, S. J.
Puckett, J. M., k.
Puckett, F. M.
Pharr, T. P.
Query, Wm. W., d.
Query, Leander, sergt., w.
Query, F. E.
Query, F. N.
Rodgers, J. R., k.
Rodgers, T. P.
Rodgers, J. W.
Roday, T. A., d.

CIVIL WAR TROOPS. 165

Rankin, C. S., k.
Rankin, W. W., w.
Russ, W. A.
Roberts, S. L.
Roberts W. A., w.
Roberts, J. L., k.
Ramsey, J. F.
Rice, J. W., w.
Rea, James, w.
Stuart, A. H.
Shaffer, W. H., w.
Shaffer, J. S., w.
Solomon, Wm. R.
Solomon, D. A., d.
Stinson, Dave, d.
Thompson, J. W.

Taylor, J. M., d.
Taylor, W. J.
Taylor, W. H.
Tarlton, James D., w.
Wilson, M. A., w.
Wilson, R. L., d.
Wilson, T. J., w.
White, James A., lieut., d.
White, E. F.
Woodall, Thos., w.
Wallace, A. W., k.
Wilson, M. N., w.
Yandle, M. N.

Total, 181; 24 killed; 35 wounded; 5 captured; 33 died.

COMPANY C, THIRTY-SEVENTH REGIMENT.

OFFICERS.

J. M. Potts, Captain.
O. N. Brown, Captain, k.
L. A. Potts, Captain, w.
J. D. Brown, Captain.
T. A. Wilson, Lieutenant, d.
T. J. Kerns, Lieutenant.
J. S. Johnston, Lieutenant.
J. L. Jetton, Lieutenant.
G. H. Beattie, Lieutenant, k.
J. W. Pettus, Lieutenant, w.
A. P. Torrance, Lieutenant, w.
B. A. Johnston, Lieutenant, k.
W. W. Doherty, Lieutenant. k.
J. R. Gillespie, Lieutenant.
J. B. Alexander, Surgeon.
G. M. Wilson, Sergeant, d.
J. A. Gibbes, Sergeant, k.
D. H. Fidler, Corporal, d.
J. A. Bell, Corporal, d.
Armstrong, M., w.
Alexander, J. H.
Alexander, D. R., k.
Alexander, T. L.
Alexander, T. R., w.
Alexander, W., d.
Armor, T. S., w.

Alcorn, T. P., d.
Bell, J. D., d.
Barritt, W. R., d.
Barnett, J. D.
Barnett, J. W.
Beard, Joseph, d.
Beard, J. C., w.

Beard, J. M., k.
Beard, J. F. M.
Black, A. J. L., k.
Black, J. C.
Black, W. A., d.
Black, S., d.
Blakely, J. B., d.
Blakely, W. F. M., d.
Blythe, J. W.
Boyles, J. A.
Brady, R. A., d.
Brown, B. F.
Brown, H. W., k.
Brown, J., d.
Britt, John.
Burleyson, Benj., w.
Carrigan, W. F.
Cathey, J. W.
Caldwell, W. W., c.
Carpenter, J., c.
Carpenter, J. C., w.
Cochrane, J. C., w.
Cox, Thomas, d.
Chrestainbury, S. D., w.
Dellinger, W.
Deaton, J. R.
Deaton, J. Z.
Fesperman, J. C., d.
Gardener, H. T., d.
Gibbs, Jack, d.
Gibson, J. J., d.
Gibson, T. A., w.
Goodrum, J. W., c.
Gardener, D., k.
Gardener, S. S.
Grier, J. S., k.
Harrison, W. H.
Hastings, W. C.
Henderson, W. F., k.
Hendrix, J. M., w.
Hendrix, W. P., d.
Holbrooks, R. S.
Hucks, S. L., w.
Hunter, H. C., c. and d.
Hunter, J. F., k.

Hagons, H. M., k.
Hamilton, J. R., k.
Houston, H. L., d.
Houston, J. M.
Howie, A. J., w.
Jenkins, A. B.
Johnston, M. F., d.
Jamison, J. R.
Kelley, A. A., w.
Kerns, J. A., a.
Kerns, T. J.
Knox. S. W., w.
Lentz, R. R.
Little, S. S.
Luckey, T. S., d.
Leach, L., d.
McAllister, C., w.
McAuley, H. E., d.
McAuley, A. E.
McCoy, Albert.
McCoy, J. F., k.
McCoy, C. W.
McFadden, John, c.
Miller, R. C., c.
Montieth, R. A., k.
Moore, R. D., d.
McAuley, D. N., d.
Morrison, W. S.
Nantz, C. R., d.
Nantz, D. J., w.
Page, J. F., d.
Puckett, E. M., w.
Reid, J. L., d.
Rhyne, J. ɔ., d.
Rodgers, John, d.
Sample, J. W., k.
Sample, W. L., k.
Sloan, T. A.
Sloan, T. C.
Stearns, A. L., d.
Stearns, W. R.
Stuart, S. J., w.
Sellers, Eli.
Solomon, D. A., k.
Stroup, C.

CIVIL WAR TROOPS.

Stroup, M., k.
Sample, E. A.
Shaver, M., k.
Shaw, A.
Todd, J. A., k.
Taylor, W. A., d.
Tiffins, M. B.
Torrance, J. A.
Torrance, H. L. W., k.
Torrance, W. W., w.
Tummice, L. G.
Weddington, J. Y.
Wallace, C. S., d.
Warsham, Alex., k.
Warsham, F. M., w.
Warsham, R. R., w.
Warsham, T. L., k.
Warsham, W., d.
White, J. H.
Wiley, J., k.
Williams, C. R., d.
Williams, F. C., d.
Wilson, T. C., d.
Wagstaff. J, R.
Walker, J. C.
Goodrum, Zeb., d.

Total, 149; died, 37; wounded, 26; killed, 27.

COMPANY I, THIRTY-SEVENTH REGIMENT.
OFFICERS.

J. K. Harrison, Captain.
M. A. McCoy.
N. M. Hart, Captain.
J. I. Elms, Captain.
Wm. M. Etitt, w.
W. D. Elms, Captain, w.
R. M. Oats.
T. K. Sammond.
E. H. Rupel.
J. G. Price.
E. M. Browell.
J. G. McCoy.
A. F. Yandle, w.
J. Wilson.
J. P. Elms, c.
H. F. Icehower, k.
D. C. Robinson, w.
D. C. Robinson, Sergeant, w.
J. C. Reed, Sergeant.
J. O. Alexander, Corporal.
D. M. Rigler, Lieutenant, w.
Lourie Adams, w.
Adaholt, M. L. w.
Alexander, A. M., c.
Alexander, J. A.
Allen, J. H.
Austin, J. W., k.
Ballard, W. H., d.
Barnhill, J. W.
Bean, J. T.
Black, J. P., k.
Black, S. J.

Blackard, Jas., k.
Blankenship, T. E., k.
Blythe, S. W.
Bridges, W. A., w. and d.
Brown, T. G.
Brown, J. K. P., c.
Bruce, Jas., d.
Burns, S. A.
Brines, J. W.
Crowell, E. M.
Carpenter, Levi, c.
Carpenter, Marcus, c.
Cathey, B. G., w. and d.
Clark, J. F., c.
Clark, J. W., k.
Clark, Jas., k.
Clontz, Ab., k.
Crocker, W. J., w.
Cross, W. D.
Devine, W. G.
Dulin, T. S., w.
Edwards, J. A.
Flanigan, B. F.
Flowe, J. C., w.
Freeman, J. J., d.
Freeman, McC., d.
Fronebarger, John, k.
Gates, M. W.
Gordon, J. P., w.
Gordon, J. R., c.
Gurley, W. D., k.
Hargett, A. J.
Hall, Jas.
Hayes, Elijah, c.
Heauly, Wm. L., d.
Henderson, J. W., w.
Henry, Berry.
Henry, Terrell.
Hipp, J. F., w.
Hipp, L. A., w.
Hood, H. C., d.
Hovis, A. J., k.
Hunsucker, J. W., w.
Higgenson, John, w.
Hunter, C. L., k.

Johnston, A. N.
King, G. W.
King, Wm., w.
Harris, N. J.
Haney, E. H.
Hunsucker, Wm., w.
Kissiah, G. W., w.
Kissiah, T. A.
Kissiah, W. M., w.
Kistler, G. H., w.
Kaiser, D. W., w.
Kaiser, T. P., c.
Kaiser, Solomon, c.
Kirkley, Thos., d.
Lawring, David.
Lawring, P. W., k.
Looker, J. C.
Lourie, S. J.
McGhee, Isaac.
McCoy, W. L., k.
Manning, Jas.
Manning, J. W., w.
Montgomery, A. F.
Moody, M. D. L.
Mosters, F. A., d.
Maxwell, D. S., w.
McCall, J. C.
McCord, D. L.
McGinn, J. M., w.
Montgomery, Jas.
Mooney, Caleb. w.
Mullis, Coleman, d.
Mason, Robt. G.
Nicholson, J. B., w.
Orr, Joe, L., w.
Orr, J. G. A.
Orr, C. M.
Orr, J. L. V., w.
Orr, W. S.
Oates, D. W.
Pegram, M. P.
Patterson, Eli, k.
Patterson, J. H., w.
Paysour, Caleb, c.
Phillips, J. A., k.

CIVIL WAR TROOPS.

Rarefield, Frank, c.
Reid, George, d.
Robinson, Jas. A., d.
Robinson, T. C.
Rudisill, Jacob, w.
Rumage, L., d.
Rupel, S. H., d. in p.
Sharp, R. A., w.
Sharp, T. A.
Shaw, D. C., w.
Shoe, Jacob, w. and c.
Simpson, C. L., d.
Simpson, Ira, P., c.
Smith, Franklin.
Spears, A. J.
Spears, J. J., k.
Stearns, Brown, k.
Stearns, Dulin.
Stearns, J. M., w. and d.
Stewart, A. A.
Stewart, P. J., c.

Stinson, D. W., d. in p.
Tagart, J. S., k.
Tally, Mike, d.
Taylor, Chas.
Taylor, Jepe.
Tally, John, k.
Todd, R. J.
Turner, S. R.
Turner, Wm., d.
Voorheis, Charles I.
Walker, Robt.
Whitley, G. M. D.
Whitley, J. H.
Williamson, G. W., w.
Woodall, W. C., c.
Wolf, E. B., k.
Young, A. J., k.
Yandle, A. F., w.

Total, 157; killed, 23; captured, 15; wounded, 18; died, 16.

COMPANY K, FIFTY-SIXTH REGIMENT.

OFFICERS.

F. R. Alexander, Captain, k.
J. F. McNeely, Captain.
J. A. Wilson, Lieutenant.
J. W. Shepard, Lieutenant.
J. W. Spencer, Lieutenant.
C. M. Payne, Lieutenant.
J. A. Lowrance, Lieutenant.
Alex. Livingston, Lieutenant.

NON-COMMISSIONED OFFICERS.

J. L. Sloon.
J. C. Faucet.
J. T. Hotchkiss.
W. B. Osborne.
J. J. McNeeley, k.
J. H. Williams.

Arney, Henry.
Alexander, A. H.
Alexander, J., k.
Alexander, J. Mc., d.
Alexander, M. D., d.

Alexander, R. A.
Alexander, T. C., w.
Allison, James.
Auten, T. J., w.
Barnett, A. G., w.

Barringer, D. A., w.
Bell, J. C.
Benson, R. P., d.
Bingham, J. M., w.
Black, Wm. M.
Bradley, J. H.
Brawley, R. W., w.
Brown, B. D., w.
Brown, J. M., w.
Brown, W. L., w.
Brown, J. C.
Burkhead White, d.
Beard, J. O., k.
Carrigan, R. A., d.
Caldwell, M. E., w.
Carrigan, Adam.
Cashion, Frank, w.
Cashion, Jas., w.
Cashion, I. W., w.
Cathcart, J. R., k.
Christenburg, Allison, w.
Christenburg, A. H., d.
Christenburg, Jas.
Christenburg, R. F.
Christenburg, Wm.
Clark, Alex.
Cork, Walter, c. and d.
Craven, W. P.
Cornelius, M. A., w.
Davis, H. W., k.
DeArmond, J. A.
Deweese, Calvin T.
Deweese, G. B., k.
Edwards, G. W., w.
Elms, J. I.
Emerson, M. H.
Faucet, J. C., d.
Fouts, J. M., k.
Garner, Henry.
Heldt, Enoch.
Hill, Jas. R. L.
Hunter, H. S., d.
Hux, John, d.
Hux, Wm. M., d.
Jackson, C. H.

Jackson, W. K., d.
Johnson, J. H.
Jones, A. J.
Jordan, Sansom, d.
Kennerly, E. M.
Kennerly, John, c.
Ketchie, Wm.
Kearns, J. F., c. and a.
Lowrance, R. W., d.
Lowrance, L. N.
Lowrance, S. L., w.
Moble, Joel.
Moble, John.
Martin, J. M., d.
Martin, John.
McAuley, J. C.
McConnell, R. A.
McGahey, Jas. A., k.
Miller, W. C.
Moore, Jas. C.
Morgan, Zac., k.
Mowery, Henry.
Nance, J. A., d.
Nelson, W., d.
Osborne, N. B., w.
Oliphant, J. R., k.
Reese, D. L.
Shepard, G. T.
Shields, A. C.
Sloan, A. C., d.
Sloan, J. Mc., d.
Sloan, W. E.
Smith, W. T. d.
Sossamon, J. P., c. and w.
Stearns, Henry M.
Sloan, D. F. A., w.
Stokes, J. J.
Stough, Rich. I.
Strider, John, k.
Templeton, J. E. D.
Templeton, J. M., w.
Templeton, R. D.
Tye, Wm. A.
Vance, W. H., d.
Watts, R. A., d.

Walls, Thos. w. and c.
Worsham, Alfred, w.
Worsham, B. A., d.
Worsham, Richard, d.
Worsham, H. J., w.

Watts, R. F., k.
Williams, J. H., w.
Williams, Rufus.

Total, 121; killed, 13; wounded, 25.

COMPANY K, FORTY-SECOND REGIMENT.
OFFICERS.

S. B. Alexander, Captain.
B. F. Wilson, Lieutenant.
A. M. Rhyne, Lieutenant, d.
Jos. H. Wilson, d.

NON-COMMISSIONED OFFICERS.

Thomas Norment.
Wm. Hecks, w. and c.
Wm. Price.
Jas. Keenan, k.
W. S. Bynum, c.
J. H. Staten, d.
S. W. Talton, w.
Ed. Day, k.
Jas. Scott, w.
T. C. Dule.
L. Adams.
Anderson, W. H. H., w.
Anderson, G. W., d.
Benfield, Dan., w.
Cullet, Ezekiel.
Coots, Jacob, d.
Dulin, W. C., k.
Dulin, W. L.
Foster, J. H., d.
Flowers, R. B.
Gilbert, Harrison,
Gilbert, Jas.
Grub, Absolom, d.
Gaston, J. A.
Griffin, B. F., d.
Hendrix, Grayson, w.
Hendrix, L. J., c.
Hendrix, Sanford, c.
Harman, Paul, w.
Helfer, P. E.
Helms, Hosea, c.
Helms, Enoch, c.
Helms, Gilliam.
Helms, D. B., c.
Helms, Albert.
Helms, John, w.
Helms, Josiah, c.
Helms, Kennel, c.
Helms, Copeland, w.
Helms, J. L.
Helms, Joshua.
Helms, Eli W.
Johnson, Matthew, d.
Milton, Francis, w.
Milton, Alex.
Mitchell, Allison.
Makaler, Frank.
Minor, H. J., c.
Norment, Charles, d.
Orrell, Sam'l.
Paul, J. L., w.
Phillips, J. B., d.

Polk, —, k.
Perry, Noah.
Privette, Wesley.
Randall, E. D.
Rindal, L. L., c.
Severs, —, k.
Singleton, Henry.
Scott, John W.
Scott, Leader.
Smith, Alex.
Staner, P. C.

Shoemaker, Lafayette, d.
Smith, John.
Stone, John, w.
Sanring, J. M.
Sharp, Isaac.
Triplette, J. H.
Walsh, G. B., c.
Walsh, J. H.
Whitley, John.

Total, 82.

COMPANY F, FORTY-NINTH REGIMENT.
OFFICERS.

Jas. T. Davis, Captain, k.
Jas. P. Ardrey, k.
John C. Grier, w.
John W. Barnett, Lieutenant, k.
R. H. Grier, Lieutenant, k.
J. G. Potts, Lieutenant.
S. R. Neal, Lieutenant.
Jas. H. Elms, Lieutenant.
W. T. Barnett, k.
L. M. Neal, k.

NON-COMMISSIONED OFFICERS.

J. A. Elliott.
R. C. Bell.
Wm. L. Manson, w.
J. A. Ezzell.
J. W. Wolf.
Robt. N. Alexander.

Alexander, E. E.
Alexander, R. W.
Alexander, J. J., k.
Alexander, T. B., d.
Alexander, W. P., w.
Allen, A. W.
Ashley, Wm.
Barnett, W. P.
Bennett, D. G., w.
Brown, J. G.
Brown, W. H.
Cruthers, T. M., w.
Crane, Job S.

Crenshaw, John, w.
Culp, John, w.
DeArmond, J. B., w.
Dunn, Jas. R., w.
Elliott, S. H., w.
Farris, J. A., w.
Fields, M. A.
Fincher, J. E., d.
Fincher, O.
Fleniken, L. B.
French, Wm.
Garrison, A. D.
Gordon, A. E.

CIVIL WAR TROOPS. 173

Griffin, Egbert.
Griffith, I. G.
Griffith, J. W.
Griffith, T. D.
Grier, Lawrence,
Hannon, J. J.
Harkey, D. E.
Harkey, J. J.
Harkey, M. L.
Harkey, Wash.
Hartis, J. L.
Hartis, J. S.
Hanfield, Jas. W.
Hennigen, J. E.
Howard, J. M., w.
Hudson, Wilson.
Jamison, Emory.
Johnson, Dan.
Johnson, J. A.
Kenan, D. G.
Kenier, J. R.
Kerr, Jas.
Kerr. Sam'l.
Kirkpatrick, S. A.
McAllister, H. B.
McRaney, Sam'l.
Miller, W. T.
Moore, W. W.
Morris, G. C.
Morris, J. W.
Neel, W. B.
Neely, Wm. A.
Newell, W. A.
Osborne, J. H., w.
Paxton, S. L.
Phifer, E. M., k.
Pierce, John, k.
Pierce, L. M.

Porter, Robt. A., w.
Porter, S. L.
Porter, Zenas.
Prataer, A. R., d.
Prather, S. F.
Previtt, Allen.
Raterree, W. L.
Rea, D. J., w.
Reid, William, k.
Richardson, J. H.
Ross, W. A.
Shaw, J. N.
Smith, E. C.
Smith, Wm. J. B.
Spratt, A. P.
Squires, M. D., w.
Stanford, C. L.
Stephenson, Wm. J., w.
Stitt, Jas. M.
Swann, J. B.
Taylor, Ed. S., w.
Taylor, J. A. R., w.
Tevepaugh, Wm.
Tidwell, W. P. A.
Turner, F. M.
Walker, E. M., w.
Warwick, J. M., w.
Watson, J. A., d.
Watson, J. B.
Watson, J. S.
Weeks, J. L., w.
Whitesides, Wm., w.
Wingate, J. P., w.
Wingate, Wm. C.
Wolf, J. W.

Total, 116; killed, 5; wounded, 23; died, 5.

COMPANY B, FIFTY-THIRD REGIMENT.
OFFICERS.

J. H. White, Captain, k.
S. E. Belk, Captain, k.
J. M. Springs, Lieutenant.

W. M. Matthews, Lieutenant.
M. E. Alexander, Lieutenant.

NON-COMMISSIONED OFFICERS.

R. J. Patterson, w.
S. M. Blair.
R. A. Davis.
A. N. Gray.
W. R. Baily.
R. H. Todd, k.
W. H. Alexander, k.
Alexander, J. W., d.
Alexander, Benj. P., d.
Alexander, Benj. C.
Anderson, Wm., d.
Atchison, Wm., c. and w.
Armstrong, Leroy, c.
Barnett, R. S.
Barnett, W. A., k.
Barnett, E. L. S.
Berryhill, W. A., c.
Berryhill, Andrew, w.
Berryhill, Alex.
Barnes, S. S. D., d.
Bruce, G. W.
Burwell, J. B.
Benton, Sam'l, w.
Baker, G. F., w.
Cochran, J. M.
Cochran, Wm. R.
Cochran, R. C.
Cotchcoat, J. H., w.
Capps, John, d.
Caton, Elijah, w. and c.
Caton, Sylv., c. and d.
Clark, W. H.
Clark, W. C.
Clark, A. W.
Collins, John, k.
Campbell, J. P.
Davis, W. A., d.
Demon, Jacob.
Donnell, W. T., w. and c.
Engenburn, J.
Eagle, John, w.
Eagle, W. H.

Epps, W. D., k.
Engel, Jonas.
Frazier, J. L.
Fincher, Asa.
Farrices, Z. W.
Frazier, J. C. R.
Grier, J. G., w.
Giles, M. O.
Giles, S. H.
Howie, J. M.
Howie, Sam'l M., w.
Howie, F. M., w.
Hall, H. L., w.
Hood, R. L., c.
Harry, W. B., w.
Hoover, F. M.
Katz, Aaron.
King, P. A., k.
Kirkpatrick, T. A.
Knox. J. S.
Leon, Lewis.
Love, D. L.
Marks, S. S., c.
Marks, J. G., w.
Marks, T. E., k.
Marks, W. S.
McGinn, Thos.
McElroy, Jas. W., k.
Mitchell, C. J.
McKinney, Wm.
McKinney, T. A., c.
Merritt, Wm. N., k.
McCrary, Jordan.
Morrison, J. M.
McCombs, A. H., w. and c.

CIVIL WAR TROOPS. 175

Maxwell, P. P., w.
McCrum, H. A., k.
Norment, A. A., k.
Otters, Cooney, c. and .d.
Owens, J. Henry, k.
Oates, Jas.
Potts, Jas. H.
Patterson, S. L.
Parks, ᴍiah, c.
Reid, H. K.
Reid, J. F., k.
Robinson, Thomp.
Russell, H. T., c.
Rodden, N. B., w.
Rodden, W. R., k.
Robinson, J. P.
Smith, Lemuel.
Sweat, J. M.
Sample, H. M., c.
Sample, David.
Sample, J. W.
Sample, J. M., c.
Springs, R. A.
Stone, W. D., w. and c.
Sullivan, W. L.

Stewart, W. S., d.
Taylor, J. W., w.
Todd, S. E.
Thomas, Henry.
Trotter, A. G.
Trotter, Thos., d.
Vickers, E. N.
Worthern, Henry, d.
Wilkenson, Neil, k.
Wolfe, C. H.
Winders, P. S., c.
Wilson, L. R., c.
Wilson, J. H., k.
Wilson, S. W., w. and c.
Wilson, J. M.
Wilkinson, R. L.
Williams, Hugh.
Williams, J. A.
Williams, A. L.
Williamson, A. L., c.
Williamson, J. M., c.
White, J. T.

Total, 110; killed, 16; wounded, 21; died, 12; captured, 20.

COMPANY E, FIFTY-NINTH REGIMENT.
OFFICERS.

J. Y. Bryce, Captain, w.
Robt. Gadd, Lieutenant.
B. H. Sanders, Lieutenant.
Wm. Bryce, Lieutenant.

NON-COMMISSIONED OFFICERS.

J. J. Misenheimer.
J. B. Savis.
J. F. Davidson.
G. F. Vickers, k.
—. —. Vickers, k.
W. H. A. Kluts.
M. L. Furr.
Noah Shore.
R. Kluts.
Blackwelder, D. C.
Biggers, William.
Biggers, Houston, d.

Biggers, Robt.
Bost, Moses.
Bost, S. C.

Bost, J. K. P.
Beattie, J. O.
Baroon, George.
Barber, Josiah.
Benson, H. A.
Broadstreet, J. R., c.
Browning, J. M., d.
Clay, J. M., c.
Cline, H. B.
Cline, W. D., c.
Carriker, S. C.
Cox, J. D.
Cruse, Peter.
Carson, J. L.
Craig, Alex., c.
Davis, W. E.
Doolan, E., k.
Eaudy, Paul.
Furr, Mat.
Furr. D. C.
Furr, Allen.
Furr, A. W., d.
Fisher, C. A.
File, J. F.
Falls, W. A.
Faggart, D. C.
Foard, E. M.
Floyd, Wm.
Fink, Peter, k.
Griffin, Wesley.
Gatlin, G. W.
Grover, Austin.
Hagler, Jacob.
Hagler, Allen.
Hagler, Nelson.
Hagler, J. A.
Hoffman, J. L.
Hoffman, J. L.
Hoffman, J. M.
Hartman, H. M.
Howell, W. E.
Hunsucker, N. J.
Johnson, J. M., c.
Johnson, G. W.
Johnson, Jacob.

Kiser, G. A.
Kiser, N. D.
Kimmons, R. M.
Lay, J. G.
Linker, Jas.
Linker, W. R.
Linker, Aaron.
Linker, Moses.
Lefter, W. H.
Lay, W. J.
Lay, A. L.
Lay, J. W.
Ledford, C. M.
McCoy, J. R.
McDaniel, E. B., k.
McDaniel, E. A., d.
McEntire, M. L., c.
Misenheimer, J. H.
Moreton, W. R., d.
Moore, Dr. T. J.
Osborne, J. F.
Osborne, Robt., d.
Plyler, F. S.
Pender, J. H.
Perkins, A.
Pace, Young.
Reaves, F. A.
Rice, Moses.
Richards, Wm.
Ray, A. D., c.
Rhyne, C. M.
Rinehart, W. D., c.
Rinehart, Thos.
Starnes, John, d.
Starnes, E. W.
Sossaman, D. G.
Sossaman, W. H.
Smith, G. F.
Smith, G. L.
Smith, J. B.
Stranter, Wm.
Stranter, John.
Stranter, T. H.
Stowe, L. P.
Smith, Frank, k.

CIVIL WAR TROOPS. 177

Smith, L. A.
Thomas, C. W.
Turner, W. D.
Troutman, Geo.
Wilson, J. M.
Wallace, J. M.

Wilson, Wm.
Wallace, J. R.
Williamson, J. M.
Williamson, J. B., w.

Total 116; died 6; killed 6; wounded 3; captured 4.

COMPANY B, FORTY-THIRD REGIMENT.
OFFICERS.
Robert P. Waring.
Drury Ringstaff, First Lieutenant.
William E. Still, Second Lieutenant.
Julius Alexander, Second Lieutenant.
Robt. T. Burwell, Second Lieutenant.

NON-COMMISSIONED OFFICERS.
Drury Lacy, First Sergeant.
Robt. B. Corble, Second Sergeant.
S. R. Johnston, Third Sergeant.
J. Harris Hunter, Fourth Sergeant.
R. T. Burwell, Fifth Sergeant.
Henry S. Presson, First Corporal.
Smiley W. Hunter, Second Corporal.
Robt. C. McGinness, Third Corporal.
Hiram Secrest, Fourth Corporal, k.

Alexander, John M.
Aycock, W. M., k.
Broom, Samron.
Broom, Solomon.
Broom, S. A.
Broom, N. W.
Broom, Calvin, k.
Broom, Wilson.
Broom, A. T.
Barnes, Bryant.
Blackwelder, D. M.
Boyd, Hugh.
Burwell, W. R.
Cochran, W. L., k.
Craft, A. J.
Allen, Dees L.
Fincher, Levi J., w.
Fowler, Moses F.
Fowler, Geo. W., k.
Griffith, J. Henry, k.
Griffith, J. L.

Grier, Paul B., k.
Griffith, Marley.
Griffith, Farrington.
Harrington, Ed. P.
Helms, Asa.
Helms, Josiah, k.
Helms, Noah.
Helms, Elbert, k.
Helms, W. M.
Helms, Alex. L.
Helms, Noah J.
Howell, W. J., k.
Hunter, Mad., k.
Hargrave, Robt. W.
Knight, W. M.
Singleton Lacy D.
Little, Bryant.
Moore, Pleasant.
McGwirt, David.
McGwirt, H. A.
Mullis, Simon.

Mannis, T. M.
Mannis, A. W.
Price, Josiah G.
Phillips, John.
Presley, John M.
Presley, Caswell.
Parsons, Larkins.
Paxton, William W.
Robinson, M. M.
Robinson, M. B.
Rea, W. F.
Reams, John W., k.
Robinson, Samuel J.
Stearns, Johnston.
Stearns, Daniel, k.
Stearns, Thos. H.
Stearns, John R., k.
Stack, Albert.
Steele, Albert, k.
Steele, Thos.
Stegall, Moses.
Stegall, Ambrose.
Stancel, James.
Stout, J. S.
Swift, Geo. W.
Simpson, H. Mc.
Sikes, Geo. G.
Sherrill, William E.
Thornburg, John L.
Womack, John.
Wilson, W. A.
Wilson, J. A.
Wilson, G. J.

Total, 89; reported killed, 20; wounded, 1; died, 7; 19 only returned home; 42 missing.

COMPANY F, SIXTY-THIRD REGIMENT (Cavalry).

OFFICERS.

John R. Erwin, Captain.
J. McWhite, First Lieutenant.
C. S. Gibson, Second Lieutenant.
W. J. Wiley, Third Lieutenant.
S. A. Grier, First Sergeant.
J. R. Kirkpatrick, Second Sergeant.
R. A. Davidson, Third Sergeant.
P. W. Lintz, Fourth Sergeant.
J. H. Henderson, First Corporal.
J. M. Beaver, Second Corporal.
H. C. Bird, Third Corporal.
C. B. Palmer, Fourth Corporal.

Armstrong, Larkin.
Armstrong, Mathew.
Alexander, H. L.
Abernathey, W. D.
Andrews, G. W.
Asbury, Eugene.
Adams, James.
Brown, J. C.
Blackwelder, James.
Blackwood, Eli.
Burroughs, John.
Brum, C. F.
Alexander, W. N.
Alexander, J. W.
Alexander, J. S.
Bowden, Louis.
Bigham, Green.
Cochran, J. C.
Cochran, R. E.
Caldwell, D. A.
Caldwell, R. B.
Caldwell, J. N.
Caldwell, H. M.
Cahill, John.

CIVIL WAR TROOPS.

Cathey, John.
Coleman, T. P.
Davidson, R. A.
Davis, J. T. A.
Downs, J. T.
Eudy, John.
Erwin, W. R.
Furguson, F. A.
Flenigan, R. G.
Ferrell, J. F. M.
Fisher, J. V.
Fisher, Alfred.
Fisher, Francis.
Fisher, E. L.
Faggot, Dan.
Gibson, D. M.
Griffith, C. F.
Grier, J. H.
Grier, Sam.
Harkey, W. F.
Howie, W. H.
Halobough, J. M.
Hunter, A. B.
Hoover, T. J.
Hannon, D. A.
Harris, J. S.
Hinson, M.
Hutchison, C. N.
Hartsell, Wm.
Jamison, J. L.
Jennings, J. H.
Kirkpatrick, W. L.
Kirkpatrick, J. M.
Kerr, R. D.
Kustler, M. E.
Love, D. L.
Love. J. M
Lentz, Aaron.
Lindsay, Thos.
Leeper, Jas.
Ludwick, S.
Ludwick, Wm.
Montgomery, R. C.
McCall, J. A.
McElhany, E. A.
McElhany, S. L.

McDonald, J. R.
McDonald, Worth.
Millen, R. A.
McKenzie, Wm.
Means, P. B.
Moore, J. M.
Miller, S.
Minus, J. S.
Nance, W. T.
Nelson, J. M.
Norwood, R. F.
Neagle, J. F.
Prather, W. S.
Quiry, Walter.
Reed, W. H.
Russell, P. J.
Roper, P. H.
Regler, J. R.
Rea, D. B.
Rea, Samuel.
Smith, D. W.
Smith, A.
Smith, R. T.
Smith, J. B.
Smith, John.
Smith, Wm.
Sloan, W. S.
Shuman, W. H.
Sharp, J. R.
Survis, T. O.
Terris, C. E.
Tiser, W. H. G.
Taylor, D. B.
Tate, T. A.
Tate, F. A.
Torrence, C. L.
Wilson, Wm.
Wilson, J. C.
White, R. S.
Weaver, J. A.
Wright, J. C.
Wryfield, Wm.
Wallace, I. N.
Younts, J. A.
Young, J. A.

Total, 127.

CHAPTER XV.

MECKLENBURG'S PART IN THE MEXICAN WAR.

Roster of the Troops in the Company Organized in Charlotte in April of 1847.*—Green W. Caldwell was Captain and He and the Lieutenants Were Honored by Seats in the General Assembly After the End of the War.—The Total Number of the Soldiers was Seventy-nine, and Eleven of Them Died in the Service.

James Knox Polk, a native of Mecklenburg county, was inaugurated President of the United States March 4, 1845, and in his inaugural address, he declared that he should defend the contentions of the United States with regard to the boundary line between Texas and Mexico. December 29th following, Texas, having adopted the proposition submitted, was formally recognized as a State of the Union.

Mexico claimed that the proper boundary was the Neuces river, while Texas claimed that it was the Rio Grande. In March, 1846, General Taylor, acting under orders of the President, advanced into the disputed territory, and the Mexican general, Ampudia, declared that Mexico accepted the advance as a declaration of war. April 26th, the first blood of the war was shed, a party of sixty-three Americans being all killed or captured by a Mexican detachment. Congress then declared war and the armies of the United States pushed forward into Mexico and soon demonstrated their great superiority as fighters. Vera Cruz was surrendered in April, 1847, and the capital city was captured September 13. The treaty of peace was signed February 2, 1848.

In April, 1847, Green W. Caldwell resigned his position as director of the United States Mint in Charlotte, to organize a company of dragoons for the war with Mexico. The company left Charlotte April 13, and went to Charleston, and from there to Vera Cruz, where they were enrolled as

---

*From the Supplement to the "Roster of North Carolina Troops, in the War With Mexico," published by the State in 1887.

UNITED STATES CURRENCY.

Troop A, of the Third Regiment of the United States Dragoons, of which the Colonel was E. G. W. Butler. This regiment engaged in a number of battles, in all of which the Mecklenburg troops participated. Captain Caldwell's company was mustered out of service at Jefferson Barracks, Missouri, July 31, 1848, and the soldiers, except the eleven who had died and, two others who were missing, returned home and many of them were for many years numbered among the prominent and useful citizens.

In the election held in 1849 for members of the General Assembly, which met in the following year, Captain Caldwell was elected to the State Senate, and Lieutenants J. K. Harrison and E. C. Davidson were elected Representatives.

ROSTER OF TROOP A, THIRD REGIMENT OF UNITED STATES DRAGOONS.*

OFFICERS.

Green W. Caldwell, Captain.
Edward C. Davidson, First Lieutenant.
John K. Harrison, Second Lieutenant.
Alfred A. Norment, Second Lieutenant.
Samuel E. Belk, First Sergeant.
James Brian, Sergeant.
Thomas D. Massey, Sergeant.
John G. Query, Sergeant.
John Harkey, Corporal.
Charles J. Titlemary, Corporal.
James T. Blair, Corporal.
Matthias W. Cole, Corporal.
John R. Glover, Corporal.
Cyrus Q. Lemons, Bugler.
James T. Warren, Blacksmith.

---

*From the Supplement to the "Roster of North Carolina Troops in the War with Mexico," published by the State in 1887.

Alexander, Charles G.
Alexander, Evan.
Alexander, Samuel J.**
Alexander, Thomas.
Beaty, William L.
Boyd, Matthew B.
Bridges, Nicholas R.
Caldwell, LaFayette.
Cody, John.
Cutler, William.
Davidson, William L.
Dougherty, Charles R.
Flenniken, Robert G.
Forbes, Archibald.
Fullenwider, John F.
Glass, James R.**
Gray, Ransom S.
Griffith, Thomas D.
Houston, William A.
Keziah, William A.**
Lemons, D
Lemons, Archibald.
Lemons, Jackson C.
Mason, Robert G.
Matthews, Hugh A.
McCall, James.**
McCall, John A.
McCall, William.
McCall, William J.
McKee, Alex. F.
McKee, Elias R.
Mulwee, John T.
Normant, Thomas T.

Parks, Henry.
Prather, John J.
Paxton, William.
Phifer, John.
Porter, Hugh G.
Rea, William F.
Reed, James B.**
Richardson, John K.
Richardson, Mason.
Robinson, Daniel E.
Robinson, James M.**
Sanders, Jesse.
Sherrill, Hartford.
Sherrell, Robert K.
Sherrell, William.
Sherrill, Absolom L.*
Sitzer, James.
Smith, Burton.
Smithy, Willis W.
Stanford, David W.
Stilwell, Henry.
Stewart, Allen.**
Stewart, Milus R.**
Teague, John.
Tye, William A.
Vipon, Nicholas.
Waitt, William E. R.
Wentz, Valentine.**
Williamson, James D.
Williamson, John M.
Williamson, Thomas J.
Wilson, George W.**

**Died in Mexico.

CHAPTER XVI.

THE SPANISH-AMERICAN WAR.

Account of the Service Rendered by Mecklenburg Troops.—Rosters of the Three White Companies and the Colored Company.*— Charlotte Soldiers Among the First Americans to Land in Havana.

February 15, 1898, the destruction of the United States battleship Maine, in Havana harbor, brought the Spanish-American hostile feeling to an acute stage. Congress declared war on Spain April 19, and on May 11, Ensign Worth Bagley, of North Carolina, was killed by the explosion of a Spanish shell while on the torpedo boat Winslow, at Cardenas. He was the first officer to die in the war.

President McKinley's call for volunteers April 23, met with a prompt response in North Carolina. The First Regiment of the State was mustered into the service of the Nation at Camp Bryan Grimes, at Raleigh, May 2. In this regiment were the two white companies which went from Charlotte. The troops left Raleigh May 22, and encamped near Jacksonville until October 24, when they went to Savannah and remained there until December 7. At that time, the regiment was ordered to Havana, arriving December 11, and being the first to land in the Cuban capital.* It was kept in Cuba until March 18, 1899, and then returned to Savannah and was mustered out April 22. George F. Rutzler, of Charlotte, was a major of the regiment, and H. M. Wilder was surgeon with rank of major. R. E. Davidson, now of Charlotte, was colonel of the First Florida Regiment.

---

*Roster of the North Carolina Volunteers in the Spanish-American War, printed by the State, 1900.
*Official Reports.

ROSTER OF COMPANY A, FIRST N. C. REGIMENT.*

Thomas R. Robertson, Captain.
Thomas L. Powell, First Lieutenant.
Herbert J. Hirshinger, Second Lieutenant.
Albert G. Prempert, First Sergeant.
James M. Edwards, Q. M. Sergeant.
Thomas Garribaldi, Q. M. Sergeant.
Egbert Lyerly, Seargeant.
Johnson Graham, Sergeant.
Paul Schultz, Sergeant.
Ripley P. Smith, Sergeant.
Gordon H. Cilley, Hickory, Corporal.
William B. Flake, Corporal.
Robert B. Knox, Corporal.
George M. Maxwell, Corporal.
Charles M. McCorkle, Newton, Corporal.
Coleman O. Moser, Corporal.
Francis D. McLeon, Corporal.
Luther M. Osborne, Corporal.
Charles M. Setzer, Corporal.
James J. Stuart, Corporal.
Patrick H. Williams, Corporal.
Ulyses B. Williams, Corporal.
John G. Wilfong, Corporal.
William K. Allen, Artificer.
John J. Ozment, Artificer.
William R. Graham, Wagoner.
Claude Miller, Wagoner.
John F. Butt, Wagoner.
James H. McLeon, Cook.

Allen, Otto A., Gastonia.
Armstrong, W. L., Belmont.
Auten, Edward M.
Boiles, E. L., Pineville.
Bennett, D. E., King's Mountain.
Brown, W. A., Davidson.**
Brown, Karl.
Burge, D. L., Rutherfordton.
Butler, N. A. Clinton.
Campbell, J. H., Newton.
Campbell, M. O., Newton.
Cannon, Dink, Marion.

Colbert, D. L., Augusta, Ga.
Crump, S. R., Mint Hill.
Crump, T. C., Mint Hill.
Delnaux, Alfred.
DeMarcus, Lucian, Davidson.
Elam, Ralph, Spartanburg.
Fink, L. A., Pioneer Mills.
Francis, W. A., Henrietta.
Frederick, W. T., Sardis.
Fry, Burt A.
Garibaldi, John N.
Garrison, John, Morganton.

---

*All enlisted from Charlotte except as otherwise stated, mustered out April 22, 1899, at Savannah.
**Died in Davidson on furlough, October 19, 1898.

STATE CURRENCY.

Ginn, G. R., Atlanta.
Glenn, R. W., Cluster.
Goforth, John F., Bethel, S. C.
Goforth, J. L., King's Mountain.
Gribble, Marcus H.
Grier, D. D., Matthews.
Grier, V. G., Matthews.
Head, R. L., Statesville.
Hennessee, S. A., North Cove.
Henning, F. A., Chicago, Ill.
Herndon, W. P., King's Mountain.
Hill, John D.
Hodges, Oliver L.
Hoke, W. P., King's Mountain.
Hord, R. M., Waco.
Huffsteller, W. T., King's Mountain.
Ivey, B. F., Rock Hill, S. C.
Jimison, M. E., Rocky Pass.***
Johnson, Wallace D.
Kale, A. E., Hickory.
Keener, H. O., Hickory.
Lewis, J. W., Marion.
Lewis, J. A., Marion.
Linton, S. E.
Lyon, J. S., Hendersonville.
Navney, R. J., King's Mountain.
Mize, R. L., Granite Falls.
Montgomery, Walter W.
Murphy, Harry, Boston, Mass.
McKay, Joseph V.
Odell, M., Bessemer City.

Parker, D. W., Spartanburg.
Pegram, William E.
Pitts, J. B., Concord.
Proctor, W. A., Lincolnton.
Reid, J. C., Sago.
Renn, E. W., West Durham.
Rhodes, J. E., King's Mountain.
Richard, C. J., Pensacola, Fla.
Roper, D. C., Spartanburg.
Roper, R., Spartanburg.
Romley, S. F., Winston.
Sells, James.
Sherrill, C. M., Newton.
Sikes, Daniel S.
Smith, O. B., Callahan.
Steadman, W. W., Ramasbur
Trimble, J. M., Monroe.
Wavra, Gus. E.
Weir, J. F., King's Mountain.
White, L. W., Augusta, Ga.
Williams, B., Marion.
Williams, J. W., Clover, S. C
Williams, W. H., Jr., Newton.
Wilson, W. M., Rhems, S. C.
Yoder, A. T., Hickory.
Yount, A. O., Newton.
Yount, L. C., Hickory.
Yount, T. E., Newton.
Yount, W. H., Newton.

Total, 114.

ROSTER OF COMPANY M, FIRST N. C. REGIMENT.*

William A. Erwin, Captain.
Hubert S. Chadwick, Captain.**
Harry Page, First Lieutenant. (Promoted.)
John R. Van Ness, First Lieutenant.***
Samuel Bell, Second Lieutenant. (Promoted.)
William H. Schroeder, Jr., First Sergeant. (Promoted.)

---

*All enlisted from Charlotte, except as otherwise stated. Mustered out April 27, 1899, at Savannah.
**Resigned December 1, 1898.
***Resigned October 30, 1898.

HISTORY OF MECKLENBURG COUNTY.

William F. Kuester, Second Sergeant.
Herbert N. Banks, Sergeant.
Eli W. Bonney, Sergeant.
Oscar D. King, Sergeant.
Lloyd C. Torrence, Sergeant.
W. C. Adams, Pennsylvania, Corporal. (Died.)
J. H. Dickson, Spartanburg, Corporal.
E. E. Williams, Steele Creek, Corporal.
C. G. Carter, Albemarle, Corporal.
W. A. Neal, Sardis, Corporal.
S. S. Pegram, South Point, Corporal.
Frederick R. Cates, Corporal.
Duncan F. Davis, Cumberland, Corporal.
Charles E. Mosteller, Corporal.
E. P. Carpenter, Gastonia, Corporal.
O. P. Bright, Greenville, Corporal.
Arthur B. Ferris, Corporal.
John W. Floyd, Corporal.
W. W. Phillips, Redclay, Ga., Artificer.
R. C. Hummel, Greensboro, Cook.
John Hardy, Wagoner.
William H. Ayers, Wagoner.
George F. Smith, Tryon, Musician.
William H. Asbury, Musician.

Alexander, William B.
Bailey, W. B., Marion.
Barkley, Enen L.
Beon, W. F., Asheville.
Bridges, Joseph R.
Cooper, F. W., Dysartville.
Cates, Lucky R.
Cauble, C. M., Asheville.
Chapman, A. F., Enola.
Cheary, J. J., Concord.
Culp, E., Fort Mills, S. C.
Collins, W. M., Greensboro.
Cozby, W. L., Greenville, S. C.
Cooper, H. L., Dysartville.
Crone, V. H., Partieth.
Davis, W. M., Fayetteville.
Davis, Edgar S.
Daniel, W. S., Greensboro.
Dunn, Rufus C.
Duncan, R. M., Marion.

Delnaux, Florian.
Finger, R. T., Crouse.
Freeman, John E.
Freeman, Neal B.
Greely, C. E., New London.
Gore, V. L., Philadelphia.
Gregory, R. E. L., Barnardsville.
Glass, J. D., Dysartville.
Graham, John M.
Grose, Ralph.
Gray, Edward S.
Hargett, F., Sharon.
Hillis, W. H., Augusta, Ga.
Hollister, G. H., Wilmington.
Hickey, R. H., Newport, Tenn.
Hendley, J. M., Marion.
Hoke, C. W., Clairmont.
Hunt, H. H., Spartanburg.
Harrett, O. H., Palm. (Died.)
Jones, Walter G.

THE SPANISH-AMERICAN WAR. 187

Jones, William H.
Kerr, E. D., Sharon.
Kissiah, Thomas.
Lander, William T.
Langford, O. S., Augusta, Ga.
Lindsay, R. T., Pittsburg, Pa.
Linear, N., Fort Mills, S. C.
Lequex, F. S., Greensboro.
McDonnell, S. K., Jr., Rock Hill, S. C.
McGowan, John W.
Moore, W. H., Lowsville.
Mace, C., Enola.
Murphy, Micjiel.
Murphy, Dennis.
Neese, John W.
Oates, W. D. S.
Osborne, John M.
Phillips, A. J., Concord.
Poplin, W. S., Stanley county.
Porter, W. H., Matthews.
Parrott, J. W., Richmond, Va.

Pegram, Walter P.
Ramsey, W. A., Durham.
Rogers, R. B., Leicester.
Revelle, J. H., Salisbury.
Sadler, Armond D. (Promoted.)
Stutts, Louis B.
Scott, Claudius.
Sandifer, E. L., Sandifer.
Shaw, G. R., Lamont.
Timmons, Harry.
Woodside, Rufus W.
Thomas, G. W., Gaston.
Williamson, C., Matthews.
Wells, J. M., Duplin county.
Wall, J. M., Marion.
Withers, M. P., Gastonia.
Walker, Charles C.
Yandle, L. S., Ranxin.

Total, 109.

ROSTER OF COMPANY G, SECOND N. C. REGIMENT.*

This regiment was mustered into the service May 26, 1898. After six weeks of camp drill at Raleigh, the companies of the regiment were separated. Campanies D and G, under command of Major Dixon, were stationed at Land's End, S. C. In October, the regiment was consolidated at Raleigh, and the troops were given a thirty days' furlough. Before the time expired an order was issued that the members of the companies should assemble at the most convenient points and be there mustered out. Accordingly, Company G disbanded in Charlotte, November 3, 1898. Rev. A. Osborne, of Charlotte, was chaplain of this regiment, and E. M. Brevard was assistant surgeon, with rank as captain.

Robert Lee Durham, Gastonia, Captain.
Plato T. Durham, Gastonia, First Lieutenant.

---

*All enlisted from Charlotte except as otherwise stated. This was known as the Gastonia Company.

Ernest N. Farrior, Second Lieutenant.
Walter V. Brem, Jr., First Sergeant.
A. A. Wilson, Mt. Holly, Q. M. Sergeant.
C. M. Isenhour, Gastonia, Sergeant.
S. S. Shuford, Gastonia, Sergeant.
G. C. Sandifer, Sandifer, Sergeant.
F. H. Wilson, Gastonia, Sergeant.
R. L. Jenkins, Gastonia, Corporal.
H. M. Miller, Athens, Ga., Corporal.
John S. Woodard, Corporal.
R. P. Elmore, Gastonia, Corporal.
Thomas H. Trotter, Corporal.
A. Lewis, Gastonia, Corporal.
W. M. Robinson, Lincolnton, Corporal.
W. L. Williams, Glenburnie, Corporal.
William F. Duke, Corporal.
H. Otter, New York, Corporal.
J. S. Vincent, Midlothian, Va., Corporal.
J. W. Horton, Washburn, Corporal.
W. A. Ray, McAdensville, Corporal.
Albert S. Savin, Musician.
T. B. Bryant, Gaffney, S. C., Musician.
Joe. F. Harris, Artificer.
William C. Hargett, Wagoner.

Alexander, A. W., Huntersville.
Ball, J. A., Washington, N. C.
Beaty, G. W., Gastonia.
Belk, E. A., Waxhaw.
Bell, W. T., Statesville.
Berrier, S. T., Gaffney, S. C.
Biggers, R. H., Rock Hill.
Black, R. L., McAdensville.
Bulwinkle, F. C., Dallas.
Bryon, L. J., Wilmington.
Campbell, Z. C., Spartanburg.
Clark, J. T., Griffin, Ga.
Candor, F. J., Stouts.
Costner, J. S., Gastonia.
Craig, E., Chitmar, Ga.
Craig, W. B., Gastonia.
Crook, W. W., Asheville.
Cummings, D., Wilmington.
Cummings, W. M., Wilmington.
Davis, A. J., Spray.
Davis, W. A., Asheville.
Donaldson, William D.
Doughty, Lester D.
Douglass, James F.
Draughton, D. D., Mt. Island.
Elms, John D.
Falls, W. T., King's Mountain.
Finger, N. F., Salisbury.
Foil, T. A., Concord.
Foard, C., Statesville.
Ford, J. E. C., McAdensville.
Forrest, A., Concord.
Gattis, J. A., Gastonia.
Green, E., Swain.
Grice, J. M., Gastonia.
Gulledge, H. M., Morven.
Halsell, H., Newton.
Hampton, G. W., Sylva.
Harmon, G. W., King's Mountain.
Haymie, C., Asheville.
Haywood, J. M., Stouts.
Heath, J. M., Gastonia.

THE SPANISH-AMERICAN WAR. 189

Hernden, J. J., Crocker.
Hernden, M. P., Grover.
Hoffman, R. Y., Lowell.
Humphreys, Charles.
Jackson, Clemens E.
Jacobson, A. L., New York.
Jenkins, G. A., Gastonia.
Jones, Ben. F.
Kennedy, Lawrence J.
Keller, Henry A.
Laubrey, A. C., Baltimore.
Lay, J. M., Gastonia.
Lewis, Fred E.
Linder, R. W., Gastonia.
Lindsey, H. L., Asheville.
Lipkind, Daniel.
Massagee, C. A., Asheville.
McClellan, Daniel C.
McGowan, James E.
Moore, Joseph D.
Nort, H. W., Atlanta, Ga.
O'Byrne, M., Centralia, Pa.
Pace, Albert P.
Parrish, Walter L.

Patten, James, Asheville.
Patten, James P., Asheville.
Pearce, Henry L.
Pryor, J. F., Knoxville.
Reynolds, J. O., Roberdell.
Rhodes, J. C., King's Mountain.
Richardson, J. M., Pacolet, S. C.
Richman, J. B., Tryon.
Russell, William E.
Sample, M. M., Begonia.
Savin, Charles E.
Sharar, Wilson A.
Sims, Gipson R.
Smith, E. M., Hopewell.
Smith, J. N., King's Mountain.
Steele, J. P. H., Lowell.
Thomas, J. B., Sandifer.
Ward, E. W., Lincolnton.
Watkins, T., Bryson City.
Wafford, C. H., Matthews.
Wood, J., Asheville.

Total, 113.

ROSTER OF COMPANY A, THIRD REGIMENT. (Colored.)*

This regiment of colored troops, of which James H. Young, of Raleigh, was colonel, came into the service of the United States July 19, 1898. Companies A, B and C, composing a battalion, were mustered in at Fort Macon, N. C., May 12. Company A, of Charlotte, belonged to the State Guard, but the other companies were composed of new recruits. The regiment was moved to Knoxville, Tenn., September 14, and from there to Macon, Ga., November 21, It remained in Macon until it was mustered out in February, 1899. This body of troops was reviewed by Secretary of War Alger, September 20, and by President McKinley,

*Died in Raleigh Hospital October 21, 1898.
*All enlisted from Charlotte except as otherwise stated. Company mustered out February 2, 1899, at Macon, Ga.

December 21, and was complimented by both the Secretary and the President. C. S. L. A. Taylor, of Charlotte, was lieutenant colonel; and M. T. Pope was assistant surgeon, with rank as first lieutenant.

William P. Stitt, Captain.
James C. Graham, First Lieutenant.
H. H. Taylor, Warrenton, Second Lieutenant.
Samuel A. Harris, First Sergeant.**
Leander W. Hayes, First Sergeant.
Ellis H. Johnson, Q. M. Sergeant.
Frank French, Sergeant.
Zachariah Alexander, Sergeant.
James Walters, Sergeant.
Cobb Burns, Sergeant.
Henry R. Johnson, Corporal.
Clarence L. Gordon, Corporal.
Isaac W. Parks, Corporal.
Fred Lander, Corporal.
Edward W. Moss, Corporal.
Robert Abernathy, Corporal.
Arbell V. Henderson, Corporal.
William Lillington, Corporal.
Charles J. Bartlow, Corporal.
John Caldwell, Corporal.
John Gray, Corporal.
Thomas B. Smith, Corporal.
Thomas M. Mills, Musician.
George Wilson, Musician.
Haywood Abernathy, Artificer.
Augustus Abernathy, Artificer.
A. D. Chambers, Asheville, Wagoner.

Abernatny, Hampton.
Abernathy, Lewis.
Adamson, Robert.
Alexander, Lee. (Died.)
Alexander, William.
Anderson, Henry.
Avery, Robert W.
Ballard, Isaac R.

Barnes, S., Wilson.
Barringer, Charles.
Beasley, James.
Beaty, George.
Benson, Edward.
Berry, Arthur.
Bland, Anthony.
Boger, John.

**Promoted at Knoxville, Tenn., November 8, 1898.

THE SPANISH-AMERICAN WAR. 191

Capus, William.
Carter, Green.
Chambers, Clarence.
Clinton, A. J., Jr.
Collins, William.
Cornelius, N., Asheville.
Cooper, Lucius B.
Cunningham, Ernest L.
Cunningham, Edward.
David, Ed.
Edgerton, Wm., Asheville. (Died.)
Ellis, Thomas.
Everhart, William.
Foreman, Rufus.
Garrison, Charles.
Gibbs, F. E., Asheville.
Gilmer, Walter.
Graham, John.
Grant, John W.
Grier, Adam G.
Hall, William.
Hamlin, Benjamin.
Henderson, John T.
Henderson, Thomas W.
Higgins. B., Asheville.
Houser, Lewis.
Houston, Simon.
Ingram, Otis.
Johnson, William.
Jones, Anthony.
Jones, William.
Kelly, Henry.
Knotts, Charles.
Lemmons, William.
Lytle, Claud.
McConneyhead, M.

McCorkle, Julius.
McFadden, W. C.
McKinney, G. F.
McMullen, William.
Moore, Bishop.
Moss, Edward L.
Neal, Brooks.
Nelson, Richard.
Newlan, Thomas.
Oglesby, F., Asheville.
Pharr, Floyd.
Phifer, William.
Robb, Fester.
Robertson, F. J.
Robertson, Reuben.
Senior, Hall.
Sims, Reuben.
Snowden, Emanuel.
Springs, Alexander.
Steele, John.
Swepson, P. J., Asheville.
Torrence, James.
Wade, Joseph W.
Wallace, Daniel.
Walls, Edward.
Watson, James.
Wheeler, Thomas.
White, James T.
White, William.
Williams, Harrison.
Williams, Richard.
Wilson, Eli.
Withers, Hayes.
Young, Samuel, Jr.

Total, 113.

CHAPTER XVII.

LIST OF MINISTERS.

Names of the Preachers who have Served the Leading Churches of Charlotte, With the Number of Years of Service of Each

TRYON STREET BAPTIST.

1855 to 1858—R. B. Jones.
1858 to 1869—R. H. Griffith.
1871 to 1873—J. B. Boone.
1874 to 1881—Theodore Whitfield.
1881 to 1885—O. F. Gregory.
1885 to 1892—A. G. McManaway.
1893 to 1896—Thomas H. Pritchard.
1896 to   —A. C. Barron.

FIRST PRESBYTERIAN.

1821 to 1826—S. C. Caldwell.
1827 to 1833—R. H. Morrison.
1834 to 1839—A. J. Leavenworth.
1839 to 1842—T. Owens, J. M. Caldwell, H. Caldwell.
1842 to 1846—J. F. W. Freeman.
1846 to 1855—Cyrus Johnston.
1855 to 1857—A. W. Miller.
1857 to 1865—Alexander Sinclair.
1865 to 1892—A. W. Miller.
1892 to 1893—E. Mack.
1893 to 1896—John A. Preston.
1896 to   —James R. Howerton.

SECOND PRESBYTERIAN.

1873 to 1874—W. S. Plumer.
1874 to 1881—E. H. Harding.

Maryland
Cecil County

Know all men by these presents y[t] I George Cathey of Millford hundred am holden & firmly bound to John Boggs of the township of Nottingham in y[e] County of Chester & Province of Pensylvania in the sum of Six pounds four shilling Currant Lawfull money of the Province aforesaid to be payed to the said John Boggs his Certain Atturney heirs Executors Administrators or Assigns to the which payment well & truly to be made I bind myself my heirs Executors & Administrators firmly by these presents Sealed wth with my Seal & dated this twenty day of November in the year of our Lord God Anno Domini 1737.

The Condition of this obligation is such that if the above bound George Cathey his heirs Executors or Administ[rs] do & shall well & truly pay or cause to be payed unto the above named John Boggs his heirs Executors Administ[rs] or Assigns the sum of three pound two shilling Currant money above s[d] at or before the sixth day of September next ensueing the date hereof without fraud or further delay then this obligation to be void & of none effect or else to Remain in full force & vertue —

Signed sealed & delivered
in the presence of
           George Cathey (seal)

John Linkie
Moses McElwee

If the above said John find a mare which is in a swap from y[e] above bound George Cathey then there is twenty five shillings to go off the said obligation if not pa[i]d by him on this order the above written bond is to stand in full force &c.

CONTRACT DATED IN 1737.

LIST OF MINISTERS.

1882 to 1886—L. M. Woods.
1886 to 1889—J. Y. Fair.
1889 to 1892—R. C. Reed.
1893 to 1895—J. H. Boyd.
1896 to 1903—J. E. Stagg.
1903 to   —M. D. Hardin.

TENTH AVENUE PRESBYTERIAN.

1890 to 1890—Jesse W. Siler.
1890 to 1891—C. W. Robinson.
1892 to 1895—F. D. Hunt.
1896 to 1897—W. G. White.
1897 to 1898—W. A. Wynne.
1900 to   —G. W. Belk.

TRYON STREET METHODIST.

1815 to 1817—W. B. Barnett.
1817 to 1818—Reuben Tucker.
1818 to 1821—Hartwell Spain, Zacheus Dowling.
1821 to 1822—Jacob Hill.
1822 to 1823—T. A. Roseman.
1823 to 1824—Jeremiah Freeman.
1824 to 1825—Daniel Asbury.
1825 to 1826—Elisha Askew.
1826 to 1827—D. F. Christenberry.
1827 to 1828—Daniel F. Waid.
1828 to 1830—Benjamin Bell.
1830 to 1832—Absalom Brown.
1832 to 1833—John J. Richardson.
1833 to 1834—J. J. Allison.
1834 to 1835—David J. Allen.
1835 to 1836—W. J. Jackson.
1836 to 1838—W. R. Smith.
1838 to 1839—W. Harrison.
1839 to 1840—Martin Eddy.

1840 to 1841—A. B. McGilvary.
1841 to 1842—C. Murchison.
1842 to 1843—C. H. Pritchard.
1843 to 1845—W. P. Mangum.
1845 to 1847—W. Barringer.
1847 to 1849—P. A. M. Williams.
1849 to 1851—J. J .Fleming.
1851 to 1853—A. G. Stacy.
1853 to 1854—J. W. Miller.
1854 to 1855—John R. Rickett.
1855 to 1857—James Stacy.
1857 to 1859—E. J. Meynardie.
1859 to 1860—J. W. Miller.
1860 to 1862—F. M. Kennedy.
1862 to 1863—Dennis J. Simmons.
1863 to 1864—C. H. Pritchard.
1864 to 1865—James Stacy.
1865 to 1866—W. C. Power and C. E. Lund.
1866 to 1867—W. C. North.
1867 to 1869—E. J. Meynardie.
1869 to 1870—E. W. Thompson.
1870 to 1871—A. W. Mangum.
1871 to 1873—L. S. Burkhead.
1873 to 1876—P. J. Caraway.
1876 to 1880—A. A. Boshamer.
1880 to 1884—J. T. Bagwell.
1884 to 1886—W. M. Robey.
1886 to 1888—F. D. Swindell.
1888 to 1892—Solomon Pool.
1892 to 1896—W. S. Creasy.
1896 to 1898—W. W. Bays.
1898 to 1901—H. F. Chrietzburg.
1901 to   —T. F. Marr.

CHAPTER XVIII.

DAVIDSON.

A Brief Sketch of the Progressive Town Which Has Grown up Around the College.—Has Macadam Streets and Factories, and a Large Business is Done.—The Corporation Dates From 1879.

The town of Davidson College was incorporated by the Legislature February 11, 1879. Its boundaries include rectangular one mile wide and one and one-half miles long. The first officials were: Mayor, W. P. Williams; Commissioners, W. J. Martin, H. P. Helper, R. L. Query, S. T. Thompson and F. J. Knox.

In 1891, the name of the town postoffice was changed from Davidson College to Davidson. When the college was established, in 1837, there was no town, but as the village grew, there arose a demand that it should be distinguished from the college; hence the name was changed. The officials at this time were: Mayor, R. W. Shelton; Commissioners, S. R. Neal, W. S. Graves, J. P. Monroe, J. L. Bratton and J. W. Summers.

With less than 150 voters, the town, in May, 1897, voted for an issue of $6,000 in bonds for street improvements. As a result, the corporation now has two and one-eighth miles of macadam streets. This has served to stimulate the progressive spirit, and elegant homes and beautiful grounds are to be seen in all parts of the town. Davidson is twenty-two miles from Charlotte by railroad and twenty miles by the county road. Of the latter, ten miles of the twenty is macadamized.

There is a local tax of one-half of one per cent. on the $100 valuation of property and $1.50 capitation tax. This brings in $1,300 annually, the assessed valuation of taxable property amounting to $253,564. In addition to this, the Davidson College property is valued at $160,000 and other exempted property at $15,000, making a total valuation of $428,564. The present officials are: Mayor, J. Lee Sloan,

Jr.; Commissioners, W. R. Grey, F. J. Knox, J. S. White, W. H. Thompson and H. J. Brown. The population, according to Census reports, was 484 in 1890, and 901 in 1900. In September, 1903, the population, including that of the suburbs, was estimated at 1,250. Only about two hundred of these are colored people.

The Linden Manufacturing Company, with 7,000 spindles, began operations in 1891. The plant is valued at $92,000, and employs seventy persons. A cotton oil mill was built in 1900 and was sold to the Southern Cotton Oil Company in 1901. It is worth $35,000. The Davidson Milling Company, manufacturers of flour, is capable of producing forty barrels of flour daily. The eleven stores have a good trade, and the surrounding country sells much produce. In 1903, one thousand bushels of peach seed, which were sold for one dollar a bushel, were shipped from Davidson to Northern markets. Two thousand bales of cotton are sold at Davidson annually and as much more at Cornelius, a mill town a mile distant. There is one hotel and numerous boarding houses in the town, and several small workshops of various kinds.

Until 1886, there was no church in the village, the college chapel being used for public worship. In that year, a part of the campus was given for a church site and a building was erected at a cost of $7,000. An equal amount was expended for improvements in 1903. The church has 220 members and ranks high among Presbyterian churches for liberality. The colored people have two churches, one a Methodist and the other a Presbyterian. Zion Methodist Church, several miles from Davidson, has a membership of nearly five hundred.

Davidson High School has been for several years a first-class preparatory school. The public school is conducted in connection with it for four months every year. The school has a good building, three teachers and an average attendance of about one hundred and twenty.

Davidson College is situated on a beautiful campus of

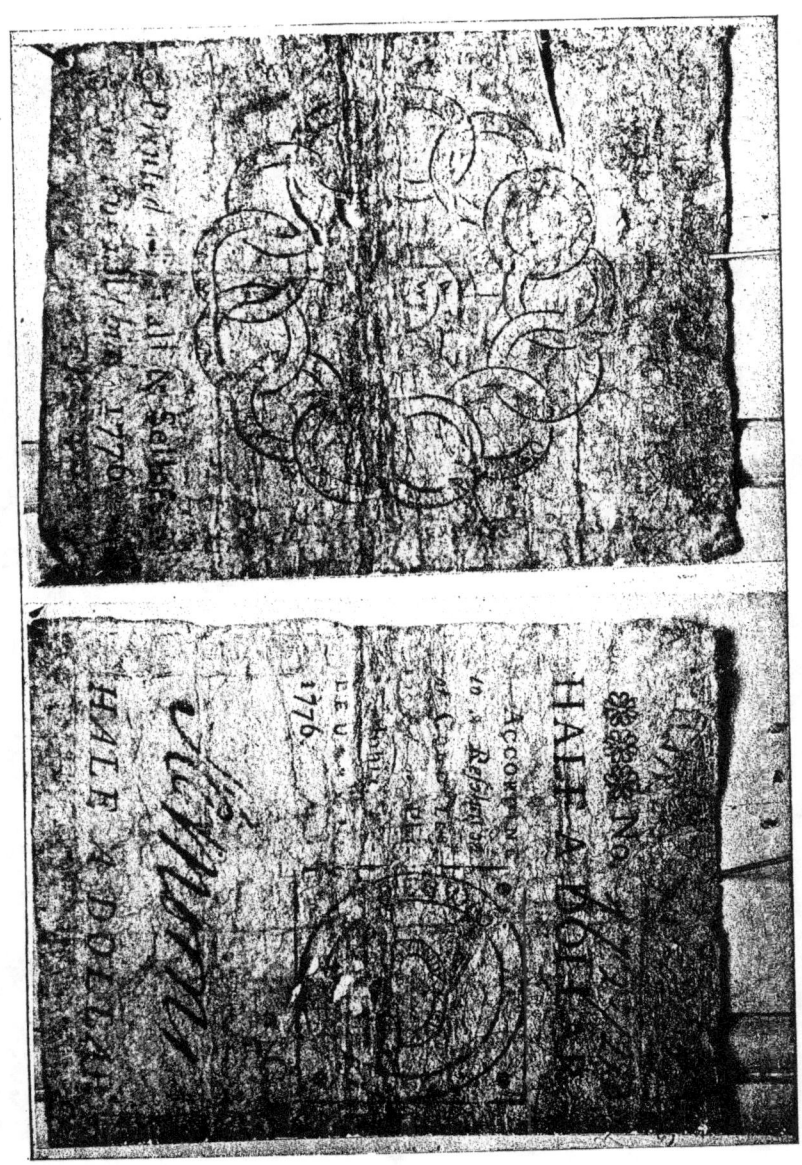

REVOLUTIONARY CURRENCY.

twenty acres, and the grove is occupied with numerous and elegant buildings. The equipment is among the best of Southern colleges and is being constantly improved. The buildings are supplied with artesian water and arrangements are being made for the installation of an electric light plant. The North Carolina Medical College is also located in the town, but it is not officially connected with Davidson College.

CHAPTER XIX.

PINEVILLE.

Brief Sketch of the Growth of the Town Which was Built Where President Polk was Born.—In Fifty Years it has Developed Into a Prosperous Community With Factories and a Population of Seven Hundred.—Creditable Churches and Schools, and Names of Some Prominent Families.

The history of the town of Pineville begins with the year 1852. In that year the railroad was completed to that point and a depot and store were established. The town was incorporated in 1873 with four commissioners: A. C. Williams, John W. Morrow, W. L. Wallis, and Samuel Younts. According to the provisions of the charter, the mayor is elected annually by the commissioners.

The population of Pineville was given at 585 by the Census of 1900. It was about 700 in 1903. Of this number of inhabitants, 125 are colored people. There are ten stores and they carry on a considerable trade. About three thousand bales of cotton are sold in the town every year, and the number has been as high as six thousand.

In 1890, the Dover Yarn Mill was established, the stockholders being nearly all Charlotte people. A weaving department was added to it in 1902 and the two factories combined employ from one hundred and fifty to two hundred hands, and have 9,400 spindles and 400 looms.

Pineville High School occupies a good building, which was erected in 1898. It has three teachers and usually about 125 students. There is no local school tax and the public school is conducted in connection with the High School. From 1896 to 1899 there was a school tax under the provision which required the receipts from it to be duplicated from the State Treasury. There are three creditable church buildings. The Presbyterians occupy a brick church which was built in 1875. The Methodist church was built in 1881, and the Baptist church in 1903. The colored people also

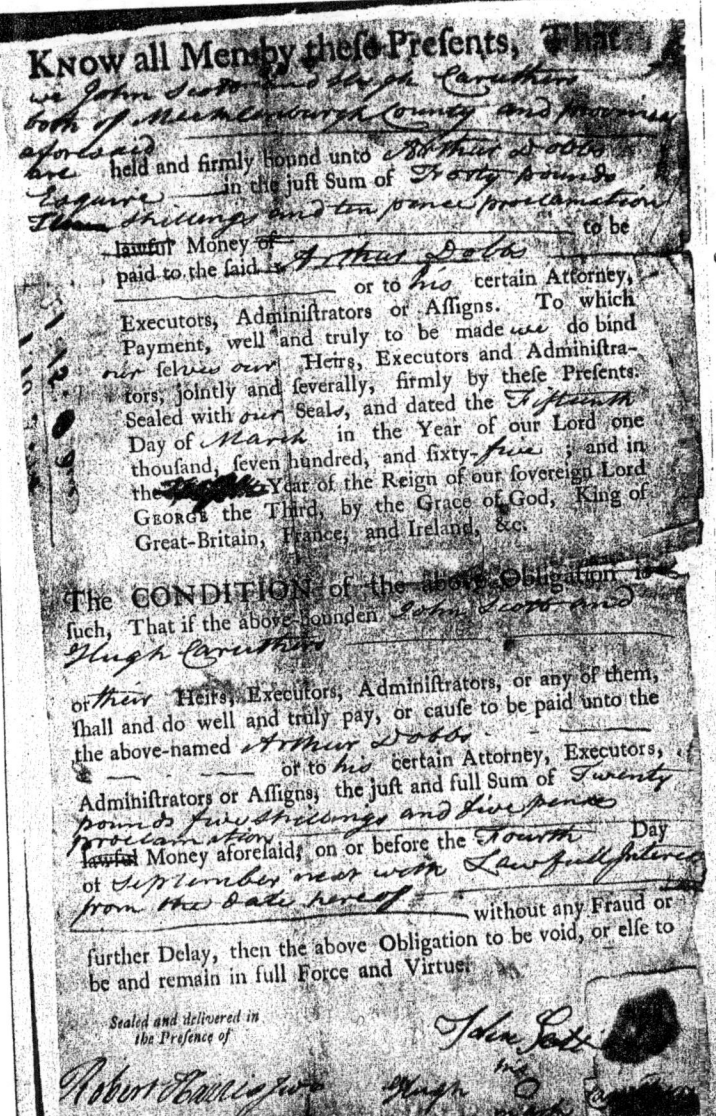

CONTRACT, 1765.

PINEVILLE.

have a Presbyterian and a Baptist church, and a school.

Since the beginning of Pineville in 1852, a number of prominent families have contributed to the growth of the town. Among them are the Alexanders, Fishers, Spencers, Morrows, Younts, Ardrews, Reids, Mansons, Dominys, Stoughs, Millers and Smiths. The town is situated in one of the best sections of Mecklenburg county, and has the distinction of being the birthplace of a President. The site of the house in which James Knox Polk was born, is one mile from the depot on the Camden road.

CHAPTER XX.

MISCELLANEOUS PAPERS.

Characteristics of the Mecklenburg Negro.—Comparative Effects of Slavery and Freedom on the Increase of Population.—Tribute to the Memory of Major Ross.—Important Dates in Mecklenburg History.—List of Mayors of Charlotte.—Acts of the General Assembly Creating Mecklenburg, Establishing Charlotte and Permanently Locating the Court House.—County Road Legislation.

THE MECKLENBURG NEGRO.

The history of Mecklenburg involves the story of three races of men, viz.: the Indian, the Negro and the White man.

The story of the Indian is of the past; that race was lost before advancing civilization as the winter snows fade before the suns of summer. There is no evidence to show that it was ever in the minds or hearts of the white race to destroy the native red race. It was simply a case of the Indian's inability to adapt himself to a civilization higher than that to which his own development had carried him. So far from having a purpose to destroy the Indian, the white man made every effort to Christianize him and to save him from destruction. Even to this day, the National Government is repeating in a sort of final effort the same supporting influences for the benefit of the Indian that have been extended by the white man ever since he landed upon this continent.

As the Indian disappeared, the white man brought into this country another race for the advantage of its labor. Of these it made slaves, and so long as slavery lasted the negro race, in a condition of slavery, was a part of the organization of the Southern social and industrial fabric. As a slave, the negro undoubtedly made great progress in respect to his moral, religious and humane nature. As a slave, he undoubtedly retarded civilization in the South. By the influ-

> Pass Briston to S. W. Meid
> advise & relieve
>   Leonard Faulkner
> July 5th 52

> Pass & repass Briston to his
> wife's house till this pass
> is taken up by me
>   Leonard Faulkner
> Dec. 22 1856.

NEGRO PASSES.

ence of slavery the civilization of the South developed as a sort of semi-feudal proposition rather than in accordance with the American Declaration of Independence and the Federal Constitution. By the influence of the negro the South lost its manufactures and largely its commerce, and became practically a purely agricultural section of the nation. The loss of manufactures and commerce weakened the territory in which slavery existed. From 1830 to 1860, there was little or no progress in wealth or in population. The story of the negro up to the time of his emancipation is a simple one. He was brought to this country regardless of his own will in the matter, he acquiesced easily, and without apparent regret subordinated himself wholly to the white man. These conditions were better than the conditions from which he came. The better element among them were willing to work without coercion. The more inferior types, like the cannibal element from the west coast of Guinea, were very easily coerced and the coercion appears to have been advantageous to them. They prospered as slaves. The freedom from responsibility seems to have been agreeable to them and their position of subordination to the white man seems also to have been agreeable.

The story of the negro as a free man is now in course of working out. The white race has no purpose to destroy the race, nor to retard its progress. As a Christian, the white man wishes in good faith to do everything possible to save and lift the negro. What the outcome will be cannot at this time be predicted. Probably the better element will survive and have a place in our Christian civilization. Probably the inferior element will go the way that the Indian went, in spite of helpful influences to the contrary. In what proportion the better element and the inferior element exist is purely speculative.

It has been said that Africa is a Mosaic of races. The highest and lowest types of these are probably as far apart in traits and characteristics as the highest of them is apart from the traits and characteristics of the white race. In view of this fact, civilization may in the future deal in one way with one element and in a totally different way with another. The white man did one thing with the Indian and another thing with the negro as a slave. The high types of negroes—the product of crossing with the Arab, Syrian and Moor, and also many of the Central African races, such as those among whom Livingstone lived in the latter part of his life, seem at this time to be making most excellent progress towards attaining to the standards of the American white man and his civilization. On the other hand the inferior types are undoubtedly retrograding and there are many instances of almost complete revertal of the descendant of the cannibal to the level of his ancestors.

Regardless of the fate of the negro, the white man will survive and will continue to be the controlling factor in all matters of advancing civilization. It has been made plain that slavery was an influence extremely hindering to the progress of the white man's civilization.

The illustrations of negro types are taken from life and give some idea of the very great varieties in the race.

The negroes of Mecklenburg county will average far above those in the "low country," which means the territory lying on the South Atlantic and Gulf coasts. The county has very few of the descendants of West Coast cannibals, or "blue gum niggers," and a large proportion of Arab, Moorish and semi-civilized pastoral negroes from Central Africa.

FREEDOM VS. SLAVERY.

In gathering and studying statistics relating to Mecklenburg county, some rather interesting facts are made clear. The accompanying table shows the population of Charlotte City, Charlotte Township, Mecklenburg county, and North Carolina, as completely as it can be obtained from 1790 to 1909. It is noticeable that the population of the county decreased between 1830 and 1860. This decrease was partly due to the creation of Union county, which took 5,000 from Mecklenburg's population, but after allowing for this, the increase would be insignificant and there would still remain a decrease of 1,800 to be accounted for between 1830 and 1840. The stationary condition during the thirty years in which the institution of slavery was dominant was mainly attributable to emigration. Many of those who believed in and advocated slavery, emigrated to the Southwest to find more land; while those who had least interest and sympathy with the institution emigrated to the Northwest.

POPULATION.

YEAR.	CHARLOTTE CITY	CHARLOTTE TOWNSHIP	MECKLENBURG COUNTY	NORTH CAROLINA
1790	325		11,395	393,751
1800			10,439*	478,103
1810			14,272	555,500
1820			16,895	638,829
1830	730		20,073	737,987
1840			18,273	753,416
1850			13,914**	869,039
1860	1,366		17,374	992,622
1870	2,212		24,299	1,071,361
1880	7,094		34,175	1,399,750
1890	11,755	15,304	42,673	1,617,947
1900	18,091	26.312	55,268	1,893,810

* Creation of Cabarros in 1792 took 4,000 from Mecklenburg.
** Creation of Union in 1842 took 5000 from Mecklenburg.

After making allowance for loss of population by the construction of Union county, the following comparative statements are found to be true.

Increase in population in Mecklenburg county in the three decades between 1830 and 1860 was practically nothing.

Increase in the three decades between 1870 and 1900 is in round numbers 125 per cent. It becomes clear that this is not merely the result of purely local conditions when the figures for the State are examined.

This table shows that the increase in population in North Carolina since the abolition of slave labor and the consequent establishment of free white labor and commerce and manufactures has far surpassed the increase in the time when slave labor was predominant.

It may be observed that the increase in the one decade from 1870 to 1880 is about the same as that in the four decades preceding 1870. This latter includes the losses incurred in the war, but there remains the comprehensive fact that in the four decades in which slavery was practically dominant, the increase in the population of the State was about the same as in the first decade succeeding the downfall of the slavery system.

Prior to 1800, the trend of emigration was to Mecklenburg county, but it was checked with the introduction of slavery about the beginning of the nineteenth century. For twenty-five years it became smaller and then the tide turned in the other direction, and until the Civil War, Mecklenburg people emigrated to the Northwest or Southwest. Since the South has turned to manufactures and the negro's value as a laborer has consequently decreased, it is probably that emigration will again turn to this section.

TRIBUTE TO MAJOR E. A. ROSS.*

"Among the men who nobly fell that desperate evening (July 1, 1864), in no feeling of partiality allow us to drop a tribute to the memory of Major E. A. Ross, of the Eleventh (Bethel) North Carolina Regiment, a promising young officer. At a point where the battle was raging most furiously, this regiment was pressing on unquailing in the face of a fearful iron and leaden storm when the colonel fell severely wounded, he (Ross) dashed to his place, and in gallantly leading his men on in the desperate charge, received a mortal wound and fell shouting his men on to victory. In the first battle of his country (that of Bethel) he had won his maiden laurels. With "Bethel" emblazoned upon his regimental flag at the instance of the State, he had seen it wave victoriously over the beaten foe on the soil of his native State (at the battle of White Hall, N. C.) And thus fell this gallant

---

*By Daniel B. Rea, of Mecklenburg, in "Sketches of Hampton's Cavalry." Major Ross was only 20 years of age. His remains were interred in the Charlotte Cemetery November 24, 1865.

Bill of Sale

This writing certifies that I have this day sold to James Smyly a negro boy named John. I guarantee the said boy to be of sound mind & body, said to be not more than 30 years old.

Price to be paid $840.⁰⁰

        Henry Arden (L.S.)

Witness.

Done Dec 14 1847
Elmwood N.C.

BILL OF SALE, 1747.

young officer, just as its tattered folds were waving over the first victory in the enemy's land, gloriously dying 'with the battle cry upon his lips and the blaze of victory in his eye.' He sleeps his long sleep on the enemy's soil; and may no fanatical foot ever press the sacred sod upon his bosom. And when the final shout of spiritual victory 'shall swell land and sea,' may his noble spirit and the many others who have died for human liberty, go up washed in the blood of Him who died for the spiritual liberty of mankind."

IMPORTANT DATES IN MECKLENBURG HISTORY.

1740—First Settlers.
1761—Creation of Tryon County.
1761, March 15—Birth of Andrew Jackson.
1762—First School Teacher.
1762, December 11—Creation of Mecklenburg.
1764—First Physician.
1765—Beginning of Charlotte.
1768—Incorporation of Charlotte.
1771—Queen's College Established.
1775, May 20—Declaration of Independence.
1780, September 26—The Hornets' Nest.
1780, October 3—Surprise at McIntyre's.
1781, February 1—Death of Gen. Davidson.
1790—Discovery of Gold.
1791, May 25—George Washington in Charlotte.
1792—Creation of Cabarrus County.
1795, November 2—Birth of James Knox Polk.
1805—Nathaniel Alexander Elected Governor.
1815—First Church in Charlotte.
1824—First Newspaper in Charlotte.
1834—Branch of State Bank Established.
1837—Davidson College.
1837—United States Mint.
1852—Railroad Completed to Charlotte.
1854—Macadamized Streets.
1858—C. M. I. Opened.

1860, December 1—County Secession Convention.
1860, April 20—Mint Occupied by Local Militia.
1865, April 15 to 20—Jefferson Davis in Charlotte.
1867—Biddle University.
1873—Graded School.
1875, May 20—Independence Centennial Celebration.
1876—St. Peter's Hospital.
1881—First Cotton Mill.
1882—Water Works Plant.
1882—Cotton Seed Oil Mill.
1884—Macadamized Roads.
1887—Street Cars.
1889—Evening *News*.
1892, February 1—Charlotte *Observer*.
1893—North Carolina Medical College.
1895—Presbyterian College.
1897—Elizabeth College.

LIST OF MAYORS OF CHARLOTTE.*

1851 to 1852—William K. Reid.
1852 to 1853—Alexander Graham.****
1853 to 1857—William F. Davidson.
1857 to 1859—David Parks.
1859 to 1861—Jennings B. Kerr.
1861 to 1862—William A. Owens.
1862 to 1863—Robert F. Davidson.**
1863 to 1864—L. S. Williams.**
1864 to 1865—Samuel A. Harris.
1865 to 1866—H. M. Pritchard.
1866 to 1867—Samuel A. Harris.
1867 to 1868—F. W. Ahrens.***
1868 to 1869—H. M. Pritchard.***

---

*This official was known as "Intendent" until 1861. Prior to 1851, there had been merely a Chairman of the Town Commissioners. The town officers were elected annually until 1881. Since then, bi-ennially.

MISCELLANEOUS PAPERS. 207

1869 to 1871—C. Dowd.
1871 to 1873—John A. Young.
1873 to 1875—William F. Davidson.
1875 to 1878—William Johnston.
1878 to 1879—B. R. Smith.
1879 to 1880—F. I. Osborne.
1880 to 1883—F. S. DeWolfe.
1883 to 1884—W. C. Maxwell.
1885 to 1887—William Johnston.
1887 to 1891—F. B. McDowell.
1891 to 1895—R. J. Brevard.
1895 to 1897—J. H. Weddington.
1897 to 1899—E. B. Springs.
1899 to 1900—J. D. McCall.
1901 to 1905—Peter Marshall Brown.

***Appointed by Gov. Holden.
**Elected to fill vacancy.
**First "Intendent" elected by popular vote.

ACT CREATING MECKLENBURG COUNTY, 1762.*

(From Iredell's North Carolina Laws, Page 210, Published in 1791.)

I. WHEREAS by Reason of the large Extent of the County of *Anson*, it is generally inconvenient for the Inhabitants to attend Court of the aforesaid County, general Musters, and other public Duties by Law required:

II. *Be it therefore enacted by the Governor, Council and Assembly, and it is hereby enacted by the Authority of the same,* That from and after the first Day of *February*, the said County of *Anson* shall be, and is hereby divided into two distinct Counties, by a Line beginning at Lord *Car-*

---

*Petition presented November 12, 1762. Bill introduced November 17. Passed December 2. Ratified December 11. Signed by Gov. Arthur Dobbs, President James Hasell and Speaker John Ashe. (Colonial Records, Vol. VI, Page 891.)

teret's Line, six Miles North-East from Captain *Charles Hart's* plantation on *Buffalo* Creek, and to run from thence to the Mouth of *Clear* Creek, which empties itself into *Rocky* River, below Captain *Adam Alexander's;* and from thence due South to the Bounds of the Province of *South Carolina.* And that all that Part of said County which lies to the Eastward of said dividing Line, shall be a distinct County, and remain and be called by the Name of *Anson County;* and that all that Part of the said County lying to the Westward of said dividing Line, shall be thenceforth one other distinct County, and called by the name of *Mecklenburg.*

ACT ESTABLISHING CHARLOTTE.*

(From Martin's Acts of the General Assembly, Pages 55 and 56, Published in 1794.)

I. WHEREAS it hath been represented to this Assembly that three hundred and sixty acres of land was granted to *John Frohock, Abraham Alexander and Thomas Polk,* as commissioners, intrust for the county aforesaid, for erecting a court house, prison, and stocks, for the use of said county; which said three hundred and sixty acres of land was afterwards by them laid off into a town and common; and that part of the said three hundred and sixty acres of land hath likewise been laid out into lots, of half an acre each, on some of which good habitable houses have been erected; and that by reason of the healthiness of the place aforesaid and convenient situation thereof for trade, the same might soon become considerable, if it was erected into a town by lawful authority; to which the said *John Frohock, Abraham Alexander and Thomas Polk,* commissioners aforesaid, who are now seized in fee of the said three hundred and sixty acres, and those who claim under them, having consented:

II. *Be it therefore enacted, by the Governor, Council and*

---

*Ratified December 3, 1768. (Colonial Records, Vol. VII, Page 921.)

ARAB-AFRICAN.
Butlers, Body Servants and Mechanics. From Northeast Coast. Color, Dark Bronze to Red Gold. Straight Nose, Thin Lips and Woolly Hair. Women Very Handsome. Arabs Ally Themselves With This Type as an Equal.

SARACEN-AFRICAN.
Preachers, Mechanics and Farm Laborers. From Highlands of Middle Africa. Color, Dark Bronze. High Forehead, Woolly Hair.

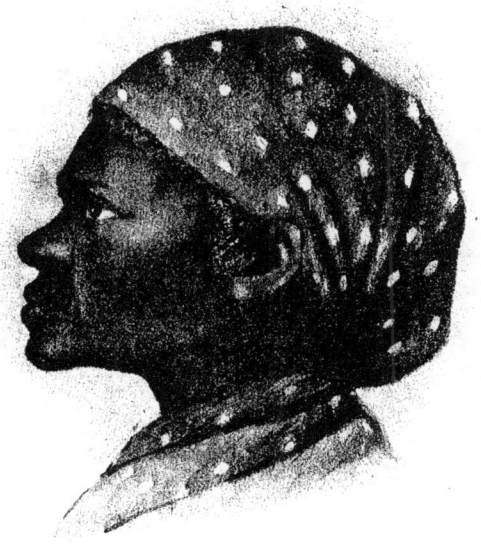

DINKA-NEGRO.
House Servants and Farm Laborers. The "Mammy" Was Usually From This Type. Pastoral People From Upper and Middle Nile. "Strikingly Long and Lean," Predominantly Dark, With Shading Toward Gray.

GUINEA-NEGRO.
Farm Laborers. West Coast. Color, Black. Flat Nose, Thick Lips, Receding Forehead, Kinky Hair. With Savage and Cannibal Instincts. Colloquially known as "Blue-Gum Nigger."

Assembly and by the authority of the same, that the said three hundred and sixty acres of land, so laid off by the commissioners or trustees as aforesaid, be and the same is hereby constituted, erected, and established, a town and town common, and shall be called by the name of *Charlotte.*

III. *And be it further enacted, by the authority aforesaid,* That *John Frohock, Abraham Alexander, Thomas Polk, Richard Berry, Esquires,* and *George Allen,* and every of them, be, and are hereby appointed directors and trustees, for directing the building and carrying on the said town; and they shall stand seized of an indefeasible estate, in fee, in the said three hundred and sixty acres of land, to and for the uses, intents and purposes, hereby expressed and declared; and they, or the majority of them, shall have full power and authority to meet, as often as they shall think necessary; and cause an exact plan of one hundred acres of the said land to be made, as near as may be, agreeable to the streets and lots already laid out, and the residue thereof shall be and remain for a common thereto; and that the said directors shall insert a mark or number on each lot; which said plan shall be kept in some convenient place in the said town, for the view of such persons who have, or incline to have a lot or lots in the same.

IV. And whereas eighty lots already laid off in the said town, have been purchased; *Be it therefore enacted by the authority aforesaid, that the said directors, or the majority of them,* shall make and execute deeds for granting and conveying the said eighty lots to the purchasers, their heirs and assigns, forever; and also to every other person who shall purchase any other lot or lots in the said town at the cost and charges of the grantee to whom the same shall be conveyed, he or they paying to the treasurer herein after appointed, the annual rent of one shilling, for each and every lot; and every person claiming any lot or lots by virtue of any such conveyance, shall and may hold the same in fee simple.

V. *Provided, nevertheless,* that every grantee of any lot or lots in the said town so conveyed, or hereafter to be conveyed, shall, within three years next after the date of the conveyance for the same, erect and build on each lot so conveyed, one well framed sawed or hewed log house, twenty feet in length, and sixteen feet wide, high in the clear, with brick or stone chimney or chimnies, or proportionable to such dimensions, if such grantee shall have two or more lots in said town: and if the owner of any lot shall not pursue or comply with the directions of this act prescribed, for building and finishing a house thereon, then such lot upon which such house shall not be built and finished, shall be vested in the said directors; and they or the majority of them may, and are hereby impowered and authorized, to sell such lot for the best price that can be had, to any person applying for the same, in such manner and under such restrictions, as they could or might have done if such lot had not before been sold or granted; and the money arising by such sale to be applied as the directors, or the majority of them, shall think proper, for the use of the town.

VI. *And be it further enacted, by the authority aforesaid,* that *Thomas Polk* be, and is hereby appointed treasurer of the said town; who shall enter into bond, with sufficient security, to the directors of the said town, in the penal sum of five hundred pounds that he will well and truly account with and pay the monies he shall receive in virtue of his office, to such person or persons as by this act he is directed: and on the death or removal out of the county of the said treasurer, the remaining directors, or the majority of them, by certificate under their hands and seals, shall nominate and appoint one other of the said directors to be treasurer of the said town: and so in like manner, from time to time, as often as the said office shall become vacant as aforesaid; and such treasurer or treasurers shall enter into bond, with security, in the same manner as the treasurer by this act appointed.

VII. *And be it further enacted, by the authority aforesaid,* that in case of the death, refusal to act, or removal out of the county, of any of the said directors, the surviving or other directors, or the majority of them, shall, and are hereby impowered, from time to time, by instrument of writing, under their respective hands and seals, to nominate some other person, being an inhabitant or freeholder in said town, in the place of him so dying, or refusing to act, or removing out of the said county; which director so nominated and appointed shall from thenceforth, have the like power and authority, in all things in the matters herein contained, as if he had been expressed by name, and appointed by this act.

AN ACT FOR ESTABLISHING THE COURT HOUSE IN THE TOWN OF CHARLOTTE, IN MECKLENBURG COUNTY, AND OF REGULATING THE SAID TOWN.*

(*From Martin's Acts of the General Assembly.*)

I. WHEREAS, by an act intitled, *An act for dividing the county of* Mecklenburg, *and other purposes,* the court of the county was directed to be held in the court house then built during the term of seven years, which said term is near expiring; and it having been represented that the removal of the seat of the court from the said court house, and the disposal of the same, agreeable to the before recited act, would be inconvenient to many of the inhabitants of the said county and discourage the trade and commerce of said town;

II. *Be it therefore enacted, by the Governor, Council, and Assembly, and by the authority of the same,* that from and after the passing of this act, the said court house already built in *Charlotte* town, be, continue, and remain the court house of the said county of *Mecklenburg,* and the inferior court of the said county shall hereafter be constantly held therein; any thing in the said act contained to the contrary notwithstanding.

III. And whereas the frequent firing of guns, running horse races, and playing at long bullets, in the said town, is found to have a dangerous tendency; to prevent which, *Be*

---

*Passed in March, 1773, but vetoed by Gov. Martin because of technical errors. Finally ratified March 19, 1774. (Colonial Records, Vol. IX, Page 862.)

it enacted by the authority aforesaid, that from and after the passing thereof, no person whatsoever shall shoot with a gun (except it be to kill cattle or hogs) or immoderately ride or strain any horse or horses, or play at long bullets, within the limits of the said town, under the penalty of paying the sum of twenty shillings for each offence; to be recovered by a warrant, before any Justice of the Peace of the said county, by one of the trustees.

IV. And whereas by an act, *for establishing a town in Mecklenburg county,* every person having a deed of any lot in the said town of *Charlotte* is required to build a house, of the dimensions in the said act specified, within three years after the date of the conveyance for the same, which is found to be injurious to the inhabitants of the said town; *Be it enacted, by the authority aforesaid,* that no person or persons shall forfeit his or their lot or lots for not building on the same, except such lots shall front on one of the main streets in the said town; any law, usage, or custom, to the contrary notwithstanding.

V. *And be it further enacted, by the authority aforesaid,* that every taxable person in the said town shall be obliged to work on the streets thereof six days in every year, if required by the overseer, or find some person to work for him, under the penalty of five shillings for every day he shall refuse or neglect; shall be recovered as is hereinbefore directed.

VI. And whereas some of the trustees of the said town are dead, and others removed out of the province; *Be it enacted by the authority aforesaid,* that *Jeremiah McCafferty, Robert Elliot, William Patterson, and Isaac Alexander,* be added to the trustees formerly appointed, and they are hereby invested with the same powers and authorities as the other trustees: anything to the contrary notwithstanding.

VII. *And be it further enacted, by the authority aforesaid,* that all fines arising in virtue of this act, shall be applied towards clearing and repairing the streets in the said town of *Charlotte.*

COUNTY ROAD LEGISLATION.*

The first legislation in connection with the movement which has resulted in Mecklenburg's good roads, was by the General Assembly of 1879. The bill enacted was introduced by Capt. S. B. Alexander, who by this and subsequent efforts in the same direction, came to be known as the "Father of Good Roads in Mecklenburg." This law, which provided for a special road tax applicable to all residents of the county, met with the disapproval of the people and was repealed in 1881.

Capt. Alexander and others continued their efforts in the county, and in 1884, Capt. Alexander was elected to the State Senate with the avowed purpose of re-enacting the good roads legislation. The bill, which is substantially the road law at the present time, was introduced into the House of Representatives by Capt. W. E. Ardrey, and was passed after a determined fight.

References: General Road Laws, Chapter 50, Laws of 1901, Page 195, Amended to General Road Law, Chapter 445, Laws of 1903, Page 788; Charlotte Township Law, Chapter 615, Laws of 1901, Page 857; Amendment to Charlotte Township Law, Chapter 380, Laws of 1903, Page 629.

---

*Chapter 36, Volume I, contains the account of "Road Building."

INDEX II

----L, W H 159
ABERNATHEY, W D 178
ABERNATHY, Augustus 190 Elig
  156 Hampton 190 Haywood
  190 J N 161 Lewis 190 Robert
  190
ABERNETHY, C W 162 Clem H
  150 E R 154 J N 162 Jas 150
ADAHOLT, M L 167
ADAIR, Thos 158 Wm 158
ADAMS, 36 45 H A 154 James
  178 John 2-3 11 L 171
  Lindsey 144 Lourie 167 W C
  186 Wm 160
ADAMSON, Robert 190
ADDEN, William 62
ADKINS, W H 160
AGNEW, Mary 78 Mr 78
AHRENS, F W 206
AHSMORE, James 61
ALBERTES, Alexander 140
ALBRIGHT, H A 150 J E 150
ALCHISON, J C 158
ALCORN, A S 162 T P 165
ALEXADNER, John Mcknitt 52
ALEXANDER, 7 199 A H 169 A M
  167 A P 163 A W 188 Abdon
  133 140 Abraham 15 17 21
  23-26 28-29 64 132 208-209

ALEXANDER (cont)
  Abram 26 Adam 17 23-26 29
  64 208 Adbon 150 Alphonso
  19 Amos 19 Aswold 158 Benj
  C 174 Benj P 174 C F 163 C
  W 144 152 Capt 98 Catherine
  65 Charles 25 64 Charles G
  182 Col 62-63 D R 165 David
  135 E E 172 Eli 135 Evan 64
  133 182 Ezekiel 139 Ezra 24
  64 F R 169 F T 142 G W 163
  George 132 H C 158 H L 178
  H Q 134 Hannah 77 Hezekiah
  19 23-26 29 64 66 Isaac 26
  64 212 J 169 J A 156 167 J B
  134 165 J G 134 152 163 J H
  165 J J 142 172 J K 163 J L
  142 160 J M 160 J Mc 169 J
  Mck 47 J Mcknitt 12 J N 152
  J O 167 J O D 162 J P 146 J
  S 178 J W 174 178 James 139
  James F 154 Jane 79 Joab
  133 John 137 John D 139
  John M 177 John M'knitt 15
  John Mcknitt 2-6 9 16-17 19
  21 23-28 32-33 43 46 50 54
  64 68 94 132 Jos M'kt 22
  Joseph Mcknitt 65 Julius 142
  177 Laid 137 Leander 163 Lee

ALEXANDER (cont)
  190 M A 152 M C 158 M D
  169 M E 142 174 M Mc 152 M
  R 144 152 M W 55 Margaret
  76 Margaret Polk 65 Mary 75
  Moses 60-61 96-97 Nathaniel
  6 65 133 205 O S P 158 Ossil
  158 Palau 136 Peter 154 R A
  169 R B 152 R C 152 R W 172
  Richard 148 Robert 76 Robt N
  172 S B 134 171 213 S D 160
  S W 163 Salamachus 140
  Samuel J 182 T A 144 T B 172
  T C 169 T P 160 T R 165
  Thomas 77 182 Thos M 163 W
  165 W H 174 W N 178 W P
  172 W S 158 William 190
  William B 186 William Baine
  65 William J 133 William
  Julius 65 129 William S 18
  Wm 148 Zachariah 190
  Zebulon 75
ALLEN, A W 172 C A 152 David J
  193 Dees R 177 George 209 H
  W 152 J H 167 J W 160 John
  140 L 152 Otto A 184 Robert
  140 Thomas 135 William K
  184
ALLISON, J J 193 James 169
AMPUDIA, Mexican Gen 180
ANDERSON, C 142 C J 162 G W
  171 Henry 190 L D 146 W H
  H 171 Wm 160 174
ANDREWS, A B 76 E M 156 G W
  178 Julia M 76
ANTHONY, Paul 108
ANTRICE, J W 146 W M 146
ARCHEY, J W 146
ARDERY, J P 144
ARDREW, 199

ARDREY, J A 65 J W 65 146
  James P 65 Jas P 172 Lydia L
  65 Margaret R 65 Mary 65
  Mary J 65 W E 65 130 134
  144 159 213 William 65
  William A 65
ARMOR, T S 165
ARMSTRONG, Larkin 178 Leroy
  174 M 165 Mathew 178 W L
  184
ARNEY, Henry 169
ASBURY, Daniel 121 123 193
  Eugene 178 William H 186
ASH, John 136
ASHBY, J T 156
ASHE, John 49
ASHLEY, M 154 Wm 156 172
ASHMORE, James 60 62-63 99
ASKEW, Elisha 193
ATCHISON, Wm 174
ATKIN, Mr 102
ATKINS, Mr 101
ATKINSON, Gov 58
AUSTIN, J W 167
AUTEN, Edward M 184 J W 163
  P S 152 S W 154 T J 169
AVERY, Humphrey 66 Mr 18
  Robert W 190 Waightstill 19
  43 66 132
AYCOCK, W M 177
AYERS, A G 148 William H 186
BADGER, Mr 45
BAGLEY, Worth 183
BAGWELL, J T 194
BAILES, G S 158
BAILEY, E D 160 J A 160 W B
  186 W H 134 Wm 156 160
BAILIFF, Fred 162
BAILY, W R 174
BAIN, J J 162

BAINE, Matthew 133
BAKER, Aaron 139 154 Abel 139
  G F 174 Green C 158 J 160 J
  B 150 J C 158 J R 163 Joel M
  154 Michael 139 Wm M 154
BALCH, Hezekiah James 19 24
  66
BALDWIN, Alfred 150
BALES, E M 160 J P 160
BALL, J A 188
BALLARD, Benj 154 F A 146
  Isaac R 190 J L 146 W H 167
BAMBOW, Peter 136
BANCROFT, 44 55-56 George 49
  51 53 Mr 4 46 54
BANKS, Herbert N 186
BARBER, Josiah 176
BARCKLEY, A C 163 H S 163
BAREFOOT, N G 160
BARFLEET, Richard 140
BARKLEY, Enen L 186
BARNES, Bryant 177 James 140
  John 136 S 190 S S D 174
BARNETT, A G 169 Amos 138 E
  L S 152 174 J D 165 J F 152
  J L 152 J W 165 John 138
  John W 172 R C 160 R S 158
  174 T E 146 W A 174 W B 193
  W P 172 W T 172 William 142
BARNHARDT, Christian 66
  Elizabeth 66 John 138
BARNHILL, J W 167 John 139
BARNS, Micajah 140 Robt 156
  William 137
BAROON, George 176
BARRETT, William M 135
BARRINGER, Ann Eliza 66
  Catherine 66-67 79 Charles
  190 D A 170 D M 67 129
  Dolly 66 Elizabeth 66-67

BARRINGER (cont)
  Eugenia 67 George 66 John
  Paul 66 Margaret 67 Mary 67
  Osmond L 67 Paul 66-67 79
  Paul Brandon 67 Rosalie 67
  Rufus 67 Victor C 67 W 194
  William 67
BARRIS, E C 146
BARRITT, W R 165
BARRON, A C 192
BARRY, Anne 67 Dickey 25
  Richard 24 67 132
BARTLETT, J H 158
BARTLETTE, W F 158
BARTLOW, Charles J 190
BASS, Buston 154 Jas A 154
BAXTER, Daniel 139
BAYS, W W 194
BEAL, Charles 154 John 154
BEAN, J T 167
BEARD, J C 165 J F M 166 J H
  148 J M 166 J O 170 Joseph
  165 Mr 18
BEASLEY, James 190
BEATTIE, G H 165 J O 176
  William 133
BEATTY, A W 162 J W 150 154
  John 162 Samuel 162 Wm
  150
BEATY, G W 188 George 190
  Isaac 135 John 139 William L
  182
BEAVER, J M 163 178
BECKER, 112
BEEK, Wm A 154
BEEMAN, G C 158
BEHRENDS, L 144
BELK, Brelon 137 E A 188 G W
  193 John 140 S E 173 Samuel
  E 181 Wm 156

BELL, 67 Benjamin 193 C E 156
159 J A 165 J C 170 J D 165
Martha 74 Mary J 65 N J 160
R C 172 Samuel 185 W T 188
BENFIELD, B E 163 Dan 171 H S
163 J R 163
BENHILL, William 139
BENNETT, D E 184 D G 172 G W
148 J G 148 Thos 162
BENSON, Edward 190 H A 176 R
P 170
BENTLEY, M W H 160
BENTON, Sam'l 174
BEON, W F 186
BERNS, George 140
BERRIER, S T 188
BERRY, Arthur 190 Jas 148
Richard 209
BERRYHILL, Alex 174 Andrew
174 J H 162 J J 158 Jas L
158 W A 174 W G 144
BIGART, Jas 156
BIGGART, W S 143
BIGGERS, Houston 175
Johnston N 138 R H 188 Robt
175 W A 163 William 175
BIGHAM, Green 178 J R 153 J W
153 M S 158 Robert Jr 139
Samuel 139
BILLOW, W H 148
BINGHAM, J H 154 J M 170
Joseph 135
BIRD, H C 178 W L 154
BISHOP, W T 146
BISSELL, Edward 121 Humphrey
121 123
BLACK, A J L 166 David H 138
Ezekiel 153 J B 156 J C 166 J
H 160 J M 152 J N 160 J P
167 J S 160 John 136 138

BLACK (cont)
Josiah 143 R L 188 S 166 S J
167 T A 160 T J 152 T N 146
W 134 W A 166 Wm M 170
BLACKARD, Jas 168
BLACKBURN, John 139
BLACKWELDER, A 158
Catherine 66 D C 175 D M
177 James 178 Margaret 79
Moses 150
BLACKWOOD, Eli 178 Joseph
133 138
BLAIR, James T 181 S M 174 S
W 156 William 62
BLAKE, S N 146
BLAKELY, A C 163 J B 166 J J
152 M F 152 W F M 166 W J
163
BLAND, Anthony 190
BLANKENSHIP, J N 156 S P 156
T E 168
BLOUNT, J M 163
BLYTHE, J W 166 S W 168
BOGER, John 190
BOILES, E L 184
BOLD, Robert 137
BOLTON, G B 148 J C 162 John
R 130
BOND, Newton 142
BONNEY, Eli W 186
BOONE, Gov 101 J B 192 J B T
143
BOOTH, Mr 22
BOSHAMER, A A 194
BOST, Daniel 138 J K P 176
Matthias 138 Moses 175 S C
175
BOURDEAUX, A J 143
BOWDEN, Louis 178 S D 158
BOWDITCH, Mr 13

BOWMAN, R 160
BOYCE, C B 156 Hugh 156 S T 160
BOYD, David 156 Hugh 177 J A 156 J B 144 J G W 158 J H 193 J J 156 Jepe A 158 John 67 158 Margaret 67 Mattew B 182 P L 146 Thomas 138
BOYLES, J A 166
BRACKETT, Wm 150
BRADDOCK, 104
BRADLEY, J H 170 J L 154
BRADSHAW, J T 154
BRADSTON, V M 160
BRADY, James A 139 R A 166
BRANDON, Elizabeth 67 Matthew 67
BRANNAN, Patrick 148
BRATTON, J L 195
BRAWLEY, R W 170
BRAY, Winfield M 150
BREFFARD, W J 146
BREM, T H 71 150 Walter V Jr 188
BREVARD, A F 58 Alexander 69 Dr 25 E M 187 Eph 35 47 Ephaim 80 Ephraim 5 17 21 23-24 26-27 33 48 65 67 70 Hamilton 135 Jane 68 70 John 68 70 Margaret 80 Margaret Polk 65 R J 207 Sally 69
BREWER, J H 160
BRIAN, James 181
BRIDGERS, W B 150
BRIDGES, Joseph R 186 Nicholas R 182 W A 168
BRIGHT, O P 186
BRIGMAN, C C 152
BRIMER, Alfred 158

BRINES, J W 168
BRINGLE, D L 144
BRINKLE, John 148 Thomas 148
BRINKLEY, H 160
BRISTOW, J C 160
BRITT, John 166
BRITTON, Ed F 144
BROADSTREET, J R 176
BROADWAY, Whitson 150
BROOM, A T 177 Allen 137 Calvin 177 N W 177 S A 177 Samron 177 Solomon 177 Wilson 177
BROTHERTON, John 162 Wm 162
BROWELL, E M 167
BROWN, A H 144 A M 156 Absalom 193 Alex 148 B D 170 B F 166 C W 158 H J 196 H W 166 I E 148 J 166 J C 170 178 J D 165 J F 163 J G 172 J J 148 J K P 168 J L 134 J M 170 J W 156 Jas W 158 John 136 139 John E 134 Karl 184 Nicholas 148 O N 165 Peter Marshall 207 R E 158 S H 163 Samuel 135 T G 168 W A 184 W H 172 W J 153 W L 170 Wm 144 Wm J 144
BROWNING, J M 176
BRUCE, G W 174 Jas 168
BRUM, C F 178
BRYAN, Joseph 137 T J 158
BRYANT, Sydney 156 T B 188
BRYCE, J Y 175 Wm 175
BRYON, L J 188
BUFF, Henry 150
BUGLIN, Patrick 148
BULKWINKLE, F C 188

BULL, Mr 101
BUNDLE, Thomas 148
BUNIER, J 154
BURGE, D L 184
BURGWYN, Fred 162 W H S 163
BURKHEAD, L S 194 White 170
BURLEYSON, Benj 166
BURNETT, J S 148
BURNS, Cobb 190 S A 168
BURRIS, J T 146
BURROUGHS, John 178
BURTON, Hutchins G 133
BURUS, Jas 150
BURWELL, A 134 J B 174 R T 177 Robt T 177 W R 177
BUSHBEY, Will 136
BUTLER, E G W 181 J T 146 N A 184
BUTT, John F 184
BUTTON, Daniel 140
BYNUM, Rufus 148 W S 171
BYRUM, James 152
CABLE, Lewis 148
CAHILL, John 178 T J 148
CALDER, Wm 144 Wm Jr 148 Wm Sr 148
CALDWELL, D A 163 178 D G 163 D P 163 D T 68 David 62 68 82 97 G M 163 G W 133 Green W 129 134 180-181 Green Washington 68 H 192 H M 178 H W 163 Harriet 68 J E 143 J M 163 192 J N 178 J P 58 J S P 156 John 135 190 Lafayette 182 M E 170 R B 143 178 R N 163 Robert 138 Robert Jr 138 S C 68 192 S P 144 Samuel C 3 Samuel Craig 68 W W 166
CALLOWAY, J C 146

CALLWALL, James 62 John 62
CAMBELL, R H 146
CAMERON, Catherine 81 Judge 48 52
CAMERSON, William 136
CAMPBELL, C M 163 Charles 55 Cyrus 138 Geo L 162 J C 156 J H 184 J P 174 J W 154 James 104 M O 184 Robert 62 100 T J 144 Thos 156 W H 153 163 Z C 188
CANDOR, F J 188
CANIPS, Henry 150 John 150
CANNEDY, Robt 143
CANNELL, Jas H 150
CANNON, Dink 184 Fred 150 Joseph 150 Sid 150 Wm S 150
CANSTER, Martin L 150
CAPPS, John 174
CAPUS, William 191
CARAWAY, P J 194
CARMICK, J 154
CARNES, John 85
CAROTHERS, James 139
CARPENTER, E P 186 J 166 J C 156 166 Jas 162 Levi 168 Marcus 168 W B 156
CARR, Julian S 58
CARRICKER, Levi 248
CARRIGAN, Adam 170 R A 170 Robert Jr 137 Robert Sr 137 W F 166
CARRIHER, Andrew 138
CARRIKER, S C 176
CARROLL, Francis 150 J H 146 John 138
CARRUTH, John 22
CARSON, J L 176 William 138
CARTER, C G 186 F B 148 Green

CARTER (cont)
 191 Jas 150 Jas N 150 R A
 145 W R 145
CARTERET, Lord 208
CARUTHERS, J A 156 J B 156 J
 K 158 Robert 60 63
CASHION, Frank 170 I W 170
 Jas 170 Thomas 148 W M 148
CASKILL, Tim L 148
CASWELL, 12-13 27 50-51 Gov
 17 49 Richard 11 15 18
CATES, Frederick R 186 Lucky R
 186
CATHBERTON, John 137
CATHCART, J R 170
CATHEY, A A 161 B G 168
 George 92 Henry 158 J L 162
 J W 144 146 166 Jean 92
 John 179 W 154 W A 162 W H
 162
CATON, Elijah 174 Sylv 174
CAUBLE, C M 186
CHADWICK, Hubert S 185
CHAINEY, Peter 141
CHALKLEY, W P 150
CHAMBERS, A D 190 Clarence
 191
CHANCY, John 148
CHANNELS, Michael 139
CHAPLE, Jesse 138
CHAPMAN, 122 A F 186 A H 150
 A J 150 Mathero 150 Peter
 150 R P 150 Robert P 130 Wm
 150
CHARLES, Ii 52
CHEARY, J J 186
CHEEK, Randolph 136
CHEERY, William 140
CHENTENBERG, C E 156
CHESHIRE, Bishop 108 C M 163

CHESHIRE (cont)
 M E 153
CHOAT, J M 158
CHOATE, A D 158 R W 158 Wm
 158
CHRESTAINBURY, S D 166
CHRIETZBURG, H F 194
CHRISTENBERG, Allison 170
CHRISTENBERRY, D F 193
CHRISTENBURG, A B 150 A H
 170 Jas 170 R F 170 Wm 170
CHRISTY, J H 154
CHUNN, Rosalie 67
CHURCH, Eli 160 Martin 160
CILLEY, Gordon H 184
CLANTON, J B 154 W D 158 W S
 130 134
CLARK, 22 A A 158 A W 174 Alex
 170 Almirive 162 J A 154 J F
 168 J T 188 J W 168 James
 148 Jas 168 John 162 Jonas
 24 68 Joshua 136 P M 156 R
 F 158 W A 156 W C 174 W H
 174
CLARKSON, Heriot 134
CLAY, J M 176
CLAYWELL, J F 148
CLEMMONS, R R 155
CLENDENNEN, J W 144
CLINE, H B 176 W D 176
CLINTON, A J Jr 191
CLISK, John 138
CLONTZ, Ab 168 Henry 137
COBB, C A 156 Thomas W 19
COBBLE, J D 146
COCHRAN, Benjamin 60 63 J C
 178 J M 174 R C 174 R E 178
 Robert 141 Robert M 138
 Thomas S 141 W L 177 Wm R
 174

COCHRANE, J C 166 J F 153 J L 163 L J 163 N R J 163 R B 163 W C 163
CODY, John 182
COFFE, B M 156
COFFEY, A S 160
COHEN, E B 144
COLBERT, D L 184
COLE, Matthias W 181
COLEMAN, T P 179
COLLING, John 148
COLLINS, Dennis 150 J F 144 John 174 W M 186 William 191
CONDER, Wiley 148
CONNELL, S C 150 Thomas 139
CONNER, James 139
CONNOR, James 133 T A 146
COOK, Dolly 66 J P 163 Nicholas 66 R W 163 Robert 140
COOKSON, Thomas 105
COOPER, F W 186 H L 186 J M 156 Lucius B 191
COOTS, Jacob 171
CORBLE, Robt R 177
CORK, Walter 170
CORNELIUS, M A 170 N 191
CORNWALLIS, 110
COSTENER, Jacob 150
COSTLEY, James 141
COSTNER, J S 188
COTCHCOAT, J H 174
COTCHKIP, Aug 156
COTLHARP, H T 160
COTTRAIM, A W 146
COUGHRAN, Eli 137
COUSAR, Mary 85
COWAN, T B 144
COWLES, Calvin J 129 Josiah D 130 W D 130

COX, Eli 156 J D 176 Thomas 166 W C L 162
COZBY, W L 186
CRAFT, A J 177
CRAIG, Alex 176 E 188 M F 146 Moses 140 W B 188
CRAIGHEAD, Alexander 68 70 104-105 Jane 70 Mr 106
CRAMER, Stuart W 130
CRANE, Job S 172 Madison C 150 Wm 150
CRAVEN, W P 134 170
CRAWFORD, James 84-86 Jane 84 Micajah 158 R R 143 Thomas 86
CRAWSON, J F 144
CREASMAN, J 153
CREASY, W S 194
CRENSHAW, John 172
CRESWELL, A H 161
CRISP, J C 74
CROCKER, W J 168
CRONE, V H 186
CROOK, W W 188
CROSS, W D 168
CROUCH, Charles 34
CROW, Grace 85 James 85
CROWEL, E M 156
CROWELL, Charles 136 E M 143 168 Israel 160 John 141 S W 158
CRUMP, R H 146 S R 184 T C 184
CRUSE, M C 146 Peter 176
CRUTHERS, T M 172
CULBERSON, J W 155
CULER, J A J 150
CULLET, Ezekiel 171
CULP, A A 160 E 186 John 172
CUMMINGS, D 188 Francis 69 W

CUMMINGS (cont)
   M 188
CUMMINS, Francis 18-20
CUNNINGHAM, Edward 191
   Ernest L 191 Jacob I 135
CURETON, Jeremiah 85-86 Lydia
   L 65 Thomas 85 William J 86
CUTLER, William 182
DAFTER, Obed 136
DALLARHIT, J D 156
DANIEL, W S 186
DARNALL, J J 158
DARNEL, David 136
DARNELL, Jack 153 John 135
   John L 135
DARTMOUTH, Lord 47
DASINGER, Francis 148
DAVENPORT, J W 162
DAVID, Ed 191
DAVIDSON, Adam Brevard 69 B
   H 148 B W 148 E C 68 134
   146 Edward C 181 Ephraim
   70 Gen 72 205 George 69-70
   Harriet 68 J F 143 175 J P A
   144 J S 150 J W 148 Jack 69
   Jane 70 John 17 27 69-70
   132 Margaret 70 Parmela 70 R
   A 178-179 R E 183 Robert 69
   Robert F 206 Sally 69 W F
   134 W L 148 William 3 18 68-
   69 133 William F 206-207
   William L 182 William Lee 69-
   70 William Lee Jr 70 Wm 17
DAVIE, 6-7 32 46 50 80
   Archibald 70 Gen 47 Gov 52
   Sarah 70 W R 16 William R 4
   12 17 William Richardson 70
DAVIS, A J 188 Black 142 Daniel
   139 Duncan F 186 Edgar S
   186 G W 160 H W 170 J C

DAVIS (cont)
   158 J G A 143 J M 163 J T A
   179 Jas T 172 Jefferson 206
   John 62 John N 134 M L 146
   R A 174 R A G 143 R B 142
   Robert 60 63 S W 134 T G 144
   W A 174 188 W E 176 W H
   163 W M 186
DAVYS, George 62
DAWNS, Robt R 151
DAY, Ed 171
DEARMOND, A L 160 J A 170 J
   B 172
DEATON, J C 153 J R 166 J Z
   166 L L 163 Sarah 74
DEGGARHART, J L 156 J V 156
DELLINGER, W 166
DELNAUX, Alfred 184 Florian
   186
DEMARCUS, Lucian 184
DEMON, Jacob 174
DENNIS, Charles 141 J T 163
   Littleton 66
DENTON, John 155
DERIVAFANOLI, Vincent 123
DEROSSET, 108
DESOTO, 109
DEVINE, W G 168
DEWEESE, Calvin T 170 G B 170
DEWEY, T W 57
DEWOLFE, F S 207
DICKINSON, 13
DICKSON, J H 186
DIEHL, Patricia S 13
DINKINS, James 139
DIXON, Col 72 H M 163 Hugh M
   156 Ira B 137 Maj 187 S L
   160 W W 155
DOBBIN, Mark H 151
DOBBS, Gov 100-101 103

DOBSON, Hiram 148 John 68
DOHERTY, Dr 68 W W 165
DOMINY, 199
DONALDSON, William D 188
DONNELL, W T 174
DONOVAN, Jeremiah 148 Philip 148
DOOLAN, E 176
DORSETT, J F 143
DOUGHERTY, Charles R 182 James 133
DOUGHTY, Lester D 188
DOUGLAS, Joseph 132
DOUGLASS, James F 188 Joseph 135
DOVE, George 138
DOWD, C 56 207 W C 134
DOWLING, Zacheus 193
DOWNS, Frank 162 Henry 70 J T 144 160 179 L W 144 W H 160 William 140
DOWNY, William 136
DOYLE, Bernard 150
DRAUGHTON, D D 188
DREWRY, A G 156
DUAN, T J 162
DUCKWORD, R 135
DUCKWORTH, G P 160 George 139 H D 153 J A 153
DUGLASS, S A 162
DUKE, William F 188
DULE, T C 171
DULIN, D H 163 Daniel 153 J C 163 J M 146 John 163 Matthias 163 R H 163 T L 163 T S 168 W C 171 W L 171 W W 163
DULS, C H 134
DUNCAN, R M 186
DUNLAP, David R 70 Jane 70

DUNLAP (cont)
  Polly 71 Sam'l N 151
DUNN, A J 160 A S 160 Geo 160 J A 133-134 J R 144 Jas R 172 John 22 Robert Jr 139 Rufus C 186 S W T 160 William 139
DUPERT, Mr 108
DURHAM, Robert Lee 187
DYER, W G 143
EAGLE, A 143 John 143 174 W H 174
EARNHARDT, C D 163 Geo 156 S O 163
EARNHEARDT, J H 153 J M 144 153 S O 153 W C 153
EATON, Professor 112
EAUDY, Paul 176
ECKFELDT, Frederick 130
EDDY, Martin 193
EDGERTON, Wm 191
EDLEMAN, T P 146
EDMIRTON, J R 148
EDWARDS, A J 146 E 146 G W 170 J A 168 J M 156 James M 184 M A 158 Marshal 155 Shepherd 155
EFIRD, J C 146 J E 146
EISENHART, Henry 92
ELAM, Ralph 184
ELLER, A 155 John 148 S W 155
ELLINGTON, Werley P 151
ELLIOT, Robert 212
ELLIOTT, H W 162 Hugh 135 J A 144 172 John B 136 S H 65 144 172 Solomon 93 Thomas 139 W A 153 William 139 Wm 148
ELLIS, Dan 156 Gov 78 Thomas 191 Wm 158

ELMORE, J T 148 R P 188
ELMS, 128 J I 167 170 J P 144 153 167 Jas H 172 John D 188 W D 144 167
ELWOOD, 122
EMERSON, M H 170
EMMONS, Professor 111-112
ENGEL, J 144 Joans 174
ENGENBURN, J 174
EPPS, W D 174
ERVING, John 162
ERWIN, A A 157 A R 158 Andrew 130 Edward 94 F L 158 Francis 135 J C 158 J M 158 J R 134 157 Jennie 71 John R 178 John Randolph 71 Mary 82 Sallie 71 W R 179 William A 185 William L 71
ETITT, Wm M 167
ETTERS, H P 162 P P 162
ETTRES, J H 156
EUDY, John 179
EVERETT, 67
EVERHART, William 191
EWING, G R 153 Nathaniel 78 Rebecca 78 W E 153
EZZELL, J A 144 172 M F 144 160
FAGGART, D C 176
FAGGOT, Dan 179
FAIR, J Y 193
FAIRES, G N 162
FALLS, W A 176 W T 188
FANCY, John 151
FANNING, Edmund 98 107
FANYGEN, M L 143
FARLEY, A 151
FARR, Henry 135
FARRA, John 139
FARRICES, Z W 174

FARRIOR, Ernest N 188
FARRIS, J A 172 M C 163
FAT, John 135
FAUCET, J C 169-170
FAULKNER, James 85 Thomas 85
FAUNT, D L 151 D M L 150 Sam'l 151
FERREL, Gabriel 139 John 139 William 139
FERRELL, J F M 179
FERRET, John Sr 136
FERRIS, Arthur B 186
FESPERMAN, J C 166 M W 163
FIDLER, 122 D H 165
FIELD, W B 146
FIELDS, M A 172
FILE, J F 176
FINCHER, Asa 174 J E 172 Levi J 177 O 172
FINGER, John 155 N F 188 R T 186
FINK, L A 184 Peter 176 Philip 138 Son 138
FINLEY, M K 146
FINSHER, Joshua 140
FISHER, 199 Alfred 179 C A 176 E L 179 Francis 179 J V 179 J W 153 William 140
FITE, J C 151 Robt D R 151 Sam'l 151 W J 156
FLAKE, William B 184
FLANIGAN, B F 168
FLEMING, J J 194
FLEMMING, George 138
FLENEKIN, J B 158
FLENIGAN, Elias 136 Michael 137 R G 179 Robert 136 Samuel E 136 William 136
FLENIKEN, L B 172

FLENNEGEN, John 24 29
FLENNEGIN, David 71 John 71
FLENNIKEN, Robert G 182
FLORE, James 144
FLOW, David 94 E 146 J M 146 John 137 R H 144 153 T J 163
FLOWE, J C 168
FLOWERS, Henry 140 Jessie 151 R B 171
FLOYD, John W 186 Matthew 108 Wm 176
FOARD, C 188 C A 163 E M 176 Henry 163 J C 163
FOBES, John 137
FOGLEMAN, P L 148
FOIL, T A 188
FOOTE, 56
FORBES, Archibald 182
FORCE, Col 45 Manning F 36 Peter 4 35-37 44 49 Samuel S 55 William 36 William L 35
FORD, J E C 188 John 71 77 W C 153
FORDS, H H 146
FOREMAN, Rufus 191
FORREST, A 188
FORSYTHE, John 140
FOSTER, J H 171
FOUTS, J M 170
FOWLER, Geo W 177 Moses F 177
FOX, Stephen 133 W T 151
FRANCIS, W A 184
FRANKLIN, 36
FRAZIER, I A 162 I S A 144 153 Isaac A 158 J C R 174 J L 174 J T 158 John 143 M L 143 Richard 158 W F 158
FREDERICK, W T 184

FREDRICK, J R 143
FREELAND, John 138
FREEMAN, Gideon 140 J F W 192 J J 168 Jeremiah 193 John E 186 Mcc 168 Neal B 186 R C 134 W H 158
FREEZE, Adam 138
FRENCH, Frank 190 J B 142 Wm 172
FRICK, Jacob 148
FROHOCK, John 208-209
FRONEBARGER, John 168
FRY, Burt A 184
FULENWIDER, Barbara 79
FULLBRIGHT, D B 151 J K 151 K 151 M 151
FULLENWEIDER, H 143
FULLENWIDER, John F 182
FULLER, John 140
FURGUSON, F A 179
FURR, A W 176 Allen 176 D C 176 John 146 M L 175 Mat 176
GADD, Robt 175
GAISESEN, W G 146
GAITHER, S 129
GALLAGHER, Arch 148 Jas 148
GALLANT, J A 158
GALLOWAY, J S 153
GAMBLE, Jas 160
GARDEN, 8 55 Alexander 5 33
GARDENER, D 166 H T 166 S 166
GARIBALDI, John N 184
GARNER, Barzilla 138 Henry 170 Wm 158
GARREN, Andrew 162
GARRETSON, Arthur 136 John 137
GARRIBALDI, Thomas 184

GARRISON, A D 172 Alex 155
    Charles 191 J S 153 J W 164
    John 184 John C 139 R W
    163
GASTON, J A 171
GASTONIA, A Lewis 188
GATES, M W 168
GATLIN, G W 176
GATTIS, J A 188
GAUGUS, Jacob 138
GAYLOR, Theophilus 137
GENTH, F A 113
GEORGE, E P 160 Iii 19 Iii King
    21 Prepley 160
GIBBES, J A 165
GIBBON, Corrina 72 J H 122
    John 72 John H 130 Mary 72
    N 134 Robert 71 Robert Jr 72
GIBBS, F E 191 Jack 166
GIBONY, David 135
GIBSON, C S 178 D M 179 J A
    144 153 J J 166 J M 164 Mr
    122 T A 166
GILBERT, Harrison 171 Jas 171
GILES, M O 174 S H 174
GILLESPIE, A M 147 J R 165 R L
    144 S A 146 T D 142
GILLETT, J H 143
GILMER, Walter 191
GILMORE, Josiah 138
GINGLES, Samuel 93
GINN, G R 185
GIRARDIN, 13
GIVENS, Samuel 137
GLASS, J D 186 James R 182
GLEASON, Jas W 148
GLENN, D P 144 153 F C 153
    Gideon 128 R W 185
GLOVER, B C 160 John R 181
    Joshua 153 T M 158

GLUYAS, 122 Thomas O 134
GOFORTH, George 139 J L 185
    John F 185
GOODLOE, Daniel R 56
GOODMAN, J E 154 John 138
    151 S C 148
GOODNIGHT, John 138
GOODRUM, C H 153 J W 166 W
    J 153 Zeb 167
GOODSEN, H M 146
GORDON, A E 172 Clarence L
    190 J P 168 J R 168
GORE, V L 186
GRADY, A M 137 Jas 148
GRAHAM, 55 Alexander 206
    Anna Eliza 75 Emmor 130
    Gen 47 50 George 6 22 72 75
    132-133 Gov 48 J R 146 J W
    160 James 150 James C 190
    John 191 John M 186
    Johnson 184 Joseph 6 20 57
    69 72 S R 143 Samuel 135
    William 24 72 William R 184
    Wm A 56 78
GRANT, John W 191 R W 149
GRAVES, A C 149 W S 195
GRAY, A N 130 174 Edward S
    186 H N 143 Jacob 140 John
    190 N 144 Nelson 139 R F
    143 Ransom S 182 Sherrod
    133 W W 153
GREELY, C E 186
GREEN, E 188
GREENE, 5
GREENHILL, Lawson 162
GREENWOOD, Mr 12
GREER, E S 156 Z B 156
GREGG, D H 162 Hugh 135
GREGORY, O F 192 R E L 186
GREY, Robt 51 W R 196

GRIBBLE, J R 144 152 Marcus H 185
GRICE, J M 188
GRIER, Adam G 191 Addie 72 Andrew 67 133 C E 151 Calvin Eli 72 D D 185 E C 134 158 J C 144 J G 174 J H 179 J M 144 J O 164 J S 166 Jennie 71 John C 172 Lawrence 173 Margaret 67 Marshal 151 Nancy 82 Paul B 177 R A 134 R H 144 172 S A 143 178 S M 158 Sallie 71 Sam 179 T H 155 Thos 158 V G 185 W L 156 W M 151 William M 72 Wm M 71 Z A 71
GRIFFIN, B F 171 Egbert 173 G 155 J H 143 J J 160 Thomas 148 Wesley 176
GRIFFITH, A E 160 C F 179 Farrington 177 I G 173 J Henry 177 J L 177 J W 173 Marley 177 R H 192 T D 173 Thomas D 182
GRIGG, B W 151
GRIGSBY, Hugh Blair 55
GROSE, 122 Ralph 186
GROVER, Austin 176
GROVES, J R 158 R A 153
GRUB, Absolom 171
GUDGER, R V 150
GULLEDGE, H M 188
GURLEY, W D 168
H----, Prof 51
HADLEY, Joshua 60 63
HAGLER, Allen 176 J A 176 Jacob 176 King 100-101 Nelson 176
HAGONS, H M 166
HAIL, W H 158
HAINANT, Henry 157
HALL, A G 160 Amzi 164 D W 145 H L 174 J F 160 James 74 76 82 138 Jas 168 Joseph 140 N C 157 R B 160 T M 164 Thomas 62 W H 158 William 191
HALOBOUGH, J M 179
HALSELL, H 188
HALSHOUSER, A R 149
HAMBLETON, James 140
HAMILTON, J R 166 Joseph 138
HAMLIN, Benjamin 191
HAMPTON, G W 188 George 133
HAND, A J 153 R H 152 Robt H 145 W L 152 W Lee 145
HANEY, E H 168
HANFIELD, Jas W 173
HANNA, George B 130-131 J M 149 J W 157
HANNEL, A R 156
HANNON, D A 179 J J 173 J N 156
HANSER, W T 145
HANSON, Stephen 140
HARBESON, James 140
HARDIN, M D 193
HARDING, E H 192
HARDY, John 186
HARGET, Harrison 147
HARGETT, A J 168 Aleg 157 F 186 H M 147 Henry 140 Osborne 147 William 141 William C 188
HARGRAVE, Robt W 177
HARKEY, D E 173 David 141 J J 173 Jacob 145 John 141 181 M L 173 P C 146 T B 147 Tom M 145 W F 179 Wash 173
HARMAN, Paul 171

HARMER, Thomas H 130
HARMON, G W 188 Levi 156
HARON, S L 157
HARRETT, O H 186
HARRINGTON, Ed P 177
HARRIS, C C 155 164 Charles 67
    72 Charles J 73 Col 60
    Corrina 72 Cunningham 133
    Edwin 67 Elizabeth 67 F R
    164 Francis 149 G W 164 H W
    134 Houston 137 Hugh 136
    Isaac 137 J C 156 J H 156 J S
    179 James 6 16 62 73 132
    Joe F 188 John 81 133
    Jonathan 133 Mary 67 Morris
    157 N J 168 N O 153 R H 156
    Rachel 82 Robert 73 Robt 96
    Samuel 62 Samuel A 190 206
    Samuel H 137 W C 153 W L
    143 William Shakespeare 73
HARRISON, Adam 135 J K 68
    134 167 John K 181 Robert
    141 W 193 W H 166
HARRY, W B 174
HART, Charles 136 208 N M 167
    W S 160 W S M 158
HARTE, John 133
HARTGRUE, R D S 155 W W 155
HARTIS, A L 147 J L 173 J S 173
    M A 147
HARTLEY, Richard 139
HARTLINE, Adam 155 Andrew
    155 D L 155 G H 155 P 155
HARTMAN, H M 176
HARTS, J H 160
HARTSELL, J M 149 Wm 179
HASELL, Chief Justice 92
HASKELL, Jas T 145
HASTINGS, W C 166
HATCHUP, A 157

HAULEY, John 140
HAWKES, F L 5
HAWKINS, Albert 151 F A 159 J
    A 151 J P 151 158 John 138-
    139
HAWKS, 44 Dr 48 50 54 Francis
    L 55
HAYES, Elijah 168 Leander W
    190 S L 162
HAYMIE, C 188
HAYS, J B 157
HAYWOOD, J M 188
HEAD, R L 185
HEADLY, Wm L 168
HEATH, J M 188
HEAVNER, J J 151
HECKS, Wm 171
HEDGEPATH, Geo 157
HEITMAN, O B 158
HELDT, Enoch 170
HELFER, P E 171
HELMER, Joel 141
HELMS, Albert 171 Alex L 177
    Asa 177 Charles 140
    Copeland 171 D B 171 E T
    155 Elbert 177 Eli W 171
    Enoch 171 Gilliam 171 H M
    147 Hosea 171 J A 147 J L
    171 J W 147 John 171
    Joshua 171 Josiah 171 177
    Kennel 171 Noah 177 Noah J
    177 W M 177 William 140
HELPER, H P 195
HENDERSON, Arbell V 190
    Archibald 65 David 135 I S
    153 J E 134 J H 178 J W 168
    James 139 John T 191 L P
    145 M A 150 Samuel 17 T M
    153 Thomas W 191 Thos 133
    W F 166 W M 143 160 W M F

HENDERSON (cont)
  147 W R 157 W T 160 William
  28
HENDLEY, J M 186
HENDRIX, Grayson 171 J M 166
  L J 171 Sanford 171 W P 166
HENLEY, Thomas 137
HENNESSEE, S A 185
HENNIGEN, J E 173
HENNING, F A 185
HENRY, B G 157 Berry 168 J B
  157 Mr 13 Patrick 12 26
  Terrell 168
HERBERT, W G W 148
HERNDEN, J J 189 M P 189
HERNDON, W P 185
HERRON, Calvin 164 G T 153
  George T 145 Green 164 J M
  153 J W 157 John 164
HERRVELL, R 151
HEWES, 12-13 Joseph 11 15
HICKEY, R H 186
HICKS, T W 149
HIGGENSON, John 168
HIGGINS, B 191
HILL, C H 157 D H 73 H H 145
  153 Isabella 73 J C 145 J W
  155 Jacob 193 Jas R L 170
  John D 185 Miles 153 Milton
  153 W J 145 W P 142
HILLIS, W H 186
HILLSBOROUGH, Lord 98
HILTON, S H 143 147
HINKLE, J L 151
HINSON, G T 153 M 179
HINTON, A J 155
HIPP, Andrew 162 J F 168 J M
  162 John 162 L A 168
  Pinkney 162 Wm 162
HIRSHINGER, Herbert J 184

HOBBS, F 153
HODGE, John 141
HODGES, C J 164 Oliver L 185 P
  B 164 W G 164
HOFFMAN, J L 150 176 J M 176
  Miles 157 R Y 189
HOKE, C W 186 W P 185
HOLBROOK, A 147
HOLBROOKS, John 137 R S 166
HOLDEN, E M 147 Gov 207
  Samuel 137
HOLDSLAW, R 155
HOLLAND, Robt 157
HOLLINGSWORTH, B 143 J B
  155
HOLLISTER, G H 186
HOLMES, B 160 Hugh 136 T
  Lindsey 145
HOLMS, T L 153
HOLTON, Charles S 74 Harriet C
  74 Harrison 74 Henry C 74
  Leopold 74 Margaret Q 74
  Mary S 74 Rachel Regina 73-
  74 Sarah 74 Thomas J 73
  Thomas Jefferson 73 Tom F
  145 Virginia W 74
HOOD, A B 160 H C 168 J M 164
  J R 164 J W 134 Junius 135
  R L 174 Reuben 141 W L 160
  W S 164
HOOKER, John 136
HOOKS, Dave 164
HOOPER, 12-13 27 122 William
  11 15 18
HOOVER, A B 162 F M 174 J D
  151 J T 151 T H 151 T J 179
  W G 151 W H 151
HOPE, Thomas 139
HOPKINS, P 147
HORD, R M 185

HORTON, J W 188
HOTCHKIP, S A 159
HOTCHKISS, J T 169
HOUSE, Jacob 138
HOUSER, Lewis 191
HOUSTON, David 138 G W 164
  H L 166 Harper C 145 J M
  166 James 132 Simon 191
  William A 182 William Jr 141
HOVIS, A J 168 Monroe 153
  Moses 162
HOWARD, J M 173 Lewis 137 R
  H 145 T M 153 Thomas 145
HOWELL, David 149 E M 143
  Jas 149 151 S A 143 W E 176
  W J 177
HOWERTON, J R 58 James R
  192
HOWEY, Geo W 145
HOWIE, A J 166 Aaron 140 F M
  174 J H 160 J M 174 S E 164
  Sam'l M 174 W H 179 Wm 160
HOWOOD, Robert 140
HOYLE, D R 151
HUBBARD, Prof 50
HUCHISON, J M 133
HUCKS, D W 164 John 164 S L
  166
HUDSON, J H 147 Wilson 173
HUFFSTELLER, W T 185
HUMBLE, David 149
HUMMEL, R C 186
HUMMONS, John 136
HUMPHREY, T L 157
HUMPHREYS, Charles 189
HUNSUCKER, J W 168 N J 176
  Wm 168
HUNT, F D 193 H H 186
HUNTER, A B 179 A G 164 A J
  154 C 56 C L 55 115 168 D P

HUNTER (cont)
  153 G S 164 H C 166 H S 170
  Henry Jr 139 Hester 164
  Hugh 164 Humphrey 56 74
  Isabella 74 J F 166 J H 143 J
  Harris 177 J M 164 J M C 164
  J P 116 J W 147 John 74 M B
  153 Mad 177 Martha 74 Mary
  74 R B 151 R C 164 R H 164
  Rebecca Wilson 74 Robert
  Boston 74 S C 164 Smiley W
  177 T H 153 Thomas 74 Wm
  May 74
HURSTON, A W 147
HUTCHINSON, Charles 138
  William 74
HUTCHISON, 22 C N 179 Cynes
  N 145 D S 146 Elizabeth 75
  84 Grace 85 J H 153 J M 134
  J R 164 James 135 Jane 84
  Jas M 145 Margaret 84 S B
  162 Samuel J 135 Sarah 85
  Wm 24
HUTSPETH, L 153
HUX, John 170 Wm M 170
HYMANS, S 145
ICEHOUR, Martin 138
ICEHOWER, H F 167 W S 152
  Wm S 145
ICENHOUR, P E 149
INGLE, Peter 157
INGOLD, E P 145
INGRAM, J 134 Otis 191
IREDELL, Margaret 81
IRVEY, Will U 137
IRVIN, Robert 17
IRWIN, 128 Caleb 133-134 G C
  164 Giles 139 John 78 137
  Mary 75 Mary A 78 Robert 6
  24 29 75 94 132-133 William

IRWIN (cont)
75
ISEMAN, Ann Eliza 66
ISENHOUR, C M 188
ISREAL, Jack R 145
IVEY, B F 185 Jess 140
JACCOUR, John 137
JACK, Capt 17 24 47 James 15 18 20 22-23 26-27 75
JACKSON, Andrew 75 82 84 86 Andrew Sr 75 84 C H 170 Clemens E 189 Elizabeth 75 84 Hugh 75 85 John 149 Margaret 82 Peavon 139 Robert 75 85 W J 193 W K 170
JACOBS, G W 143
JACOBSON, A L 189
JAMES, Paul 148
JAMESON, J W 155 T J 155
JAMISON, E A 159 Emory 173 J L 179 J R 166 S N 148-149
JANNISON, R J 149
JARRETT, Samuel 162
JARVIS, Gov 81
JASWA, L R 143
JEFFERSON, 3 36 45-46 Mr 17 37-38 54 Th 14 Thomas 2 11 55
JENKINS, A B 166 Aaron 151 David 153 Edward 151 G A 189 Jacob 153 Miss 71 R L 188 Sam'l 151 Tillman 151
JENNINGS, C J 147 G W 160 J H 179
JETTON, J L 134 165
JIMISON, Arthur 135 M E 185
JOHN, E Edward 149 Will 136 William 140
JOHNSON, Dan 173 Daniel 151

JOHNSON (cont)
Dr 46 Elijah 29 Ellis H 190 G W 176 H F 159 Henry R 190 J A 173 J F 146 J H 170 J J 164 J M 176 J W 157 Jacob 176 James 28-29 Joseph 45 151 Matthew 171 R L 151 Rufus 149 T A 162 Thomas 149 W P 147 W R 76 Wallace D 185 William 191
JOHNSTON, A N 168 Alfred 153 Anna Eliza 75 B A 165 Cora J 76 Cyrus 192 D E 160 D H 162 F E 162 Frank G 76 G W 160 J H 155 160 J S 165 John 138-139 Joseph 4 Julia M 76 M F 166 Mary E 77 Mitchell 136 Robt W 145 Rufus 138 S A 160 S R 177 Samuel Jr 139 William 75 139 207
JONES, 13 49 55 A J 170 Anthony 191 Ben F 189 David 149 Edmund 71 H C 58 134 Isaac W 129 Joel 139 Milton 143 R B 192 Rachel Regina 73-74 Rebecca Wilson 74 Sarah 70 Walter G 186 William 191 William H 187
JORDAN, 115 B F 147 Mc H 164 Sansom 170
JULIN, Jacob 139
JUNDERBUSK, John 140
KAISER, D W 168 Solomon 168 T P 168
KALE, A E 185
KALORAM, Thos 151
KANAPUM, A E 149
KARY, William M 135
KATZ, Aaron 174 Jacob 145

KEAN, J B 151 J H 151 R F 151 S W 151
KEARNS, J F 170
KEASEY, Thomas 100
KEELOUGH, Ebenezer 138
KEENAN, Jas 171 John 164 Peter 157 Robt 145
KEENER, H O 185
KELBY, William 4
KELL, J T 134 159
KELLER, Henry A 189
KELLEY, A A 166 Lawrence 149
KELLY, Henry 191 William 138
KENAN, D G 173
KENEDY, Joseph 35
KENIER, J R 173
KENNEDY, F M 194 Jepe 149 Joseph 25 47 Lawrence J 189 Wm 153
KENNERLY, E M 170 John 170
KENNON, Col 18 Mr 21-22 William 76
KENTY, George 137
KERNS, J A 166 J D 153 T J 165-166 T M A 164
KERR, Adam 140 E D 187 J T 159 Jas 173 Jennings B 206 John B 159 Professor 112 R D 179 R O 157 Sam'l 173 William 139 Wm J 143 148 154
KESIAH, Wm 143
KESTLER, P H 155
KETCHIE, Wm 170
KEY, Albert 157
KEZIAH, William A 182
KILOUGH, Ed 164
KILPATRICK, W F 157
KIMBALL, J L 159
KIMMONS, Joro 137 R M 176

KING, Andrew 140 C C 153 Ezekiel 162 G 155 G W 168 J A 153 157 Oscar D 186 P A 174 R R 147 Thos 162 Wm 168
KINNEY, B 153
KINSEY, Jack A 145
KIRBY, P J 148 Patrick 149
KIRK, J C 164 John 134 Wm 164
KIRKLEY, Thos 168
KIRKPATRICK, H Y 160 J F 159 J M 179 J R 178 S A 173 T A 174 W L 179
KISER, Frederick 137 G A 176 N D 176
KISLER, Wm 149
KISSIAH, G W 168 T A 168 Thomas 187 W M 168
KISTLER, G H 168 Wm H 145
KIZZIAH, J W 146
KLUTS, R 175 W H A 175
KNIGHT, W M 177
KNIPPER, Thos 153
KNOTTS, Charles 191
KNOX, F J 195-196 J D 159 J H 145 J M 156 158 J N 159 J S 174 Jas F 158 Robert R 184 S W 166 T N 159 W H 157
KNUIPE, Henry 151
KUESTER, William F 186
KURTZ, P K 149
KUSTLER, M E 179
KYLE, P H 155
KYLES, Fielding 155 Wm 155
LACY, Drury 177
LAMB, Mike 151
LAMBERT, J M 155 Richard 141 Wm 155
LANCEY, Charles 137
LANDER, Fred 190 William T 187

LANDLER, Orminer 143
LANE, A D 149 Andrew M 136 J D 151
LANGFORD, O S 187
LATHAN, John 85 Sarah 85
LATTIMER, A M 151
LAUBREY, A C 189
LAUGHLIN, D P 151
LAWING, A W 151 J M 161-162 J S 162 J W 151
LAWLER, John 151
LAWRING, David 168 P W 168
LAWSON, 103 Hudson 155
LAY, A L 176 J G 176 J M 189 J W 176 W J 176
LEACH, L 166
LEAVENWORTH, A J 192
LEDFORD, C M 176 John 151
LEDWELL, David 155
LEE, 5 D P 159 J A 160 J M 143 J T 160 S B 160
LEEPER, Jas 179
LEFTER, W H 176
LELAIN, Al 148
LEMMOND, William L 136
LEMMONS, Robt 134 William 191
LEMONS, Archibald 182 Cyrus Q 181 Jackson C 182
LENTZ, Aaron 179 R R 166
LEOMS, D 182
LEON, Lewis 174 Louis 145
LEOPOLD, Jacob 145
LEQUEX, F S 187
LESLIE, Samuel 85 Sarah 85
LEVI, J C 145
LEWELLYN, J 146
LEWING, Andrew Jr 139 John 139
LEWIS, C J 147 E 152 Fred E

LEWIS (cont)
189 J A 185 J M 147 J W 185 Lindsey 155 W H 160 William 52
LIBERMAN, C S 159
LIGHT, John 138
LILLINGTON, Col 49 William 190
LILYCROP, 122
LINDER, R W 189
LINDSAY, R T 187 Thos 179
LINDSEY, H L 189 W G 151
LINEAR, N 187
LINEBARGER, Marshall 155
LINEBERGER, J M 151
LINKER, Aaron 176 George 138 Jas 176 Moses 176 W R 176
LINTON, S E 185
LINTZ, P W 178
LIPKIND, Daniel 189
LITTLE, Bryant 177 S S 166
LIVINGSTON, Alex 169
LLOYD, Margaret 78
LOCKE, Elizabeth 79
LOFTAIN, Samuel 62
LOFTEN, Martin 155
LOGAN, Andrew 61-62
LONG, J C 134 John 137 Margaret 67
LOOKER, J C 168
LOSSING, 44 55 Benjamin J 56 Benson J 45
LOURIE, R B 156-157 S J 168
LOVE, Christopher 139 D L 174 179 J M 179 Joseph 135
LOWRANCE, J A 169 L N 170 R W 170 S L 170
LOWRIE, J B 143 156 Judge 71 78 Lillie 78 Margaret 76 Mary 76 P J 156 Polly 71 Robert 76 Samuel 76 133

235

LOWRIEE, Samuel 133
LUCAS, Allen 135 H C 162
LUCKEY, T S 166
LUDWICK, S 179 Wm 179
LUND, C E 194
LUTHER, Daniel 138
LYERLY, Egbert 184
LYNCH, Robt 162
LYON, J S 185
LYONS, Patrick 150
LYTLE, Claud 191
M'CLURE, Matthew 24
MACE, C 187
MACK, E 192
MACON, Nathaniel 3 20
MADDAN, G W 155
MADDEN, J P 157
MADISON, Mr 10 President 5
MAGLAUCHLIN, John 140
MAKALER, Frank 171
MANESS, J A 159
MANGUM, A W 194 W P 194
MANNING, J W 168 Jas 168
MANNIS, A W 178 T M 178
MANSON, 199 Wm L 172
MAPE, Peter 136
MARKS, J G 174 S H 159 S S 174 T E 174 T H 159 W S 174
MARR, T F 194
MARRABLE, W M 151
MARSHAL, Jas H 151
MARSHALL, 13
MARSHBURN, J M 157
MARTIN, 3-4 6-7 33 55 211
   Alexander 76 Edward 138 147
   Francis Xavier 5 11 Gov 2 8
   38-39 43 45 47 50-51 Hugh
   76 Jane C 76 John 170
   Josiah 98 Judge 32 46
   Samuel 17 76 132 Samuel A

MARTIN (cont)
   76 W 155 W J 195 William 137
MASON, J J 164 R C 164
   Richard 135 Robert G 182
   Robt G 168 W B 149 Wiley J 149
MASSAGEE, C A 189
MASSEY, Benjamin 85 Henry 133 Thomas D 181
MASSINGALE, R H 160
MATHISON, Jas 155
MATTHEUS, W M Jr 142
MATTHEWS, Hugh A 182 John 140 W 134 W M 174
MAXWELL, Carrie 77 D G 77 163 D S 168 George M 184 Guy 76 Mary E 77 Nancy A 77 P P 175 R H 146 W C 77 207 W M 164 William 76
MAYES, W D 134
MAYGEEHEE, William 140
MAYS, William 137
MCADEN, Hugh 104
MCALLISTER, C 166 H B 173
MCALROY, Hugh 140
MCAULEY, A E 166 D N 166 H E 166 J C 170
MCBEAN, John 149
MCCAFFERTY, Jeremiah 212
MCCAIN, Hugh 138
MCCALL, Alex 162 C N 164 D H 164 J A 147 153 179 J C 168 J D 134 207 J M 147 James 140 182 Jas 162 John A 182 Josiah F 164 Matthew 140 R W 164 William 182 William J 182 Wm 147
MCCALLAN, Robert 62
MCCALLOK, Elias 136

MCCARVER, Alex 147 Jas 147
MCCAUL, James 61 63 99
MCCAUSLAND, W B 151
MCCEWON, J M 164
MCCLELLAN, Daniel C 189 W A 149
MCCLURE, C A 155 Matthew 76
MCCOMBS, A H 174 James 138 Jas 164 Samuel 127 133
MCCONNELL, A M 149 J F 153 J H 153 Jas H 159 R A 170 T A 149 T M 164 T Y 153 Thomas 149
MCCONNEYHEAD, M 191
MCCORD, D L 168 W C 162
MCCORKLE, Charles M 184 H P 155 J G 144 152 John 137 Julius 191 R B 143 Robt 151 T J 164
MCCOY, Albert 166 C W 166 J F 166 J G 167 J R 176 M A 167 W L 168 William 140
MCCRACKEN, Elisha 139
MCCRARY, Jordan 174
MCCRUM, H A 175
MCCULLOCK, John 140
MCCULLOH, 87
MCCURRY, J A 161
MCCUTCHEON, John 94
MCDANIEL, E A 176 E B 176
MCDILL, Mary 74
MCDONALD, Allen 143 D W 154 D Watt 145 J H 154 J R 179 John H 145 Worth 179
MCDONNELL, S K Jr 187
MCDOUGHALL, M 147
MCDOWELL, F B 57-58 134 207 Hugh 139 Nancy 77 R W 77 Robert 93
MCELHANY, E A 179 S L 179

MCELROY, Jas W 174 S J 152 Sam'l J 145
MCENTIRE, M L 176
MCFADDEN, John 166 W C 191
MCGAHEY, T C 162
MCGARAR, Wm W 149
MCGHEE, Isaac 168 J T 162 Joe B 162 T J 162
MCGILVARY, A B 194
MCGINN, I H 159 J M 168 J N 159 N C 159 R F 153 Thomas F 145 Thos 174 W A 159
MCGINNESS, Robt C 177
MCGINNIS, George 149 J J 164 John 147 R C 143 S A 153 T M 164
MCGOWAN, James E 189 John W 187
MCGRAW, James 138
MCGUIRE, John 149
MCGWIRT, David 177 H A 177
MCIRE, Thomas 136
MCKAY, Joseph V 185 Robt W 164
MCKEE, Alex F 182 David 132 Elias R 182
MCKEEVER, Wm 145
MCKELLERAND, Joseph 139
MCKELVIA, William 138
MCKEMEY, George 82 84-86 John 86 Margaret 82
MCKENZIE, 68 Wm 179
MCKINLEY, John 145 President 183 189
MCKINNEY, J W 160 R M 161 Sam'l 151 T A 174 Wm 174
MCKNIGHT, Robert 139
MCKNITT, 13 J 19 Joseph 17
MCLAUGHLIN, J J 164 W J 164
MCLEAN, Dan W 150 H W 164 J

237

MCLEAN (cont)
  D 157 J L 159 Thos 160
MCLEARY, Michael 77 133
  William H 133
MCLEOD, J M 147 M D L 146
MCLEON, Francis D 184 James
  H 184
MCLOYD, Daniel 136
MCLURE, J 155 James 164 Jas
  M 148 John 136
MCMALLEN, J H 161
MCMANAWAY, A G 192
MCMILLAN, J C 157
MCMULLEN, William 191
MCMURRAY, Robert 62
MCNEELEY, J J 169
MCNEELY, J F 169 T N 147
MCQUAIG, J 161 James 157
MCQUAISE, Jas 157
MCQUAY, S 155 W H 155
MCRAE, Thomas 135
MCRANEY, Sam'l 173
MCREA, James 161
MCRELEY, Roderick 137
MCRUMB, S J S 159 S W 159
MCWHIRTER, Agnes 78
  Alexander 78 Elizabeth 85
  George 85 J H 153 James 153
  Jane 68 Samuel 85
MCWHITE, J 178
MEAGHIM, W H 151
MEANS, Catherine 67 G W 162 J
  K P 162 J S 154 James 139 P
  B 179 W G 67 W N M 143 W N
  S 154
MEEK, James 139
MEGAHEY, Jas A 170
MEHOLERS, John 143
MENTEITH, James 139
MEREDITH, J 149 Stephen W

MEREDITH (cont)
  149
MERRITT, Wm N 174
MEYNARDIE, E J 194
MILES, Augustus 139
MILLEN, R A 179
MILLER, 199 A W 192 Claude
  184 D M 161 H M 188 H M W
  164 Henry 138 J F 155 J M
  146 164 J W 194 R C 166 S J
  164 Svminus J S 179 Thomas
  137 W C 170 W T 173
MILLS, Thomas M 190 W T 162
MILTON, Alex 171 Francis 171 J
  G 161
MINCEL, Willis 157
MINOR, H J 171
MISENHEIMER, J H 176 J J 175
MITCHA, John 155
MITCHELL, 112 Allison 171 C J
  174 Professor 111 116
MIZE, R L 185
MOAD, John 151
MOBLE, Joel 170 Johnvmartin J
  M 170
MOLLAY, Thos P 148 Tim P 148
MONROE, J P 195
MONTEITH, H L D 153 M O 153
  Moses O 145 R J 153 Tobt J
  145
MONTGOMERY, A F 168 J H 153
  J P C 164 Jas 168 Leander
  164 R C 179 Robert 139
  Samuel 29 Walter W 185
MONTIETH, R A 166
MOODY, M D L 168
MOONEY, Caleb 168
MOORE, Alexander 135 Bishop
  191 David 140 Dr T J 176 J M
  179 J W 134 146 James 135

MOORE (cont)
  Jas C 170 Joseph D 189 Mary A 78 Pleasant 177 R D 166 T J 134 W H 187 W W 173 Walter S 58
MORETON, W R 176
MORGAN, Zac 170
MORRIS, D W 164 G C 147 173 J C 164 J S 151 J T 161 J W 173 Martha 77 Nancy A 77 Solomon 137 W G 164 W T 161 William 77 Zebulon 77
MORRISON, Alexander 77 133 D M 164 Eugenia 67 Isaac Jr 139 Isabella 73 J E 159 J M 174 James 62 77 141 John 62 138 140 Marshall 164 Neal 77 Neel 141 Neil 24 Neill 25 29 R H 67 73 192 Robert C 138 S N 164 W S 166 W T 157 Washington 77 133 William 77 132
MORROW, 199 B F 159 Benjamin 133 J L 146 John W 198
MORTON, Mr 106 Rev Mr 107
MOSELEY, M 143
MOSER, Coleman O 184 H S 159 Henry 137
MOSS, Edward L 191 Edward W 190
MOSTELLER, Charles E 186
MOSTERS, F A 168
MOTZ, Mayfield 151
MOWERY, Henry 170
MOYLE, 122 Henry 145
MULLIS, Coleman 168 Simon 177
MULSON, Robt 149
MULWEE, J W 159 John T 182

MUNDAY, O M 155
MUNSEY, John 149
MUNTEETH, William 136
MUNY, T N 143
MURCHISON, C 194
MURDOCK, W D 155
MURPHY, Daniel C 151 Dennis 187 Harry 185 Micjiel 187
MURRAY, James W 150
MYERS, J S 134 James 161 W R 134 161
NAIL, Richmond 149
NANCE, J A 170 W T 179
NANTZ, A E 149 C R 166 Calvin 151 D J 166 R E 151 R R 151
NARSON, J G 155
NAVNEY, R J 185
NEAGLE, J F 179 Jas H 159
NEAL, A G 134 Brooks 191 G A 153 155 Hannah 77 L M 145 172 Louisa 77 Martha D 77 Mary 77 Nancy 77 P A 77 145 S R 145 172 195 S W 77 Susan 77 W A 186 W B 77 164 Wm B 145 Wm H 77 Z C 77
NEEDHAM, Thos 151
NEEL, W B 173
NEELE, Andrew 138 James 138 Samuel 141
NEELEY, Samuel 139
NEELY, J J 157 T W 152 Thos W 145 Wm A 173
NEESE, John W 187
NELSON, J H 161 J M 179 R A 164 Richard 191 T J 164 W 170
NESBIT, John 78 Mary 78
NESBITT, J G 155
NEVINS, J G 159

NEWELL, A H 153 D S 164 W A 173
NEWITT, William 138
NEWLAN, Thomas 191
NEWTON, Eli 149 John 149 Meredith 149 Robt 151
NICHOLAS, J S A 154
NICHOLS, B G 161 J S 143
NICHOLSON, J B 168 J R 159 John 162
NILE, 55
NITZE, 112
NIXON, A 100
NOLES, A T 147 John 164 W A 147
NONE, John 137
NORFLEET, Mary 76 Robert 76
NORMAN, William S 139
NORMANT, Thomas T 182
NORMENT, A A 143 175 Alfred A 181 Charles 171 G M 161 Isaac 145 153 Jack 145 153 Thomas 171
NORT, H W 189
NORTH, W C 194
NORTHEY, 122
NORWOOD, R F 179
NULL, J T 155
O'BYRNE, M 189
OATES, Brawley 77 Coowy 143 D W 168 David 78 Jas 175 Jas H 143 Lillie 78 Margaret 78 Mary 78 W D S 187
OATS, R M 167
OCHLETREE, Duncan 17
ODELL, G W 162 J C 162 M 185
OGLESOY, F 191
OKELY, C 159
OLIPHANT, J R 170
OLIVER, Calvin 149 James 18

OLMSTED, 112 Professor 116
OPPENHEIM, S 145
ORMAN, J E 145 153
ORMAND, Adam 137
ORMOND, Samuel 137
ORR, C M 168 D K 146 Franklin 164 G B 159 J A 147 J F 153 J G A 168 J J 147 J L V 168 J T 145 Jas T J 133 Joe L 168 N C N 153 N D 147 159 S H 143 T J 161 W S 168
ORRELL, Sam'l 171
OSBORNE, Adlai 78 Agnes 78 Alexander 78 Col 96 E K P 134 Edwin J 78 F I 134 207 Frank Irwin 78 Harvey 164 J F 176 J H 173 James W 78 Jas W 129 134 Jean 78 John L 145 John M 187 Judge 57 Luther M 184 Margaret 78 Mary 78 Mary A 78 N B 170 R D 78 Rebecca 78 Rev A 187 Robert A 139 Robt 176 W B 169
OSTWALT, Francis 155
OTTER, H 188
OTTERS, Cooney 175
OVERSTEIN, Catherine 66 Christian 66
OVID, 19
OWENS, H C 129 J Henry 175 T 192 W A 142 William A 206
OWREY, Michael 138
OZMENT, John J 184
PACE, Albert P 189 Young 176
PACKARD, John 149
PAGE, E M 147 Harry 185 J F 166
PAINE, Tom 11
PALMER, C B 178

PAREDOE, S M 143
PARISH, Nicholas 135
PARKE, George 140
PARKER, D W 185 Hugh 133
  James 135 John 139 S S 159
  Wm 151
PARKS, D K 159 David 206 G L
  159 George 162 Henry 182
  Isaac W 190 J L 147 John Sr
  139 Miah 175 Samuel 139
PARRISH, Andrew M 139 Walter
  L 189
PARROTT, J W 187
PARSONS, Larkins 178
PARTON, 84
PATILLO, Henry 96
PATTEN, James 189 James P
  189
PATTERSON, Eli 168 J E 149 J H
  168 M S 161 R J 174 S L 175
  William 212
PATTON, Benjamin 24 79
PAUL, J L 171
PAXTON, S L 173 William 182
  William W 178
PAYNE, C M 169
PAYSOUR, C 153 Caleb 168
  Peter 153
PEACH, H 147
PEARCE, Henry L 189
PEARSON, Judge 67 R M 75
PEGRAM, M P 168 S S 186
  Walter P 187 William E 185
PELT, Simon V 139
PENDER, J H 176
PENMAN, Thomas 123
PENN, 13
PENNIX, J A 155 J W 155
PEOPLES, Isabella 74 J N 150
  Mary 77 N H 77 R R 150

PEOPLES (cont)
  Richard 139
PEPPEN, John 157
PERKINS, A 176
PERRY, Francis 139 Noah 172
PETIT, Jas 149
PETRE, Wm 164
PETTUS, H M 153 J W 153 165
  Mack 145 Stephen 153
PHARR, Floyd 191 H N 134
  Susan 77 T P 164 Walter W 77
PHELPS, H M 143
PHIFER, Barbara 79 Caleb 79
  132 Capt 63 Catherine 79 Col
  16 E M 173 Elizabeth 79 Jane
  79 John 23-25 43 47 60 79
  96-97 108 132 182 Margaret
  79 Martin 79-80 132 Martin
  Jr 79 Paul 79 R 143 William
  191 William Fullenwider 80
  William W 115
PHILLIPS, 142 A J 187 J A 168 J
  B 171 J J 162 John 135 140
  178 S A 145 W W 186
PHOLAN, J 147
PICKENS, Israel 52-53
PICKERELL, J H 162
PIERCE, J M 161 J R 161 J W
  161 John 173 L M 173 Orren
  L 161
PIRANT, William 137
PITKIN, 56
PITT, Isaac V 135
PITTS, J B 185
PLATO, T Durham 187
PLUMER, W S 192
PLYLER, F S 176 R C 149
POLK, ---- 172 Capt 60 Charles
  80 132-133 Col 46 52 Ezekiel
  17 80 J G 45 James 80 James

POLK (cont)
   Knox 80 180 199 205 John 80
   Margaret 80 Susan 81
   Susannah 80 T 14 Thomas 6
   9 17-20 23-26 35 43 47 61 65
   68 70 80 96 107 132 208-210
   Thomas G 133 Thos 62
   William 6-7 16 18 22 25 74 80
   132 Wm 45 50
POOL, A W 151 G S 155 J T 151
   Solomon 194 William 137
POPE, D Kirby 130 M T 190
POPLIN, W H 187
PORTER, Hugh G 182 James 139
   R C 157 Robt A 173 S A 159 S
   L 173 W H 187 Zenas 173
POTTS, A W 151 C A 147 J G 172
   J M 134 165 J W 143 Jas A
   151 Jas H 175 John 65 John
   G 145 John W 134 Jonathan
   108 L A 165 Lamson A 145
   Lydia L 65 Margaret R 65 T E
   147 Wm M 145 Wm P 151
POWELL, A T 159 Dan 153
   Thomas L 184
POWER, W C 194
PRAG, W J 159
PRATHER, E L 159 John J 182 S
   F 173 W S 179
PRATNER, A R 173
PREMPERT, Albert G 184
PRESLEY, Caswell 178 John M
   178 W A 157
PRESSON, Henry S 177
PRESTON, John A 192
PREVITT, Allen 173
PRICE, Anne 67 Isaac 138 J A
   157 J G 167 John 139 Joseph
   143 Josiah G 178 R S 143
   Robt 142 Wm 171

PRIFLY, Valentine 137
PRIM, Andrew 139 T A 153
PRITCHARD, C H 194 H M 134
   206 Thomas H 192
PRIVETTE, Wesley 172
PROCTOR, J A 162 W A 185
PRYOR, J F 189
PUCKET, T J 155 W C 155
PUCKETT, E M 166 F M 164 J H
   162 J M 164 S J 164
PUGH, J M 146
PURSER, Moses 140
PURVINS, Antheris 136
QUEARY, John 24-25 29 81
QUEEN, Joseph 151 Laban 151
QUERY, Calvin M 145 F E 164 F
   N 164 John G 181 Leander
   164 R L 154 195 R W 143 S F
   154 Wm W 164
QUINN, Jas 149
QUIRY, Walter 179
RACHELLE, J B 157
RAE, John 77 Martha 77
RAFFERTY, Thos 149
RALEIGH, Walter 110
RAMSAY, 13
RAMSEUR, Addie 72 Gen 72
RAMSEY, J F 165 J G M 28 55 W
   A 187
RANDALL, 44 E D 172 H L 54
   Henry S 53 Thomas G 55
RANKIN, C S 165 W W 165
RANSOM, R M 134
RAP, J N 161 W J 161
RAPE, Samuel 140
RAREFIELD, Frank 169
RATCHFORD, E C 154
RATERREE, W L 173
RAY, A D 176 J M 161 John 133
   W A 188

RAYBORN, M B 154
RAYNER, L 161
REA, D B 145 147 D J 173 J L 147 J M 147 J R 145 James 165 John 133 R R 147 Robt 147 Sameul 179 W A 147 W F 178 W P 143 Will 137 William F 182
READ, William 5 33
REAK, Edward 141
REAMS, John W 178
REAVES, F A 176
REDFORD, William 137
REECE, David 64
REED, Conrad 110 David 139 J C 167 J W 159 James B 182 Joseph 140 R C 193 R S 161 Rev Mr 106-107 Solomon 140 W H 179 William 140
REENHARDT, J F 147
REESE, D L 170 David 25 81 Rev Dr 20 Susan 81
REGLER, J Rvrea D B 179
REID, 199 George 169 H K 175 J C 155 185 J F 175 J L 166 J S 134 J W 134 Robt S W 162 S W 134 W M 157 William 173 William K 206
RENER, Samuel 140
RENN, E W 185
REVELLE, J H 187
REYNOLDS, J O 189 John 149
RHINE, A M 157
RHODES, J C 189 J E 185 Wm 149
RHYM, A M 142
RHYNE, A M 171 C M 176 David 155 J ---- 166
RICE, J S 157 J W 165 John 136 Moses 176

RICH, Daniel 140
RICHARD, 122 C J 185 J W 151
RICHARDS, Wm 176
RICHARDSON, J H 173 J M 189 John J 193 John K 182 Mason 182 W W 161
RICHLEY, W L 155
RICHMAN, J B 189
RICKETT, John R 194
RIDDICK, H L 149 J A 149
RIELER, G H 143
RIGGINS, Robt 149
RIGHT, George 138
RIGLER, D M 167 John 130
RINDAL, L L 172
RINEHART, Jacob 138 Thos 176 W D 176
RINGSTAFF, Drury 177
RITCHIE, 12
RIVEN, Prof 51
RIVES, J R 155
ROBB, Fester 191
ROBERTS, J L 165 J W 151 Peyton 154 S L 165 W A 165
ROBERTSON, F J 191 James 137 140 Reuben 191 Thomas R 184 Will 136
ROBEY, W M 194
ROBINSON, 22 C W 193 Cora J 76 D C 167 Daniel E 182 J P 175 J R 161 James M 182 Jas A 169 John 78 81 M B 178 M M 178 Margaret 78 Miles J 133 Rev Dr 65 Rob't 24 Robert 81 Samuel J 178 T C 169 T R 76 Thomp 175 W H 161 W M 188 W W 157
ROBSON, G M 147
RODAY, T A 164
RODDEN, J J 162 N B 175 T B

RODDEN (cont)
    151 W R 175
RODEN, Upton 135
RODGER, Mary 72
RODGERS, J R 164 J W 164
    John 166 T P 164
RODMAN, J L 84 86
ROGER, 50
ROGERS, J C 149 James 141
    Jas 149 R B 187
ROLMER, W C 149
ROMLEY, S F 185
RONE, James 140
ROPER, D C 185 P H 179 R 185
ROSE, W C 143
ROSEMAN, T A 193
ROSICK, G W 162
ROSS, E A 81 144 152 204
    James 137 Jas W 134 R A 154
    157 W A 173
ROTHE, 112
ROWE, Henry 138
ROZZELL, J T 155 W F 143 154
RUDDOCK, B M 154 B W 154 T
    C 152 Theo C 145
RUDISILL, Jacob 169
RUIS, W R 155
RUMAGE, L 169
RUMELL, J C 157
RUNFELT, Wm H 150
RUPEL, E H 167 S H 169
RUSS, W A 165
RUSSELL, H T 175 J C 157
    James 62 John 62 P J 179
    Robert 62 W D 161 William E
    189
RUTHERFORD, Gen 69 74
    Griffith 79
RUTZLER, George F 183
SABINE, 51

SADLER, Armond D 187 John
    139 Julius 143 Minor 142
SAMMOND, T K 167
SAMPLE, David 175 David I 145
    E 167 H M 175 J M 175 J W
    166 175 John W 145 M M 189
    W L 166 Wm 161
SANDERS, B H 175 G W 149
    Jacob 157 Jesse 182 W H 147
SANDIFER, E L 187 G C 188 T T
    134
SANFORD, J M 163 Jas O 163
SANRING, J M 172
SAVILLE, J C 161 J M 156
    James M 145 R D 156 W H
    145
SAVIN, Albert S 188 Charles E
    189
SAVIS, J B 175
SAWYER, Archibald 137
SCHNEIDER, G 147
SCHROEDER, William H Jr 185
SCHULTZ, Paul 184
SCOTT, Claudius 187 Jas 171
    John W 172 Leader 172
    Nelson 151 R S 157 W A 163
    Will 136 William 62
SEAGLE, G W 151
SEAGRAVES, A C 149
SECREST, Hiram 177
SEIGLE, T L 150
SELLERS, Eli 166
SELLS, James 185
SENIOR, Hall 191
SETZER, Charles M 184
SEVER, 122
SEVERS, ---- 172
SHAFFER, J S 165 W H 165
SHAFTEBURY, Lord 50
SHANK, Martin 138

SHANNON, Robert 137
SHANNONHOUSE, F M 134
SHARAR, Wilson A 189
SHARP, Cunningham 136 Isaac 172 J R 179 R A 169 T A 169 William 136
SHARPE, R A 143
SHARPLY, William 135
SHAVER, Jacob 136 M 167
SHAW, A 167 Alex 161 D C 169 G R 187 J G 151 J N 173 James 140 L W A 143 Wm 151
SHEFFIELD, J M 159
SHEHORN, Morris 140
SHELBY, D H 161 J L 163 J M 151 Miss 64 Moses 62 W W 150 William 140
SHELTON, R W 195
SHELVEY, William 139
SHEPARD, G T 170 J W 169
SHEPHERD, Thomas 135
SHEPPARD, J W 143
SHERIDAN, John 149
SHERRELL, Robert K 182 W 155 William 182
SHERRILL, Absolom L 182 C M 185 Hartford 182 N J 149 William E 178
SHIELDS, A C 170
SHIPP, Bartlett 81 Catherine 81 Margaret 81 W M 81
SHOE, Jacob 169
SHOEMAKER, Lafayette 172
SHORE, Noah 175
SHOTWELL, R A 134
SHUFORD, S S 188
SHUMAN, W H 179
SIKES, Daniel S 185 Geo G 178
SILER, Jesse W 193

SIMESON, John 25-26 47
SIMIANER, John 79 Margaret 79
SIMMIMER, James 136
SIMMON, Jacob 138
SIMMONS, ---- 161 Dennis J 194
SIMMS, J M 152
SIMPSON, C L 169 H Mc 178 Ira P 169 J 161 J W 154 M S 161 R F 154 Robt Frank 145
SIMS, Gipson R 189 J Monroe 145 Natheil 137 Reuben 191
SINCLAIR, Alexander 192
SINGLETON, Henry 172 Lacy D 177
SITZER, James 182
SIZER, Wm E 145
SKINNER, S L 149
SLOAN, A C 170 Allen 136 D F A 170 G W 159 J Lee Jr 195 J Mc 170 J W 152 James 139 Robt 152 Sam'l 152 T A 166 T C 166 W E 170 W S 179
SLOON, J L 169
SLOOP, Alex 157
SLOUGH, David 62
SMART, Elisha 140 Geo W 133 Osborn 140
SMITH, 199 A 179 A J 157 Alex 172 Alexander 136 B R 207 Burton 182 C Ed 145 D H 159 D J 155 D W 179 Daniel 138 E 158 E C 173 E M 189 Ed 159 Frank 176 Franklin 169 G F 176 G L 176 George 152 George F 186 J A 152 J B 176 179 J D 161 J N 189 J P 150 J Perry 143 J S 154 161 J T 156 J W 147 157 159 Jacob 152 Joan 172 John 179 John L 157 L A 177 Lemuel 175 M

SMITH (cont)
   H 145 O B 185 R T 179 Ripley
   P 184 S B 145 161 T J 157
   Thomas 62 Thomas B 190 W J
   B 145 W M 152 W R 193 W S
   161 W T 170 William 137-138
   Wm 179 Wm J B 173
SMITHY, Willis W 182
SMYTH, Dr 46 48
SNEAD, Frank 157
SNEED, Reuben 138
SNIDER, J A 157
SNOWDEN, Emanual 191
SOLOMON, D A 165-166 Drury
   136 Wm R 165
SOLON, John 135
SOSSAMAN, D G 176 W H 176
SOSSAMON, J P 170
SPAIN, Hartwell 193
SPARROW, J S 147
SPAWL, A B 149
SPEARS, A J 169 J J 169 Wm H
   149
SPENCER, 199 Clark 159 J W
   169
SPER, William 62
SPRATT, A P 173 C E 78
   Margaret 78 Susannah 80
SPRAVEY, Benjamin 140
SPRINGS, Alexander 191 E B
   207 J M 173 John 64 69 R A
   175 Richard A 145
SPRINKLE, Mary S 74
SQUIRE, J A 157
SQUIRES, J B 143 161 J W 161
   M D 173
STACK, Albert 178
STACY, A G 194 James 194
STAGG, J E 193
STALEY, C R 144

STALY, John 149 W Y 149
STANCEL, James 178
STANCIL, A G 161
STANER, P C 172
STANFORD, C L 173 David W
   182 M T 161
STANIS, J B 147
STANNING, Wm 149
STANT, S G 152
STARNES, E W 176 John 176
STARNS, C R 147 Frederic 140
   Jacob 136 Nathaniel 140
STATEN, J H 171
STATLER, Peter 108
STEADMAN, W W 185
STEARNS, A L 166 Brown 169
   Daniel 178 Dulin 169 Henry
   M 170 J B 146 J M 169 John
   R 178 Johnston 178 Thos H
   178 W R 166
STEEL, A F 161 M 146 M D 143
STEELE, Albert 178 Gen 52 J
   154 J P H 189 James 139
   John 139 191 Thos 178 W
   145 W G 147
STEGALL, Ambrose 178 Moses
   178
STEPHENS, A B 163 M 149 R T
   163
STEPHENSON, J F 161 Wm J
   173
STERLING, J W 159
STEVENSON, Adlai E 58 Hugh
   136 Mr 8
STEWARD, Capt 102
STEWART, A A 169 Alexander
   140 Allen 136 182 Andrew
   136 Matthew 62 Milus R 182
   P J 169 Thos A 149 W S 175
STILL, William E 177

STILLWELL, Jacob 152
STILWELL, Elias 141 Henry 182
STINSON, D W 169 Dave 165 J B 155
STITT, Jas M 173 William P 190
STOCKTON, Commodore 123
STOKES, Gov 6 45 52 J J 170 Montfort 9
STONE, A 155 John 172 W D 175 Wm D 145
STORY, David W 140 James Sr 141
STOUGH, 199 Rich I 170
STOUT, J S 178
STOWE, H D 134 J C 154 J M 154 Jim M 145 John 143 L P 176 R A 159
STRANGE, W F 130
STRANTER, John 176 T H 176 Wm 176
STRIDER, John 170
STRONG, Charles 81 Dr 113 John Mason 81 Nancy 82 Rachel 82
STROUP, C 166 David 149 M 167
STUART, A H 165 James J 184 S J 166
STUCKER, Christian 147
STULY, J J 152
STUNFORD, Moses 137
STURGAN, C S 159
STUTTS, Louis B 187
SULLIVAN, D C 149 W L 175 William 135
SUMMERS, J W 195
SUMMERVILLE, J W 152
SUMNEY, George 157 J B 157
SUMTER, Gen 69
SURVIS, T O 179
SUTER, Mr 108 Rev Mr 96-97

SWAIN, 55 D L 51 53-54 David L 49 David Lowry 44 George 44 Gov 4 45
SWANN, J B 173 R L 158
SWANNE, Moses 95
SWEAT, J M 175
SWEPSON, P J 191
SWIFT, Geo W 178
SWINDELL, F D 194
SYMON, 122
TAGART, J S 169
TAGGART, J C 157
TALLENT, Daniel 152
TALLY, John 169 Mike 169
TALTON, S W 171
TARBIFIELD, Jas 157
TARLTON, James D 165
TART, Henry 161
TATE, A H 143 F A 179 Henry 143 Hugh A 145 T A 179
TAYLOR, A A 159 A W 147 Art 147 C S L A 190 Chas 169 D B 179 Ed S 173 Gen 180 H H 190 H S 154 J A 147 J A R 173 J C 147 J M 147 165 J Q 154 J W 143 175 Jepe 169 John L 44 R C C 154 W A 167 W B 144 152 W F 147 W H 165 W J 159 165 Wilson 140
TAYLOUS, John S 138
TEAGUE, John 182
TEDDER, Sid 161
TEMPLETON, J E D 170 J M 170 R D 170
TEREPAUGH, J H 152
TERRES, Edward 130 James 163
TERRIS, C E 179 Henry 144
TEVEPAUGH, Wm 173
THOMAS, C W 177 G W 187 Henry 175 J B 189 W B 161

THOMASON, J C 154
THOMASSON, J L 161
THOMBURG, F B 159 G J 159 H M 159 S L 159
THOMPSON, Benjamin 136 E W 194 Henry 140 J M 147 J W 165 James 137 Jas 161 Joe 157 L 161 Lee 161 Lewis 161 R 143 R G 147 S T 195 W H 196 W J 159
THORNBURG, John L 178
THUNER, E A 157 J T 157
TICER, R C S 159
TICKNOR, Mr 13
TIDDY, J F 143 R A 143
TIDWELL, W P A 173
TIFFINS, M B 167
TIMMONS, Harry 187
TISER, W H G 179
TITLEMARY, Charles J 181
TODD, C B 163 D S 163 G C 163 G F 163 G N 163 Hugh 135 J A 167 J A W 159 J L 162-163 J W 158 163 Jas A 162 Jas C 161 L N 163 R H 174 R J 169 S E 145 175 Wm 145 152
TOMBERLEN, E M 147
TOMBERLIN, Moses 141
TOMLIN, J 147
TORRANCE, A P 165 H L W 167 J A 148 167 W W 167
TORRENCE, C L 179 George 143 James 191 Lloyd C 186 W B 159
TOVAN, William 143
TOWEY, Lewis 149
TRADEWICE, N P 159
TRAIN, James 140
TREDERMICK, J R 147 N P 147 W S 147

TREDINICK, 122
TRELOAR, 122 John W 145
TRIMBLE, J M 185
TRIPLETTE, J H 172
TROTTER, A G 175 T B 144 Thomas H 188 Thos 175
TROUTMAN, Geo 177
TROWER, T J 161
TRYON, Gov 19 48 60-62 97 106-108
TUCKER, George 55 Mr 46 Reuben 193
TUMMICE, L G 167
TURNER, F M 173 J W 155 S R 169 W D 177 W S 154 Wm 169
TUTOR, George 141
TYE, W B 147 William A 182 Wm A 170
UALLE, P O 147
UNDERWOOD, David 152 J O 152 J R 152 J S 152 Jas 152 Reuben 152 S M 147
VAGORER, J V 143
VANCE, J C 147 Richard 149 W H 170 Z B 57
VANNESS, John R 185
VANPELT, J N 147
VARKER, Wm 149
VAUGHN, Benjamin 36 H J 149 John 35 37 44
VENO, 122 Francis 152
VICK, Moses 140
VICKERS, ---- ---- 175 E N 175 G F 175
VINCENT, J S 188 Jas B 149
VINSON, Groves 140
VIPON, Nicholas 182
VIVIAN, 122
VOORHEIS, Charles I 169

WADDELL, Gen 60 Hugh 63
WADE, Joseph W 191
WAFFORD, C H 189
WAGSTAFF, J R 167
WAID, Daniel F 193
WAITT, William E R 182
WALKER, Andrew 135 139 B 155
   Charles C 187 E H 134 E M
   173 H J 158 J B 147 J C 167
   J H 155 James 82 136 Jas H
   155 John 82 133-134 L J 159
   L L 155 Matthew 94 P L 157
   Robt 169
WALKUP, S H 84
WALL, J M 187
WALLACE, A W 165 C S 167
   Daniel 191 I N 179 J M 177 J
   R 177 M L 147 Matthew 135
   W 134 W A 154 William 3 Wm
   147
WALLIS, Joseph 139 Matthew Jr
   139 W L 198
WALLS, A A 152 Edward 191
   Thos 171
WALSH, G B 172 J H 172
WALSTON, S L 161
WALTER, Charles 138
WARD, E W 189
WARING, R P 82 134 Robert P
   177 Robt P 129
WARREN, James T 181 R S 157 T
   W 157
WARSHAM, Alex 167 F M 167 R
   R 167 T L 167 W 167
WARWICK, J M 173
WASHAM, Alexander 135 J B
   149
WASHINGTON, 36 Gen 18
   George 205
WATKINS, T 189

WATSON, J A 173 J B 173 J S
   173 James 136 191 Samuel
   Brown 82 W A 147
WATT, B Frank 145 C B 157
   Charles B 145 J B 77 Louisa
   77 W T 159
WATTERS, Allen 157 J C 163
WATTS, C L 152 Charles 152 R A
   170 R F 171
WAVRA, Gus E 185
WEAVER, G H 159 J A 179 Wm
   149
WEBB, Lewis 141 Wm 161
WEDDINGTON, J H 207 J Y 167
WEDLOCK, W 148
WEEKS, J L 173 R B 161
WEIDNER, Henry 108
WEIR, Howard 136 J F 185
WELLS, J M 187 Samuel Adams
   12
WENTZ, Valentine 182
WERNER, L 147
WEST, J L 154 Matthew 139 Wm
   161 Wm F 152
WESTON, Job 18
WHALON, Roderick 149
WHEELER, 44 48 55 John C 56
   John H 129 Thomas 191
WHITAKER, H A 148
WHITE, A S 152 D W 152 E F
   165 J H 167 173 J S 147 196
   J T 175 James 60 James A
   165 James Jr 61 63 James T
   191 John 139 John Jr 60 63 L
   W 185 R S 179 W G 193
   William 60 62-63 191 Wm 159
WHITESIDE, Joseph 139
WHITESIDES, Wm 173
WHITFIELD, 105 Theodore 192
WHITLEY, G M D 169 J H 169

WHITLEY (cont)
  John 172 R D 134
WHITNER, Henry 108
WHITSETT, Wm 94
WHITSIDES, John 95
WIAT, John 136
WILDER, H M 183
WILEY, 49 Hugh 135 Isaac 137 J
  167 J C 159 John 145 Oliver
  62 Samuel 136 W J 143 178
WILFONG, John G 184
WILHITE, James 29
WILKENSON, Neil 175
WILKERSON, J H 149 Jno 157 W
  149 W H 157
WILKES, Admiral 123
WILKINSON, Osborne 140 R L
  175 W C 130
WILL, John 152
WILLIAMS, A B 150 A C 198 A L
  175 B 185 C R 167 E E 186 F
  C 167 Harrison 191 Henry
  Bartlett 82 Hugh 175 J A 175
  J H 169 171 J J 134 J M 147
  J W 185 Joseph 139 L S 142
  206 P A M 194 Patrick H 184
  Richard 191 Rufus 171 S H
  154 Ulysses B 184 W E 161 W
  H Jr 185 W L 188 W P 195 W
  S 143 Wm S 150
WILLIAMSON, 9-10 A L 175 C
  187 D J 149 Dr 8 13 50 52 E
  Y 155 G W 169 Hugh 6-7 16
  52 J A 147 J B 177 J M 175
  177 J W 143 James D 182
  John M 182 M B 134 Martha
  D 77 Thomas J 182
WILLIFORD, T F 147
WILLSON, William 17
WILSON, A A 188 B F 171

WILSON (cont)
  Benjamin 139 Catherine 65
  David 132 David B 135 Eli
  191 F H 188 G J 178 G M 165
  George 190 George W 182
  Hugh 141 J 167 J A 169 178
  J C 179 J E 159 J H 57 134
  175 J M 175 177 J R 155
  James 138 John 82 133 136
  140 147 John Jr 139 John
  Mckemey 82 Jos H 171
  Joseph 65 82 L R 175 Lewis
  149 M A 165 M N 165 Mary
  82 R L 165 R S 154 S W 175
  Samuel 27 T A 165 T C 167 T
  J 165 W A 178 W M 154 185
  Wm 177 179 Zaccheus 83
  Zachias 24
WILY, Samuel 101
WINDERS, P S 175
WINDLE, M F 143
WINECOFF, J T 149
WINES, William 138
WINGATE, Angus 154 C C 145
  154 J 155 J P 173 Jas R 158
  M 154 N J 159 R G 157 T 155
  Wm C 173
WINSLOW, Jean 78 Moses 78
WINSTON, C W 163
WIRT, 13 Mr 26
WITHERS, B A 154 Hayes 191 M
  P 187
WITHERSPOON, J G 159 M T
  161
WLATERS, James 190
WOLF, E B 169 G D 161 J N 161
  J W 172-173 R B 161
WOLFE, C H 175 George 144 T D
  145 T J 145
WOLFER, H F 159

WOLLES, William Jr 139
WOMACK, John 178
WOOD, J 189 Robert 136
WOODALL, Thos 165 W C 169 William 140
WOODARD, John S 188 W L 149
WOODS, L M 193
WOODSIDE, Rufus W 187
WORSHAM, Alfred 171 B A 171 H J 171 Richard 171
WORTHERN, Henry 175
WRIGHT, Gov 47 J C 179 Taylor 154
WRYFIELD, J R 159 Wm 179
WYATT, J H 142
WYLIE, James 93
WYNENS, John 138
WYNNE, W A 193
WYNNS, Ann 139
YANDLE, A F 167 169 L S 187 M
YANDLE (cont) N 165
YANDLES, Jesse 137
YARDLE, J B 148 W A 148 W H 148
YATES, 123 W J 83
YAUDLES, David B 140 Samuel 140
YEARGAN, W 161
YERBY, William 140
YODER, A T 185
YORK, G W 155
YOUNG, A J 169 J A 161 179 J H 157 James H 189 John A 134 207 S T 161 Samuel Jr 191
YOUNGBLOOD, F C 158
YOUNT, 199 A O 185 L C 185 T E 185 W H 185
YOUNTS, J A 179 R C 155 Samuel 198

www.ingramcontent.com/pod-product-compliance
Lightning Source LLC
Chambersburg PA
CBHW070904300426
44113CB00008B/931